TALKIN' MOSCOW
BLUES

TALKIN' MOSCOW BLUES

Josef Škvorecký

Edited by Sam Solecki

LESTER
&ORPEN
DENNYS
PUBLISHERS

FIRST EDITION

CANADIAN CATALOGUING IN PUBLICATION DATA

Škvorecký, Josef, 1924–
    Talkin' Moscow blues

Bibliography: p.
ISBN 0-88619-196-3

I. Solecki, Sam, 1946–   . II. Title.

PS8537.K86T34 1988   C891.8′64   C87-095341-9
PR9199.3.S55T34 1988

Printed and bound in Canada

Lester & Orpen Dennys Limited
78 Sullivan Street
Toronto, Canada   M5T 1C1

Artists hold out the mirror to the bruises
on the face of the world.

> Josef Škvorecký,
> *All the Bright Young Men and Women*

Contents

—

Introduction

Talkin' Moscow Blues brings together the best of the essays and reviews Josef Škvorecký has published since leaving Czechoslovakia in the wake of what he calls the "ambush" of August 21, 1968. As is often the case with a novelist's nonfiction, the majority of these pieces were commissioned by either magazine editors or conference organizers; the rest were written in response to some news item that sufficiently provoked Škvorecký to make him pause in his work on a novel, and turn to journalism. The result is that public writing a novelist does between chapters when, in his heart of hearts, he knows he should be working on his fiction. Collected as a volume, the pieces are that pleasant surprise described by Russian émigré poet Joseph Brodsky* as the book "that was never meant to be".

If 1968 marks the beginning of Škvorecký's exile, it is also the point at which he stepped into the North American culture. Prior to the Soviet-led invasion, he was a Czech novelist, essayist, editor, scriptwriter, and translator—in other words, a Czech man of letters; in the two decades since, as these essays and reviews testify, he has become a North American one. A measure of this transition is the fact that, with the exception of his monthly Voice of America broadcasts, Škvorecký wrote most of these articles in English, although he still writes his fiction in Czech.

The relative ease with which Škvorecký has made a space for himself within North American writing—publishing in such journals as *The New Republic*, *The New York Times Book Review*, *The Canadian Forum*, and *Canadian Literature*—will seem less surprising if we keep in mind that English has always been his favourite second language, and that since adolescence he has been passionately interested in American literature, jazz, and culture. As a result—like Joseph Brodsky, fellow Czech Milan Kundera, and the young Polish poet and critic Stanislaw Barańczak—he was able to make a substantial intellectual contribution to his new society from early on. Like Brodsky, who has astonished both English and Russian critics by writing poetry in English, Škvorecký is a good example of the émigré writer for whom exile unexpectedly creates a second linguistic and cultural home. In this he is very different from Alexander Solzhenitsyn, who has suffered a double exile: for political reasons he is barred from the Soviet Union, and by reason of language and temperament he remains almost completely isolated within the United States. Solzhenitsyn has no role in Western intellectual and cultural affairs—and one can't quite imagine him wanting one. A literary titan, almost a world historical figure, he has little direct connection with any living national culture.

Škvorecký, in contrast, is very aware of the part he can play in his new society. For one thing, there is the inevitable function of contributing information and ideas about "the other Europe". A not insignificant aspect of his writing is simply the context it provides for East and Central European events and affairs, from the viewpoint of one who lived "over there" for many years. Essays like "The Good Old Drinking Poet", "Jiří Menzel and *Closely Watched Trains*", "Reading Between the Takes", and "Prague Winter" can be read as instalments in an ongoing corrective to those official versions of contemporary Czech life in *Rudé Právo* (the Czech equivalent of *Pravda*) or in naive fellow-travelling accounts offered by Western tourists. These detailed reports of (respectively) government harassment of the Nobel Prize winner Jaroslav Seifert, of various attempts to suppress jazz, of the post-1968 fate of New Wave directors like Jiří Menzel and Věra Chytilová, and of "literary and film diplomacy in the corridors of dictatorship power" are indispensable reading for anyone interested in the political and social history of what Škvorecký calls the "Soviet *gubernia*", and in the nature of the more quotidian aspects of totalitarianism itself.

Paradoxically, it is only because of the painful fact of exile that a writer like Škvorecký can fulfil this sort of function, in which, of necessity, he "looks east but writes west". Edward Said has written that while "most people are primarily aware of one culture, one setting, one home, exiles are aware of at least two, and this plurality of vision gives rise to an awareness of simultaneous dimensions, an awareness that—to borrow a phrase from music—is contrapuntal." In Škvorecký's case this means, for example, that when he thinks of 1968 he remembers both the Chicago Democratic Convention and the Soviet invasion of his homeland. This dichotomy often shows in his vocabulary, as phrases migrate from one language to another, rather like points of conjunction between parallel universes. In his essays we often find the complex situation of a major Czech novelist, banned in Czechoslovakia, writing about his homeland in English but occasionally borrowing from German or Russian. The interaction of the three languages with the unspoken Czech can almost be read as a metaphor for Škvorecký's life and Czechoslovakia's history. English, as Škvorecký often tells us, is his language of choice, and his various Anglo-American epigraphs and allusions serve as reminders that for him "Bohemia [is] a land of Western culture." German, although also a language of the West, is more ambiguous; it recalls the rich Germanic heritage characterized by Goethe and Rilke (see *The Bass Saxophone*), but it is also the language of six years of brutal Nazi totalitarianism. And finally there is Russian, an unambiguous symbol of the continuous boot in the face over nearly half a century of Soviet imperialism. Seen from this viewpoint, the German and Russian elements in Škvorecký's work are linguistic scars of invasions, while English is the language of "what if"—what if, that is, Czechoslovakia's history had been different.

But if language in Škvorecký's essays and novels inevitably involves history, it is also impregnated with politics—to the point that, although *Talkin' Moscow Blues* divides his essays into four categories—jazz, literature, film, and politics—one could just as easily, and with strong justification, see them all as ultimately, if reluctantly, political. The book can be read as showing the extent to which all writing not only *within* but also *about* life under a totalitarian government is involved with political and ideological issues. This is as true of Škvorecký's fiction as it is of his essays, although the politics of the essays are always more explicit than those of the novels.

In the essays Škvorecký is able to state his views directly to
his English-speaking readers, to make them aware of some aspect of life under a totalitarian regime and to persuade them
of the validity of his judgements. The speaker in these pieces
is a man who, having survived both the right and the left extremes of ideology, prefers an empirical and humanistic attitude
towards history and politics, and remains permanently suspicious of slogans, dogmas, and abstractions without a basis in
everyday life. Terms like "history", "revolution", and "class justice" are to his skeptical mind what the proverbial red cape is
to the bull. Against them, as well as against politicized explanations of history, he brings a clear-headed view that is witty
and ironic—though never cynical or intolerant—and a memory of problematic events not easily reconciled with the grand
claims of ideology. Thus, to armchair Marxists (Vargas Llosa's
"intelleftuals") who prattle on about class warfare and the necessity or inevitability of revolution, Škvorecký points to history
and reminds them of what revolutions have traditionally done
to their children. To those attempting to forget or whitewash the
genocides and human rights violations of the left while pointing a distracting finger at the right, he quotes Nathanael West's
sobering commonsense reminder, "If against Fascism, why not
against Communism?" And to those who ask, "What makes you
so sure?" his answer is simply Huck Finn's "I been there before."
     For it is Škvorecký's own experience that has made him
suspicious not only of "the absurd dream of justice called Communism", as he calls it, but of any accounts of reality not rooted
in common experience. When he does use commonplace terms
like Fascism, Communism, socialism, and totalitarianism, he
insists on the ballast of specific personal or historical events.
(One of the consequences of this is that he tends to be blind to
the meanings socialism has in countries like France, Britain,
Sweden, and Canada, where it is radically distinct from Communism and National Socialism and is almost always an aspect
of social democracy.)
     Of the essays included in *Talkin' Moscow Blues*, I suspect
that Škvorecký probably found the more directly political ones
among the most difficult to write, even though three of them,
"Are Canadians Politically Naive?", "A Revolution Is Usually
the Worst Solution", and "Prague Winter", strike me as among

his best. (The title of the first, incidentally, echoes a line in Czeslaw Milosz's classic *The Captive Mind*—"Are Americans really stupid?") In each of these Škvorecký finds himself compelled to restate tactfully something that he finds obvious, something that should be self-evident to anyone except the most blinkered fellow-travellers or those whom Lenin contemptuously labelled "useful idiots". In "Are Canadians Politically Naive?", for example, he finds it inexcusable that a Canadian would write a gullible account of the 1983 Czechoslovak World Assembly for Peace and Life against Nuclear War, as Leslie Hughes did for the *Winnipeg Sun*. Yet, typically, the essay shows him controlling his annoyance, explaining yet again how certain governments manipulate official visitors to such conferences, and ending with the wry observation that he really wanted "to write about this beautiful land; about its golden skyscrapers silhouetted against the skies of Indian summer.... But damn politics got me like the blues, and the naivety of so many of my fellow Canadians does not help me out."

If there is a note of exasperation in the passage just quoted, there is in the next sentence a reiteration of the writer's traditional duty to his society and to humanity: "I am far from being of the stuff that Sisyphus was made of, and yet, again and again, I push this boulder up the steep slope of incomprehension." Implicit in this is a view of writing as a witnessing that helps "to keep the memory of certain things alive, in this fast-forgetting world." This idea of the writer's moral reponsibility—"the dimension of mission in a writer's vocation"—is more explicitly and forcefully stated in one of Škvorecký's favourite quotations from Ernest Hemingway: "The writer's job is to tell the truth."

But the writer as political essayist can only be useful if he can engage the reader in a dialogue; and a significant part of Škvorecký's art lies in his ability to do just that. The essay on Canadian political naivety, for example, could easily have been a shrill, sarcastically condescending, and self-justifying performance. But Škvorecký begins the process of involving the Canadian reader by turning the potentially offensive title into a question, and then disarms the reader entirely by insisting, in the very first sentence, that it is a "stupid" question. And so he goes on to qualify the question, and ultimately he *seems* to offer the essay as just a set of observations from an Old World point of view. The slightly world-weary tone (one can almost hear the accented English of *Casablanca*'s Victor Laszlo), the Orwell-like appeals to history and common sense, the dramatic anecdotes drawn from his own life, and the engaging "speaking" voice—all are part of his attempt to convince the reader to give the provocative argument a hearing. A complacent polemic, by contrast, would have appealed only to the already converted; all others would have stopped reading early on. The only effect would have been a reinforcement of the status quo—precisely the result of Solzhenitsyn's jeremiad at Harvard in 1978. Incidentally, a third approach is indicated by Miloš Forman's comment "I don't argue about certain things any more. I know a person who hasn't seen some things and some contents from close up, for himself, simply cannot comprehend them." Unlike the more impatient Forman, Škvorecký remains the inveterate if reluctant Sisyphus, trying to create the conditions under which dialogue and understanding can be established.

Although the essays are, as one would expect, more expository than the novels, they often recall Škvorecký's fiction in the way they introduce arguments and ideas concretely and dramatically through references to real people, events, situations, and places. In both, political ideas are inseparable from characters, happenings, and the texture of daily life. The novelist persuades us to prefer one way of thinking and being over another by showing the private and public lives of the characters—their emotional stresses, intellectual reflections, and social and moral choices. Škvorecký as essayist also involves us with characters, manners, and events, but they happen to be real. Essays like "Red Music" and "Talkin' Moscow Blues", which deal with the censoring of jazz by Nazi and Communist regimes respectively, begin with personal anecdotes and proceed with references to often forgotten people and events; the first culminates in a movingly elegiac apostrophe to the past—always present, always lost—and the second in Abraham Lincoln's philosophical "You can fool all of the people some of the time...." In both cases the emphasis is not on censorship, repression, and totalitarianism as abstractions or theoretical elements (that can be left to political theorists) but as realities with practical consequences in the daily lives

of the extraordinary "ordinary people" evoked so movingly by
Škvorecký.

Škvorecký's occasional reminders that he participated in
many of the events he describes lend a note of authority to the
essays. He was an eyewitness; when he writes about the Nazi
occupation of Bohemia, Stalinist purges in Czechoslovakia, and
the Prague Spring, he can say, in passing, "I was there." In one
particularly impressive passage he reminds us that

> I have experienced all existing political systems of
> twentieth-century Europe: liberal democracy until 1939,
> Nazism from 1939–45, the uneasy democratic social-
> ism of 1945–48, Stalinism between 1948 and 1960, the
> liberalization of Communism from 1960–67, the crazy
> attempt to square the circle in 1968, and the Attila-the-
> Hun solution of the *Panzers* in August 1968....

If we complete his catalogue by adding that in 1968 he went
into exile, and if we recall Brodsky's comment that "Displace-
ment and misplacement are this century's commonplace," then
Škvorecký can be seen as a representative twentieth-century
European.

The essays dealing with Škvorecký's years as an émigré are
less dramatic, almost inevitably anticlimactic. It's not without
significance that they are often imbued with a nostalgic tone,
and leave us with the impression that, despite all disclaimers,
the emotional and intellectual motive force of his life has its
origins less in the here and now than in the past. He is like
an Orpheus caught halfway between the Eurydice of the Czech
past, which will never quite disappear, and the daylight of the
Canadian present which he will never fully enter. Škvorecký
is unquestionably sincere in telling us that he prefers living in
Toronto to living in today's Prague, yet Prague, past or present,
makes for better, more fascinating copy. I find somewhat the
same quality in two recent autobiographical books by Soviet
émigrés, Vladimir Voinovich's *The Anti-Soviet Soviet Union*
and Vassily Aksyonov's *In Search of Melancholy Baby*. Each
writer's positive comments about his present life (in Munich
and Washington, respectively) are gently undermined by the
text's darker emotional undercurrents whose origins are in

memories of the irretrievably lost past; the prose flows in two opposite directions, which may be an apt metaphor for the lives of writers who find themselves stranded midstream between languages and cultures.

Škvorecký deals most explicitly with this simultaneous sense of gain and loss in the essays dealing with being an émigré and an ethnic writer. In "Between Two Worlds", for example, he offers a personal account of the complex problems facing a writer who moves to a country in which other émigrés may constitute the primary, even the *only*, audience for his work. On the one hand, he celebrates the freedom he has found to write and publish without the threat of censorship, as well as the pleasantly surprising reception his work has met with in the West. On the other, he recognizes that not all writers have been as fortunate as himself in finding a new audience, and reminds us that for some the move to the West is a leap from official censorship to near silence, and to permanent marginality in both the old and the new culture.

The loss of a homeland entails losing not only one's natural audience but also full contact with one's native tongue. It's typical of Škvorecký that, even as he acknowledges this aspect of emigration, his ultimate emphasis is on some of the unexpected positive aspects of exile. He points out that a writer "surrounded by the strange sounds of a foreign language" may, like

> such expatriates as Hemingway, Fitzgerald, or Henry Miller,...develop a greater sensitivity to the beauties and subtleties of the language in which he feels at home. He becomes afflicted by a kind of beneficent nostalgia for his verbal homeland, and potentialities of his medium, which he tended to miss while the acoustic milieu was familiar, begin to dawn on him.

According to Škvorecký, another of the ambiguous linguistic pleasures of exile is the experience of listening to the creative corruption of one's native tongue as, within the space of a single generation, it begins to respond to the daily pressure of English. Not surprisingly, he rejects "linguistic purism" and insists that North American Czech be treated as "simply another dialect of our Mother Tongue" and that a "Czech writer living on these shores...use North American Czech in the same way as novelists at home use Prague slang or Moravian dialect." If we recall that a support of tolerance, pluralism, and negative liberties is at the heart of Škvorecký's humane politics, then it isn't surprising that even in the small matter of North American Czech he is on the side of the language as it is used in daily life, and opposed to he dogmas of "old schoolmasters" and "normative grammars".

The point is a small one but representative. I emphasize it because one of the consequences of Škvorecký's consistently anti-Soviet position in foreign affairs has been the curious tendency of some reviewers and columnists to categorize this essentially liberal writer as just a typical émigré conservative or reactionary. This is usually done on the odd assumption that the meanings of terms such as Liberal, Socialist, and Conservative depend exclusively on one's attitude to the Soviet Union. That Škvorecký is anti-Communist and anti-Soviet is undeniable— but then, so are Irving Howe and Saul Bellow, neither of whom can be called a reactionary. My own impression is that the worst one can say about Škvorecký's position on foreign affairs is that it tends to be intransigent and predictable. Still, it is more coherent and carefully thought out than those of his critics. If I had to affix a political label to him—a label taking full account of the complexity of his political position—I would be tempted to call him a skeptical liberal democrat, with perhaps a sentimental attachment to the passive anarchism of Jaroslav Hašek's "Party of Moderate Progress within the Bounds of the Law."

It's a loosely defined and eclectic position, but it reflects a lifetime's direct engagement with history. Its main tenets include "a sensitive uncertainty...about the value of ready-made answers"; a skepticism about ideologues and ideologies; an insistence on "liberal freedoms" such as free speech, tolerance, and political pluralism as essential to any truly free society; an unfashionable willingness to defend the historical contribution of the bourgeoisie to the development of democracy; an aversion to revolutions and revolutionaries; and, finally, the suspicion that "capitalism is probably good, liberalism may be right, democracy is the closest approximation to the truth, and parliamentarism a vigorous gentleman in good health, filled with the wisdom of ripe old age".

Like E. M. Forster's two cheers for democracy, Škvorecký's humane political position is not one to set people marching. It simply reminds us that we need to cherish certain hard-won and irreplaceable attitudes, values, and ideas because "if they are forgotten, the results may be tragic." That the reminder should come from "a new Canadian from the Old World" is ironic—but perhaps inevitable.

Sam Solecki,
St. Michael's College,
University of Toronto,
May 1988

* The quotations from Joseph Brodsky are from an interview in Partisan Review *(Vol. LIV, No. 4, 1987) and from the essay "The Condition We Call Exile" in* The New York Review of Books *(January 21, 1988). The quotation by Edward Said is from his essay "Reflections on Exile" (*Granta, *No. 13, 1985). All quotations from Josef Škvorecký are from essays reprinted in* Talkin' Moscow Blues.

A Note on the Text

With the exception of a section of "Between Two Worlds", "The Czechs in the American Civil War", "On the Intricacies of Adapting Fiction for the Screen", and "Venice Biennale", all of these essays, reviews, and interviews have been previously published. Several have been reworked for this volume, mainly for reasons of length and repetition, and in two cases two essays have been joined into one. The only essays not written originally in English are "An Interview in Prague" (translated by Peter Kussi); "Introducing Bohumil Hrabal" (the first part translated by Káča Polačková Henley, the second by Paul Wilson); and "Red Music", "The Incomprehensible Faulkner", and "Venice Biennale" (all translated by Káča Polačková Henley).

The editor's work has consisted in selecting and arranging the essays, ensuring a typographical continuity in pieces published in magazines and journals with often differing house styles, suggesting cuts when two essays dealt with the same material, offering translations or explanations of terms not immediately accessible to the ordinary North American reader, and transferring, as often as possible, the information contained in original footnotes into the body of the text. I would emphasize that no cuts, additions, or changes were made without the approval of the author.

Readers should note that whenever Škvorecký has referred to both the Czech and English titles of a work I have put the Czech title first if the book is available only in that language, and the English first if the book is available in both: for example, *Tankový prapor* (*The Tank Corps*) but *Closely Watched Trains* (*Ostře sledované vlaky*). Since he regularly refers to many of his own still untranslated books by English titles, readers should note that at present only the following are available in English: *The Cowards, The Bass Saxophone, Miss Silver's Past, The Mournful Demeanour of Lieutenant Boruvka, The Swell Season,*

The Engineer of Human Souls, Dvorak in Love, All the Bright Young Men and Women, and *Jiří Menzel and the History of the Closely Watched Trains. Sins for Father Knox* will be published in 1988, and *The Miracle Game* and *The End of Boruvka* are expected to appear shortly thereafter.

Anyone interested in reading the original versions of these essays will find their place of first publication in the acknowledgements following the text. The original manuscripts of the essays will be in the Škvorecký collection at the Thomas Fisher Rare Books Room at the John Robarts Library, the University of Toronto.

Finally, I would like to thank Paul Wilson, Josef Škvorecký's superb translator, who helped with some useful suggestions when the volume was first taking shape; Mrs. Audrey McDonagh, who kindly undertook, always on very short notice, the retyping of many manuscripts made almost indecipherable by either the author's handwriting or the editor's; Gena Gorrell, the book's attentive editor at Lester and Orpen Dennys; and of course Josef Škvorecký himself, who answered all questions and editorial problems with his familiar tact, patience, and Old World *laskavost*.

Pronunciation

Czech Vowels (a,e,i,o,u) are long under the diacritical sign ´ but the sound remains essentially the same. *Ů* is also long. All consonants marked with a hook or *hacek* (˘) are soft. *Č* corresponds to the English *ch*, *s* to *sh* (Škvorecký is pronounced "Shkvoretski"), and *ž* to the *z* of *azure*. *Ř* is a sound peculiar to Czech and combines a trilled *r* and a *sh* or *zh* sound—as in the name Dvořák ("Dvorzhak").

Stress, which is usually light, always falls on the first syllable of a word; it does not lengthen a vowel.

Y is a variant spelling of the Czech *i* (pronounced "ee").

I Was Born in Náchod....

I WAS BORN IN NÁCHOD....

———

This charming and wry account of Škvorecký's life was written in 1984 for the Contemporary Authors: Autobiography Series. *No other essay of Škvorecký's is as rich in detail about the autobiographical background of the "Smiřický" novels and stories*—The Cowards, The Bass Saxophone, The Swell Season, The Engineer of Human Souls, *and so on.*

I WAS born in 1924 in Náchod, a small town on the north-eastern border of Bohemia, the westernmost part of Czechoslovakia. The name of the place can be translated as "point of entry": since time immemorial the mountain pass where my birthplace is located has been used by caravans of traders and by armies of invaders. Through the narrow cleavage between the mountain peaks they penetrated into the vast valley of Bohemia inhabited, at the beginning of our Christian era, by Celtic peoples who apparently were never subdued by the Roman Empire, but later partly mixed with, partly were forced out by, an assortment of adventurous Slavic tribes who had pushed farthest west from their cradle somewhere on the outskirts of Asia. Of these the most capable of survival proved to be the Czechs, who came to dominate the valley and give their name to almost all its inhabitants. Among the few exceptions who retained their tribal names the most colourful seem to have been the Chods, a spearhead of the Slavic march into Central Europe. These free and bellicose warrior-farmers colonized the mountain range overlooking the Germanic lands in the west. The Czech kings cleverly exploited their proud independence by establishing them as border guards, subject to no one except the royalty, and in exchange for their martial services granted them various privileges: above all, freedom from any kind of feudal servitude. My beautiful mother was a Chod.

In my early childhood, history spoke to me from all sides and in many diverse tongues. The Renaissance castle towering over the town was built on the ruins of a fortress dating back to the eleventh century; remnants of its stone walls, winding down the steep rock, ended in a smelly turret believed to have been the castle's donjon, and allegedly still full of ancient bones. Nearby one could sit at a stone table with a shallow depression for gambling dice: Jan Žižka, the commander of the ferocious Hussite rebels of the fifteenth century, reportedly used to kill time at this table during his year-long, unsuccessful siege of the castle. Its lord, a staunch Catholic, defended well his faith and his property against the heretics.

In the town square, in front of the early Gothic church with its absurdly baroque steeples, stood an object of spicy mystery: the sandstone statue of a naked man, manacled to a post, with a dog at his side holding in its mouth what apparently was a pair of testicles. According to the venerable Father Meloun, our religion teacher, the man was a Christian martyr and the balls were "an instrument of torture". According to pub lore, the man was a local sixteenth-century playboy who received his just punishment from the hands of infuriated husbands of fickle wives.

In a military cemetery on the hill overlooking the exit from the mountain pass, one could lose oneself in thought over the tombstones of soldiers killed for the Austrian emperor in the lost Prussian War of 1866. Beyond it, heaps of weatherbeaten rocks were all that was left of the castellets of the robber-barons who in the time of Richard the Lion-Hearted thrived on murdering traders. And about twenty miles to the east loomed the steeples of another medieval town by the name of Braunau which earned Adolf Hitler his derogatory nickname of *der böhmische Freiter*—the Czech corporal—coined for him by Chancellor Hindenburg. The Chancellor was weak on geography and confused our neighbouring town, with its crowds of magnificent sandstone statues eaten away by rain and wind and looking therefore almost modern, with another Braunau, in Austria. History appeared to me as a paradoxical montage; it spoke to me also in the very contemporary terms of the iron and concrete wall stretching all around the town and consisting of huge bunkers and big-gun sites: the Czech Maginot line, abandoned after Munich. At the beginning of the war, its flanks were detonated by SS army engineers, ripped open, and the inner steel turrets were taken into Germany, melted, and reshaped into the Tiger and Panther tanks whose charred carcasses were soon to mark the battlefields of Europe.

Náchod, however, was the only border town in Bohemia which had not been annexed after Munich. Only seven German families lived in this community of about 12,000 souls; most of them were decent people, remarkably immune to the lure of ideology. Nationally, if not racially, Náchod was pure: non-German. In fact, Czech was spoken on the other side of the border, in the county of Glatz that had been lost to the Prussians in yet another war—this one mismanaged by Maria Theresa in the eighteenth century. After the Great Aryan got into power in Germany, the Glatz Czechs had to adjust very fast, or else. They did it by sending their children to German schools and by giving them ultra-German first names: Horst, very fashionable then, in the country of Horst Wessel, or Gudrun, after some kind of female from some sort of Wagnerian myth. They couldn't do much about the patronymics so when, after the war, I taught school in that region, I was in charge of urchins sporting names like Horst Vohňousek, Gudrun Skočdopolová, Heidemarie Smrkáčová, or Klaus Vopice, and talking a kind of Black-Sambo Czech.

Náchod was also a town of cotton mills. Exhaust pipes removed the debris from the machines and pushed it up into peculiar little towers on the factories' roofs, from where the dust was puffed out into the air. The smog was so heavy that if, towards evening, you climbed the mountains surrounding the valley, the town lay in what looked like thick pea soup. But in those days nobody knew there was such a thing as smog. It was a constant puzzle for the local doctors that, in spite of the healthy mountain climate, so many people suffered from respiratory trouble.

I was one of them. After a brief career as right defence in a soccer minileague, I fell ill with pneumonia. This was before the days of antibiotics, and one could easily die. I very much did not want to die and promised, therefore, to say ten Our Fathers and ten Hail Marys daily if I survived. As the days, made hazy by fever, dragged on, I kept raising the numbers until I ended up with a burden of about a hundred Our Fathers and Hail Marys per day. In the year that followed my recovery I tried to live up to the promise. For hours I knelt beside my bed, night after night, and in the morning I looked like a child suffering from a bad hangover. This intense religiosity exhausted me so much that in another year I had another bout with pneumonia. This time I was wiser. I only vowed that, if I recovered, I would— at the age of eighteen—enter a monastery. When the deadline was approaching I postponed the day until twenty-one. A girl— two, in fact—were unwittingly involved in that decision. With my twenty-first birthday closing in on me, I shifted the date once again: to twenty-five. Eventually, it was the Communists who saved me for secular life. When they took over the country, one of their first acts of class justice was the closing down of all monasteries.

Religion played an important part in the groping around of my childhood. Before our First Communion, we third-graders searched our souls, then counted our sins and compared. With fourteen sins to unburden myself of in the confessional, I was apparently the greatest sinner in my form. Berta Grym, the richest boy in the class, committed only four and was, therefore, a model of saintly purity. Moreover, among my sins was one called "Doubts about the Articles of Faith". When I mumbled this phrase into the big ear of Father Meloun, he looked up at me through the grille of the confessional and asked in a tone of astonishment: "Which one?" "That the world was created in seven days," I stammered. I had read a book about dinosaurs, and somehow it stimulated my imagination more than Moses. "That's not an article of faith," said Father Meloun comfortingly. Instead of relief I felt confusion. Why does the Bible contain misinformation?

   Yes, religion has been a force with me all my life, and under the strangest of circumstances. My parents used to send me to a summer camp called Onkel Otto und Tante Blanka, in order to perfect my German. Since that language was mandatory in the camp, everybody tried to speak Czech as much as possible. Ninety per cent of the inmates were Jewish. Ninety per cent of them perished a few years later. When I spent my first summer with Onkel Otto, I already knew a little about the Jewish religion. I had been taking German lessons from the cantor of the local synagogue, but I met with him only twice a week, whereas now I was in daily touch with Jews and learned a lot about their traditions and rituals. The custom that fascinated me most was circumcision. With amazement I realized that I had never given a thought to what had actually been done to Jesus. Circumcision was just a word with no image attached to it. Now the word was made flesh: at night it was projected by means of an electric torch onto the wall in the boys' dormitory, its length and thickness ascertained by a measuring tape. A boyish idea: the contest for the longest and thickest member, needless to say, was not a part of the official "Olympics" in which we participated during the day.

A group of Orthodox youngsters did not compete in the penis-Olympics. They indulged, instead, ceremoniously, in long prayers, with their cicitls affixed to their foreheads, and also held various fasts. Suspiciously many fasts, but I had never been a suspecting boy. There was one Quido Hirsch, apart from Alex Karpeles my closest friend in the *pension*, an enormous blob of a fatso who was fasting practically all the time. The reason was not theology, but doctor's orders; however I did not know that. Quido gave his fastings various Hebrew-sounding names, and I was envious. In order to beat him at his game, I invented a three-day Catholic fast of total abstention from drinking anything, and I almost died of thirst. But it was Quido who was to die, a short three years later.

Alex Karpeles was one of the few who did not perish in Auschwitz. His family left the country in time, and after the war Alex returned—for a brief time—in a British uniform. He then went back to Palestine, and if he survived all the ensuing wars, he may still be alive. He was responsible for my literary debut.

I became a writer in the classic Freudian way. Due to my two bouts with pneumonia I developed into a sickly, overprotected child, accompanied to and from school every day by an anxious mother, and forced to wear a shameful knitted headgear that looked like Spiderman's mask and was to prevent my catching cold. Bereft of activities, I began to dream about activities. One day I put one such dream on paper. It happened after I read— in a Czech translation—the first two parts of an unfinished trilogy by James Oliver Curwood. Many years later, when I came to Canada, I was surprised that nobody there knew this master. Although Curwood had been American-born, he had written many romantic novels featuring red-coated Mounties and beautiful Indian girls: the Rose-Marie stuff. Frustrated because the happy ending was missing, I completed the saga as *The Mysterious Cave,* and for the first time in life experienced the bliss of creation. My second novel, inspired by a Canadian, Ernest Thompson Seton, and describing a war between the French and the British in America, was called *Men of Iron Hearts* (under the spell of feminine beauty the hearts melted). It was this novel which Alex mimeographed in a magazine he edited for the Club of Young Zionists at the Prague English Grammar School. After the Communist coup in Czechoslovakia, I wisely refrained from mentioning my debut.

As I grew into puberty, there followed a series of novel fragments no longer inspired by Canadian literature. All featured a young Czech actor who makes it big in Hollywood and vows eternal friendship to one Freddie Bartholomew.

I am the very opposite of a gay person, but apparently most young people go through a phase of platonic homosexuality. I was enchanted by the (probably pretty horrible) Hollywood boy-star after seeing him in a tearjerker based on *Little Lord Fauntleroy.* For the next summer, the local cinema announced another opus starring Freddie: *Captains Courageous.* Without explanation I staunchly refused to spend my vacations in Switzerland where, at a *pension* near Geneva, I was to learn French. I was afraid I would miss that saccharinized distortion of Kipling. Well, I did not—nor did I see Switzerland until some thirty-five years later, by which time the dimple-cheeked Freddie had long faded into dim memory.

For some time after that ingloriously spent summer the fragments continued, but after *Thoroughbreds Don't Cry* the Czech hero's counterpart became a girl by the name of Judy Garland. She remained the staple female character of a third set of fragments, in which the Czech actor turned into a nightclub tenor sax player.

For, like a revelation, jazz, that strange way of making music, entered my life. It is the only revelation I have ever experienced. I am not a mystic. My religious life has been all in the brain. I have been indifferent to marching men waving flags, to slogans, to little girls kissed by statesmen, to arms raised in Roman or proletarian fashion. But....

My initiation into jazz later proved to have been the beginning of my decisive step into literature as well. I talked my father into buying me a tenor sax, and tried my luck with several local student swing bands. But I did not have much more luck as an active jazzman than as a lover of Judy Garland. A sentence from Faulkner's *The Unvanquished* has always struck me as fitting my case extremely well: "Those who can, do, those who cannot and suffer enough because they can't, write about it." I could not, I suffered, and eventually I wrote *The Cowards*—the novel that unmade and later made me.

Judy Garland, like Freddie before her, soon dropped out of my fragments, yet she influenced my future in an important way. To be able to write her a letter, I started to learn English from a teach-yourself book, and badly neglected my French lessons with an expensive tutor. Finally, the expensive tutor told my disappointed mother that a student less talented for the language of Racine would be hard to find—although, she added, why a youngster so proficient in German should prove to be so thick-skulled in acquiring French was beyond her. But even before I was thus dismissed in disfavour, the celluloid girl of my dreams had been replaced by flesh-and-blood beauties from Náchod, and the locale of my fictional fragments shifted from California to my hometown, which became the Kostelec of my books. The melancholy superstar of the nightclubs on Sunset Boulevard assumed humbler proportions and turned into a cynic by the name of Danny Smiřický.

The choice of that name was not accidental, and curiously enough I owe it to the politics of the Great Aryan. My mother was very roots-conscious, and since her maiden name was Kuráž, a Czech phonetization of *courage*, the story went about that she was descended from a French aristocratic family which had fled France after the Revolution. (Hence my private French

lessons.) But until the Nuremberg Laws were applied in Bohemia, it had been just an unconfirmed story, deriving perhaps
from that vain side of my beautiful mother's character which
made her so proud of her easily verifiable Chod ancestry—
so majestically proud, in fact, that whenever she wanted to
put down my father, she switched from regular Czech to her
hard-sounding Chod dialect. My father, on the other hand,
was a class-unconscious democrat to the marrow of his bones,
and didn't give a damn about his forebears. He was a typical product of T.G. Masaryk's Americanized First Republic.
Although a card-carrying member of the ultra-conservative National Democratic party, he used to drink beer with the local
Socdems and Commies and neither he nor they found anything
unnatural about it. Although my father's party is now described
by the Fascists of Czech *Realsozialismus* as "semi-Fascist", the
majority of his close friends were Jews, and nobody saw anything strange in this either. In fact, my dad was something
of a philo-Semite, due mainly, I suspect, to a Jewish aunt of
mine of whom he was inordinately fond. This dark-eyed beauty,
whom I remember in long black pants (only suffragettes wore
pants in those days) and smoking from a three-foot cigarette
holder, combined, in her attractive person, capitalism and Communism. She was a millionaire, and an active member of the
Party, in which she invested most of her free capital: a true
parlour Bolshevik. When the Nazis came she fled to the Soviet
Union, where they promptly put her behind bars. Only one letter arrived from her, over which I found my father in tears that
he tried to hide from Mother. Auntie Marie asked him to send
her a Czech-Russian dictionary. After that we never heard from
her. In a book my wife published forty years later in Canada,
about Jews in the Czech Eastern Army, auntie is mentioned as
a *politruk* in Stalingrad. But she never came back.

Although my father had no interest in his ancestry, the
Nazis had: like everyone else we were required to prove our
Aryan origin. The proof, partly obfuscated, was provided by
my father's brother, who was a Catholic priest and liked to
research old parish registers. Three surprising things came to
light. First, the legend of my mother's French background was
confirmed, though not much to her liking. On her father's side
she was indeed descended from a Frenchman. But this man's

only connection with aristocracy was his profession. He was a butler who accompanied his master into the count's temporary exile in a West Bohemian château, succumbed to the charms of a Chod girl from a nearby village, and defected from the nobleman's service. If this was something of a disappointment to my mother, my venerable uncle's second discovery was, in the light of the new law, embarrassing. It appeared that the maiden name of one of my father's grandmothers was Silbernagel. The chances of a Silbernagel being Aryan are slim, but fortunately, in the wedding entry of the parish register, the lady was listed as "of Catholic faith". Of course, the Nazis didn't care about a Jew's religious beliefs, and the pathetic efforts of some Jews in Náchod to save themselves by asking the ever-ready Father Meloun to baptize them proved absolutely futile. But according to the Nuremberg Laws, if a grandparent's race could not be established beyond reasonable doubt, but the person was listed as Catholic or Protestant, he or she was to be regarded as Aryan. My uncle, having slightly tampered with the evidence, cunningly proved that this was Granny Silbernagel's case, and we were safe.

My uncle's third discovery was a pleasant surprise for my aristocratophile of a mother. The Škvoreckýs were apparently an extremely old family, first mentioned in the fourteenth century as yeomen who owned a castellet east of Prague, in the village of Škvorec. An ancestor, Martin Škvorecký, a turncoat who switched from Protestantism to Catholicism after the defeat of the Czech Protestants in the battle of the White Mountain in 1620, was even of some importance to historiography. He had managed the estates of Count Czernín, one of the biggest landholders in Bohemia, and his weekly reports on the state of the count's farms survived and serve as a priceless source for the study of the economy of the Thirty Years' War. Martin ended his life miserably, though. His seventeen-year-old second wife, at that age already the mother of two sons, ran away with Swedish soldiers, and the old husband went mad. The "Swedish" soldiers were, most probably, Protestant Czechs who fought in the Swedish army in the hope of reconquering their land. When they saw their case was hopeless, they at least took Czech girls with them to Sweden, irrespective of their marital status, to become their wives, the mothers of their children, and the cooks who would nourish the fading memories of the old fatherland with dumplings, pork, and sauerkraut.

The Škvoreckýs were a sort of sideline to the powerful Smiřický family, one of the most prominent aristocratic houses in Bohemia. Hence Danny Smiřický.

He, however, was not born until after the war. During the first four years of that *Götterdämmerung* I attended the local *Realgymnasium*, a very traditional institution with mandatory Latin and mathematics as the two main subjects at matriculation exams. In the course of those four years, Czech grammar schools were quickly Germanized, first by increasing the number of German classes from three to seven per week, then by decreeing that such ideologically important subjects as history and geography be taught in German. It was the Nazis who introduced the term "ideology" into our vocabulary; can anyone wonder why, ever since, I have mistrusted that word and all the varying contents it signified? Something called *Die deutsche Ideologie* became part of our German instruction, and was reluctantly taught by a pretty Sudeten-German, Eva Althammer, who racially forgot herself by marrying a Czech with the hopelessly non-Teutonic name of Švorčík. She did it, however, before the war: such a mésalliance would not be permitted after the establishment of the Protektorat Böhmen und Mähren. The German *Ideologie* consisted mostly of memorizing biographies of the leading Nazis: "*Adolf Hitler, der Führer und Reichskanzler des Grossdeutschen Reiches, wurde in Braunau geboren.... Reichsmarschall Hermann Göring hat sich im ersten Weltkrieg als Jagdflugzeugführer auserordentlich ausgezeichnet.*" More fun was provided by *Die Rassentheorie* taught, as part of history, by a gentle old spinster lady whose German was so poor that— although in Czech she was an excellent lecturer—she had to instruct us by reading slowly and with many mispronunciations from mimeographed sheets. The theory was quite something. We learned that the Germans, far from being a "pure" race, were in fact a "*Rassenmischung der besten Germanischen und Nordischen Elemente*": a top-quality race cocktail. The "pure" race was the Jews. No admixture of noble blood there, only a parasitic instinct, greediness, and thick lips drooling at the sight of Aryan girls.

Aryan girls were objects of interest also to the *Rassen-forscher*, the racial researchers from the Institut für Rassen-forschung, housed in the former Faculty of Philosophy of Charles University in Prague, which had been closed by the Nazis in 1939. Sometime in 1941 all fifteen-year-old Czech girls in Prague were summoned to the Institute where the scientists photographed them in the nude and took measurements of their skulls, hips, and bosoms. About a year later, during a visit to Prague, I bought a set of nude photographs from a waiter. To my surprise, among the shy-looking lovelies I recognized my niece. The race researchers apparently were not above a practical application of their theories.

What a science, this racial theory! We learned that the noblest among the Germanic tribes were the Vandals, since they best preserved the warrior traditions of immemorial myth. The military achievements of Rome should be credited to an admixture of German blood in the veins of the Roman legionnaires. The same blood was the better ingredient in the bodily juices of the English; symptomatic of that was, for instance, Shakespeare's best play, *The Merchant of Venice*. The Japanese allies were skipped over as "Aryans of the East", and within the German nation itself there existed several racial types. Our good teacher stammered the ultralong words describing the ideal type—tall, blond-haired, narrow-skulled, grey-eyed—and Lexa, who later became an inextricable part of my novels, asked, as if innocently, in German: "Why then, Professor, is the Reichspropagandaminister Herr Doktor Josef Goebbels dark and short?" The teacher was taken aback and promised to look up the mystery for the next class. She kept her word and came up with the characterization of Dr. Goebbels as belonging to the type of *nachgedunkelter Schrumpfgermane*; a staggering label which I am unable to translate. "A secondarily darkened Shrivelgerman", perhaps? Anyway, this gave the impetus to a game of names we used to play from then on, giving Germanic-sounding names to our own racial types: *Riesenbauchgermane*—Giantbelly-German, or *Rotundogermanus Goeringi* in Latin—being for instance the one given to the amiable fat trumpeter of the Zachoval jazz band, who became the Benno of my novels. Years later, in a book on Goebbels which I read while ghostwriting the autobiography of the minister's famous mistress, Lída Baarová, I found out that *nachgedunkelter Schrumpfgermane* was a defamatory nickname given to the little doctor by some not-so-orthodox SA men.

So we had fun, too, in those grim times: we had our swing bands, and the town was full of lovely mountain-climbing girls. When my novel *The Swell Season* appeared in Canada, some critics doubted its authenticity. Why, they wrote, he describes life under the Nazis as almost devoid of hardships and rather full of merriment. In fact, like life anywhere. One critic found the occasional intrusions of the Nazi threat into the idyll of Kostelec "rather unexpected".

This bewilderment comes, I suppose, from seeing too many trashy films about Nazism, and from forgetting about the irrepressible ability of youth to enjoy life under almost any circumstances. My late friend J.R. Pick wrote a humorous novel about the Theresienstadt ghetto, which functioned as a gate to the hells of Auschwitz, Maidanek, Treblinka. It is called *The Society for the Prevention of Cruelty to Animals* and features a group of Jewish youngsters who catch and eat the pets of the SS guards to protect the beasts from exposure to their Nazi masters. Gallows humour, to be sure, but humour nevertheless. Most of the models for Pick's characters perished in the gas chambers. He himself survived, but lost one lung. He died, at the age of fifty-seven, of heart failure.

Of course, the horrors of Auschwitz did exist. But when you were sixteen, seventeen, not Jewish and therefore not in any immediate danger, you did not think about the horrors all the time. Besides, the knowledge of them was vague. The Nazis kept their secrets well. Also, their rule in Bohemia was less conspicuously bloody than in some other occupied lands. Bohemia—unlike, for instance, Poland—was a heavily industrialized country, famous for its armament factories, and the Nazis needed to maintain production of the Škoda three-purpose guns, of the Panzerjäger armoured attack vehicles, and other fruits of Czech weapon design. The boss of Bohemia, SS Obergruppenführer Reinhard Heydrich, posed as a convinced socialist and a protector of the working class. That's why the terror in the Protectorate was not as indiscriminate as elsewhere—except, of course, during the weeks after the Czech and Slovak paratroopers from England had killed the workers' friend.

After that spectacular event of the Second World War, people were at first jubilant. Then the executions started—about five thousand of them, announced on red posters every day, day after day. The villages of Lidice and Ležáky were erased from the face of the earth, all males older than fifteen years of age shot, all women transported to the Ravensbrück concentration camp, all small children sent for adoption by childless German families. A truly apocalyptic time—with, however, a Czech encore. The only man of Lidice who survived was a murderer who, at the time of the Holocaust, had been serving twenty years in jail. He was a decent, well-behaved fellow who had murdered his young wife not with premeditation but in a fit of jealousy. The Czech prison guards liked him and spared him the knowledge of what had happened. They neglected to tell him even when he was released, about a year before the end of the war, and he searched for his disappeared birthplace in vain. Eventually he found out, and something happened to his mind. He went to the Gestapo and demanded an execution. He was a citizen of Lidice and a man, he argued, and hadn't the Germans, with proper Prussian thoroughness, picked up all citizens of Lidice, no matter where they lived at the time of the tragedy, and shot them as well? The Gestapo men considered the apparently crazy fellow a joke and did not fulfil his wish. When Lidice was rebuilt and the women who had not died at Ravensbrück moved in with their new husbands (their marriage prospects greatly increased since, at a time of desperate housing shortage, they became owners of brand-new family houses), the poor murderer claimed his right to a house too. He was chased out of the village by the furious ladies. Soon afterwards he drank himself to death.

Yes, during the Heydrich terror life in Náchod did not differ much from that of the Warsaw ghetto. But at other times it went on as normally as can be during a war and in a town far removed from the battlefields. Now and then the Gestapo took someone, usually an intellectual or a former professional soldier. Some returned after a few months—my father among them—some after the war. Some did not return. But death was not as indiscriminate as in Poland or in the Balkans. You learned to live with the ordeals of the situation, and you were sixteen, seventeen. Totalitarian regimes are not only bloody but also pompous. Pomposity is always ridiculous. Consequently, every bloody dictatorship has its comic aspects. Do you remember the *Paradeschritt* of the SS? Their absurd goose-stepping to lyraphone music? When people saw it for the first time in occupied Prague they burst out laughing—and some were arrested right away, and some never came back.

In 1943 I passed my matriculation exams—by that time the school was so Germanized that even Czech examinations had to be conducted in German—and my coming of age coincided with the announcement of the *Totaleinsatz*, according to which all able-bodied Czech men and women were drafted into the armament industry. "All" in dictatorships always reads as "except the more equal", and the greater equality may be acquired in different ways. It applied mostly to people who knew where to pull strings and had enough French cognac saved from pre-war times to bribe an influential Nazi or quisling. My father, unfortunately, was a teetotaller, and whenever he tried to pull he did so, reliably, in the wrong direction. I was drafted and was to be sent to Bremen, then one of the prime targets for carpet bombing raids. According to a Czech saying, however, if the devil is unable to do a job, he substitutes a woman. Or perhaps it is the Good Lord who is the ladies' man. Utterly dejected, I was walking away from the *Arbeitsamt* in the district capital of Hradec Králové with an order to report for transport in three days when I ran into the jolly wife of my confirmation godfather. She was a model of neither marital fidelity nor Czech propriety, and that afternoon she was compromising herself with a man in a German army officer's uniform: at least he was not an SS. "Why so gloomy, young man?" she teasingly asked me, and with a savage look at her consort, I told her why. "Thank God it's not a broken heart!" she laughed. "This can be fixed. Go home."

And she fixed it. I never asked her how, but she did. I never saw her again, but instead of going to Bremen I was dispatched to the Metallbauwerke Zimmerman und Schilling, a Messerschmitt subsidiary in Náchod. I don't even know what

became of that "auntie" of mine. After the war my godfather
lived alone.

Was she a sexy guardian angel sent by the Lord? There were
such angels. I knew another one: she used to be a young local
wench of easy virtue, a pretty proletarian girl who preferred
bedding with gentlemen to working on a selfactor machine in
one of the cotton mills. Shortly before the war she successfully
seduced our Jewish landlord's innocent fatso of a son, a passionate hunter of hares. As soon as she reached the status of
a converted Jewish matron, she resumed her old lifestyle. She
became one of the scandals of the town, and the fat hunter
its principal cuckold. But when the Nazis came, the spread-leg
lady refused to leave her husband, although divorcing a Jew
was easier than getting a haircut. Otherwise, however, she did
not mend her ways, and to immorality and infidelity she added
the sin of bed-quislingism. She would be seen in the elegant
Café Beránek in the company of cheek-scarred, ramrod Prussian officers, laughing unashamedly over privileged champagne
bubbling in glasses on marble-top tables, while the hunter was
inconspicuously surviving the war, stuck away in the cottage
of the courtesan's parents: Jews married to Aryans were not
sent to the camps. Nevertheless, every busybody in town was
preparing for the day of liberation which was to be celebrated
by, among other things, the public shaving off of the hair of
the harlot. About a month before the end of the hostilities the
harlot disappeared. She re-emerged on the ninth of May, sitting in an open, horse-driven carriage next to a scarred and
bemedalled ramrod officer of the Red Army. She retained her
hair and only moved, with her liberated husband, to Prague,
where they lived happily ever after, both having resumed their
old hunting hobbies.

C'est la vie. In the summer of 1943 I became a *Hilfsarbeiter*—
an auxiliary worker—in the Messerschmitt factory in Náchod.
Quite a shock for a pampered middle-class youngster whose
only physical exertion up till then had been the pressing of
the keys on his tenor saxophone. But it started a new chapter
of my education which, some years later, culminated with my
army service, and made me into what I am: a writer who, as
some of my readers kindly say—and I can only hope they are
not entirely off the target—has been able to portray, with equal

verisimilitude, a wide assortment of Czechs not only of both sexes but also of all walks of life.

It was a unique experience. There were fourteen-hour shifts which we tried to spend mostly in the latrine, partly to escape the boredom of mass production, partly to avoid working for the Nazis. The company that assembled in those smelly and smoky rooms was a classless amalgam of all classes, more so than in a jail: textile workers, students, bank clerks, tailors, gardeners, businessmen, barbers, lawyers, waiters—all turned welders, locksmiths, drill-operators, and *Hilfsarbeiter*. The discussions were profound, lively, and on many subjects; sometimes the shitting room resembled a philosophy seminar.

There was also a pathetic working-class girl, toiling on a drill, who helped me to get rid of the young man's burden. She also almost became the end of me. Since she made me feel like a man, I tried to behave like a man, which in those days meant like a war hero. She was a very patriotic kind of girl prepared, I am sure, to die for her country without much ado. I wasn't. But I realized that only after I had figured out and executed a rather clever act of sabotage, described in detail in *The Engineer of Human Souls*, which was aimed at radically reducing the firepower of the Messerschmitt fighter plane. Luckily enough, the sabotage was discovered by the Czech foreman, who did not inform the Gestapo but tried to cover up the deed. He explained to me quite unequivocally that my little stupidity could indeed turn into an act of heroism, sanctified by death on the gallows. I did not become a Dostoevsky only because I do not possess Dostoevsky's talent. But my mortal fear, I guess, was equally strong.

I survived. The girl did not. She wasn't hanged, though. She died of the classic illness of her class: tuberculosis. And soon I was to witness another TB death. But that wasn't until after the war, in the sweet, sunny spring of 1945. I was helping out at the hospital, and there a young survivor of Auschwitz was dying. She appeared to me like a living skeleton. She was beyond help. She survived the horror only to die amid the jubilant lilac blossoms of that spring, amid universal rejoicing and eager expectations of the glories of the newly won freedom. I almost despaired. Lying in my comfortable bed at night, I felt that nobody had the right to enjoy life while there, behind the antiseptic partitions, that quintessence of hopeless sadness lingered on, expiring slowly, day by day, until she faded out into nothingness. That sweet, sad summer of 1945 I enrolled at the medical school of Charles University. It seemed to me, young and inevitably idealistic, that only selfless service to those who suffer desperately could justify my own survival. Very few young men, I believe, ever decided to study medicine who were worse equipped for that strenuous vocation than I. My service to my fellow men—if service it was—would be of an entirely different kind.

Náchod was the scene of probably the last fighting at the end of the war in Europe. On the tenth of May, the SS rearguards of Marshal Schörner's army made a last stand on the outskirts of the town to inflict some last-minute casualties on the advancing spearheads of the Russian army under Marshal Malinowski. The army was Russian in name only. For sure, the officers looked Russian. But the draftees were soldiers from the Asian republics of the USSR.

The fighting was soon over, the surviving SS were savagely butchered by the Czechs, and after the Soviet spearheads, thousands upon thousands of horse-driven buggies rolled into town, followed by vast herds of captured horses. I had never seen so many equines in my life. The meat ration tickets, which even during the war entitled one to a double portion if the meat chosen was horsemeat, shot up in value like shares on a stock exchange gone crazy. Half a kilo of horsemeat for a hundred-gram coupon. Then two kilos. Then five. Then fifteen. In the first days after the war my native town must have devoured the equivalent of a century of four-legged participants in the Kentucky Derby.

But there was not only the memory of the dying Jewish girl in the hospital; there were other shadows, too, among the bright lights of that spring and summer. A few months earlier, while the war was still on, a leaflet issued by a local Communist cell had fallen into my hands. In this document, the comrades were exhorted to be ready for a liquidation of the "bourgeois resistance groups" as soon as the war was over. I was a member of one such group, and this was my initiation into Marxist-Leninist dialectics. The article was the first I had read which used the word "bourgeois" as a synonym for "bad, wrong, despicable". Since then, this usage has been mindlessly accepted by far too many in the West. And yet, in my opinion— and I have an incurable tendency to base my opinions on experience and solid reading, not on hearsay and ideology—the bourgeoisie are not worse than any other class. In fact, many things incline me to suspect that they, the middle class, neither rich enough to become decadent nor poor enough to become enfeebled, are the backbone of every society. I know of far too many who faced deadly situations during the Hitler years, and then again during the Stalin years, with coolness, courage, self-sacrifice, and honesty. I met quite a few perfumed and red-nailed girls, with the sweet charm of the bourgeoisie, who survived courageously the degrading conditions of Communist camps. I do not subscribe to that synonymous usage.

Soon I received another lesson in dialectics. I became the editor of a local youth weekly published by the newly founded Union of Czech Youth. Covertly this was a Communist-front organization from the very beginning, but overtly, in 1945, it was still nonpartisan. For the launching issue I wrote a lead article entitled "Goodbye, Mr. Churchill", an enthusiastic tribute to the great war leader who had just lost—inexplicably to me—the first post-war election. For the second number I contributed a "critical" analysis of the works of a young local painter who specialized in expressionistic portraits of girls, including my two great and, of necessity, platonic loves, Irena and Marie. In my article I defined Art as Love, inspired by the gentle colours of Marie's portrait—which was, indeed, a product of love. Like myself, the painter was pining for the inaccessible lips the colour of mellow strawberries which adorned the lovely face of that merry but chaste Catholic lass. Before the third issue was out I was summoned to the union's headquarters in Prague, where some grim-looking functionaries told me that Churchill was a Warmonger and a Reactionary, and that Art was not Love but Class Struggle. Unfortunately for them—fortunately for me—I had already read the definition of Churchill as a warmonger, in the display window of the Náchod Hitlerjugend Club. This little incident put something of an equation mark in my mind between Communism and National Socialism which I have never been able to erase—probably because reality is ineradicable.

That was the end of my career as a Youth Union editor.

At medical school I lasted exactly one semester. Memorizing the Latin names of all the bones in the human body proved to be an insurmountable task. I switched over to philosophy, where you can talk yourself out of any problem and successfully pass any exam without knowing anything; at least not by heart. Instead of attending lectures—all I needed for the colloquia was to borrow notes from diligent colleagues—I threw myself into the life of the big city. I also started writing seriously and made a few literary discoveries. My mentors were a shopgirl who called herself Maggie, and Ernest Hemingway.

Although, among other subjects, I was nominally taking phonetics with the celebrated Professor Trnka, one of the founders of the Prague Linguistic Circle, it was the grandiosely loquacious young Maggie who made me aware that language as it is actually spoken differs considerably, often radically, from what appears on the printed page—or used to in those days. The gap is—or was—much greater in Czech than in post–Mark Twain American English. Maggie was a natural-born raconteuse, unable to recount anything except in the form of a dramatic scene. Her basic narrative mode relied on the frequent use of the verb *povídat* (to say), which invariably introduced her masterful renditions of conflicting dialogue. "*Já povídám...von povídá*"— "I says...he says." But she condensed the three-syllable Czech verb into its bare essentials and connected it and the pronoun into a single word: "*Jápám...vonpá.*" Like Archimedes, I jumped out naked from the restricting corset of classical Czech usage and produced a novel called *The Nylon Age*. On paper it looked like the phonetic transcriptions of Daniel Jones. Having discovered that there is no letter for the "ng" sound which, in Czech, is a nasal, I considered actually using Jones, but abandoned the overintellectual idea. Nevertheless, the result was a hardly readable text. It told—with thousands of apostrophes—about a love affair between a university student and a shopgirl; as you can see, the content was realistic too. The story was presented in a series of dramatic scenes encased in the heroine's endlessly talkative monologues. And then I read *A Farewell to Arms*.

In my many fragmentary Hollywood novels I had been pretty good—as is every young adept of fiction—at describing nature and creating mood, preferably of the gloomy-sentimental variety. My evocations of Los Angeles must have been second only to Chandler's. But when it came to dialogue—well, my characters were wooden and lectured to each other with all the animation of shop dummies. Over the pages of Hemingway I realized that people in a novel can talk about nothing particularly important, and yet their dialogue can be amusing, captivating, full of nuances, and, when you come to think about it, quite profound. So Hemingway taught me to write dialogue, and Maggie acquainted me with the use of the vernacular. The girl's lesson proved to be the more fateful one, for it eventually led to charges of imitating decadent naturalists like Louis-Ferdinand Céline, and of irreverence for the mother tongue.

But it was poetry, not prose, that prepared my eventual entry onto the Prague literary scene, underground variety. In 1945 I penned a long Whitmanesque poem entitled "Don't Despair!", its title taken from a line by the surrealist poet Jindřich Heisler. It was in all respects a very derivative poem, and I submitted it to the jury of a poetic competition in 1946. Instead of a prize I received a letter from František Halas, who expressed a wish to see me.

To my mind Halas was hardly a lesser poet than, say, William Carlos Williams or W.H. Auden. But because he performed his rhymed miracles in a small, unknown tongue, and translators with the poetic talent of a T.S. Eliot as well as an intimate knowledge of Czech are rare, internationally Halas is a nobody. To Czech poetry and to me however.... In a trembling voice I made an appointment with the poet's secretary, and a few days later I entered his office on shaky legs. As is the common lot of poets, Halas had to make a living as a bureaucrat. He began by telling me that he had not recommended my poem for a prize because—and here I interrupted him: "Oh, I never intended to have it published!" A transparent lie, of course. Halas looked at me with mocking eyes, then said: "C'mon! The defloration must come one day!" The sentence from his gentle lips silenced me, and he proceeded to explain that he feared that, should the poem come out, I would be slaughtered by the critics of both the right and the left.

It may be that he was only trying to make the denial of a prize more palatable to me. Anyway, I didn't understand him then. Why, in my poem I just tried to present the world as I saw it! To express my feelings as they were! My aesthetics were simpleminded indeed. In my inexperience I had no idea that simple realism is the last thing ideologically minded critics want. And in those days, the vast majority of critics were ideologically minded. Their concept of the writer's subject—of the world and of the human life in it—was a combination of idealization and diabolization. Reality was not their friend. It never is. It never fits their visions.

That was my third major literary lesson: through no fault or virtue of mine, I was apparently walking some sort of tightrope which neither the right nor the left cherished and approved. Halas spoke from personal experience. He was one of those kind but fallible Catholics who, moved by genuine social feelings in the years of the Great Depression, had joined the Communist party. In the sweet, tragic summer of 1945 he travelled, for the first and last time in his life, to the Soviet Union. He returned a broken, desperate man. Three years later he died, only a few months after the coup d'état of 1948. Before his death he wrote a testament which was circulated in the underground in the fifties and, after many years, published abroad. It is a compassionate confession of the big mistake he made, and a bitter critique of the absurd dream of justice called Communism.

Halas also left his notebooks to his friend and factotum, the literary and art critic Jindřich Chalupecký. In one of them he had jotted down a few remarks about myself and my poem. And so I received another letter, this time from Chalupecký, inviting me to attend an informal meeting of friends in the apartment of the poet and artist Jiří Kolář.

Thus I became a member of one of the very few circles of underground literature of the early fifties—the time of hangings and of the Soviet-operated Czech uranium camps. You qualified for hanging either by really doing something against the new dictators—trying, for instance, to carry on the activities of the banned Socialist party, like Milada Horáková, the only Czech woman ever hanged by her own people for political "crimes"—or by being Jewish and high up in the Communist party hierarchy, and therefore conspicuous to the evil eyes of Stalin and his Czech sycophants—like Rudolf Slánský and his "Zionist co-conspirators". For the uranium mines, simple bad luck sufficed. Two or three times I had good luck, while others were arrested.

One of the most remarkable members of the Chalupecký–Kolář circle, surrealist painter Mikuláš Medek, whose family had taken care of the little daughter of Kafka's Milena during the war, once actually painted the evil eyes of Stalin. Surrealism was, naturally, strictly taboo; painting like Magritte or Toyen, i.e., indulging in *entartete Kunst* or "degenerate art", as *Genosse* Goebbels had called it, could be punishable, and so poor Medek had to do his real work in secrecy and offer his hack services on the socialist market. In the latter field, though, he cannot be regarded a success. His first commission was for a poster advertising a bedbug-killing powder. Medek produced a beautifully realistic human torso, surrealistically bitten all over by bedbugs (*before*), and shining with mysterious inner light (*after*). He almost got himself arrested because one of the wise men of the Approving Committee found the bitten torso slanderous, and usable by enemy propaganda as referring to housing conditions in Socialist Czechoslovakia.

But soon afterwards Medek seemed to have struck it lucky. He received two commissions at once: one a thirty-metre-high portrait of Party Secretary Rudolf Slánský which was to be used during the Barnum-like First of May celebrations in Wenceslas Square, and the other a private order from a minor Party secretary. In the Cloister Hluboká, where the comrades assembled art objects from all the cloisters they had closed—after first sending the nuns and monks to the concentration cloister in Braunau—this luminary had seen a baroque painting of the Saviour whose eyes, due to some trick of the painter's craft, followed him all around the room. The secretary expressed a wish to have such a picture for his office, only of Stalin, not of Christ. Mikuláš was a perfect craftsman, and the trick was no secret to him. The Stalin he produced was a most penetrating study of the killer, and when I walked around the easel to try out how the eyes worked I felt my knees trembling. Mikuláš was in for a nice bundle.

But then blow came upon blow. First, a few days before the Barnum–Bailey–Marx–Engels–Lenin–Stalin hit parade, Slánský was unmasked as a Zionist spy; the comrades didn't pay Medek for his work, and he had to congratulate himself that they had not included him, as a fellow traveller, in the conspiracy. He got paid for the Stalin with the movable eyes, but a mere couple of years later Stalin too was unmasked (though not as a Zionist), the minor secretary was arrested, and his precious picture was confiscated. Again, Mikuláš had to congratulate himself. Not all creators of Stalin's likeness got off so easily.

A case in point is Švec, the sculptor who made the World's Greatest Statue of Josef Vissarionovich, the one that for about six years loomed over Prague. The Party ordered the monument to be blown up in October 1962. But they had trouble carrying out the order. They could not liquidate the Thing by just one powerful charge because the explosion could have damaged a considerable portion of downtown Prague. So the pyrotechnicians nibbled him away, bit by bit, in a series of mini-explosions. It took them, I think, a couple of weeks: the statue got gradually thinner, less and less realistic, until it looked quite modern. The whole process was preserved on film by a photographer who, from the windows of the Writers' Union, took pictures daily. They document a gorgeous experiment in pop art, or maximal art, or whatever. Švec, however, took his life when he saw how his realistic Goliath was changing slowly, step by step, into a Giacometti-like monster.

The unlucky sculptor was really more a victim of malicious fate than of just Stalinism. Only one item of his oeuvre survives. It stands in the garden of the Art Academy in Prague and captures a motorcycle driver taking a sharp curve—a most unusual, exquisitely beautiful rendition of motion in stone. It is an early work. After it, the gifted student began to get commissions. A huge T.G. Masaryk for some town square; an even huger John Huss, the fourteenth-century religious martyr, for another; Franklin Delano Roosevelt, right after the Second World War. The first two were destroyed by the Nazis. The Roosevelt monument was never completed because the Communists came to power. When Švec was asked to participate in the nonpublic competition for Stalin's monument, he had already been pretty frustrated and thought that he stood no chance anyway, with all the National Artists for competitors. So he reportedly concocted a model in the course

of one single afternoon, with the help of two bottles of vodka—
and he won. It seems that the National Artists—none of them
real Communists, just radishes (like a radish, red only on the
surface)—who stood a dangerously good chance of prostituting
themselves in a gigantic manner, either did not send any
models, blaming the failure on feelings of inadequacy to meet
the awe-inspiring task, or spent even less time and even more
vodka on their entries. That's how the story, or perhaps the
folksy legend, of the World's Biggest Stalin goes.

The times were lunatic. We would meet at Kolář's, read unpublished and, under the circumstances, unpublishable stories
aloud, talk about literature and art, and indulge in similar sub-
versive activities. Jiří Kolář presided; he is now well known for
his collages, etc., and lives in exile in Paris. Bohumil Hrabal
read the first version of the story which later became world-
famous as the Oscar-winning film *Closely Watched Trains*; the
first draft was definitely *entartete Kunst*. Hrabal still resides
in Bohemia, in close contact with troublemakers such as the
Jazz Section of the Musicians' Union, in and out of trouble,
protected solely by the love of his hundreds of thousands of
readers. Věra Linhartová, the pretty art historian and experimentalist of fiction, lives in exile in Paris. So does Jan Vladislav,
the poet and translator of, among many other things, Shakespeare's sonnets. Jan Rychlík, the modernistic composer, jazz
theoretician, and percussionist, died early. Jan Hanč, the existentialist athlete and poet, followed him to the grave a few years
later. Zdeněk Urbánek, the Shakespearian translator, became
a Charter 77 signatory. Jiřina Hauková, a poet and close friend
of Dylan Thomas, and her husband, Jindřich Chalupecký—we
were a stubborn lot, and we survived.

It was in this underground circle that I first met my future
wife, Zdena. In fact, the meeting was cunningly arranged by
my friend František Jungwirth, a translator and author of
mystery stories who once travelled to Moscow for the sole
purpose of stealing some American detective novels unavailable
in Czechoslovakia from the American Exhibition held there
as part of the rapprochement of the late fifties. This reckless
adventurer became engaged to Zdena's sister. Deeply in love, he
was extolling his prize when he mentioned that his fiancée had

a sibling who was a "hot dish". "A dancer, you know?" he said, and gave me a dirty-old-man wink. Naturally I was interested. The interest proved fatal. The fatality, however, was of the best sort.

I wrote several books during those dark and colourful years: *The Cowards* in 1948–49, right after the putsch; *The Tank Corps* after my discharge from the army in 1954; *The Stories of the Tenor Saxophonist* in 1955–56. And with P.L. Dorůžka, a jazz historian and musicologist, and Ludvík "Louis" Šváb, a psychiatrist by profession but the guitarist of the Prague Dixieland Band by vocation, I put together a musical show called *Really the Blues*, the very first jazz revue to be produced after the Communist takeover. All these efforts spelled trouble; some brought me within reach of the prison gates. But I was lucky. Or maybe I had a good guardian angel.

The Stories of the Tenor Saxophonist fell into the wrong hands, those of a young lady portrayed in several of them, one of the femmes fatales of the fifties who loved to associate with characters in the underground, and were to them an excellent source of information; after all, very prominent people in the aboveground also loved to associate with such females. This particular sexbomb, whom I called Lizzette in my stories, was the object of the amorous yearnings of, among others, Pavel Kohout (*Poor Murderer*), the then young star of literary Stalinism. After the death of his God he started to have doubts, and was in the habit of confessing them to Lizzette. She promptly reported them to me so that I was able to be pretty accurate when I portrayed Pavel in my various works. Pavel eventually metamorphosed from a vain Stalinist hack and manufacturer of ideological platitudes into a consummate playwright and novelist, with the inevitable consequence of such status: exile.

An even more influential friend of Lizzette was Václav Kopecký, the ultra-Stalinist minister of information and the overlord of film, art, and propaganda. This proletarian leader liked to collect things, and among his prize exhibits was a genuine countess, a nonagenarian who lived in one of the old palaces in Malá Strana and did not even know we had become afflicted with Communism. The minister supplied her with cigarettes and paid her a pension out of his own pocket so that she, with her nonagenarian chambermaid, could live blissfully ignorant of the blessings of the dictatorship of the proletariat. Kopecký also had a private screening room in the Wallenstein Palace, a baroque affair with pink and gold wallpaper and silk rococo chairs where, two or three times a week, he screened American westerns for himself and for a few invited sycophants and ladyfriends. Each of them was entitled to invite one guest, and that's how I witnessed a memorable showing of John Ford's *Stagecoach*, during which the minister almost suffered an attack of apoplexy when Red Indians threatened the lives of Claire Trevor and John Wayne. Quite a sight, high-ranking comrades shouting jubilantly when the US cavalry came to the rescue. At that time, audiences in the regular cinemas of Prague watched dramas about the fulfilling of industrial quotas.

But *The Stories of the Tenor Saxophonist* put an end to my friendship with Lizzette, at least temporarily. She was mad at me, not because I portrayed her as a cunning, high-class courtesan—of that she was rather proud—but because I wrote that her ass was too big. She threatened to take the manuscript to the StB, the Czech version of the KGB, and it took some effort to pacify her.

Strange how people behave. There was a certain corporal Střevlíček who paid dearly for his two years in the army. He entered the service as an unattached lad, then knocked up a village girl and decided to save her honour. He was quite cheerful about it. "I'm a blacksmith, I can support a family!" became his self-confident slogan. Then the wife bore him triplets. "I'm a blacksmith, I can...." His optimism continued unabated until he was finally granted a furlough to see that family of his. When he returned he was still optimistic, but less than before. It came out that this wife had had two illegitimate children by previous lovers, one of whom had been a gypsy. Střevlíček, an unattached lad only a year and a half earlier, was now a father of five. That night, in the local pub, he fed his optimism by imbibing, then ordered the band to play his favourite song. "I'm a blacksmith...," he repeated, whereupon he jumped onto the dancing floor, stamped his foot—and collapsed with a broken leg. A miraculous or maybe surrealistic event.

Well, I put the story into my book *The Tank Corps*, and about three years later whom do I run into on Wenceslas Square but

Střevlíček. He was a big, burly blacksmith with the look of a quarrelsome bulldog. Grinning maliciously, he put his heavy palm heavily on my shoulder and said, "I read your book. My sis is a typist and she had to copy it for her boss." (The sis naturally copied an unpublished typewritten *samizdat* copy.) My God, I thought, and I said a few quick prayers to the Lord, for I expected to be dead, or at least mortally beaten up, within the next few seconds. "A jolly good book, partner!" said the blacksmith. "You got me right! Ho ho! Did we have fun in the old tank corps!" Then he dragged me to the Pinkas beer hall, paid for everybody at the table, told the story with quite a few embellishments, and concluded that, since his discharge from the army, he had added four more brats to his collection: two sets of twins, all "cracked up down below" he added somewhat sadly, but immediately cheered up again. "I'm a blacksmith, I can support...."

Yes, people do react unexpectedly. Irena stopped talking to me after *The Cowards*, although I wrote so beautifully about her in that book, and even straightened her bandy legs. My mistake, perhaps, for as Poe knew—and she, like every intellectual girl in Bohemia, was an ardent reader of Poe—"there is no exquisite beauty without some strangeness in the proportion." On the other hand, Marie, after she had read a smuggled-in copy of *The Swell Season* back in Náchod, sent me a sweet letter. "Oh, Danny, did we have fun those many, many years ago!" And she even enclosed an old photograph of herself as she looked in the good old times.

None of the works of my young maturity came out until much later. *The Tank Corps* had to wait until 1969, when Gallimard brought it out in French as *L'Escadron blindé*. In Czechoslovakia a chapter was printed in a magazine with disastrous results; in a fit of rage, the political commander of the army issued orders forbidding any Czech magazine to print any kind of satire on any aspect of army life. In the year of Alexander Dubček the novel was printed, but then the Russians came and the entire printing was destroyed before publication. It was first brought out in Czech in 1972—eighteen years after I had written it—by my wife's firm, Sixty-Eight Publishers in Toronto.

When the tanks arrived in Prague in August 1968, one of their first objectives was to occupy the building of the Writers' Union, which also housed the offices of the union's publishing house. After about three weeks the Red Army withdrew and the editors moved back in. They found nothing missing except some felt pens and the original of one of the illustrations for *The Tank Corps*. It was the frontispiece drawing, showing a group of army officers' faces in magnificently cheeky caricature. But then one of the editors found the drawing. It was stuck among some old proofs and the man who had put it there had obviously got scared of what he had done to it. Under the most repulsive-looking officer's head there was a careful inscription: *"Eto golava prjaklyatoy svini, generala Antona Antonovitche Gretchka"*—"This is the head of that fucking pig, General Gretchko". The general was the commanding officer of the invading Soviet forces. Apparently Good Soldier Švejk has his siblings even in the World's Best-Disciplined Army.

Speaking of Švejk: many people say that *The Tank Corps* is a kind of *Good Soldier Švejk* in a Communist army. The name of Švejk (often transcribed as Schweik) is known to most western readers, but I wonder how many have actually read the classic novel, and know who Švejk is and what he stands for.

He is, to put it briefly, one of the major embodiments of passive resistance: the essence of one of the few ways open to the powerless who intend to survive the dangers of living under the powerful. Whenever Švejk is called upon to do something that a loyal citizen of an authoritarian state is supposed to do, he does it not just obediently, as most subjects would, but with exemplary enthusiasm. Whenever he is given an order, he is overeager to carry it out to the letter. He ostentatiously displays an unshaking and unshakable belief in every authority and every piece of wisdom emanating from that authority's mouth. He is an energetic shouter of officially approved slogans. In short: by always behaving as a model citizen, an exemplary soldier, a super-obedient orderly, he exposes the impossibility of such behaviour. The good soldier is too good to be true. To define his philosophical meaning—for he has a very deep one—he shows the absurdity of ideological orthodoxy.

The name of Švejk's creator, Jaroslav Hašek, is, I suspect, much less known in the West. Hašek was a spineless but extremely talented man. He betrayed everyone and everything—but he wrote *Švejk*. Having made a name for himself as an épateur of the bourgeoisie and a professional alcoholic, he was drafted into the Austrian army, defected to the Russians, and joined the Czech legion that was fighting for secession from Austria. As editor of the legion's paper he enthusiastically supported T.G. Masaryk, the future president, in his efforts to organize the Czechs for a fight, on the Russian side, against the Germans. Then the Bolshevik Revolution broke out, a Czech Red Army unit was formed, and Lenin signed a separate peace treaty with Germany which put the Czech cause in jeopardy. Hašek, foreseeing the victory of the Bolsheviks, promptly ran over to them, made a career as an editor and political commissar, and married a Russian lady, although he already had a wife in Prague. Under fire he showed solid cowardice; he once ran away from the battlefield disguised as a woman. Nevertheless, after the war the Bolsheviks sent him as their agent to Czechoslovakia, where he was to organize a Communist movement in the coal mines around Kladno. As soon as he set foot on his native soil he forgot about his mission and resumed his former life as a popular, story-telling derelict. He worked on *Švejk*, but over its unfinished pages drank himself to death. Not a savoury character, but, oh my, what a writer! And what an épateur! Among his pre-war pranks was also the founding of a political party under the name The Party of Moderate Progress within the Bounds of the Law. At about that time my uncle co-founded the Catholic People's Party, of which he eventually became the deputy chairman. During election times he had been involved in several public debates with Hašek and used to relate this experience until the end of his days, half a century later. Until then, too, he believed that out of those debates he had come victorious. "Just imagine!" my pious uncle would tell me. "Have you ever heard of a party with a sillier name? The Party of Moderate Progress within the Bounds of the Law! Who would ever vote for such a party! I tell you, Josef, the man may have been a good writer, but he was a political ignoramus!"

I wonder which of the extremely numerous characters in Hašek's *magnum opus* is a portrait of my late uncle, the

Catholic deputy. He himself, naturally, had never stooped to reading the ignoramus's masterpiece.

The ironic fact is that at the time I wrote *The Tank Corps* I had not read *Švejk* either. Certainly I was aware of its existence; I knew some of its episodes from oral renditions by enthusiastic connoisseurs. But I had never really perused the work—which corroborates a hypothesis I have that *The Tank Corps* is not literary satire, but plain realism. I certainly did not intend to write satire; I just endeavoured to capture experience. I was not inspired by a world-famous book, but by a worldwide phenomenon: the army and its inherent absurdities. The basic absurdity is similar to *Švejk*'s: the discrepancy between ideological concepts and reality. But I wasn't even aware of that principle when I was writing the book. It's *post factum* knowledge, or rather analysis, revealed to me by a clever lady critic in Sweden.

The major disaster of my literary career came with the publication of *The Cowards*. I had written the novel in 1948–49 and did not offer it to a publisher until ten years later. In it I made a conscious effort to produce a work of "magic realism". What I had in mind, however, was not the type of magic performed by some South American novelists—such as Gabriel García Márquez, who uses gag-like surreal exaggerations to stress the craziness of the world he describes, or simply distorts historical facts to serve his ideological purposes. The term had been coined before the war by a Czech poet, Josef Hora, who meant an infusion of poetry into epic prose. What I had in mind was recreating events in my past life so that they would, as if magically, return to me; so that, as Hawthorne had written, they would be "etherealized by distance". But I knew all too well that the only permissible kind of realism in the early fifties was socialist realism, a type of socialist western, and I was not very good at that genre.

Curiously enough, my first published work *was* a western. I only ghostwrote it, together with a friend who soon afterwards died of a brain tumour. We did it for a professional hack who was trying to cure himself of alcoholism in the spa of Běloves, on the outskirts of Náchod. This derelict fell in love with my hereditarily beautiful sister Anna, and since he spent all of his time either drinking the curative waters or playing tennis with Sis, he had none left to fulfil his obligation of one western novel per month for a kind of penny-dreadful weekly called *Rodokaps* (*Pocketnovels*). When he learned about my literary aspirations from my sister, he offered me a deal: he would provide me with a synopsis, I would put some flesh on its bones, he would then paint it over and we would split the profits fifty-fifty. The opus—called, I think, *The Guns of Rio Presto*—had a plot that must be called classic. It featured a Rancher and his beautiful Daughter and a band of Thieves who were stealing his cattle. The incompetent local Sheriff was helpless. Then a Stranger appeared, first against the rising sun on the Horizon, later in the local Saloon. He saw the Daughter and offered help. He shot up the Thieves and saved the Rancher from penury. However, the Daughter then revealed to the Stranger that she was engaged to a Young Rancher, the owner of the neighbouring Circle B Ranch. The Stranger left first the Saloon, then the county. He was last seen against the setting sun on the Horizon.

This, of course, is also the formula of the socialist realist novel of the Stalinist era, which invariably features a factory or collective farm Manager and the beautiful local Schoolteacher or Doctor. A gang of hard-drinking and soft-working Workers is infiltrated by CIA Agents who are stealing material from the factory or farm. The incompetent local Chairman of the town council is helpless. A Secretary appears, first in the Railway Station, then in the Party Secretariat. He turns out to have been sent from Prague (or Moscow, or Warsaw, or Sofia). He sees the Doctor or the Schoolteacher, and offers help. He uncovers the Agents, reforms the Working-class Alcoholics, and thus ensures the fulfilment of the Production Quotas. However, the Doctor or Schoolteacher then reveals to the Secretary that she is engaged to the Young Stockworker in the factory or on the farm. The Secretary leaves first the Secretariat, then the county. He is last seen at the Railway Station. As you see, only the rising and setting suns are missing.

As I said, I knew that the only magic permissible to realism in those days was the twisting of reality to suit ideological purposes. Therefore the first book I offered for publication in 1956, after Stalin had safely died, was another novel I naively considered safe, called *The End of the Nylon Age*; a spinoff of my unpublished tribute to Maggie the shopgirl. It was quickly seized by the censors and banned before publication as "pornography", due to my use of the word "bosom" to describe a woman's (certainly not bare) breasts. When I suggested to the lady censor that I could replace it by "tits", as that was what the working people called it, she threw me out of her office. It therefore came as a surprise to me when the censorship office raised no objections to *The Cowards*, which I had offered for publication thinking that, after the disaster with my pornography, I had nothing to lose. I had no idea that the amazing liberalism of the press supervisors came only after the Stalinist faction in the Party's Presidium had decided to use me as a tool in their backstage struggle with the liberal faction, then on the ascendancy. They needed a blatant example of where liberalizing the censorial policies would lead: a novel that fitted their concept of decadent naturalism and reactionary individualism. Later I learned that their first choice had been Karel Ptáčník's highly political fictional pamphlet *The Town on the Border*. But Ptáčník had been awarded a state prize for his first novel, and moreover he was a Party member. I was a non-Party man, never previously published, and the story, which presented an important historical event not from the "objective" (i.e., Marxist) point of view, but through the eyes of a sax-blowing bourgeois youngster, was ideally suited to become the target of righteous fury.

Which it duly became. For two weeks, day after day, reviews appeared in all the national papers and journals, and then the hunt continued in local weeklies. The director of the union's publishing house was fired, as was the editor-in-chief, together with six other editors. A journalist who managed to sneak in a favourable review was dismissed as well. I lost my job on the staff of *World Literature* magazine. Then the president himself condemned the novel at a Party congress and my mother-in-law, a simple woman of the people, offered to hide my valuables and bankbooks. My wife transported my manuscripts to my father in Náchod, who hid them with a friend in a mountain village some twenty miles from my native town. It looked as though I would get a belated opportunity to become a uranium miner.

But Stalin had been dead for six years, so I missed my chance and indeed became an overnight literary celebrity. Scandals have always been the best publicity gimmicks. When policemen were dispatched to bookshops to seize unsold copies, they found them already taken up. In actual fact, they had been carefully hidden by the enterprising store managers, and when the immediate danger was over they were sold at many times the original price.

In one bookstore, the disgusted manager told the cops that he had catered all his copies to the cultural secretary of the Prague Dairies. As part of the tradition of socialist enterprise, at the end of the year all companies honoured their best employees by presenting them with books with a handwritten dedication by the branch chairman and with the official Party rubber stamp. This ritual gave booksellers a good outlet for at least some of their unsaleable stock: the *Selected Works of Lenin*, for instance. When *The Cowards* came out, the protective blurb on the jacket described the book as a "caustic satire on the cowardice of the bourgeoisie". This seemed to put the novel in a category of saleability with Marx and Lenin, so this bookseller got rid of his stock before the attacks (or the sales) began. Seeking revenge, he sent the cops to the dairies, but there a magical event had taken place: all those honoured by the gift of my novel had lost their copies, and the police left empty-handed.

Dozens of such stories became part of the literary folklore of Prague at the end of the fifties. Not all, however, came to such happy endings. In 1960 I was in the hospital with a bad case of hepatitis, contracted during a hernia operation. There was a young doctor there, a pretty woman who spent much more time at my bedside than was required. Chatting with her about literature, film, etc., I thought she was just another medic compensating for her cultural inferiority complex with a notorious writer—but she wasn't. One day she confessed to me that her husband had been the one who attacked my novel on the national radio network. He, poor man, had been an army officer, editor of an army cultural journal, and had been on duty that fateful night when he received orders to dispatch one man to the radio station to perform a special task. For one reason or another he had no man under his command that night, so he set out for the station himself. In the studio he was given a text to read over the waves: a savage tearing apart of a reactionary novel he had not read. Being a soldier, he decided to obey orders first and read the book afterwards. Somehow he got hold of a copy, read it, and was shocked. He liked the work! And yet he had abused it in the mass media! One can find righteous men even in the ranks of a Stalinist army. For some time he was making up his mind to write to me and apologize, explain. Then he was sent to manoeuvres in the Soviet Union, where his plane was struck by lightning and crashed. In his case, the Good Lord may have been overly harsh. But perhaps the unfortunate officer is now in heaven.

On New Year's Eve of 1959, a few weeks before the critical barrage exploded, we received several hundred New Year's cards. One year later only a few dozen came. Nothing extraordinary. Those were the times that tried friends' souls. One day when my fortunes were at their lowest, the doorbell rang, but instead of the expected visitors two unexpected ones stood in the doorway: the period's most famous Czech film star, Jana Brejchová, and her totally unknown husband, Miloš Forman. I had known Miloš in the war: he had been a little boy then, staying in Náchod with his uncle who was a grocer and my mountain-climbing buddy. Miloš's parents had been sent to a concentration camp from which they never returned, and so he spent most of the war "visiting" with various uncles. He was pitied by all, but he was too young for me to take any particular interest in him, and he pursued his own childish pursuits—not girls, like me. Now, not so many years later, he reappeared in my life with a wish: he'd like to write a script from a story of mine, "Eine kleine Jazzmusik", and make it into his first feature film; he had just graduated from the Film Academy. The story had appeared in the first *Yearbook of Jazz*, which, partly because of it, was immediately banned, but Miloš got hold of a copy saved by the printers. I was moved by this demonstration of fearless loyalty and reminded of the war and of the little grocery shop where Miloš used to steal sauerkraut from a big barrel. Why should I say no? We set to work. In those days, each script had to be approved by a dramaturgical body of about seventy members. Since they were paid for their membership, they considered it their duty to suggest changes. We titled our script *The Band Has Won*, and the story was about a student swing band that outwits the Nazis. It was subtitled "A Musical Comedy". After a year of comments and suggestions from the seventy sages, the script, still bearing the same title, no longer had a swing band in it, and instead of a comedy it was a tragedy about working-class anti-Nazi sabotage in an armament factory. However, parallel to this metamorphosis, the political climate changed. At the end of that year one of the seventy wizards pointed out that although the screenplay was called *The Band Has Won*, there was no band in it, and although it promised to be a musical comedy, it called for no music at all and was practically a tearjerker. We set to work again, and after less than a year the band was back, the tragedy was out, and the script bore unmistakable touches of Forman's situations and of *The Cowards'* dialogue. By then the political climate had turned almost pleasant, and one night our work was approved. In an elated mood we walked down Wenceslas Square, Miloš fantasizing about casting his wife's sister in the leading role (she eventually became the star of *Loves of a Blonde*) and I walking silently in amazed disbelief. My feeling proved to be right. That night, my friend the president listened to the ten o'clock news. An enterprising newscaster smuggled in an item about a new director and his first film to be shot, based on a story by Škvorecký. In the president's mind, only one story was associated with my name. The very first thing he arranged in the morning was to decree that filming Škvorecký was out of the question, and any efforts to do so would be considered a serious political provocation. Miloš tried to get an appointment with the president and explain the matter to him, but he only got to one of his secretaries who told him confidentially, "Comrade, we know the boss made a mistake. But who do you expect will have the guts to tell him so?"

Incidentally the Party decided to permit a new edition of *The Cowards*, and I was officially launched on a literary career. The novel quickly went through several editions and sold well over 100,000 copies in hardcover; this is the equivalent of about two million copies sold in the United States. I became a successful novelist, and everybody was eagerly expecting my next book.

Six years later, in the summer of 1968, Miloš and I wrote a synopsis of *The Cowards*, which was to be filmed in the summer of 1969 with Irena's daughter cast in the role of Irena. But the Russians came, Miloš left for Hollywood, and I for Canada.

I wonder if any artist has ever been absolutely sure that what he was doing was good, whether any has felt that he has mastered his art and that the process of creation from now on will be pure joy, unmixed with doubts. What I often find expressed in writers' confessions is that with every new book the author is faced with a brand-new problem for which there is no ready-made solution, that all his previous experience, though useful, does not guarantee a success once again. I catch myself in this frame of mind over and over again, and I most certainly found myself in that mental anguish after the success of *The Cowards*. In Bohemia, it is customary to address an established writer as "Master". The word, however, is also the traditional appellation of any master craftsman: a blacksmith, a cabinetmaker, a tailor. Whenever somebody calls me Master, I feel uneasy. What am I really a Master of? Of doubts, probably. And hearing some of my colleagues discuss, in all seriousness, their "art".... Craftsmanship, perhaps. But can I really be sure that what I am doing is art?

One has to strive for certainties. I certainly had to, after the Big Bang over my first novel. That was one reason why I started writing detective stories, first under a pseudonym, later under my own name—to prove to myself that I was at least something of a master craftsman. The pseudonym was the name of my dear old friend, the poet and translator Jan Zábrana. We plotted the novels together, then I wrote them and he contributed most of the many little poems and song lyrics we used in the text. Altogether we produced three overlong novels: *Murder for Luck* (1962), *Guaranteed Murder* (1964), and *Murder by Proxy* (1967). The latter was reissued in 1983, so I am probably the only blacklisted émigré writer to have a book published in Prague in the eighties. And I can prove my claim—the first letters of the many chapters of this almost endless detective yarn make an acrostic: *Škvorecký et Zábrana fecerunt ioculum* (Škvorecký and Zábrana made this joke).

We also wrote a children's book together, *Tanya and the Two Gunmen* (1966). This was the fruit of an idea of mine that never materialized. I had suggested to the State Publishing House of Pedagogical Literature that I would write an English-language textbook in the form of a detective story. Lesson One: "This is a knife. This is a body. The knife is in the body. It is murder," etc. They liked the idea but said that the first book of this sort would, of course, have to be a Russian-language text. I told them I knew no Russian, and they advised me to get a collaborator. So I got Jan and we devised a story about a Russian girl, Tanya, who gets lost in the woods on an excursion to Czechoslovakia and meets two Czech boys who play gunmen and escort her to Prague, hitch-hiking. Since she speaks no Czech, they use a Russian which the boys have learned—very imperfectly—at school, and Tanya keeps correcting their errors. The book was made into a feature film which won the first prize at a children's film festival in Moscow. Incidentally, Tanya was played by a girl born in Prague to White Russian parents. She became the darling of Moscow because the Muscovites found her Russian incredibly beautiful; it was the language of Tolstoy, preserved in Czech exile.

Anyway, I soon discovered that my uncertainty would not be cured by writing about fictional crimes. It may not be much of an art, but it is a hell of a craft. Yet *one* kind of certainty my detective stories did give me. In Czechoslovakia, both those written under my own name and those published under the pen-name were extremely popular. The sales, in hardcover, went easily into six-digit figures, and anything that is bought in such quantities must be at least partially read, not just displayed on bookshelves in the sitting room. And it is not only the quantity that counts. I received a letter from a blind girl who had read *Miss Silver's Past* in braille, and declared she had never had a better time in her life. Again: it may not be art that appealed to the blind girl, but for her the book apparently had some kind of human value. The big sales and letters like this one simply convinced me of one thing important for the writer's inner balance: fiction, if you give it all you can, no matter how lowbrow the genre may be, can be pretty useful for many people.

Then came *Emöke*, the romantic story of a frustrated love affair, and *The Menorah*, seven stories in commemoration of the forgotten ones from Onkel Otto und Tante Blanka's summer camp. After that I published the first crime fiction under my own name, *The Mournful Demeanour of Lieutenant Boruvka*, and by the mid-sixties I was a successful and exceedingly popular writer.

At the height of my popularity two events occurred that could have landed me in deep trouble again, but didn't; times had changed. The thaw of the early sixties enabled the cautious publication of a few works which a few years earlier would have been anathema. To push such pieces through the vigilant censorship was still a hard and risky labour, but the censors began to be confused, and occasionally one succeeded. Working as an editor in the Odeon publishing house I spotted a beautifully written and moving American novel about teenage gangs in Harlem, *The Cool World* by Warren Miller, and convinced my surrealistically minded editor-in-chief—who did not read English—that we should commission a translation. There's little doubt that had the book been read by someone who believed in what then passed for Marxist aesthetics, its publication would have been vetoed. On the one hand, the story pictured one of the darkest sides of American life—the destitute world of the black metropolis. On the other hand, it portrayed life in that metropolis without omissions. Its characters spoke as they speak in Harlem, which is certainly not the language of socialist realism; they did the things that are done there, that is, they drank, smoked marijuana, prostituted themselves even on the gay market; and there was not one single Marxist *Besserwisser* (know-it-all) among them to point out the only correct way out of their misery. As I learned later, the author was actually a fellow traveller of the most radical sort, but that only added piquancy to what followed.

I did the translation under the name of Jan Zábrana, the same friend who had signed my detective novels; he is dead now, so I can disclose the secret. I did not want to endanger the already risky project by adding my own name to it. I "edited" the text and eventually took it to the secretary of the publishing house whose duty it was to put a rubber stamp on it and take it to the printer. Unfortunately this lady, one Marie Šavrdová, was a human being whose sole purpose in life was to make trouble for other human beings, an ideal cadre for the builders of better societies. It did not escape her sharp eyes that I had been emotionally involved with one of the tenants in her apartment house (yes, the ardent comrade was the former owner of a huge apartment house in the Kobylisy district of Prague) who had been arrested as a French spy, and she was also well read in the critical literature about *The Cowards*. Therefore she knew that I was a naturalist and formalist, Titoist and Hitlerite, Trotskyite and Fascist, immoralist and Catholic, decadent, racist and philo-Zionist, and she harboured grave doubts about both my literary taste and the sincerity of my editorial intentions. As soon as I stepped out of her office, she opened the manuscript and found five four-letter words on one page. She turned over a few pages and spotted a description of human copulation. Another turning of the leaves revealed a homosexual lovemaking. That sufficed; full of righteous class rage, she ran to the editor-in-chief. This former surrealist was a genuine working-class boy and therefore decent, but he was as afraid of the monster-lady as everyone else. Although he was the boss of the publishing house, she was the chairperson of its Party organization, and therefore the boss's boss. She made a scene, and instead of sending the manuscript to the printer, the poor boss forwarded it to the cultural department of the Central Committee of the Party. The thing quickly developed into a major scandal which began to threaten the position of the editor-in-chief, the reputation of the totally innocent "translator", and my recently won acceptability. I was even brought to the secretary of the Minister of the Interior in a black limousine. To my surprise he was rather amused, and as a souvenir gave me a few American books with inscriptions from various American relatives to various Czech recipients: apparently the loot of the post office censors. But the affair dragged on for two years and through many meetings on different levels of power and ideological importance. Warren Miller, the author, inquired several times about the delay; I don't think he ever understood why his novel of social criticism ran into trouble in a country as staunchly socialist as Czechoslovakia. Eventually, apparently after some advice from American comrades, the Department of the Central Committee decided that the muckraking novel would be published in a limited edition of a few hundred, not available to the general public, but distributed only among trusted "literary and pedagogical workers". These "workers" naturally had untrustworthy sons and daughters. Soon *The Cool World* was hit number one in Prague.

At that time Jan himself was working on a Czech version of Allen Ginsberg's *Howl*. His English was far from perfect, so I did a rough translation for him. But my own English was far from adequate for the task of unravelling the many allusions in Ginsberg's verses, incomprehensible to a non-American, and the numerous words that came into use long after my obsolete dictionaries had been published. We exchanged a few letters with Ginsberg and he enlightened me on the enigmas in the poem. Then, one night in early winter, the phone rang. "This is Allen Ginsberg speaking." "Oh—are you calling from New York?" "No. I'm at the airport here, in Prague." We drove to the airport, picked up the bearded guru, and brought him to Jan's flat. He had just been thrown out of Cuba, where he had made some sexually irreverent comments about Che Guevara, and in those days if you wanted to fly from Havana to New York you had to go via Prague.

Next day we took Allen to the Viola winecellar, the Prague equivalent of a San Francisco jazz-and-poetry café.

In the next few weeks he became one of the best-known figures in the Prague underground and a hero of student dormitories. Therefore it was easy for me, when Allen returned from a short visit to Moscow—where he did not find people as congenial as in Prague—to convince the students to nominate him for King of the May, which is an ancient tradition at Charles University. As expected, Allen won a landslide victory. But when he was sitting on the throne, about to be mock-married to the Queen of the May, Mr. Jiří Hendrych, the dreaded Party secretary for cultural matters, entered the hall. By that time the Party had already decided to expel the mystic for socratic reasons ("corrupting socialist youth"). His crowning at the students' festivities, observed by such a witness as Comrade Hendrych, only speeded up the execution of the decision. Shortly before they picked him up at his hotel and took him to the airport—just as in Havana—in a police wagon, I had lent him some Czech money. The guru, in his American honesty and political innocence, asked the cops to do him a favour: return the money to his friend J.Š., for he had not been able to spend it, and Czech crowns were not convertible. The cops obliged with pleasure.

About two years later, when I was going to the States to attend a literary conference at Long Island University, the cops okayed my trip on condition that I not seek out the corruptor of socialist youth. I had no intention of doing so, for I wanted to travel to America again in the future, but Murphy's Law intervened. On my first night in New York, I ran into Allen in the restroom at Grand Central Station.

I don't know whether the cops ever found out about my doings with the guru and his companions in New York City. But even if they did, when I returned to Prague, Czech society was knee-deep in the sixties, and that made all the difference.

In many respects, the sixties were a glorious time. Some of the enthusiastic former Stalinists finally realized that, in their revolutionary fervour, they had assisted in the destruction of certain very vital things, and that without these things life couldn't really be good, no matter how much economic socialism had been achieved. They now busied themselves with trying to reintroduce those once rejected items into the life of Czech society: intellectual freedom instead of the Party line, safety instead of political vigilance, plain justice instead of class justice. Remembering those dialectical efforts, it sometimes seems to me that the Marxist revolution is a kind of monstrous punishment devised by the Lord to teach the naughty child called Humanity about priorities.

The sixties in Prague were indeed a glorious time, except in one respect: they were also a time of unparalleled literary snobbism. A Franz Kafka conference was held at the château of Liblice in May 1962; it rehabilitated the Prague Jewish writer who, up till then, had served the Marxist establishment as the prototype of decadence. Marxist scholars now argued— with ample, hitherto hushed-up evidence—that alienation, the mode of Kafka's existence, was the monopoly neither of the Jews nor of capitalism. In fact, profound existentialist feelings were widespread in a country where political prisoners were mining uranium used for the manufacture of Soviet atomic weapons, and where children were led to proclaim their disbelief in Santa Claus and their faith in Grandpa Frost, Santa's Soviet substitute. If alienation did not disappear when private ownership of the means of production was eliminated, as Marx had assumed, then Kafka was not necessarily irrelevant to the socialist reader.

So far so good. However, the reluctant acceptance of Kafka opened the door for more authors, and suddenly the pages of magazines were flooded by a parade of names of long-time victims of socrealistic taboo: Beckett, Robbe-Grillet, Ionesco, Sarraute, Butor, Artaud, and Barthes, Lévi-Strauss etc., etc. Suddenly much of this forbidden fruit was also in bookshops, and everybody hastened to taste it. Not perhaps so many readers, but far too many critics, became heavy addicts of the drug of rediscovered modernity. The cultural atmosphere of Prague underwent a dialectical change. A few years earlier, unless you told an absolutely comprehensible story with black and white characters you were considered a political reactionary. Now, if you told a comprehensible story with realistically drawn characters you were a literary reactionary. Unless you sounded like Nathalie Sarraute or some unpalatable West German experimentalist, you were passé. Outdated. Uninteresting for the new, Kafkaesque literary establishment.

The most Kafkaesque aspect of that establishment was that it included numerous literary arbiters—and practitioners— who, well within human memory, had insisted on a *deus ex machina* in the form of a wise Party secretary to resolve any problems in your novel, public, private, or sexual.

How did I stand, once chastised for slandering the icons by describing them in their emperor's clothes, now chastised again for telling, in the same age-old realistic manner, my tales about jazzmen and about the sweet charm of the bourgeoisie? Even stooping to formula fiction? Oh sure—these Marxist literary rediscoverers would say condescendingly—he *is* a good storyteller; in the traditional mode, that is. Quite funny, too. Certainly popular. And of course, he is *historically* important. After all, his first novel *was* a turning point in the development of modern Czech fiction.

So I became an important item of literary history. But if you are a writer worth your salt you don't want to be important for authors of textbooks. You want to feel like—and be recognized as—someone who has something to say not to history, but to your contemporaries. It is nice to have Ph.D. theses written about your turning-point novel. It is nicer to see that novel, in cheap paperback, on display in drugstores.

In those days of the anti-realist witch-hunt I did a lot of soul-searching. Was I perhaps guilty of neglecting the chances of the new liberalism in arts? Of turning my back on experiments? I had never written a piece of fiction in order to please a tendency, a literary movement, let alone an intellectual fashion or political party line. But shouldn't I try something in the manner of, let's say, a *nouveau roman*? Suppress my tendency to tell a good story well, possibly with a twist in its tail? Strive for more shapelessness which, allegedly, imitates life better than old Poe's structural concepts? Stop writing my little satirical stories for the Paravan cabaret *Textappeals*, for which my friend Jiří Menzel, the youth who had just made *Closely Watched Trains*, reprimanded me, partly under the spell of the times, partly because he recognized himself in one of the stories and did not take it as well as Corporal Střevlíček?

At that time a dear buddy of mine was working on a desk-drawer translation of that old, crazy, disgusting Fascist but, alas, poet of the first magnitude, Ezra Pound, not quite recognized yet by the establishment. There, in Canto LXXXI, I found lines that took my breath away: "What thou lovest well remains, the rest is dross / What thou lov'st well shall not be reft from thee / What thou lov'st well is thy true heritage...." Here was the answer to my dilemma. In the frenzy of three ecstatic days I wrote *The Bass Saxophone*. I never had to change a line in that text. It was all about what I loved well. It was about jazz. About art. It was about the sense of life; at least, of my life. An *apologia pro vita mea*.

Then came the *annus mirabilis, annus horribilis* of 1968, when the sobered-up comrades tried to put the stupid clock of history back, with predictable results. The Orwellian boot of the Soviets that tramples on the human face—forever—stepped on the face of my country, and brought about a *finis Bohemiae* as a land of Western culture. My place was no longer there.

And so we left, my good and charming wife and I, and settled in Toronto, in the province of Ontario, Canada. My lifelong devotion to the masters of American fiction paid off: I got a job at the University of Toronto, teaching American literature. Poe,

Hawthorne, Twain, James, Hemingway, Fitzgerald, Faulkner, Lewis, Chandler, that remarkable procession of men who—somewhat like myself, who was born in a mountain village into a nonintellectual family—confronted a nonintellectual continent and produced their magnificent responses to the rawness, freshness of life. Within the limits of my capacities I tried to emulate them.

My wife founded and through hard labour and perseverance built up a publishing house, Sixty-Eight Publishers, which to date (1988) has brought out more than 190 titles: books by contemporary Czech and Slovak fiction writers, poets, playwrights, and essayists, living both in exile and at home, all banned in their own country. There are altogether about 600 such authors: imagine an American literature with some 8,000 of its contemporary writers McCarthyized. In addition to that hardly imaginable workload, she wrote two successful books of fiction, *Summer in Prague* and *Ashes, Ashes All Fall Down,* and became the darling of Czech and Slovak readers in exile and in Czechoslovakia, where her—and my—books are smuggled in considerable quantities. I continued writing as well, and managed to finish and publish more volumes in my first fourteen years in Canada than in my twenty-five years of creative life in the old country. How is that possible? The answer is very simple. This is a free country—a clichéed explanation, but clichés are not necessarily untrue. Quite often original concepts are nothing but elaborate lies.

We found uneventful peace in this lovely country, and that's all you need if you are a writer and have entered the downhill road of your life. You don't need the country of your birth any more; you don't even have to hear the everyday sounds of your native tongue. Against the background of an acquired language the fine qualities, the subtleties, the music and the charm of the words you write stand out; you become more aware of the unique properties that only that particular language has—and every language has unique qualities of its own. As a novelist I love, above all, to dwell in the world of my youth; but as a human being I know that that age, that landscape even, that community, are for ever lost. As a man brought up in the traditional—or conservative, if you wish—concepts of human life, I am not sentimental about the past which has disappeared into the realm of memories. I loved my native town and all the pretty girls in it. But they are grandmothers now. I was quite fond of the Prague of the sixties. But it does not exist any more. It's now the provincial capital of a Soviet *gubernia*. You cannot enter the same river twice. You can't go home again.

Some of my new countrymen who have visited my old country express pity for me. They think I must miss the land where I can never return, not even for a visit, since the Colonial Office called the Ministry of the Interior revoked my and my wife's citizenship for "activities that harm the interests of the State abroad." "It's such a beautiful country!" say my Canadian friends. But why should I—or anybody for that matter—miss the beauty of Central Europe in a region as visually beautiful as Canada? Or am I perhaps a sort of callused cosmopolitan who feels at home nowhere and everywhere? It seems to me that the beauty of one's homeland is replaceable. What is much harder to replace are the buddies you left behind, the shared common background, the unique atmosphere of your culture, the emotional experience that shaped you—all these things. But they are no more—even *there* they are no more. A remarkable Slovak poet of the nineteenth century, Jan Kollár, wrote, long ago: "Don't give the holy name of homeland / To the country where we dwell. / The real homeland we carry in our hearts, / And that can be neither violated, nor stolen from you." The original is a beautifully rhymed sonnet. And that's how it is.

And since passing the halfway point of my life, it has been here, on this continent of Poe, Twain, and Faulkner, that I set out to recapitulate my life in fiction. You can be a great poet at twenty, die at twenty-four, and remain alive, because for lyrical poetry all that is necessary are fresh, strong emotions and a sensitivity to words. But to be a ripe epic novelist at twenty requires a miracle. For that you have to retain the freshness of emotions well into your declining years when you have accumulated a wealth of experience: the hundreds of real-life stories of which you were a part, the hundreds of characters— sweet and funny, sad and obnoxious—who crossed your way, the decades of historical upheavals, political somersaults, the wisdoms and stupidities of your age.

So I set out to write *The Miracle Game* in 1969–72, and *The Engineer of Human Souls* in 1975–77. And I faced problems, mainly technical, I had not encountered before. The time span covered by these fictions is about thirty-five years, the action takes place in different and very dissimilar places on the globe: in Bohemia, in Germany, in the United States, in Canada. There is the traditional chronological method which was useful in the previous century, when people lucky enough to be living in the numerous places on earth that were not in the way of marauding armies, and where benevolent rulers were not interfering in their domestic affairs and in their aesthetics, could live long, quiet, orderly, uneventful lives. There were many such people; if not a majority, then quite possibly many more than in our own century. For our age, where the craziness of wars and parochial despots spreads throughout countries and continents, I felt the chronological portrayal of fates against a background of the era was inadequate. Joseph Conrad, one of the very best modern writers, introduced "deliberate confusion" into psychological portrayal, aiming for greater verisimilitude, greater realism. A character was to be presented to the reader not in the orderly fashion of old novels, from the cradle to the grave, but in the manner we learn to know people in real life: we meet a man who is fifty, then find out, from a discarded mistress, how he was at twenty, and later, from a schoolfellow, we hear about his pranks as a boy. I thought about Conrad, and then I pondered the inexpressible, surreal atmospheric change I experienced when, on board an Air India Boeing, I left Prague on a dark January afternoon, the day after the funeral of the self-immolated student Jan Palach. On my way to the airport I saw the gloomy, dejected groups of university students holding a vigil on Wenceslas Square—and then, a mere hour later, at sunny Heathrow airport in London, I observed a group of giggling girls in their school uniforms who were cheering another bunch of teenagers disembarking from a Swissair jet, apparently coming home from a holiday in the Alps. Both events were part of the same, allegedly indivisible world.

And then I thought of the political history of my country: I was then only forty-five years old, and yet, within that short life span, I had experienced all existing political systems of twentieth-century Europe: liberal democracy until

1939, Nazism from 1939–45, the uneasy democratic socialism of 1945–48, Stalinism between 1948 and 1960, the liberalization of Communism 1960–67, the crazy attempt to square the circle in 1968, the Attila-the-Hun solution of the *Panzers* in August 1968, the colonization of *Regnum Bohemia*e which had begun before we left. All my compatriots went through this rigmarole of history. A writer does not and cannot write just about himself. That fact has nothing to do with romantic, patriotic concepts of being a "spokesman for one's people". It is the kernel of writing. Some writers may *think* their only subject is themselves: if they are any good they are in fact telling the history of their times and of their people in the form of a self-portrait. For the self-portrait has an open landscape in the background, with little human figures toiling and frolicking in it, the way the Dutch masters used to paint. If all a writer manages is a picture of himself against a blank curtain he is just a miserable scribbler who never grew out of puberty, no matter how much fucking he includes.

How to get the chaotic dialectics, this point-counterpoint of an aleatoric symphony of my life and times, onto the pages of a novel? The dissimilarity of fates, and the similarity, yes, the sameness of the humaneness of people? Those rosy-cheeked lasses from the Manitoba prairies, playing the same games, in the very same manner, that the strawberry-lipped wenches used to play thirty years ago, although that was in another country, on another and very distant continent?

Hundreds of stories went through my head, dozens of plotless plots; they refused to arrange themselves into neat patterns. I jotted down episodes, conversations, images, on little pieces of paper, then I sat down on the floor, and as if I were putting together a giant jigsaw puzzle, I began shifting those shreds of the past around. I grouped them by contrasts, by similitudes, linked them by tone and meaning; I tried to create a world out of the mess of my life in our messy century. Finally, some sort of pattern emerged. I joined together the deliberate confusion of disjointed episodes by means of several series of chronologically arranged letters by writers from different walks of life, typed up the fragments from the pieces of paper on sheets, and had a skeleton of a story. Then I started putting the flesh of words onto the skeleton.

Did I succeed? It would hardly be proper for me to judge. What is it really that I have written about?

In discussions I have with readers concerning the final phrase of *The Bass Saxophone*, the question pops up frequently: What *exactly* is the "memento" of the bass saxophone? If I knew what the story of the giant hookah meant *exactly*, I, being the realist writer I am, would have written it in a way that would render its *exact* meaning. But perhaps one possible meaning of the novella—of all my writings, of any sincere efforts in fiction— is this. We do not know *exactly* what life is all about. But the moment we lose our sensitivity for this central and mysterious question of our existence, our humanity is diminished. We set out on the easy road towards the mindless acceptance of mindless opinions, of unexamined assertions, of fossilized ideas about people, their society, and their lives. Something brought the giant saxophonist to the pink pool of the bathtub, and he endeavoured to express that something by savagely blowing his horn. Perhaps the essence of a writer is a sensitive uncertainty. Not just about the value of what he is doing, but also about the value of all ready-made answers. There are so many of them in this world of ours. Literature that accepts such answers at their face value is a very debased genre indeed. Much more debased than the cheap thriller, the saccharine romance, the unashamedly commercial pornography. It is the inability to say the final word that is human. All else is delusion, often dangerous delusion. *Endlösungen* (final solutions), as we know by now, are all false. In the end they solve nothing. They only increase suffering and multiply death.

A curious thought occurs to me as I conclude this autobiographical sketch. Except for my latest book, *Dvorak in Love*, which recounts the fortunes in America of Antonín Dvořák, the composer, I have never written a historical novel. Most of my efforts charted out the adventures of Danny Smiřický as he bumbled through life. These novels represent, if you wish, the serious line among my attempts. Another line, my detective fiction, follows the misadventures of a sad homicide squad lieutenant named Borůvka through three decades of history. And that's the word! Suddenly I realize that, in a certain way, the history of Danny, and even that of the melancholy sleuth, is in fact the history of my people. My God—am I a historical novelist after all? Was my real teacher the ancient and paradoxical voice of my native town?

The Nazi protectorate: in my works that is *The Bass Saxophone, The Menorah, The Swell Season*. The great divide at the end of the war: *The Cowards*. The horrible fifties with their police brutality, which were at the same time the beautiful age of Danny's young manhood—the subject of *The Miracle Game*, of *The Tank Corps*, and of numerous stories from unpublished volumes such as *Stories of the Tenor Saxophonist*, collected in a book entitled *The Bitter World*. The time of the thaw in the sixties: *Miss Silver's Past* is about that. The year of Alexander Dubček, of the unrealistic hopes—*The Miracle Game* again. And eventually Canada and the fate of my compatriots there: *The Engineer of Human Souls* and my only play, *God in the House*. Over the years I have even written three volumes of satirical stories, collected now in Czech under the title of *From the Life of Czech Society*; the first volume, *From the Life of Better Society*, is an evocation of my boyhood in pre-war Czechoslovakia. The title of the second one, *From the Life of Socialist Society*, is self-explanatory, and so is the third, *From the Life of Emigré Society*. Except that this last sequel is written not in standard Czech but in American Bohemianese.

And oh my! *The Mournful Demeanour of Lieutenant Boruvka* and *Sins for Father Knox*—the sixties. *The End of Lieutenant Borvuka*—the year 1968 and the seventies. *The Return of Lieutenant Boruvka*—Toronto, where the unlucky former sleuth now works as a parking lot attendant, but solves his obligatory murder nevertheless.

I never intended to write satire—yet ended up producing something that is indistinguishable from satire. I never thought of myself as a dissident writer—yet I was stripped of my citizenship because of literary dissent. I never dreamt of writing history—yet perhaps a stranger perusing my saga about the cynical tenor saxophonist would get a more or less continuous picture of the last four decades of Czechoslovakia's history.

What sort of writer am I?

As Veronika, the sad heroine of *The Engineer of Human Souls*, put it: "Let's leave it to the horses to figure out. They have bigger heads."

An Interview in Prague

—

*In 1968, two years before he fled Czechoslovakia,
Škvorecký was interviewed by the Czech film critic Antonín Liehm as part of a series Liehm did with Czech
and Slovak writers and intellectuals like Milan Kundera,
Ludvík Vaculík, and Václav Havel. The collected interviews were published in Prague under the title* Generace,
and in the United States as The Politics of Culture.*

Knowing of Škvorecký's lifelong interest in Ernest
Hemingway, Liehm began the interview with a discussion
of Hemingway and his critics.*

*Do you think that criticism is important, either for a writer or
for culture in general?*

Criticism is essential, there's no getting around it. It is needed
for a variety of reasons but it should always be aware of its
dangerous potential. Even with the best of intentions, it may do
harm. Every artist must overcome tremendous problems with
himself; he generally knows his own weaknesses only too well,
they torment him and make him hypersensitive. Hemingway
stylized himself into the likeness of a tough boxer, but in reality
he was a bundle of tender emotions. The impact of criticism on
such a person may be so violent as to destroy him as an artist. Of
course, there are other destructive forces as well. Hemingway
was not a spontaneous writer, and he spent a tremendous
amount of thought on how he should write. He didn't worry
much about what to write, but how. I recall statements made
about culture a few years ago to the effect that one sign of
greatness in an artist is that he is mainly concerned with not
the *how*, but the *what*. In my opinion, the truth is just the

opposite. The literary giants know perfectly well what they want to say; they practically overflow with their subject, it's in them and can't be held back; but they desperately struggle with the *how*, the form, how to tell it, how to organize it. After prolonged and persistent thinking Hemingway finally evolved a style that influenced everything in subsequent Anglo-American literature. Some people think I exaggerate, but in my opinion Hemingway's significance to literature is equal to that of Picasso's to painting. And yet this very man struggled with fantastic problems in his work. He continually crossed out and rewrote—he rewrote a single chapter thirty-eight times—and he never gave up. He kept wrestling with the material, with what he had seen, experienced, and carried in his head; and when they suddenly began to tell him that his writing had gone bad, this took its toll.

It is extremely important for a writer to believe in himself. Take that famous author of detective stories, Raymond Chandler. He wrote some beautiful letters about literature which convinced me that the only reason he hadn't written so-called "serious" novels was that he didn't believe in himself. He wrote only detective stories, though actually in this way he produced more literature than many a "serious" author. Chandler too inveighed against the critics. In the West, critics have a notorious influence on a writer's commercial success. You know, he used to say that critics understand a work of art too, but with a totally different kind of understanding from the author's. Perhaps it's like a football game. The spectators and referees know the game, but their understanding is quite unlike that of the players on the field.

Chandler once wrote a very fine article: "The Simple Art of Murder". It was a sharp attack on the contemporary English detective story, on its lack of realism. And then he wrote a letter saying that the article shouldn't be taken too literally, because he could equally well have written a piece defending the English detective story and showing how American realism had ruined the genre, how the old form was actually superior.

So that actually....

Art is art because nobody has yet quite grasped the art of doing it. To achieve complete certainty in this area is impossible. And I am not defending the golden mean, either. There must be extremes, there must be avant-garde writers who act like voracious pikes in a pond, and they are needed even if they don't always speak the truth. Their job is to provoke—arrogantly, even using lies when necessary. They're needed to chase the lazy carp that wallow at the bottom and grow fat.

I myself have never belonged to any group. It's not my nature, even though I am extremely attracted to certain movements, such as surrealism. I like to cite the American journalist Joseph Barry, who wrote on the occasion of Henry Miller's obscenity trial in California: "The artist must go too far, so that others can go far enough." Extremist manifestations in life such as the beatniks have tremendous importance; they serve a vital function because they destroy conventions that threaten to retard or stifle life. Those artists who have done the same iconoclastic job may not all have been the greatest creators, but they have played a very important role.

So you see, I am by no means advocating the idyllic, the golden mean, the careful avoidance of insulting somebody or other. That is unrealistic; it doesn't do justice to life. But there is always a kind of mainstream, even in jazz, and people who are concerned with theory must realize that, in matters of art, a certain continuing relativity obtains. It is therefore good to have both types: opinions that are purely theoretical and extreme, along with exponents of sober wisdom—the wisdom of those who merely observe the passions and try to form objective judgements about them insofar as it is possible to do so within the limits of art....

Don't you think that criticism plays the role of maintaining "mental hygiene"?

Wherever criticism comes across a dishonesty that tries to seduce the taste of some segment of society, it must act with great vigour. It must be able to distinguish that which is offered honestly from that which merely panders; it must recognize fraud and expose attempts at superficial effect. I believe that style is a reliable hallmark, style behind which one feels the author's personality. To paraphrase Chandler again: style is the greatest thing an artist can bequeath to his era. Style is the projection of personality. But of course, this presupposes a genuine personality to begin with. There are quite a few authors who succeed in everything they do, readers like their work, yet personality is missing.

On the other hand, take someone like "New Wave" film director Věra Chytilová. She herself boasts that each of her films is entirely different, yet the trademark of her personality is unmistakable. And even though I intensely dislike certain things she does, I find her work as a whole quite fascinating; one senses that behind it there is a human being with urgent things to say. That's personality.

One often hears people talk about the beneficial effects that external pressures and obstacles have on creative work. Oddly enough, even artists themselves often express this opinion. You know a lot about this subject, and not just from theory.

I believe that this idea is just a myth. Of course, people vary. There are some who need a punch in the nose to wake up, and there are others who would be knocked out cold.

Let's examine the great authors. Look at Shakespeare, for example. We know—in spite of what occasional articles may say to the contrary—more about Shakespeare than we do about a great many other great writers. Shakespeare, then: he was successful, lived well, wrote fairly good plays, made money, and died. In Elizabethan England there was little cultural pressure put upon the artist; this particular writer, though he never got into any real trouble, produced worthwhile work. On the other hand, consider Edgar Allan Poe. Life gave him a terrible beating. He lived in wretched poverty, he was sick, his beloved died, he was an unhappy man through and through. And he himself says that the circumstances of his life were such that he couldn't accomplish in literature what he would have liked. I suspect, though, that even under better conditions he would have written just about the same things. An explosive talent and yet a true builder too. For he invented the detective story, and since his time nobody has discovered anything really new to add to this genre. That's Dorothy Sayers' opinion, and she ought to know. The ones who came after Poe made all the money, of course. God only knows what Poe would have written if he had made all that money himself.

You do a lot of translating. Many writers throughout the world translate, even though they are under no financial necessity to do so. Why is it that there are only a few such writer-translators in Czechoslovakia?

There are some. I know at least one, Jan Zábrana. A fanatic. He falls in love with an author and then turns the world upside down to make sure he gets published. Some time ago he did that with Isaac Babel. He read some Babel in the 1950s and didn't rest until he had translated all of his work. Later, he translated Allen Ginsberg and Lawrence Ferlinghetti. I honour such devotion. When you love a certain author, it is a delight to translate him. I feel that way about Hemingway and Chandler. Translating poses a great danger to a writer, though. When you translate something, you feel somewhat like a co-author. And that is a psychological illusion. But the effect is to turn an author into a translator. And there is another reason why translation is attractive to a writer: the best way to read a book is to translate it. Then you may learn to like even those aspects you couldn't appreciate at first. For me, Faulkner's *A Fable* is a case in point. At first I thought the book rather drawn out, full of mysticism, and to this day I have the feeling that I may be the only person who has truly read it. And yet how powerfully Faulkner's personality begins to emerge! How much that man knows! I worked on it for four years. I lost a lot of money on the project, had to have the whole manuscript retyped four times, and yet the work was a great pleasure and in the end it even proved to be useful.

It is said, even by some writers, that contemporary literature is boring.

Obviously, literature must never be boring. But that is no argument against certain new forms, such as the *nouveau roman*. If it seems boring to me personally—well, that's my affair, but there are others who may find it interesting. Boredom is an objective phenomenon but its sources are subjective. It is nonsense to use the argument that this or that work does not take the reader into account. It always turns out in the end that authors of such works actually addressed themselves to a rather broad public.

Sometimes I think that the old method of publishing had a good feature; every author found a publisher. It never occurred to anyone to take Kafka to task for being dull. After all, society is made up of minorities. And a publishing monopoly has a tendency to discriminate against certain types. No matter how cultured the men at the top of such a monopoly may be, they cannot possibly be so liberal as to erase their own prejudices and tastes and accept everything. Read the autobiographies of writers. How many times did Erskine Caldwell have to make the rounds of publishers with *God's Little Acre*? Think of the trouble Faulkner had before he found a publisher! Even Hemingway practically had to publish some of his stories himself.

We once discussed the question of universality....

I think about this problem quite often, because I'm fairly well acquainted with Anglo-American literature and it is read all over the world. And I ask myself how many of these writers would have a world-wide reputation if they wrote in Czech, and how many of our own writers would be known abroad if they wrote in English. I know that this smacks of sour grapes or a kind of Czech chauvinism of which I want no part. And yet we sometimes encounter this situation as an objective fact. For example, Karel Poláček [a writer and journalist who died in a Nazi concentration camp] is in my opinion a writer who deserves an international audience, yet he will never become recognized as such because he was never translated and probably never will be. Who in the world translates Czech, anyway? Imagine what would happen if our country gave birth not to just one writer of international merit, but to a whole literature of world significance! There would still remain the very prosaic problem of how these authors could become known to an international public; who would translate them and publish them? It is true that Czechoslovak films have achieved a world-wide reputation, but film people have the great advantage that they are not so closely bound to language.

You come from a small Czech town. What role did this play in your development?

The small-town atmosphere is closely connected with my youth, and I live above all from my childhood experiences. My youth still has a magic power over me. What is *The Cowards*, anyway? The story of a small town, its jazz, its student life, the end of the war.... Whenever I wrote anything I tried with all my might to relive my memories, and at the same time I wanted my writing to have the magic, to be truer than truth, as Hemingway put it. I think I know what he meant. While we are living it, an experience means little, but when it is recalled it becomes beautiful. I wrote that the war years were the most beautiful years of our lives. And I was severely criticized for this statement. But we were young in those days, everything was encompassed by a halo, we promenaded in the square surrounded by pretty girls. In a small town, people know each other; countless tales and legends float through the atmosphere and a kind of unexpressed enchantment fills the air. I hope that one day I'll be able to write a book about the war, about forced labour, about the huge underground hall, about how people tried to goldbrick, about the beautiful girls, and the days when we sat for hours in the men's room debating about politics and art. These experiences are still extremely vital for me. I tried to capture some of this magic in *The Bass Saxophone*. But before writing a novel about it, I'll probably try to do it as a musical. Actually the theme lends itself better to a musical.

Your relation to jazz is, of course, a very special one.

It's like this: sometimes I feel lonely, suddenly I hear jazz and it affects me like a shot of some powerful stimulant. It isn't only a matter of aesthetics. Jazz goes deeper; it is a psychological force, a beautiful force which gives me joy and pervades my whole emotional life. It is a source of never-ending pleasure, one of the things in my life which time has not spoiled for me. I am not a collector, I don't sit in a corner and listen to records. I probably couldn't give the right answer to a single question on a jazz quiz. But I love that anonymous music. Recently I realized that I haven't written a single book in which jazz doesn't play some sort of role. Jazz, and everything it symbolizes, represents for me a key to all human striving. There are other currents that enter into my attitude to jazz, too—certain wartime associations, the role that jazz played for us during the bleak war years, the fact that it was semi-forbidden music, but all this is relatively unimportant. Jazz is, above all, a kind of fraternity.

But you want biographical data. First the Gymnasium, then forced labour, then medicine. The trouble was that I couldn't stand being an intern. Even autopsies were better than having to watch people dying and not being able to do anything about it, not being able to help even though many were still quite young. I'm no good at putting on an act, at solacing people, and so I became terribly depressed. To this day I am convinced that a certain amount of callousness is necessary to survive in this world. In one of my pieces I wrote that indifference is our salvation, our mother as well as our nemesis. Just imagine—if we didn't have a bit of indifference in us, how could we face the idea that in this century, though life has reached pinnacles of civilization, there are still millions who are hungry and naked.... Without a bit of callousness, we would be continually screaming and revolting, and this would probably not help much but would only lead to chaos.

From my university days I especially remember the lectures of Prof. Vladislav Vančura on American literature. He had a habit of talking with a kind of dry English objectivity and wit, and yet it was obvious that he loved his subject very deeply. Except for the lectures of Vaclav Černy [professor of comparative literature at Charles University], these were the only ones I attended with any regularity. In 1949 an order was issued to the effect that everyone who had passed the state exam should serve for a period of time in the border regions. I was the sort of person who thought that laws meant what they said, so off I went. Of course, many of my colleagues realized that laws were made to be broken and stayed in Prague. But I have no regrets. I had graduated with a major in English and a minor in

philosophy, but both subjects had disappeared from school curricula around that time, so I ended up teaching social studies
in a provincial girls' school. There were, of course, no textbooks,
no curricula, nobody knew exactly what social studies meant,
but the school was supposed to be "socially oriented" and so social studies became the main subject. They assigned it to me,
and I taught it, four hours a week. I don't remember how we
passed the time in class; we probably just chatted a lot. But
suddenly an order came stating that compulsory certification
exams would include my subject, and I was to prepare seventy
questions at once. Somehow I managed to lay my hands on a
few pages from an old textbook which mentioned that hospitals
were founded as early as the Middle Ages and that mediaeval
monks used unscientific methods of treatment. From this single
source I sweated out seventy different-sounding questions, and
I believe that this test belongs among my most inspired literary
accomplishments.

During the oral exam each student was given a different
question, but they all gave pretty much the same answers because all their learning came from the same few pages of the
same book. By the time the fifth student started out on her
by now familiar recitation, things started to look rather embarrassing, even though the chairman of the examining board
didn't seem to be aware of what was going on. Fortunately, these
girls were resourceful. The school was no bourgeois finishing
school; it was run on a more practical basis, and the girls also
learned how to sew and cook. The cooking instructor was fabu-
lous, a real artist who had written several books on the subject.
Naturally, during the exams the kitchen was going full blast,
and every two hours relays of girls in white aprons trooped into
the examination room bringing trays of luscious delicacies the
examiners had never dreamed existed. And so the exam became
one long banquet and social studies were completely forgotten.

There was a sculpture school in town, too, and ours was full
of pretty girls between the ages of seventeen and twenty-two;
I myself was twenty-seven and I was supposed to chaperone
them when they went dancing. So you see, here it is again: the
early 1950s, the second beautiful period in my life.

But I didn't feel like making teaching my career; I longed to do something connected with literature. I was a docile student, though, and I thought that I must first complete my doctorate before I could consider doing anything else. So after I received my degree and served my hitch in the army, Zdeněk Urbanek,the author and translator, helped me get a job in the State Publishing House.

But hadn't you started writing much earlier?

I had written *The Cowards* while I was still at university. At the "social school" I retyped the manuscript and showed it to one of my colleagues, a woman, who was so disgusted by it that I never showed the book to anyone again until finally I gave it to Zdeněk Urbánek, who restored my courage.

When I was at university, I submitted a piece to a university-sponsored contest. It was called "New Canterbury Tales" and was about a gang of boys. One of them mentions that it's Chaucer's birthday—though of course nobody really knows when Chaucer was born—and then they start recounting tales about their wartime experiences. I won the contest, under the pen name Fred Errol. This name has its roots in my subconscious. When I was ten years old I fell madly in love with Freddie Bartholomew, and he played the part of Cedric Errol, little Lord Fauntleroy. You see, quite infantile.

Anyway, the results of the contest were announced three days before the political upheaval of February 1948, and first prize was to be a two-month trip abroad. But because of the political events, the entire contest was called off. František Halas tried to send me over to the magazine *Kytice* to see Jaroslav Seifert, but by the time I got there Seifert was gone and so was the magazine. From all this work I was able to salvage only "Rebecca's Story", which eventually came out in the collection *The Menorah*.

I had participated in a contest even earlier, in 1945, sponsored by the Czech Academy. A man from Náchod, my home town, had won the contest the year before—a good omen. I sent them a kind of surrealistic novel with the significant title *Inferiority Complex*. I won honourable mention and then a group called the Society of Czech Writers nominated me for membership in their organization. It was an odd group. Only one of the members had actually published anything, and he wore spats. Another member, a lady named Carmen, collected stories about the Prague Uprising which she cut out of popular magazines. It was my first experience with literary groups.

After Halas died in 1949, Jindřich Chalupecký [a philosopher, critic, and art historian] invited me to come to see him and introduced me to Urbánek and to [poet and artist] Jiří Kolář, [author and composer] Jan Rychlík, and Bohumil Hrabal. We sat around together and debated about art. Kolář acted as a kind of intellectual centre and source of continuity. I remember Hrabal reading his first stories to us, which the bibliophile Kolář was the first to publish, though few people nowadays know this. (Kolář played the same role of patron and publicist that Pound played for Hemingway.)

Here I developed respect for the avant-garde, although I myself did not share their viewpoint, and I learned to admire people who love art so much that they are willing to sacrifice everything for its sake. To live it day after day, to remain steadfast to certain ideals, that's a rare and precious thing. Too many people aren't loyal to anything, not even to their favourite authors. And it was this loyalty which, more than anything else, fascinated me about the surrealists. Once I heard a semi-secret lecture on surrealism given by the art critic and historian Vratislav Effenberger. It was held in the psychiatric faculty, but the hall was crowded with all sorts of gentlemen who looked more like policemen than poets, and that was the end of that. It is beautiful to see people who are capable of total sacrifice. One surrealist even worked as a driver for a brewery.

I myself am not much of a theoretician, my mind is more drawn to the spontaneous and the intuitive. Not that I don't think about literature, you understand, but when I succeed in writing something it's like a successful jazz improvisation. Inspiration is a phenomenon that used to be explained in all kinds of mystical ways. But I believe in it; I think it is real and exists widely. Not universally, of course. There are rational kinds of writers, too, and perhaps they are the more valuable ones.

Unfortunately, I belong to those who must write thousands of pages before hitting on the one thing that seems to have some inspiration in it, that on rereading makes me doubt that I was actually capable of writing it. This is my method, or perhaps I should say "my disease". Some things are simply the result of inspiration, while others are created from elements that one inherits and that one develops somehow or other later on. As I said, I would be much happier if I could write in a more rational way. But I think of writing as a pathological manifestation; anyway, it certainly isn't part of normal life.

In 1956 I began to edit the magazine *Světová Literatura* [*World Literature*], a review devoted to publishing translations and reviews of contemporary writing. I loved doing it, it was a wonderful job.

The Cowards came out quite smoothly, without any problems. In fact, on the very day the book was being distributed, I heard—just by chance—that the cultural ideologists had read my novel and, by God, they said, that was some book. I expected to be attacked for excessive naturalism, slang, some of the erotic scenes, and I was ready to defend myself on literary grounds. But I never would have dreamed that I might become the target of attacks for having sullied things that are holy and glorious—no, this was the last sort of thing I expected, I assure you.

For a long time after publication, nothing much happened. *Literární Noviny* gave it a fairly favourable review; Jiří Lederer, writing in the Prague newspaper *Večerní Praha*, noted that the book showed talent. And then somebody came up to me and said, "Have you seen this?" waving an article from the trade unions' daily *Prace* which contained Václav Běhounek's review entitled "A Slap at the Living and the Dead". Right after that came Josef Rybák's piece, "Rotten Fruit", and soon each day brought a new attack.

Just then, when verbal bombs were falling all around and many people refused to see me altogether, I got an invitation from Alfréd Radok, the film and stage director, one of the founders of *Laterna Magica*, whom I hadn't known at all until then, and this gave me a big lift. In the end, though, except for being forced to leave *Světová Literatura*, no real harm came to me. Jan Řezáč took me right back into the editorial offices of the State Publishing House.

As I now reconstruct the whole affair, I believe this is what happened: a number of reviews of *The Cowards* were scheduled to appear, and as far as I know many had already been written, but they never came out. In this way, an artificial and distorted critical atmosphere was created. Lederer's review caused quite a scandal all on its own. On Thursday his favourable review of *The Cowards* came out in *Večerní Praha*; on Saturday an article appeared in the same newspaper denouncing "this politically unreliable person" and Lederer got the axe. Step by step, the same thing happened not only to Fikar and Kocourek but also to Jan Grossmann, Josef Hiršal, and finally even to Kamil Bednář—the last three, like Fikar and Kocourek, were on the staff of the Writers' Union Publishing House—whose only sin was to praise the book at the office. Ironically enough, the axe job was done by the same people who only a short time before had been praising *The Cowards* to me to the sky. This climate didn't affect only people; literary works fell victim to it too. Hrabal's *Pearls on the Bottom*, Lubomír Dorůžka's book about jazz—all such works were set aside and had to wait a number of years before they could return to grace. A conference on criticism was called, at which Ladislav Štoll, the ultra-orthodox Party ideologist and critic, delivered his famous denunciation of my book, and so on. In short, it was a victory for the conservative elements who felt that things had gone too far. But now comes the paradox. A year after this purge which was supposed to result in the production of healthy and constructive literature, everybody began to write and publish books that actually went much further than *The Cowards*.

I had already had similar experiences in 1945 in Náchod. I used to edit a publication there. I put out three issues, and you wouldn't believe how fast I got fired. Then a friend of mine took over, and he got away with all sorts of things that I never would have dreamed of trying. That's always the way it goes, I suppose. Still, I'm surprised that people go along with this farce.

Why do you think it was The Cowards *rather than some other book that caused the roof to fall in?*

The Cowards was, in its time, a real innovation—a fact which was due less to my genius than to luck. I had been studying English, and so at a time when others were struggling through typical Stalinist-era works such as *Knight of the Golden Star*, I was able to read literature of a higher order. I was surrounded by fine examples of writing, and this includes Marx and Engels as well. These classics were not required reading at the time, but I saw that these men knew how to write, that they knew how to create a system, present an idea. I have not read any political writings since. I found no difficulty in reconciling Marxist ideology with the literature of sincere, truthful exposition as practised in England and America. But even this was somehow an unusual idea at the time.

It often happens in art that something totally new—or, as in the case of *The Cowards*, relatively new—makes its appearance in the midst of scandal. A scandal attracts people, and the bigger the furor the more people it lures and seduces. All prohibitions are in vain once the devil has appeared; as is well known, only God can prevail against the devil. That's why, in such cases, theoretical victories are usually promptly followed by crushing practical defeats. All the initial excitement about *The Cowards* was stirred up by an edition of approximately 10,000 copies. Since then, 120,000 copies of the book have been printed, and the world still hasn't come to an end.

All art is a manifestation of a more or less critical attitude towards society. Artists usually have a strong moral consciousness and dislike producing "on demand". And when their works are wronged, though they cannot fight back and struggle in the same way as other people, their opposition hardens all the same. That's just a normal dialectical process. Those who hate repression—and they are in the majority—don't react to it with the thought "we will obey", but on the contrary, "we will disobey". That's because they realize that otherwise they would lose their identities. A decent person never criticizes those who are defenceless.

To come back to foreign writers: you are probably our best authority on Hemingway and Faulkner. You have a very special relationship to these two Americans.

That is a complicated and rather personal matter. The magic of Hemingway's style reached me, at one point of my development as a writer, and profoundly affected my sensibilities. I kept reading more of Hemingway, I thought about him and studied works written about him. I think I was so fascinated by him because he managed to merge literature and life, because literature became his fate, his destiny. He felt that if he stopped writing, even for a while, his life would stop too. And then, in the early 1950s, I was struck by his absolute sincerity: "The writer's job is to tell the truth." That is as simple as a commandment, and it is a commandment that is difficult to evade.

For me, there is no basic difference between Hemingway and Faulkner. In Faulkner I found once again the magic, luminous text. And once again I got a peek into the author's life, and a number of details drew me even closer to him. For example, his love for detective stories. Until 1946 he spent several months each year in Hollywood writing movie scripts. For rather commercial films, too, I believe. He used to say that if he were ever to write himself out, to lose his inspiration, he would write detective stories and get by on pure skill and craftsmanship. I am impressed by his broad taste, his refusal to turn up his nose at anything. His brother, John Faulkner, tells how William once entered the local drugstore and saw a stack of detective stories on the counter. They had been picked out by a prominent Oxford citizen, but when this gentleman saw Faulkner enter the store he felt ashamed of his plebeian reading habits and pretended to be busily examining some serious books. "These yours?" asked Faulkner, pointing at the detective stories. "Certainly not," answered the gentleman. Whereupon Faulkner started to rummage avidly through the stack and bought a handful on the spot.

There is another reason why I am so fond of Hemingway, Faulkner, and Greene. Who was it who said he'd give his life for a good aphorism? In their books you will always find, at a crucial point, some key words, some truth that would make the book precious even if it contained nothing else. For example, in *A Farewell to Arms* there are two such moments that make the book unforgettable for me. The first is the idea that the world breaks almost everyone, and those it cannot break it kills. This is not a philosophical discovery. Writers aren't philosophers, they simply formulate in a better way what starlings twitter to each other across rooftops. The second great comment comes in the scene in which the military police are shooting deserters: "The questioners," writes Hemingway, "had that beautiful detachment and devotion to stern justice of men dealing in death without being in any danger of it."

And Graham Greene! In *The Heart of the Matter*, when Scobie kills himself after committing a long series of sins, his wife is convinced that he will be denied salvation. And yet in answer to the priest's question, she replies that she herself no longer feels any bitterness towards her late husband. "And do you think God's likely to be more bitter than a woman?" asks the priest. I love an author for such lines, and I am willing to forgive a great deal for their sake alone.

JAZZ

RED MUSIC

—

*The Bass Saxophone, Škvorecký's first book to be pub-
lished in English after his arrival in Canada, contains
two novellas,* Emöke *and* The Bass Saxophone. *He wrote
this essay about the fate of jazz under two totalitarian
governments to provide his non-Czech readers with a
social and historical context for the second of the novellas.*

IN THE days when everything in life was fresh—because we were
sixteen, seventeen—I used to blow tenor sax. Very poorly. Our
band was called Red Music which in fact was a misnomer, since
the name had no political connotations: there was a band in
Prague that called itself Blue Music and we, living in the Nazi
Protectorate of Bohemia and Moravia, had no idea that in jazz
blue is not a colour, so we called ours Red. But if the name itself
had no political connotations, our sweet, wild music did; for jazz
was a sharp thorn in the sides of the power-hungry men, from
Hitler to Brezhnev, who successively ruled in my native land.

What sort of political connotations? Leftist? Rightist? Racial-
ist? Classist? Nationalist? The vocabulary of ideologists and
mountebanks doesn't have a word for it. At the outset, shortly
before the Second World War, when my generation experienced
its musical revelation, jazz didn't convey even a note of protest.
(Whatever shortcomings the liberal republic of T.G. Masaryk
may have had, it was a veritable paradise of cultural tolerance.) And no matter what LeRoi Jones says to the contrary,
the essence of this music, this "way of making music", is not
simply protest. Its essence is something far more elemental: an
élan vital, a forceful vitality, an explosive creative energy as
breathtaking as that of any true art, that may be felt even in
the saddest of blues. Its effect is cathartic.

But of course, when the lives of individuals and communities are controlled by powers that themselves remain
uncontrolled—slavers, czars, führers, first secretaries, mar-
shals, generals and generalissimos, ideologists of dictatorships
at either end of the spectrum—then creative energy becomes
a protest. The consumptive clerk of a working-man's insurance company (whose heart had reportedly been moved by
the plight of his employer's beleaguered clients) undergoes a
sudden metamorphosis to become a threat to closely guarded
socialism. Why? Because the visions in his *Castle*, his *Trial*, his
Amerika are made up of too little paper and too much real life,
albeit in the guise of non-realist literature. That is the way it is.
How else explain the fact that so many titles on Senator Joe Mc-
Carthy's index of books to be removed from the shelves of U.S.
Information Libraries abroad are identical to many on the one
issued in Prague by the Communist party early in the seventies? Totalitarian ideologists don't like real life (other people's),
because it cannot be totally controlled; they loathe art, the product of a yearning for life, because that too evades control—if
controlled and legislated, it perishes. But before it perishes—or
when it finds refuge in some kind of *samizdat* underground—
art, willy-nilly, becomes protest. Popular mass art, like jazz,
becomes mass protest. That's why the ideological guns and
sometimes even the police guns of all dictatorships are aimed
at the men with the horns.

Red Music used to play (badly, but with the enthusiasm of
sixteen-year-olds) during the reign of the most Aryan Aryan
of them all and his cultural handyman, Dr. Goebbels. It was
Goebbels who declared, "Now, I shall speak quite openly on the
question of whether German radio should broadcast so-called
jazz music. If by jazz we mean music that is based on rhythm
and entirely ignores or even shows contempt for melody, music
in which rhythm is indicated primarily by the ugly sounds of
whining instruments so insulting to the soul, why then we can
only reply to the question entirely in the negative." Which was
one reason we whined and wailed, rasped and roared, using
all kinds of wa-wa and hat mutes, some of them manufactured
by ourselves. But even then, protest was one of the lesser
reasons. Primarily, we loved that music that we called jazz, and

that in fact was swing, the half-white progeny of Chicago and New Orleans, what our non-blowing contemporaries danced to in mountain villages, out of reach of the *Schutzpolizei*, the uniformed security service. For even dancing was forbidden then in the Third Reich, which was in mourning for the dead of the Battle of Stalingrad.

The revelation we experienced was one of those that can only come in one's youth before the soul has acquired a shell from being touched by too many sensations. In my mind I can still hear, very clearly, the sound of the saxes on that old, terribly scratchy Brunswick seventy-eight spinning on a wind-up phonograph, with the almost illegible label, "'I've Got a Guy', Chick Webb and His Orchestra with Vocal Chorus". Wildly sweet, soaring swinging saxophones, the lazy and unknown voice of the unknown vocalist who left us spellbound even though we had no way of knowing that this was the great, then seventeen-year-old, Ella Fitzgerald. But the message of her voice, the call of the saxes, the short wailing and weeping saxophone solo between the two vocal choruses, they all came across. Nothing could ever silence them in our hearts.

And despite Hitler and Goebbels the sweet poison of the Judeo-Negroid music (that was the Nazi epithet for jazz) not only endured, it prevailed—even, for a short time, in the very heart of hell, the ghetto at Terezín. The Ghetto Swingers...there is a photograph of them, an amateur snapshot, taken behind the walls of the Nazi-established ghetto during the brief week that they were permitted to perform—for the benefit of the Swedish Red Cross officials who were visiting that Potemkin village of Nazism. They are all there, all but one of them already condemned to die, in white shirts and black ties, the slide of the trombone pointing diagonally up to the sky, pretending or maybe really experiencing the joy of rhythm, of music, perhaps a fragment of hopeless escapism.

There was even a swing band in the notorious Buchenwald, made up for the most part of Czech and French prisoners. And since those were not only cruel but also absurd times, people were put behind barbed wire because of the very music that was played inside. In a concentration camp near Wiener Neustadt sat Vicherek, a guitar player who had sung Louis Armstrong's scat chorus in "Tiger Rag" and thus, according to the Nazi judge, "defiled musical culture". Elsewhere in Germany several swingmen met a similar fate and one local *Gauleiter* issued an extraordinary (really extraordinary? in this world of ours?) set of regulations which were binding for all dance orchestras. I read them, gnashing my teeth, in Czech translation in the film weekly *Filmový kurýr*, and fifteen years later I paraphrased them—faithfully, I am sure, since they had engraved themselves deeply on my mind—in a short story entitled "I Won't Take Back One Word":

1) Pieces in foxtrot rhythm (so-called swing) are not to exceed 20% of the repertoires of light orchestras and dance bands;

2) in this so-called jazz type repertoire, preference is to be given to compositions in a major key and to lyrics expressing joy in life rather than Jewishly gloomy lyrics;

3) as to tempo, preference is also to be given to brisk compositions over slow ones (so-called blues); however, the pace must not exceed a certain degree of allegro, commensurate with the Aryan sense of discipline and moderation. On no account will Negroid excesses in tempo (so-called hot jazz) or in solo performances (so-called breaks) be tolerated;

4) so-called jazz compositions may contain at most 10% syncopation; the remainder must consist of a natural legato movement devoid of the hysterical rhythmic reverses characteristic of the music of the barbarian races and conducive to dark instincts alien to the German people (so-called riffs);

5) strictly prohibited is the use of instruments alien to the German spirit (so-called cowbells, flexatone, brushes, etc.) as well as all mutes which turn the noble sound of wind and brass instruments into a Jewish-Freemasonic yowl (so-called wa-wa, hat, etc.);

6) also prohibited are so-called drum breaks longer than half a bar in four-quarter beat (except in stylized military marches);

7) the double bass must be played solely with the bow in so-called jazz compositions;

8) plucking of the strings is prohibited, since it is damaging to the instrument and detrimental to Aryan musicality; if a so-called pizzicato effect is absolutely desirable for the character of the composition, strict care must be taken lest the string be allowed to patter on the sordine, which is henceforth forbidden;

9) musicians are likewise forbidden to make vocal improvisations (so-called scat);

10) all light orchestras and dance bands are advised to restrict the use of saxophones of all keys and to substitute for them the violoncello, the viola, or possibly a suitable folk instrument.

When this unseemly decalogue appeared in that story of mine in Czechoslovakia's first jazz almanac (it was in 1958), the censors of an entirely different dictatorship confiscated the entire edition. The workers in the print shop salvaged only a few copies, one of which got into the hands of Miloš Forman, then a young graduate of the Film Academy in search of material for his first film. After several years of writing and arguing with the censors, we finally got official approval for our script, whereupon it was personally banned by the man who was at the time the power in the country, President Antonín Novotný. That was the end of our film. Why? Because the decrees of the old *Gauleiter* were once again in force, this time in the land of the victorious proletariat.

But back in the days of the swastika it was not just that one isolated German in the swing band at Buchenwald, not just the few imprisoned pure-Aryan swingmen—many far more reliable members of the master race were tainted with the sweet poison. How vividly I recall them, in their blue-grey Nazi uniforms, recently arrived from Holland with Jack Bulterman's arrangements of "Liza Likes Nobody", in exchange for copies of which we gave them the sheet music for "Deep Purple" and the next day they were off to Athens, where there were other saxophones swinging, underlined with Kansas riffs. I can see those German soldiers now, sitting in a dim corner of the Port Arthur Tavern, listening hungrily to the glowing sounds of Miloslav Zachoval's Big Band, which was the other, far better swing band in my native town of Náchod. Vainly did I dream of becoming one of Zachoval's swingers. Alas, I was found lacking in skill, and doomed to play with the abominable Red Music.

How naive we were, how full of love and reverence. Because Dr. Goebbels had decided that the whining Judeo-Negroid music invented by American capitalists was not to be played in the territory of the Third Reich, we had a ball inventing aliases for legendary tunes so that they might be heard in the territory of the Third Reich after all. We played a fast piece—one of those forbidden "brisk compositions"—called "The Wild Bull", indistinguishable to the naked ear from "Tiger Rag"; we played a low tune, "Abendlied" or "Evening Song", and fortunately the Nazi censors had never heard the black voice singing, "When the deep purple falls over sleepy garden walls...." And the height of our effrontery, "The Song of Řešetová Lhota", in fact "St. Louis Blues", rang out one misty day in 1943 in eastern Bohemia, sung in Czech by a country girl, the lyrics composed so that they might elaborate on our new title for W.C. Handy's theme song: "Řešetová Lhota... is where I go... I'm on my way... to see my Aryan folk...." In fact, we were fortunate that the local Nazis had never seen Chaplin's *The Great Dictator*, never heard the bullies sing about the "Ary-ary-ary-ary-aryans." Neither had we, of course—"The Song of Řešetová Lhota" was simply an indigenous response to Nazism.

It was, like most of our songs, ostensibly the composition of a certain Mr. Jiří Patočka. You would search for his name in vain in the lists of popular composers of the time since he too was a figment of our imagination. That mythical gentleman's large repertoire also included a tune indistinguishable from "The Casa Loma Stomp". In our ignorance we hadn't the faintest idea that there was a castle of that name in distant

Toronto. We believed that Casa Loma was an American band
leader, one of the splendid group that included Jimmy Lunceford, Chick Webb, Andy Kirk, the Duke of Ellington (Ellington
had been placed among the nobility by a Czech translator who
encountered his name in an American novel and decided that
this must be a member of the impoverished British aristocracy, eking out a living as a bandleader at the Cotton Club),
Count Basie, Louis Armstrong, Tommy Dorsey, Benny Goodman, Glenn Miller—you name them, we knew them all. And
yet we knew nothing. The hours we spent racking our brains
over song titles we couldn't understand... "Struttin' with Some
Barbecue"—the definition of the word "barbecue" in our pocket
Webster didn't help at all. What on earth could it mean: "walking pompously with a piece of animal carcass roasted whole"?
We knew nothing—but we knew the music. It came to us on
the waves of Radio Stockholm mostly, since that was the only
station that played jazz that the Nazis didn't jam. Swedish
style: four saxes, a trumpet plus rhythm—perhaps the first distinct jazz style we knew, except for big band swing. Curiously
there was one film, also of Swedish provenance, that among all
the Nazi war-propaganda films, the *Pandur Trencks* and *Ohm
Kruegers*, escaped the eyes of the watchmen over the purity of
Aryan culture. In translation it was entitled *The Whole School
Is Dancing*. The original title appealed to us more, even though
we understood no Swedish: *Swing It, Magistern!* In the territory
of the Third Reich, that was the movie of the war. We all fell in
love with the swinging, singing Swedish girl called Alice Babs
Nielsson, another reassuring indication that though we lacked
knowledge we at least had an ear for jazz: much, much later
she recorded with Ellington. But that film—I must have seen it
at least ten times. I spent one entire Sunday in the movie theatre, through the matinée, through the late afternoon show and
the evening show, inconsolably sad that there was no midnight
mass of *Swing It, Magistern!*

"Swing It, Magistern, Swing It!" became one of the standard
pieces played at public concerts in obscure little towns in eastern Bohemia, much to the joy of fans of swing. But of course,
enemies of jazz and swing were also to be found among our
Czech contemporaries. The milder ones were the jazz conservatives to whom swing was an outlandish modern distortion.

They would just boo loudly at our concerts. The radicals, the polka buffs, did more than that. They threw apple cores at us, rotten eggs, all kinds of filth, and the legendary concerts in the legendary hick towns often ended in a brawl between the polka buffs and the fans of swing. Then the band would have to flee by the back door to save their precious instruments, irreplaceable in wartime, from the wrath of the protectors of the one and only true Czech music: the polka—played, horror of horrors, on an accordion.

The polka buffs never dared throw eggs at our Ella, though. Yes, we even had our own Goddess, our Queen of Swing, Girl Born of Rhythm, Slender Girl with Rhythm at Her Heels, our own Ella. She was white, of course, and her name was Inka Zemánková. She distinguished herself by singing Czech lyrics with an American accent, complete with the nasal twang so alien to the Czech language. My God, how we adored this buggering up of our lovely language, for we felt that all languages were lifeless if not buggered up a little. Inka's theme song was something entitled "I Like to Sing Hot", not one of Jiří Patočka's ostensible compositions but a genuine Czech effort. The lyrics described a swinging girl strolling down Broadway with "Harlem syncopating in the distance". It contained several bars of scat and concluded with the singer's assertion, "I like to sing Hot!" This final word, sung in English, alerted the Nazi censors, and on their instructions Inka had to replace it with the equally monosyllabic expression "*z not*"—a charmingly absurd revision, for although it rhymes with "hot" the expression means exactly the opposite of singing hot music: it means singing from sheet music, from the notes.

Far from Harlem, from Chicago, from New Orleans, uninformed and naive, we served the sacrament that verily knows no frontiers. A nucleus existed in Prague that published an underground magazine entitled *O.K.* (an abbreviation not of *Ol Korekt* but of *Okružní Korespondence*, i.e. Circulating Correspondence). Pounded out on a typewriter with about twenty almost illegible carbon copies, this underground publication (really underground, its very possession punishable by a stint in a concentration camp) was our sole source of reliable information. It was distributed through the Protectorate by lovely

krystýnky on bicycles, the bobby soxers of those perished times.
I can see them in their longish skirts, dancing and "dipping"
in the taverns of remote villages, with one fan always standing
guard at the door, on the lookout for the German police. When
a *Schupo* appeared over the horizon, a signal was given, and all
the *krystýnky* and their boyfriends, the "dippers", would scurry
to sit down to glasses of green soda-pop, listening piously to the
Viennese waltz that the band had smoothly swung into. When
the danger had passed, everyone jumped up again, the Kansas
riffs exploded, and it was swing time once again.

Then the Great War ended. In the same movie theatre where
I had once sat through three consecutive showings of *Swing It,
Magistern!* I sat through three screenings of a lousy print of *Sun
Valley Serenade*, with Russian subtitles. I was impervious to the
Hollywood plot, but hypnotized by Glenn Miller. The print had
found its way to our town with the Red Army, the film badly
mangled by frequent screenings at the battlefront, the damaged
sound track adding Goebbelsian horrors to "In the Mood" and
"Chattanooga Choo-choo". None the less, I had the splendid
feeling that, finally, the beautiful age of jazz had arrived.

My mistake. It took only a lean three years before it was back
underground again. New little Goebbelses started working diligently in fields that had been cleared by the old demon. They
had their own little Soviet bibles, primarily the fascistoid *Music
of Spiritual Poverty* by a V. Gorodinsky, and I. Nestyev's *Dol-
lar Cacophony*. Their vocabulary was not very different from
that of the Little Doctor, except that they were, if possible, even
prouder of their ignorance. They characterized jazz and jazz-
inspired music by a rich assortment of derogatory adjectives:
"perverted", "decadent", "base", "lying", "degenerate", etc. They
compared the music to "the moaning in the throat of a camel"
and "the hiccupping of a drunk", and although it was "the music
of cannibals", it was at the same time invented by the capitalists "to deafen the ears of the Marshallized world by means
of epileptic, loud-mouthed compositions". Unfortunately, these
Orwellian masters soon found their disciples among Czechs,
who in turn—after the fashion of disciples—went even further
than their preceptors, declaring wildly that jazz was aimed at
"annihilating the people's own music in their souls". Finally the
aggressive theoreticians even organized a concert of "model"

jazz pieces composed to order for the Party's cultural division. It was an incredible nightmare. Band-leader Karel Vlach, the greatest among Czech pioneers of swing, sat in the front row, going from crimson to ashen and from ashen to crimson again, probably saying a prayer in his soul to Stan Kenton. Beside him sat an unholy trinity of Soviet advisers on jazz (led by, of all men, Aram Khachaturian, colleague of Prokofiev and Shostakovitch), gloomy, silent, and next to them a senile choirmaster using a hearing aid. And yet not even the emasculated musical monster presented to them satisfied the Soviet advisers. They criticized its "instrumental make-up" and described it as "the music of a vanishing class". Finally, the old choirmaster rose, and we heard him add the final chord: "Now, take the trumpet. Such an optimistic-sounding instrument! And what do those jazz people do? They stuff something down its throat and right away it sounds despicable, whining, like a jungle cry!"

After that Vlach was unable to refrain from a few heretical remarks: if they didn't give him something better than Stan Kenton, said he, he would keep on playing Stan Kenton. Which is perhaps what he did in the travelling circus to which he was shortly thereafter relegated along with his entire band. The Party also proclaimed the creation of an "official" model jazz band, and in the Youth Musical Ensembles the most avid ideologists even tried to replace the hybrid-sounding (therefore supposedly bourgeois) saxophones with the non-hybrid (therefore more proletarian) violoncello—but it takes at least five years to learn to play the cello passably, while a talented youth can master the saxophone in a month, and what he wants to do is play, play, play. But ideological thinking follows paths free from the taint of reality. In place of Kenton, they pushed Paul Robeson at us, and how we hated that black apostle who sang, of his own free will, at open-air concerts in Prague at a time when they were raising the socialist leader Milada Horáková to the gallows, the only woman ever to be executed for political reasons in Czechoslovakia by Czechs, and at a time when great Czech poets (some ten years later to be "rehabilitated" without exception) were pining away in jails. Well, maybe it was wrong to hold it against Paul Robeson. No doubt he was acting in good faith, convinced that he was fighting for a good cause. But they kept holding him up to us as an exemplary "progressive jazz man", and we hated him. May God rest his—hopefully—innocent soul.

But in the early fifties, although the bishops of Stalinist obscurantism damned the "music of the cannibals", they had one problem. Its name was Dixieland. A type of the cannibal music with roots so patently folkloristic and often (the blues) so downright proletarian that even the most Orwellian falsifier of facts would be hard put to deny them. Initiates had already encountered isolated recordings of Dixieland during the war, and after it ended a group of youths heard the Graeme Bell Dixieland Band performing at a Youth Festival in Prague. They created the first Czechoslovak Dixieland Band, and soon there was a proliferation of Louisiana-sounding names: Czechoslovak Washboard Beaters, Prague City Stompers, Memphis Dixie, and dozens of others. Uncle Tom music was really the only form of jazz suffered at the depressing congregations called youth entertainments, where urban girls in pseudo-national costumes got up and sang bombastic odes to Stalin in the style of rural yodelling.

An apostle of Dixieland, Emanuel Uggé, took the Czechoslovak Dixieland on the road. Once again, obscure little towns in the north-east of Bohemia resounded with loud syncopations, wound around with the boring, hyperscholarly commentaries of this devoted *Doctor Angelicus* of Dixieland who, for the ears of the informers attending the concert, succeeded in interpreting the most obscene tune from the lowest speakeasy in Chicago as an expression of the Suffering Soul of the Black People, waiting only for Stalin and his camps where re-education was carried out directly for the other world. But it turned out that going on the road with Dixieland was a double-edged move. On the one hand it kept the knowledge of jazz alive, but on the other hand what the more enlightened and therefore less brazenly orthodox supervisors in Prague had passed off as a "form of Negro folklore", the true-believing provincial small fry recognized for what it was: an effort to "smuggle western decadence into the minds of our workers.... Such orchestras conceal their vile intentions in music that has no educational merit," says a letter from the town council of Hranice to the management of

the Hranice Cement Workers. "Eighty per cent of what the en-
semble played was westernist, cosmopolite music which had an
eccentric effect, going so far as to cause one of the soldiers to
come up on the stage and do a tap dance." Horrors! A soldier in
the Czech Red Army, tap-dancing to some Nick La Rocca tune!
Years later I recalled this Harlemized soldier when I read in an
article by Vassily Aksyonov (author of the epochal *A Ticket to
the Stars*—but who in the West has heard of him? Who knows
that the liberating effect of this novel, written in Moscow slang,
had perhaps a more profound influence on contemporary Russian prose than *Doctor Zhivago*?) about a big band that existed
somewhere in Siberia during Stalin's last days, and played "St.
Louis Blues", "When the Saints", "Riverside Blues".... Another
chapter in the legends of apostles who were often martyrs.

Even Inka, our idolized Queen of Swing, became one. After
the war she had put aside her career in order to study singing
professionally. Five years later, she decided it was time to make
her comeback. The concert agency booked her for a Sunday
matinée at the Lucerna Hall in Prague. She sang one song just
before the intermission and was to sing another one after. It
was an old swing tune, and while Inka's sense of rhythm had
remained, her vocal range had doubled. She was rewarded by
thunderous applause, gave them an encore, and this time sang
one whole chorus in scat. The applause was endless. "When
I stumbled offstage," she told me years later, "I thought to
myself—there, I've made it again! But there was a guy there,
in one of those blue shirts, you know, I think they called them
the Young Guard, all scowling and furious, and he yelled at me,
'That's it! Out! I can assure you you'll never sing another note
in public.' And in fact, that's what happened, they didn't even
let me sing my second number after the intermission." At that
moment I couldn't help thinking about Vicherek and his scat
chorus in "Tiger Rag" during the Nazi occupation.

However, with the passage of years political events threatened the unlimited rule of the provincial small fry (and the
blue-shirted Communist Youth storm trooper) and also the validity of their musicological opinions. We began to consider how
we might get permission for the Czechoslovak Dixieland Band

(now metamorphosed into the Prague Dixieland Band) to perform in public again—and found unexpected and unintended
help from the U.S. An American bass player named Herbert
Ward had asked for political asylum in Czechoslovakia, "delivering another serious blow to American imperialism", the Party
press announced. It also said that Ward used to play with Armstrong. We immediately looked him up in his hotel in Prague
and talked him into playing a role of which he was totally unaware and which is referred to in Stalinist slang as "shielding
off". In fact, we used him ruthlessly. We quickly put together a
jazz revue entitled *Really the Blues* (title stolen from Mezz Mez-
zrow), printed Herb's super-anti-American statement in the
program, provided the Prague Dixieland to accompany Herb's
homemade blues about how it feels to be followed by American secret-police agents (a particularly piquant blues in a police
state where everybody knew the feeling only too well), dressed
his sexy dancer-wife Jacqueline in original sack dresses borrowed from a Prague matron who had lived it up in Paris in the
twenties, then settled down to enjoy her dancing of the eccentric, decadent Charleston. Since Herb's terribly shouted blues
had anti-American lyrics and because Jackie's skin was not entirely white the authorities didn't dare protest, and left us alone
with our towering success. The show finally folded as a result
of difficulties of a more American nature. Herb and Jacqueline wanted more money. The producer, bound by state norms,
was unable to give them more, and *Really the Blues* died a pre-
mature death. Later on, Herb and Jacqueline went the way of
many American exiles: back home to the States, the land where
the words "you can't go home again" generally seem not to apply. Apply they do, though, for other countries, the ones that
send their own writers into exile, to prison, or to their death.

Really the Blues was the end of a beginning. Jazz had grown
to resemble the Mississippi, with countless rivulets fanning out
from its delta. The Party found other targets: Elvis Presley,
little rock'n'roll groups with guitars electrified and amplified on
home workbenches, with a new crop of names recalling faraway
places—Hell's Devils, Backside Slappers, Rocking Horses—new
outcries from the underground. By the end of the fifties, a group
of young people had been arrested and some of them sentenced
to prison for playing tapes of "decadent American music" and

devoting themselves to the "eccentric dancing" of rock'n'roll. (Again, the spirit of Vicherek was present at their trial.) And because the mass of young people had turned to follow other stars, jazz proper, be it mainstream or experimental, was no longer considered dangerous, and so the sixties were a time of government-sponsored International Jazz Festivals. The stage at Lucerna Hall in Prague echoed with the sounds of Don Cherry, The Modern Jazz Quartet, Ted Curson.... We applauded them, although, for the most part, this was no longer the music we had known and loved. We were the old faithfuls. The broad appeal of the saxes was gone, either this was esoteric music or we had simply grown old.... Jazz is not just music. It is the love of youth which stays firmly anchored in one's soul, for ever unalterable while real live music changes, for ever the calling of Lunceford's saxophones....

That was when I wrote *The Bass Saxophone*, and I was writing about fidelity, about the sole real art there is, about what one must be true to, come hell or high water; what must be done to the point of collapse, even if it be a very minor art, the object of condescending sneers. To me literature is for ever blowing a horn, singing about youth when youth is irretrievably gone, singing about your homeland when in the schizophrenia of the times you find yourself in a land that lies over the ocean, a land—no matter how hospitable or friendly—where your heart is not, because you landed on these shores too late.

For the steel chariots of the Soviets swung low, and I left. Jazz still leads a precarious existence in the heart of European political insanity, although the battlefield has shifted elsewhere. But it is the same old familiar story: a spectre is again haunting Eastern Europe, the spectre of rock, and all the reactionary powers have entered into a holy alliance to exorcize it—Brezhnev and Husák, Suslov and Honecker, East German obscurantists and Czech police-spies. Lovely new words have emerged from the underground, like the *krystýnky* and the "dippers" of the Nazi era: now there are *Manichky*, "little Marys", for long-haired boys, *undrooshy*, from the Czechified pronunciation of the word "underground", for rock fans of both sexes. Anonymous people hold underground Woodstocks in the same old obscure hick towns, gatherings often ruthlessly broken up

by police, followed by the arrest of participants, their interrogation, their harassment, all the joys of living in a police
state.

And so the legend continues...and the chain of names. The
Ghetto Swingers, the nameless bands of Buchenwald, the big
band in Stalin's Siberia, the anonymous jazz messengers in
Nazi uniforms criss-crossing Europe with their sheet music,
the Leningrad Seven—nameless aficionados who in the Moscow
of the sixties translated, from the Czech translation of original American material into Russian *samizdat*, the theoretical
anthology *The Face of Jazz*—and other buffs and bands, even
more obscure, blowing away for all I know even in Mao's China.
To their names new ones must be added, the Plastic People
of the Universe, and DG307, two underground groups of rock
musicians and avant-garde poets whose members have just
been condemned (at the time I am writing this) to prison in
Prague for "arousing disturbance and nuisance in an organized
manner". That loathsome vocabulary of hell, the vocabulary of
Goebbels, the vocabulary of murderers....

My story is drawing to a close. *"Das Spiel ist ganz und gar
verloren. Und dennoch wird es weitergehen...."* The game is
totally lost. And yet it will go on. The old music is dying,
although it has so many offspring, vigorous and vital, that will,
naturally, be hated. Still, for me, Duke is gone, Satchmo is
gone, Count Basie has just barely survived a heart attack, Little
Jimmy Rushing has gone the way of all flesh....

> ...anybody asks you
> who it was sang this song,
> tell them it was...
> he's been here, and's gone.

Such is the epitaph of the little Five-by-Five. Such is the
epitaph I would wish for my books.

*Editor's note: "I Won't Take Back One Word" was published fi-
nally in 1966 as "Eine kleine Jazzmusik". The detailed story of
the intrigue surrounding "Eine kleine Jazzmusik" may be found*

in Josef Škvorecký's All the Bright Young Men and Women.

TALKIN' MOSCOW BLUES

In 1983 The New Republic *asked Škvorecký to review* Frederick Starr's Red and Hot: The Fate of Jazz in the Soviet Union 1917–1980. *The review published was a slightly shortened version of the following essay.*

SOMETIME IN 1957 or so, my friend Jan Zábrana travelled to Russia. He was a professional translator and spoke the language with ease. Like all Czech tourists in those days, he deposited, amid his underwear, a good supply of brassieres, and put on a layer of three raincoats made of a kind of transparent plastic that the popular mind had nicknamed "condom-coats". To divert the attention of the Soviet customs officers from his valuable black-market goods, he displayed, on top of his belongings in his luggage, a British edition of Hemingway's *For Whom the Bell Tolls*. The ruse worked. After longish consultations, the customs men confiscated the still dubious book of the recently rehabilitated writer and failed to notice both the incongruous articles of clothing in a single man's bag, and the triple layer of plastic on his perspiring body. My friend then sold his brassieres in Moscow, exchanged some for internationally accepted female services, but kept one of his condom-coats for Odessa. He had just begun translating Babel, then in the process of partial rekosherization, and wanted to see the setting of his stories. In a crooked street of the ancient harbour he showed his wares to a group of young, modish-looking men. Instead of money he was offered—a record. "A record?" "Yes," said the prospective buyer, and added with awe: "It's an Eddie Rosner!"

The owner of the coat knew nothing about Rosner and very little about jazz. But the fact that the youngster apparently held the record to be the market equivalent of the commodity then in greatest demand indicated to him the status of Rosner on the Soviet jazz Olympus, and he remembered me. Obviously, the precious disc would make a nice present for a jazz buff. In a moment of selfless magnanimity he accepted the deal. Had he persisted in his intention to bring me a souvenir from Russia I would have heard the music of the legendary Soviet swing star (he was a German Jew, chased by political disasters from his native Berlin to Warsaw, to Moscow, to the Gulag). However, things turned out differently, and I have yet to hear the sounds that fascinated Kolyma.

Late at night that day, returning to his hotel, my friend found the doorman, in his resplendent uniform, dozing off in a chair next to the empty front desk. He woke him up and asked for the key to his room. The doorman opened his eyes, for a while listened incredulously, then got up, stretched his limbs, inflated his giant chest, and, in the glitter of several rows of medals, metamorphosed into—a Soviet army officer. *"Ya genieral!"* he said threateningly. Then his eyes rested on the record in my friend's hands. It was in a homemade brown paper sleeve, on which the proud previous owner, in shaky *azbuka*, had inscribed the holy name: Eddie Rosner. The general reached for the disc. My terrified friend did not put up any resistance. But the general's gesture was not one of confiscation. He offered a sum for the contraband that made my friend forget about friendship and succumb to greed.

I include this story by way of example of the kind of associations aroused in the mind of a graduate of the two European totalitarianisms by Frederick Starr's unique history of jazz in the land of the Soviets. *Red and Hot: The Fate of Jazz in the Soviet Union 1917–1980* is full of stories of this and similar kind, often reaching the level of top-quality surrealism. Veritable bicycles on the operating table. Imagine, for instance, Graf Werner von Schulenburg, the Nazi envoy to Moscow, scribbling an amazed secret report for Ribbentrop in Berlin: at a very official diplomatic party, celebrating the seventeenth anniversary of the Bolshevik Revolution, the count had just witnessed Marshal Voroshilov foxtrotting with his wife in front of the entire assembled Politburo, to the wild sound of a Czech jazz band imported from Prague. Imagine professional Soviet saxophonists who, after the banning of Adolphe Sax's bourgeois invention, are forced to turn in their horns at the Musicians' Union offices, and are issued bassoons and oboes instead (not bourgeois, because feudal); apparently they had to requalify overnight for their assigned instruments if they wished to remain members of their union. And what about the notorious Lazar Kaganovich, one of Stalin's dreaded henchmen, as the author of a successful textbook entitled *How to Organize Railway Ensembles and Jazz Orchestras*?

But Starr's book is not merely a collection of anecdotes and absurdities, and I would not like to create that impression. It is an absorbing and exhaustive work of scholarship; indeed, a pioneering work because, as the author accurately observes,

> The impact of the Bolshevik Revolution on American politics, diplomacy and literature has been the object of much study. The impact in Russia of America's democratic and liberationist upheaval in popular culture remains terra incognita.

Not quite incognita after Starr's book.

The history of the two phenomena starts with an ironic coincidence; during the same week in November 1917 the Bolsheviks conquered the Winter Palace in Petrograd and, in New Orleans, the brothels of Storyville were closed down. The first occurrence inaugurated the October Revolution, the second caused the exodus of jazzmen up the river and into the world. Soon the two revolutionary movements were to meet and, inevitably, clash in Soviet Russia—for one of them represented the elitist approach that strove to shape mass attitudes "from above", the other spontaneously shaped mass tastes (and attitudes) "from below".

Lenin was a master of "scientifically" exploiting existing spontaneous tendencies for his own purpose; his successors, instead of exploiting, more often than not simply tried to suppress. They too did it in the name of "science". And so the history of jazz in the Soviet Union runs parallel to the histories of other arts in that country. It drags on in a kind of yo-yo movement, alternating between periods of relaxation and periods of clamp-downs. During benign times, a Soviet marshal swings to the call of the saxophones; during seasons of frost, a pioneer jazzman like Valentin Parnakh is arrested for exceeding the permitted percentage of syncopation, and perishes anonymously in the Gulag. A nauseating story that nauseatingly yo-yos to this very day.

There are little ironic twists. In the full frost of Stalin's last years, the Obratsov Puppet Theatre is thronged every night because the nasty satire on decadent Hollywood on the stage is accompanied by jazz from genuine American records. Can the censor object? How could he? The decadent music is part of the biting satire on U.S. decadence. A rather nonsensical British film comedy set in the Second World War also plays to full houses. Why? Because its hero, a British jazz-bassist–spy, uses his bowless rhythmic plucking to transmit coded messages over the radio. The ban on plucking clearly does not apply in this case. And at the time Parnakh is dying in the Gulag, Eddie Rosner and his band, all of them arrested, arrive in the same Gulag only to be summoned immediately to the camp commander. It turns out this man used to listen to Rosner's jazz in the trenches—a memory obviously stronger than whatever political convictions the commander has now. Rosner and his men are issued instruments and spend the next five or six years playing as convicts in various camps, until they attain the status of what is virtually a feudal court orchestra of serfs in the house of the all-powerful Alexander Derevenko, the grand duke of the entire camp system in the East. His 250-pound wife Galina loves to do the swing.

Stories like these indicate why the Soviet efforts to eradicate spontaneous art forms remained unsuccessful although they caused much suffering, and even death. As Starr puts it, one unique thing about Soviet jazz is that the attempt to purge it was the only Stalinist purge that failed.

What went wrong?

It has to do again with the shibboleth of "science": with the peculiar nature of "scientific" (as different from "utopian") socialism, better known in the West as Marxism-Leninism.

Nothing against science. All modern societies make use of it, even contemporary shamans of mediaeval obscurantism fly the friendly sky, and they are not carried by flying carpets either. The trouble with Soviet science—at least in the humanities, and occasionally in natural and technical sciences as well—is that it is a strange pseudo-intellectual structure that combines two incongruous elements. First, there is science proper; "bourgeois" science, i.e., the only real science there is. This is the heritage of Marx who, in this and in other senses, was profoundly bourgeois, and though he sometimes relied on sources of dubious validity (as, for example, when he was drooling over the successes of nineteenth-century American communes, obviously unaware of Hawthorne), he, as a rule, respected verifiable reality.

Then there is "class" science, or the "class approach" to science—the tragic and grotesque inheritance of Lenin. There is no doubt that Lenin was a genius of political organization, of subversion, of manipulation. But perhaps the essential part of his bequest—unwitting, maybe—is the unacknowledged (at times—at other times fully acknowledged) *Führerprinzip* that permeates the entire structure of the Party and eventually of society. Power in such a structure emanates from the führer, the leader, *el lider*, *duce*, chairman, whatever his title may be. It willy-nilly begets lesser führers, not only in the political sphere but in all branches and walks of life. Participating in the power from above, most of them succumb to the illusion that the source of power is also the source of infallible wisdom—scientifically infallible wisdom—and that they participate in this wisdom as well. And so it happens that the führer likes a charlatan dabbler in genetics who dislikes the founder of genetics, *ergo* the founder could not have been a scientist, *ergo* the science based on his theories is a nonscience: a bourgeois science. Or the führer is not fond of syncopation, *ergo* the only good jazz is one without syncopes.

In essence, this is a vulgarized form of the scholastic method of referring to the *auctoritates*. In the Middle Ages it produced such curious situations as the mandatory belief in the horse's heart being in its right side, contrary to the evidence of the battlefield, because Aristotle taught so. Its Soviet form,

as Starr notes, leads often to devising elaborate arguments intended to prove that the führer's dislike of an instrument's
timbre is a scientific assessment of that timbre's decadent nature directly attributable to the disintegration of the outdated
bourgeois *Weltanschauung*. The history of Soviet jazz is, therefore, also the story of incredible, often absurd meanderings of
the ideologue's "scientific" false consciousness.

In the first decade of Soviet power, marked by attempts to marry
the revolution to modern art, jazz was part of the package; it
was seen as a radically new, and therefore progressive, art form.
Science had to wait for Maxim Gorky. In his epoch-making article "On the Music of the Gross", he made a discovery: jazz, far
from being revolutionary, was in fact counter-revolutionary—a
characteristically bourgeois type of music. After all, wasn't it
played exclusively in the plush salons of international hotels
for the enjoyment of the rich? Moreover, jazz breathed out an
unbridled sexuality: a clearly decadent feature, typical not of
the struggling working class but of the ladies and gentlemen
of leisure. "Listening for a few minutes to these wails, one involuntarily imagines an orchestra of sexually driven madmen
conducted by a man-stallion brandishing a huge genital member." (These early Soviet artists seem to have been obsessed
with the idea of a superpenis. As you will remember, the prudish
Upton Sinclair withdrew his financial support for Eisenstein's
Mexican film after he had discovered some of the filmmaker's
drawings: one of them showed the Calvary scene with Jesus's
penis winding snakelike around the cross and up the cross of
the crucified criminal on his right who is engaged in an act of
oral sex with the Saviour's member.) To account for the fact
that so many Negroes, men and women of a clearly oppressed
class, were prominent among the creators of this decadent music, Gorky reached into the very heart of the dialectical method:
these Negroes "undoubtedly laugh in their sleeves to see how
their white masters are evolving towards a savagery which
they themselves are leaving behind." To this gem of insight
Lunacharsky, the Commissar of Public Enlightenment, added
another pearl of his own: jazz, according to him, was a deliberate capitalist plot "to make man live through his sexual organs,

so that during the intervals between work he will be preoccupied with these sides of his existence" and will forget about class
struggle. Jazz is simply a replacement of religion, the old opium
of the people, now semi-banned.

Gorky was an authority of the first order, and so was
Lunacharsky. Nothing short of an even more scientific proof—
because delivered by an even more authoritative authority—
could save jazz in the USSR now. The result was the first jazz
witch-hunt. In Moscow several school girls were expelled from
school for admitting their love for jazz. People were fined for
possessing jazz records.

But those incorrigibles who wanted to listen to the music,
progressive or decadent, were on the lookout, and eventually
found new authorities—and consequently new proofs: in this
case authorities sanctified by the fact that they were both
ardent Communists and native-born Americans, i.e., fellow-
countrymen of the black originators of the controversial music.
From men like Charles E. Smith and the notorious Mike Gold
they borrowed the idea that there was not just one jazz, but two.
(Gold formulated a theory that must have been a godsend to the
other arch-enemy of jazz, the Nazis: jazz, according to him, was
created not just by the Negroes, but by the two most oppressed
ethnic groups in America together: the Negroes and the Jews.
In other words, it was a Judeo-Negroid music—which was the
term actually used by the Nazi critics.) There was the bourgeois,
decadent, sex-laden type of jazz, performed in the salons by
and for the gross—and the folksy, proletarian one, devoid of
eroticism and played somewhere in the South. Calling this type
"hot" jazz, and opposing it to the "sweet" charming jazz of the
bourgeoisie, Gold and Smith claimed that the prototype of the
correct form was the music of the New Orleans Rhythm Kings,
the Wolverines, etc.; in short, early Dixieland, and the music of
their black successors that stemmed from it. The Manichaean
distinction led to, among other things, new scientific discoveries
such as the presentation of Duke Ellington as a proletarian
practitioner of folk.

It was this proletarian hot jazz that was to be imitated
and emulated. And so people like Alexander Tsfasman, Georgi
Landsberg, Alexander Varlamov, Yakov Skomorowsky, Leonid

Utesov, and others imitated and emulated. The first witch-hunt ended in a victory for jazz, and for another decade or so the saxophones wailed to the buff's heart's desire. However, one must be tone deaf, or a eunuch, not to hear the pulse of sexual joy in "hot" jazz. There was apparently something wrong with the theories of the apologists. Stalin himself sensed a flaw and Soviet science soon found an explanation. Yes, jazz was basically a music of the oppressed black proletariat; however, it contained both healthy and decadent elements, such as the overwhelming sexuality. These were an expression of the otherwise joyless life under capitalism. The task for the Soviet jazzmen, who lived under conditions of almost pure bliss, was to sift the music through the filter of their "new" reality, keep what was healthy, and eliminate the "inheritance of the past". In 1938, at the height of the purges, an orchestra was founded for that specific purpose and endowed with two million rubles: the State Jazz Orchestra. The irreformable Alexander Tsfasman declined to have anything to do with the abomination, but eleven of his fourteen men were simply dragooned into government service, "like serfs being moved from one estate to another". Two musicians were even released from the Gulag to assure the group's quality. No doubt it was a group of quality: it must have been with all the science that went into its creation. Unfortunately, unenlightened audiences failed to detect any jazz in it, save for that in the band's name. An eyewitness comments:

> The indignation...was stormy and the fiasco complete....
> A large contingent of Red Air Force pilots drove over to
> the show and were infuriated at the absence of jazz....
> Booing, hissing and shouting ended in near riot. The
> musicians considered themselves lucky to have escaped
> with their lives.

After a series of such débâcles the State Jazz Orchestra lingered on for some time—and then was saved by the war. Science was forgotten and, by popular demand of the fighting soldiers, jazz bands proliferated; not just "hot" bands but apparently all kinds of bourgeois mixtures. Even the State Orchestra resumed syncopating.

After the victory, however, this state of affairs became intolerable, and renewed scientific fervour resulted in a new analysis. The old comments of Gorky were dusted off by Victor Gorodinsky in what must be the culmination of Soviet music scholarship: a book entitled *Music of Spiritual Poverty*. "Only a slanderer," concluded Gorodinsky, "could assert that jazz was America's folk music.... One cannot speak of styles in jazz... 'sweet', 'hot', 'swing', 'boogie woogie', etc."— they are all the same. The American *Daily Worker* added more information: "The musical language of American folk music and jazz not only are different, but they are opposed to each other in principle." Finally, the case was sealed by the greatest—because black American—authority of them all: Paul Robeson. Writing in *Soviet Music* (and "blatantly feathering his own nest," adds Starr), Robeson argued that the only true Negro music of America was vocal, i.e., spirituals and the blues. Instrumental jazz was played only by "debased Negroes" and it "prostituted and ruthlessly perverted the genuine expression of folk life."

With Paul Robeson, science said its last word, and the police took over. Parnakh, Sergei Kobasev, and others perished; Rosner, Piatigorsky, Alekseev, Gorin, Landsberg, Sapozhnin, and a great number of Latvians, Lithuanians, Azerbaijanis, and other second-class citizens of the USSR disappeared for long years into the Gulag. Tsfasman was stripped of his post as director of the Radio Orchestra, and the State Jazz Band was ordered to forget about syncopation once again. Prokofiev's *Lieutenant Kijé* was struck from the repertoire because its score called for a saxophone.

A comedy of errors—and terrors. Then Stalin died, eventually Khrushchev took over, the story dragged on. There was relaxation, proliferation, crackdowns, the success of jazz festivals in fringe republics (the very first jazz festival in the world was held in Tallinn in Estonia in 1948, when virtually all jazz was forbidden in Moscow, and six years before the first Newport Jazz Festival), the emergence of the first sophisticated Soviet jazzmen, then accommodation with the government, new conflicts, simply the old yo-yo, and, eventually, emigration of many to America. In the end, as everywhere else, jazz as mass music died a natural death. A new form—rock'n'roll—invaded the paradise of proletarian purity, and the attention of the scientist was turned towards this new target.

A hopeless story of a dreary, decades-long struggle, told excitingly by a man who knows what he is writing about. Against its backdrop, Starr projects the lives of the protagonists. Essentially they are all tragic lives, with, perhaps, one or two exceptions: theoretician Joseph Schillinger who, after frequent interrogations by the GPU (forerunner of the KGB), managed to emigrate to the States in 1928, where he developed his unique theories and became the esteemed teacher of many jazz greats, from Benny Goodman and Tommy Dorsey to Gerry Mulligan and John Lewis. But otherwise, these lives range from death in the Gulag to the frustrated cynicism of the old pioneers who have had too many ups and downs, or have made too many degrading compromises not to feel exhausted, and often disgusted, even disgusted with themselves. A *pars pro toto* is Leonid Utesov, one of the most famous ones, whose early tongue-in-cheek skit which made the argument that jazz had been invented not in New Orleans but in rowdy and brawling Odessa, his native town, turned out to be emblematic of the progress of Soviet musical science. Utesov obviously loved the music dearly, but he did not have the guts of his colleague and rival, the great Alexander Tsfasman, who, at the height of Stalinist terror, when everybody else was trembling in ideologically correct *rubashkas* at Musicians' Union's meetings, used to strut through Moscow's cafés in a tailor-made maroon suit with a dove-grey Stetson on his head. When attacked by the dangerous Association of Proletarian Musicians as a "musical prostitute", Utesov quickly dropped his "St. Louis Blues" and fled under the protective wings of Shostakovich, who provided his band with a few tame and uninteresting foxtrots. And, as if that were not enough, Utesov talked Isaac Dunaevsky, the "optimist" of Soviet light music (he eventually committed suicide), into the delivery of four orchestral fantasies based on "Soviet" folk songs. Then he completed his capitulation by a savage attack on Duke Ellington in 1939, the year of the Stalin–Hitler treaty and other horrors.

Like Peter, he denied his Christ when things got precarious; but when the dangers abated, he showed his true face. In

1971, during Ellington's visit to Moscow, he had himself photographed with the Duke, and eulogized him with passion and sincerity. Turning seventy, he described his schizophrenic situation, which, in fact, is the predicament of every creative "new Soviet man":

> Do you think [he told an American visitor] we Soviet musicians don't know what jazz is? For ourselves, when we are alone, we play in a style that Benny Goodman would envy. Believe me, I'm not bragging: I know what I'm talking about. But for the public we play something different, something "lively". We are forced to pull our left ear with our right hand and our right ear with our left hand. We work as, in ancient times, Comrade Aesop worked.... But what else can we do? What can we do when the censor doesn't allow us to breathe; when a certain Apostolov sits on the Central Committee, a stooge who studied with a military bandmaster; when a certain Vartanov sits in the Ministry of Culture, a creep of a clarinet player; when there is a stone-hearted group of song-hacks and tunesmiths in charge of the Union of Composers? Yes, that is how it is.

Reading laments like these, one thinks of identical complaints in the famous Dovzhenko diaries, of Solzhenitsyn's *The Oak and the Calf*, with its detailed documentation of editor Tvardovsky's ordeals, of the many memoirs published in languages inaccessible—alas—to a vast majority of North Americans. Without idealizing the situation of Western jazzmen, writers, filmmakers, and artists in general, one must, I think, in the end agree with Miloš Forman when he explains why he prefers emigration to Communism: "...there is always the chance that you will find some fool who will let you have the money you need."

Yes, it is a hopeless, dreary story of a decades-long struggle. A mere variation on the story of all creative arts in the Soviet Union. The sad story of a revolution based on the principle of an avant-garde of *Besserwissers*.

Fortunately, in every society, including the scientific ones, another principle is also at work which, so far, has always saved art. It was formulated by a man who himself was not a scientist, merely a country lawyer turned politician. According to him, you can fool all of the people some of the time, and some of the people all of the time. But you cannot fool all of the people all of the time. Frederick Starr's remarkable and exquisitely readable book is a good illustration of the workings of that principle.

HIPNESS AT NOON

———

This essay was written in 1984 in response to the Czechoslovak government's continuing persecution of those daring enough not only to be jazz fans but to establish a Jazz Section of the Czech Musicians' Union, to publicize concerts and publish a jazz newsletter. Together with "Red Music" it chronicles the fate of jazz in Škvorecký's native land during the past half century.

The leading members of the Jazz Section were put on trial in the spring of 1987, and were sentenced to various terms in jail. With the coming of glasnost, though, there is talk in Prague that the Jazz Section may be permitted to function again, under a different name. Only time will tell.

THE NAME OF the organization was innocuous: the Jazz Section of the Czech Musicians' Union. Its membership was restricted to 3,000—a mere club of aficionados of a type of music which long ago had ceased to excite the masses, and was therefore taken off the Party list of dangerous social phenomena. When, after thirteen years of existence, the Jazz Section was for all practical purposes finally forced out of existence, the event went unnoticed in the U.S. *Time* did publish a story but ran it only in its European edition. In America this act of "minor" repression was apparently not considered newsworthy. And indeed, the bloodless demise of a small group of jazz lovers pales in the reddish light of a world where even genocide is quickly reaching the status of newsunworthiness.

Yet for the student of "really-existing socialism", as the system in Czechoslovakia now defines itself, the brief history of the bunch of Czechs who liked syncopation more than their government provides an ideal insight into the workings of "people's democracies".

After sixty years of the Soviet state's struggle against art it should be obvious that Marxists in power never ask questions about aesthetics but only their variation of the perennial query from the Jewish joke: "Is this thing good for the Jews, or bad for the Jews?" Apparently jazz, that generous gift of America to the world, has never been good for Communists in power, although before they grabbed it jazz did help them to recruit quite a few young men and women. However, once the Communist cause metamorphosed from liberating people to closely watching them the jungle sounds of freedom became suspect: sometimes they were deemed supremely dangerous, at other times only alien to the new socialist man. The criterion was simple: if a music fills a football stadium with raving youngsters, it signals danger; if it fills only a smoky jazz club with nostalgic middle-aged men, it is just a nuisance. A well-entrenched Marxist state can tolerate such nuisances. Therefore, in Czechoslovakia, jazz was under fire only until Elvis Presley and the hippy shake reached first the proletarian, then the new upper-class dance halls. After that, the ideological gunmen switched their attention from the saxophone to the electrified guitar.

But in 1982 something happened. In the course of the two following years the Party media orchestrated a clamorous witch-hunt directed overtly against punk rock, but covertly against the Jazz Section. For two years the public was treated to dozens upon dozens of articles and letters to the editor, styled in classical Stalinese, presenting the pop-and-jazz scene in Czechoslovakia as a hotbed of anti-socialist conspiracies. The campaign closely followed the model of the fifties: the victim, still at large and even holding some kind of office, is being prepared for the knock on the door, for the public confession, for the gallows.

Why suddenly so much ado about a small musical nuisance?
I suppose one has to go back to Lenin. This evil genius
of a cause that, to many, once seemed so good realized one
thing: well-entrenched establishments are rarely overthrown
by spontaneous, undirected mass movements. But if a group of
intelligent organizers channels the pent-up strength of popular
feelings in the right direction, thrones will fall. From this it
follows that once the well-directed power of the masses has
achieved the aims of its leaders, the leaders must see to it
that no more spontaneous movements emerge, or that if they
do they are made non-spontaneous by guides appointed "from
above". In the dictionary of victorious Marxism, spontaneity has
become anathema: a crime against really-existing socialism.

However, one cannot very well prevent spontaneous interest
in various uncalled-for things, such as jazz, especially among
the young, and it is hard to make them non-spontaneous.
Such interest always arises "from below", another term of op-
probrium for something that is simply natural. A group of
youngsters becomes excited by Elvis Presley, gets hold of a few
guitars, tries them out in an abandoned barn. Other youngsters
come to the barn to listen, and eventually a new amateur band
plays for free in the local pub, crowded with rocking'n'rolling
teenagers. A spontaneous movement has emerged. In America, the band makes a few records and then either disappears
into obscurity, or is catapulted into stardom and money. In the
Communist states, in the good old days of Uncle Joe, the police raided such pubs and arrested such players. However, that
kind of directness creates martyrs and raises interest in the
forbidden fruit. Nowadays it is used only against the most hardened and incorrigible thought-criminals. Remembering Lenin,
the Party has established organizations such as the Socialist
Union of Youth to channel spontaneous movements into controllable riverbeds "from above" by means of "interest groups". It is
hoped that under the guidance of Party-installed overseers the
jazz-and-rock–loving youth will listen to the trimmed sounds
of discs carefully preselected by an ideological committee, and
play de-decibelled rock that will sound sweet even to the ears
of the Communist big shots or *papalashes*.

This is hoped for but it never happens. Real interest cannot be
controlled by faked interest. All that the Youth Union achieves

is that the amateur band moves from the abandoned barn into the state-provided club room, and instead of making them work for the money needed for equipment, the man "from above" buys the synthesizer with the money from the Culture Fund. There is a tremendous scarcity of dependable men from above; the really-existing ones are moved by hard syncopation much more than by the "Holy Writ", i.e., Marxism-Leninism.

As long as an interest group is only a local phenomenon, its deviations can be handled. When worst comes to worst in Hicksville, the Hicksville cops move in, beat up a few lads, crush a few guitars, and there is peace in Hicksville for another couple of months. But if a central group in Prague appears "from below"— a sort of Central Committee of aficionados—and starts building up a network of Hicksville rock groups all over the country, oh boy, are we in serious trouble!

The Jazz Section developed into such a central committee. It was headed by volunteers who received no pay: another anathema in really-existing socialism. The permitted 3,000 members supported them with enthusiasm, and they were remarkably disciplined. A spontaneous movement came into existence, directed by leaders who were not appointed from above, and were therefore "spontaneous" themselves!

It got out of hand.

It started in 1971, three years after the Soviet ambush. After that exercise in historical dialectics all artists' unions were disbanded and new ones, presided over by carefully chosen, Party-nominated "chairmen", were cautiously being established: among them also the Czech Musicians' Union. A group of jazz enthusiasts applied to the Ministry of the Interior for permission to form a separate Union of Czech Jazz Musicians. The ministry turned them down and recommended that individual jazzmen join the Musicians' Union. The functionaries of that organization interpreted the ministry's decision not as advice that jazzmen merge with the others in a universal faceless group, easily controllable from above by a few reliables, but as permission to form, within the union, a special interest section. The statutes permitted it, and the union already had, for instance, a Music Critics' Section. In this way the Jazz Section established itself, and elected a chairman. The Ministry of the Interior, which had neglected to pre-select someone for that position, restricted itself to setting the *numerus clausus* of 3,000 for the membership: a figure certainly quite insignificant in a nation of 11 million. Right at the beginning an interesting legal situation was thus created: the Ministry of the Interior had not approved an independent organization, and so—since the Jazz Section did not originate with the ministry—the cops had no legal power to disband it; that was the unpleasant prerogative of the Musicians' Union. Later, this circumstance played a part in prolonging the section's life.

The fact that an organization not permitted *de jure* emerged nevertheless *de facto*, and that though formally dependent on the Musicians' Union it acted with remarkable independence, was made possible by the existence of what I like to call the Grey Zone. It is only another word for the "gigantic conspiracy to outwit the abysses of darkness" about which Kenneth Tynan was writing in the fifties. He, of course, did not have in mind the darkness that calls itself really-existing socialism. There, the Grey Zone is the conspiracy of normal people who stand between the fanaticism of the orthodox and the cynicism of the pragmatic on the one side, and the abnormal moral courage of the dissidents on the other. The overt solidarity of these men and women is to Caesar, but their covert sympathies belong to God. They hang portraits of the consecutive Big Brothers over their desks but right under their eyes they read Orwell and listen to Charlie Byrd. They have no organization, unless human decency is an organizing principle. All ministries, all offices, all schools, all factories are infiltrated by them, and the Musicians' Union was no exception. They are the Grey Zone which makes really-existing socialism livable. In fact, they make it work.

At first, the section limited itself to what such groupings are permitted to do. It issued *Jazz*, a not-for-sale, members-only bulletin. It sent lecturers to cultural clubs, held jam sessions and disc-jockey shows. It sponsored the yearly jazz festivals entitled *Prague Jazz Days*, distinguished at first by strict jazz-orthodoxy and therefore not attracting multitudes. The authorities watched, occasionally grumbled, but did not interfere much. Their sights were set on rock'n'roll.

Slowly, then quickly, all this changed in the mid-seventies, when jazz-rock appeared on the scene and when a half-forgotten positive phenomenon of the fifties was rediscovered and soon achieved previously unheard-of proportions. The Grey Zone conspiracy always find loopholes in the armour of orthodoxy, and in the fifties it detected a gap in censorship. Officially sanctioned organizations were allowed to print newsletters and, occasionally, little booklets for their membership. Such materials could not be sold to the public, but the censors applied much lighter criteria of orthodoxy to them, and sometimes did not even require that they be submitted for inspection. This may appear to be an incredible leniency, or perhaps oversight, but it was neither. The Party simply relied on the fright that the terror of the early fifties had put into everybody. The idea that, let's say, the Association of Keepers of Aquarium Fish would print a volume of surrealist poetry seemed—well, surrealist. And yet one of the very best surrealistically inclined modern Czech fiction writers, Bohumil Hrabal—the author of *Closely Watched Trains*—made his literary debut in precisely this way. For years he had been known to everybody interested or working in literature, but since he was labelled a decadent non-Marxist naturalist, no publisher would touch him. Then, in 1956, prominent poet and artist Jiří Kolář convinced the Greyzonists of the Bibliophiles' Club that one issue of their members' newsletter should contain, as a supplement, a little book of Hrabal's stories, *Hovory lidí* (*People Talking*). The booklet came out—for members only—and, encouraged by this event, in 1959 the Writers' Union Publishing House attempted to bring out Hrabal's collection *Skřivánek na niti* (*Lark on a String*) for the general public. The censors immediately killed the book and sent it to the thresher.

In the fifties, *People Talking* was an isolated phenomenon. In the mid-seventies, however, the loophole was suddenly stretched wide by the Jazz section and its audacious chairman, Karel Srp. To the bulletin *Jazz*, the section added two more for-members-only publications: a paperback series, *Jazzpetit*, and a line of art monographs, *Situace* (*Situations*). Both became the haven of authors, artists, and art theoreticians interested in genres and trends that, for all practical purposes, were outlawed. Surprisingly, the old exemption that said membership publications need not be submitted to the censorship office held—perhaps because the Grey Zone has a branch even in the cop ministry.

The *Situations* series focused exclusively on what that old really-existing socialist Dr. Goebbels would call *entartete Kunst*: the stuff made from old wire and feathers, the strange-looking and soon-disappearing holes in the earth, the publicly performed self-tortures, etc. I feel reasonably sure that the rank-and-file jazz aficionados did not particularly care for such artefacts, but these things have always existed not only for their intrinsic value but also to *épater les bourgeois*. However, whereas the bourgeois, that splendid liberal creature, that basis of every decent society, grew tolerant after the initial shock, the Nazis and the Communists have never ceased to see red at the sight of a woman's face painted in profile with her eyes *en face* (unless the face was found in an Egyptian pyramid). I am reasonably sure that, however little the aficionados savoured the rusty-wire-cum-smelly-eggshells masterpieces, they enjoyed the fact that these Apples of Eden were gathered by the industrious gardeners of the Jazz Section. Such are the dialectics of history.

The *Jazzpetit* series was more diversified. It included, for instance, an anthology about New York's "Living Theater" compiled by Jaroslav Kořán, the well-known translator of Kurt Vonnegut, Jr., Ernest Hemingway, and other American writers; another anthology called *Minimal + Earth + Concept Art*, edited by the son of the section's chairman, Karel Srp; a sophisticated essay, "The Body, the Thing and Reality in Contemporary Art", by Petr Rezek; a beautiful monograph of the photographic oeuvre of the leading pre-war surrealist painter Jindřich Štýrský; a book-length study of E.F. Burian, a pre-war Communist jazzman and stage director; a fascinating study of how, facing death, the Jews of the Terezín ghetto managed to lead an incomparably more cultural life than the Wagner-adoring Nazis could ever boast of, entitled *Music of the Theresienstadt Ghetto* by Ludmila Vrkočová. There was a book, *John Lennon*, edited by Tomáš Kraus and Lubor Šonka, with a series of photographs of the Prague John Lennon Wall, another spontaneous creation of youngsters, covered with graffiti of grief which the police smeared with whitewash every night and which the Lennon-mourners replaced with fresh ones every day. There was *Czech Rock'n'Roll* by Vladimír Kouřil, a history of rock music in Czechoslovakia that contained even photographs of stars who had left the country without permission and were therefore non-persons.

By an irony of fate the whole enterprise climaxed where the concept of membership publications had once started: with a book of Bohumil Hrabal. The post-ambush establishment had managed to break this old man of Czech non-conformism, forced him to give a recantatory interview, and then permitted the publication of carefully expurgated editions of the writer's least controversial works. However, there were a few manuscripts which the Master refused to have disfigured, among them the hilarious novel *Obsluhoval jsem anglického krále* (*I Waited on the King of England*). And that's where the Jazz Section came to help. The book was issued in a handsome, large-size, for-members-only paperback and the conforming non-conformist gratefully dedicated the work to the "Readers of the Jazz Section so that they may have some fun". The longhand dedication, printed in facsimile, appeared on the title page, and the cup of the cops' indignation overflowed: Hrabal was called to order, threatened that if he continued to perform such rascalities no more books of his would be published, and allegedly forced to sign a statement claiming that the Jazz Section had published the novel without his knowledge. The facsimile dedication was left unexplained—but logic never played an important role in the statements of the victims of the arrogant stupidity of power.

Finally, Karel Srp edited a book, *Graphic Music and Phonic Poetry*, and all cups overflowed. The Ministry of Culture received an order to put an end to this outrage—remember, it was the Musicians' Union, a province of the Ministry of Culture, and not the cops who had brought the section to life. So to acquire scholarly arguments for the banning of the organization, the ministry commissioned a number of analyses of the shocking book by Marxist specialists. Some of the Greyzonists in the ministry, I'd like to think, hoped secretly that at least a few of the arguments might be used for an effort to save something from the wreckage. Indeed, some readers' reports contained very Marxist arguments.

> Analysis? Why organize a wise men's dance around goose-shit? Doesn't the Music Department of the Ministry of Culture have more important things to do than prepare "specialists' analyses" of what should be clear at first glance to every man in his right mind, not to mention educated Marxists? One could say that what we are here concerned with are negligible stupidities if they did not have a clear and transparent political background. One knows, doesn't one, what the Jazz Section *is*, what it is *engaged* in, to *whom* it addresses its publications, and what are its *real* aims.

Obviously the conspirators in the ministry, if any, could not use this argument.

The publishing activities of the Jazz Section were one factor in the deepening drama. The other was, as I said before, the emergence, in the mid-seventies, of jazz rock, and the consequent shifting of the section's interest from pure, orthodox jazz to hybrid forms and finally, under the pressure of events, to rock.

Parallel with this development ran a gigantic rise of interest in the section's activities. True, new members could be accepted only if someone dropped out, but the 3,000 possessors of *Jazz* and *Jazzpetit* did not keep them to themselves. According to conservative estimates, each volume had about 100,000 readers. It was not exceptional for an especially appealing title to be read by the entire student body of a high school (including most teachers), even if only one of its students was a section member. The attendance at the Prague Jazz Days also multiplied so that, in the end, some 15,000 people bought tickets and listened to jazz rock, New Wave, rock-in-opposition, and modern jazz. After various molestations and much bureaucratic chicanery, after the veto against any mention of the Jazz Section in the media, the Jazz Days were finally banned—characteristically, neither by the Ministry of the Interior nor by the Ministry of Culture but by an "individual", the Prague cultural inspector František

Trojan—under the pretext that "public disturbances" were expected. Indeed they were to be expected, for the ban came on the eve of the event, with several bands from abroad already in town and with thousands of young fans from distant country villages already in Prague, some bivouacking in the city's parks. In hastily printed leaflets the section explained the situation to the enraged crowds of youngsters and asked them to abstain from any display of anger. Miraculously—measured by Western standards—the crowds, containing quite a few punks, maintained discipline, and the disturbances for which the cops yearned did not take place. But the section had to provide refunds to many patrons and pay the foreign bands. The resulting financial difficulties opened a new road towards a "legal" method to curb and eventually stop the section's endeavours, which the cops used a couple of years later.

Next the section committed another grave sin: instead of making appeals to "above" it asked for support "from below", and got it: in letters, in proclamations, in bold displays of the section's statements on billboards in high schools and in the club rooms of the Socialist Union of Youth. A graffito even appeared on the walls of the Ministry of Culture, with the challenging exclamation: *We Shall Not Let You Kill the Jazz Section!* And the section made another provocative—and clever—move which further complicated the life of the bureaucrats: it applied for membership in the International Jazz Federation, which is an organization of the Music Department of UNESCO, and it was admitted. The Ministry of Culture did not acknowledge this membership, arguing that the application had not been accompanied by the ministry's recommendation, but the statutes of UNESCO do not require any such thing, and the section was definitely a member. To ban an organization that is part of an international setup is naturally much more difficult than to liquidate a pest that is only domestic. Very probably, the UNESCO angle also prolonged the section's life.

Caught unprepared, the ministry again resorted to chicanery. It started denying exit visas to the section's delegates to international meetings of the Jazz Federation; it began to spread rumours that the aficionados were "subsidized from the West"; it even mailed a faked announcement to all county councils saying that the section had been abolished by the Musicians'

Union. It didn't work. And so, since the Interior Ministry still
did not want to interfere directly, since the Cultural Ministry
was unable and the Musicians' Union unwilling to perform the
killing, eventually the Party itself had to step in.

It did so by launching a campaign of defamation which was
to prepare the ground for the final "administrative measures".
The campaign was triggered by an article in the Party's politico-
cultural weekly, *Tribuna*, in March 1983, titled "New Wave with
an Old Content" and signed by one Jan Krýzl, a pseudonym
for two Interior Ministry employees. It tried to sound knowledgeable but didn't quite succeed, and became a source of
amusement for the section's thousands of supporters. Then the
section itself made another unorthodox move. It started yet one
more series, called *Dokumenty* (*Documents*), with a pamphlet
in answer to Krýzl entitled *Rock na levém krídle* (*Rock on the
Left Wing*). With elegant doses of irony the booklet corrected
the many mistakes of the Krýzl twins, from subtleties apparent
only to the initiated to gross errors in dates, critical judgements,
and personalities. For instance, Krýzl presented Pete Seeger as
a famous rock star of the early fifties; Krýzl also gave an original interpretation of the punk phenomenon: apparently punk
rock was invented by capitalist manipulators to convince young
people that they should identify with life under capitalism, and
not revolt. In other words, early punk rock was a rightist creation serving the interests of the most reactionary circles in the
West. This display of Marxist thought gave the section an opportunity for a counter-offensive: it was not difficult to prove
that punk rock started as genuinely proletarian music, created
not by the sinister plotters of some British Tin Pan Alley but by
unemployed amateurs. Rock had always been a left-wing phenomenon, claimed the section, and in the concluding lines of the
pamphlet its writers accused Krýzl of the gravest sin a Communist can commit: spreading right-wing concepts and therefore
"harming the interests of the Communist party". To indicate
graphically what the section thought about Krýzl-Marxism, the
pamphlet's title on the cover was superimposed on a crumpled
page of *Tribuna* with Krýzl's brainchild printed on it.

I often wish Westerners knew "small" languages such as Czech.
If they could read the debate that followed this clash of minds

they would shed all illusions they might still have about the
quality of intellectual life under *reálný socialismus*. The term
itself, coined by the French Communist Party after the Soviet
ambush of Czechoslovakia, has implications that are ideologically damaging. The Marxists, fond of catch phrases, slogans,
and bon mots, have always explained the difference between
socialism and Communism by a couple of those marvellous
simplifications of which they are such masters: in socialism
"everybody contributes to society according to his capabilities,
and is rewarded according to his achievements." Clearly, in
socialism something non-ideal, non-utopian, still survives. In
Communism, however, "everybody contributes according to his
capabilities, and is rewarded according to his needs." The first
stage was officially reached in Czechoslovakia in the late fifties,
when the name of the republic was changed from "Czechoslovak
Republic" (CSR) to "Czechoslovak Socialist Republic" (CSSR),
and when the president announced that what the country had
was *"dovršený socialismus"* or, approximately, "completed socialism". Since in Communist states everything gets better and
better, we should have reached at least the beginning of the
next and final stage sometime in the early seventies—after all,
it took the Communists only ten years to change the country
from a capitalist to a socialist one. Instead the Czechoslovak
Communist Party accepted the ideological sobriquet coined by
the French, which should be translated not as "real socialism"
but as "really existing socialism" or perhaps "realistic socialism". There is something fishy about the sequence of events
and terms. First socialism was "completed", indicating that the
country had arrived at the gate to the paradise of Communism;
then socialism became "realistic", indicating that the portal
reached was not the gate to Utopia but the back door to pragma-
tism. What else is this but a confession that the promised world
of slogans is just a naive remnant of early nineteenth-century
socialist ideas, and that the only socialism we will ever have is
what we have in Czechoslovakia now?

What do we have in Czechoslovakia? Something that in many
respects is closer to that other "realistic" socialism they had in
Germany in the late thirties and early forties than to Owen's
concepts or even to Brook Farm. The *Tribuna* campaign against
rock illustrated this well, and demonstrated that totalitarian

thinking, and the resulting diction, are common to all who believe in the iron rule of any sort of party. In one of the many letters published in *Tribuna* after the débâcle of the Krýzl article, a comrade Beran writes that the punks appear to him like "animals that bear only a superficial likeness to human beings". This very phrase, of course, was frequently used on the pages of *Der Stürmer*. This is how Jews appeared to *Parteigenosse* (comrade) Streicher. And the final solution offered by Beran's friends, whom he quotes in the article, is this: Command these crowds of half-wits, adorned with their cowbells and chains, to form columns and make them march in the direction of the foundries of Kladno, Ostrava, Košice! All that is missing is a suggestion to build showers for the arriving humanoids.

Another witch-hunting article in *Tribuna* tells about a rock concert in Hořice. Halfway through the show, the percussion man of the rock group Letadlo (The Airplane) stripped to the waist and put on a chain with a padlock. In today's Czechoslovakia a chain with a padlock may have many meanings. Be that as it may, the youthful extempore demonstration had serious consequences. A meeting of what sounds like a Court of Inquisition was called, attended by a three-man delegation from Prague, the chairman and two other functionaries of the Socialist Union of Youth of Hořice, the vice-chairperson of the town council, the chairman of the cultural department of the same council, the director of the Workers' Club of Hořice, and the MP for the district. After their conference, Letadlo ceased to exist.

Another group willing to expose themselves to the lions' teeth was the legendary Plastic People of the Universe, whose English-singing vocalist was the Canadian Paul Wilson, the translator of several of my books. In 1976 they were all put on trial charged with "creating public disturbances" and "singing indecent songs". In their repertoire was a song addressed to an anonymous but apparently (self) important citizen which culminated in the following lines: "What do you resemble in your greatness? / Are you the Truth? / Are you God? / What do you resemble in your greatness? / A piece of shit, a piece of shit, a piece of shit..." repeated eight times. The state prosecutor and the three judges (the Czech court consists of one professional and two amateur judges; the latter, like jury members, serve for a certain number of months) did not harangue against the insults to an unnamed public personality but against the use of the scatological expression. The courageous defence attorney JUDr. (Doctor of Law) Štěpánek delivered a learnèd speech demonstrating that scatological words not only were common in the life of the working class but had always been an indelible part of folksong vocabulary. He cited a seventeenth-century folksong from the collection of Jan Jeník z Bratřic which went, "He was shitting, shitting, shitting, / holding on to grass. / Grass gave way, / he fell into his shit, / and smeared his ass." In the days of counter-reformation—that is, at the time of the reactionary rule of the Jesuits, went on the poker-faced attorney, a Jesuit song-collector changed the lyrics of this song to "He was smiling, smiling, smiling, / holding on to grass. / Grass gave way, / he fell and hurt himself." He further quoted from the works of Hašek, Chaucer, and other luminaries of literature to show that, in certain situations, "shit" was irreplaceable if the message was to come across. The public in the courtroom, represented by proxy by plainclothes policemen, grew duly enraged, and the judge ruled that the use of "shit" in songs was a criminal offence under socialism.

The Czechs in the band were sentenced to a year and a half in jail, and Paul Wilson was expelled from the country. The Canadian ambassador might have asked disagreeable questions about the legality of sending a Canadian citizen to jail for singing a ditty about shit.

However, the jailing of the Plastic People in 1976 led directly to the emergence of Charter 77, a petition by a group of daredevils from all walks of life which challenged the government to respect the Czechoslovak Constitution. Far from respecting that piece of paper, the government clamped down on them and sent some to jail—among others, the playwright Václav Havel, who got four and a half years and barely escaped death in prison. Nevertheless, the cops were never able to completely eradicate the Charterists, and so in 1983, at the peak of the witch-hunt, the group issued an open letter entitled "About Popular Music". Its main thesis—and I think a very valid one— was that the "controversial" song lyrics of contemporary Czech rock are probably the first example of genuine folklore since the nineteenth century, and that they were provoked by the cliché-ridden banalities of the censor-approved repertoire. Although such impotent products flood the radio and television shows, they do not appeal to the young because they do not reflect the reality of Czechoslovakia. No wonder young rockers resorted to self-help. The result was that "people's creativity", which for many years had been only a propaganda myth, suddenly became a fact—but a spontaneous fact. And such facts do not have the approval of the people's government.

At this time, which was expected to climax in resolute action, a most unexpected group came to the section's help. The Critics' Section of the Musicians' Union composed an open letter which they asked *Tribuna* to print. It took several months and, I am sure, countless meetings of cop and Commie functionaries before the letter—rewritten many times, cut and edited—finally appeared in the journal. It was not presented as originally intended, as a collective opinion of the Critics' Section, but was signed by three individuals, Lubomír Dorůžka, Ivan Poledňák, and Petr Zapletal—the three most eminent jazz musicologists and folklorists in today's Czechoslovakia. Their main thesis was:

> We indulge in cultural protectionism...we indiscriminately refuse any influences from the outside; but if such influences are strong they will penetrate our defences anyway, and then we are not prepared.... We care too much about nobody stepping out of line (and this line usually expresses only the average taste), about not making a mistake, about not introducing anything improper, incorrect.... It is a big question whether the present attack on the ideological diversion by rock music is as effective as it is loud. The main direction of this ideological diversion can be found not in the form of rock excesses but elsewhere: it is realized by the mass and frontal operations of the bourgeois model of culture and music, by accepting bourgeois taste, by supporting the production of cheap and commercial pop songs which benumb people and divert their attention from the problems of life.

This is as far as you can go in a totalitarian state if you want to tell the plain truth. Using the obligatory Party lingo ("bourgeois" instead of "bad" or "kitschy"), the critics reiterated the objections of the few genuine spokesmen for the young whose letters *Tribuna* had incautiously printed at the beginning of the campaign. They ended their exposé with what sounds, and was I think meant to sound, like a warning: "The generations that follow one another identify quite strongly with the music of their youth, and it remains *their* music throughout life." In other words, if you make enemies of young people by suppressing the sounds they love, they will hate you until their dying days.

Such views and observations may be true but they do not contain the *sine qua non* of "Marxist" analysis: the "class" approach, which is more important than any truth, any reality. *Tribuna*'s answer opened with a categorical statement: "Art is Party- and class-conditioned. There can be no discussion about that!" Such an opening, naturally, precludes any discussion, and the rest of the article boiled down to a ritual restatement of well-known Stalinist dogmas.

Yet not even this stopped the rescue operations. Thoroughly unexpected help came from what I believe are the Greyzonists at the Ministry of Culture itself. True, the publisher of the brochure is identified as the Theatrical Institute in Prague, but the text bears the indelible stamp of the ministry's ponderous writing style. It is yet another rephrasing of the few early letters in *Tribuna* and of the critics' article, couched in cautious and ambiguous language, making frequent use of what Václav Havel once termed "dialectical metaphysics": "On the one hand this thing is bad, but on the other it is also good." Just one of the pamphlet's many profound observations: "If we, on any level, in any place of work, are faced with phenomena that work against the interests of our socialist society, we have to deal with them resolutely, but at the same time also sensitively, so that we do not suppress hopeful talents, hopeful creativity which, after proper redirectioning, can have the prerequisite of successfully asserting itself." And so on.

But the ministerial brochure appeared too late. By then somebody somewhere had made the decision, and the ministries of Culture and of the Interior finally took "administrative action". First, dozens of rock groups were forced to disband—the most outrageous was the ban on the excellent experimental jazz-rock orchestra of Michael Kocáb, Pražský výběr (Prague Selection). Others were forbidden to perform in Prague. Dozens of musicians were asked to take "requalification exams" which they naturally failed; without passing such exams, you cannot perform in public, even as an amateur. Then the editorial board of the only officially approved pop and jazz monthly *Melodie* was totally purged. *Melodie* had never openly supported the section or the punk rockers, but by providing excellent objective information about the world's jazz and rock scene it became guilty of a lack of class, that is, Party approach. Since its circulation was enormous, it was a continuous pain in the neck for the really-existing socialists. The journal's editor-in-chief, Stanislav Titizl, was fired, and so was the already mentioned editorial board member Lubomír Dorůžka. These and other men and women who are lifelong students of jazz were replaced by a comrade Miroslav Kratochvíl, whose occupation is that of "professional director". The meaning of the term will become apparent if I briefly recount this obscure man's career. In 1968 he was made director of the newly established Star Radio which, while purporting to be a clandestine station of the "true Marxists" broadcasting from somewhere in Dubček's revisionist Czechoslovakia, was really filling the air with virulent anti-Dubček and often anti-Semitic propaganda from somewhere in the south of the German Democratic Republic. After the ambush it was transferred to Czechoslovak territory and changed into a pop music station in the manner of Radio Luxembourg. The pop songs—naturally only the toothless, odourless kind— are interspersed with brief doses of propaganda, thought to be more palatable when set off by electronic sounds. Kratochvíl lasted for several years as Star's director, and turned his post into a profitable business: no songs went on the air unless their authors came up with hefty bribes.

Eventually the professional director overdid it and got the sack. But "reliable comrades" like him never stay unemployed. Kratochvíl was merely punished with the job of editor-in-chief of the astronomy journal *Říše hvězd* (*The Realm of Stars*). From astronomers he could not expect the astronomical bribes of pop-song writers, and since he did not grumble—thus proving his reliability—he was eventually rewarded with the chief editorship of *Melodie*. His assistant, nicknamed Krahe (KRAtochvíl's HEmorrhoid), let himself be heard saying that from then on a photo on the cover of *Melodie* would cost a pop star 5,000 crowns; Kratochvíl can expect a considerable increase of income. This con artist, by the way, is a Candidate Member of the Central Committee of the Communist party of Czechoslovakia and, naturally, an employee of the Interior Ministry.

The destruction of *Melodie* was only a side-line action. A direct hit against the section followed. Its dedicated chairman, Karel Srp, was fired from his editorial job with a printing company under the pretext of a reorganization which eliminated the need for his post. In Czechoslovakia this is one of the few valid reasons to dismiss an employee. However, as soon as Srp left a new man was hired to fill his position. In perfect agreement with the law of the land, Srp sued the employer. The judge, a woman specializing in political trials and utterly uninterested in the facts of the case, dismissed the suit. Since Srp is now unemployed he not only has no income (there is no unemployment insurance in Czechoslovakia because theoretically there is no unemployment) but he may be charged with social parasitism. Moreover, the Ministry of Culture resorted to the proven method of liquidating nuisances. In the old days, the trumped-up charges at their trials were political. In really-existing socialism non-desirables may be *attacked* for political deviations, but when they are actually put on trial the charges are invariably economic or criminal. The Committee of People's Control seized the section's accounting books and is now busily meddling with them. By a strange coincidence, as soon as the commission confiscated all bookkeeping files, bills for quite unbelievable amounts in unpaid taxes since 1980 started to arrive from the Revenue Office. These unexpected taxes—about three million crowns—were to be paid immediately from the section's account, which was closed for all other purposes. The section could easily have proven that the tax demands were incorrect, for it had never had an income that would lead to taxes to the tune of a million per year, but for that they would have needed their bookkeeping files—to which they now had no access.

As I said earlier, the section is a part of the Prague Division of the Musicians' Union. In February 1984 this division had been told to stop all activities. In actual fact the order was an effort to stop the doings of the Jazz Section, but since the decree did not explicitly mention the Jazz Section, the section carried on. The annoyed authorities sent an explicit command to the Prague Division to abolish the section immediately. The division duly responded that, having been ordered to stop *all* activities, they could not carry on *any*, and could not therefore oblige.

Everybody is having fun. But through the laughter sinister rumours may be heard: a trial of the leading figures of the section is in preparation. As is customary in Marxist states, the sentences have already been agreed upon and approved by the Party: fourteen years for Karel Srp, ten years for Josef Skalník, the graphic designer of the section's publications, and shorter terms for minor perpetrators of thought crime.

However it all ends, the efforts by the cops of the Interior Ministry, the true holders of power in Czechoslovakia, to hide behind the smokescreen of administrative measures undertaken by the Musicians' Union, and when that did not come off, by the Ministry of Culture, have failed. In the end the Interior Ministry was forced to emerge from behind the smokescreen and on July 19, 1984, it curtailed all activities of the Musicians' Union for three months. After that period, i.e., October 1984, this curtailment is to be lifted if the following conditions are met: the union will stop publishing any books, pamphlets, or periodicals; it will dissolve its Jazz Section; it will discontinue any work, theoretical or otherwise, in the field of jazz music; it will refrain from founding new orchestras, bands, and musical groups. At the time of this writing only God knows how the union will react—or what will remain for it to do, if the draconian conditions are met.

The Jazz Section is not the only branch of the Musicians' Union which was working in the field of jazz and rock. There is the Section of Young Music which sponsored two excellent membership periodicals, *Triangl* and *Kruh* (*The Circle*), under the editorship of the popular singer and song writer Jan Burian, the son of the same pre-war Communist jazzman and stage director E.F. Burian whose biography, mentioned earlier in this article, came out in the series *Jazzpetit* and was found objectionable by the official publishing houses. There is the Jazz Society of Czechoslovakia, organizer of the Summer Jazz School, attended this year by over a hundred students, among them several members of Czech symphony orchestras who play jazz as a hobby—certainly a most unsuitable pastime for a really-existing socialist Philharmoniker. In fact, the swinging philharmonians were among those severely criticized in the *Tribuna* campaign for having generated too many decibels at a jazz-rock concert in Prague. If the conditions of the Interior Ministry are met, the further existence of all these and many similar regional groups will be in grave jeopardy.

But at least the power will have shown its nakedness.

I have written this article for those who share my view that if what exists in Czechoslovakia is socialism, I would rather be a capitalist. But I am aware that many in the West are always ready to give the benefit of the doubt to any regime that calls itself socialist, except to German national socialism, discredited because it lost a war. I also know that anyone who is no longer ready to give the socialist cops the benefit of the doubt is likely to be labelled a reactionary, and that the jazzmen and rockers of whom he writes with sympathy will—perhaps subconsciously— become suspect of anti-socialism, indeed, of Fascism or, what's worse, of pro-Americanism. In an article entitled "What It's Like Making Rock'n'roll in a Police State" (*Musician*, February 1983) my translator Paul Wilson recounts his experience in London, soon after his expulsion from Czechoslovakia:

> It was in the summer of 1977 and punk rock was in full swing, joyful exuberance in grimy clubs, mindless week-end punch-ups on Sloane Square, instant analysis in the *New Society*. The same bands that the Plastic People had been inspired by ten years ago—the Velvets, Captain Beefheart—were now being rediscovered. I went to an early Slits/Sham 69 gig where the new Sex Pistol documentary was shown, full of arrests, protests, rage and *lèse majesté*. Afterward I approached someone in the Pistols' entourage with a suggestion: why not smuggle

a copy of the film into Czechoslovakia, give the Plastic People a lift. "The Plastic People?" he responded in a dead-eyed, cocky public school whine. "They're anti-socialist. I don't support fascist rock bands. I'd rather send the film to South Africa." Ah yes, images of Sid Vicious smelling his socks to raise consciousness in Soweto. I was sorry I'd asked.

How is it really? Are the Czech punks, the thousands of supporters of the Jazz Section, the hundreds of thousands of readers of *Melodie*, anti-socialists?

I have known many, and some like Karel Srp—something I can't comprehend—are convinced Communists even after all the pogroms. Most of them are—well, I would say they have no interest in capitalism, only in the freedom it offers. They have, in principle, nothing against socialism, which means in principle having nothing against the system. Having nothing against the system is the normal human stance. Only fanatics support establishments wholeheartedly and under any circumstances, and surely the many critics of capitalism in the West agree in principle with its liberal and democratic structure. The Czech aficionados of jazz and art have nothing against socialism as long as it does not annihilate what they love and what has inherently nothing to do with politics, economic systems, or ideologies, but what may assume political overtones if an oppressive establishment endeavours to crush it. These youngsters are not blind to the advantages of even really-existing socialism: job security, for instance—that is, job security as long as you behave. But neither are they blind to the disadvantages: the arbitrary rule of the police, the lawlessness of the courts, the heavily curtailed freedom of the press, of literature, of the arts in general. The terrible nepotism, the political discrimination (called by the less offensive term "class discrimination") when you apply for admission to a university or for a job, the brutality towards those who do not keep their dislikes to themselves. The new-class greediness of the *papalashes* in governmental and ministerial posts, self-appointed through the ritual of "elections". Can any decent person, socialist or non-socialist, really like such things?

Fortunately, decent persons are everywhere and sin daily against orthodox socialist behaviour. The following story is taken from a letter I received from an amateur rock musician who recently escaped from Czechoslovakia and lives now in the United States. With a group of friends he intended to attend a private jam session and lecture in a little village near Karlsbad. As they walked from the railway station to the village they passed a lorry of the state construction company. The driver, a typical working-class character, stopped, leaned out of his booth, and warned them: "Boys, don't go there! The place is swarming with them! They've got wagons ready for you, they've got German shepherds and submachine guns!" By "they" the man of the people naturally meant the cops. The boys ignored his warning, went there, and were promptly arrested and subjected to a long process of chicanery and interrogations which resulted in their fleeing the country.

Was the lorry driver a reactionary?

No, he was merely a decent man. A member of the Grey Zone. The kind of person who makes life bearable even in such disgusting places as the police states of really-existing socialism.

LITERATURE

As editor (1956–59) of *World Literature* magazine

AN EAST EUROPEAN
IMAGINATION

—

Published in Mosaic *in 1973, this was one of Škvorecký's
first essays to appear in an English-language journal. His
treatment of the topic should be compared with Milan
Kundera's magisterial essay "The Tragedy of Central
Europe" (*The New York Review of Books, *July 19, 1984)
and with George Konrad's* Antipolitics.

IS THERE SUCH a thing? I don't know. What I do know is that
there is something called Central Europe, comprising Germany,
Switzerland, Austria, and Czechoslovakia. And I do know something about that. Perhaps also about the imaginations of that
unquiet corner of the world. Yes, I use the plural. For, to my
mind, there are at least two major imaginations in this hotbed
of modern political schizophrenias, based on two major experiences, beside several minor ones. And of course I may be quite
wrong; probably I am biased. Political exiles often are, as everybody knows. They are also often right, as not everybody
acknowledges.

In late 1968, in a West German town, there was a film festival. A movie was shown about the events of the 1968 Reform
Movement in Czechoslovakia. It included unique shots of steel
monsters rolling into the streets of Prague, surrounded by
weeping girls in miniskirts. A dead youngster lay on the
national flag. A slightly embarrassed, but menacing, Soviet
politruk pointed his pistol at a man; the man bared his breast to
the *politruk*'s gat. Also—filmed by a hidden camera—a Soviet
private, crouching behind a fence, avidly (and clandestinely)
read a Dubčekist leaflet printed by the Czechs in Russian;
he looked more afraid than the soldiers, in another shot, who

were trying to extinguish a burning tank set on fire by Molotov cocktails.

These dramatic scenes followed sequences showing what had preceded them. A priest released from a concentration camp celebrates his first mass. The prime minister discusses government politics with a huge crowd of youngsters on the Old Town Square. A cantor in the Old-New Synagogue of Prague laments for the many dead citizens of that city who perished because a pseudoscience in the service of political power deemed their blood in some non-biological way inferior to the blood of a moustachioed maniac, a fat thief of valuable paintings, and a limping midget. And another shot: a group of citizens lay flowers on the graves of General Patton's soldiers who were killed in action on East Central European territory in 1945.

It was this last-mentioned shot that mainly excited the West Central European audiences at the festival. They remained calm during the steel monster scenes; they were not visibly moved by the cantor's incantations. But Czechs who fondly remembered US soldiers infuriated them. There was booing, stamping of feet. To the imagination of these people, this was the final proof that the Russian *White Book on Counterrevolution in Czechoslovakia* was right—that the Czech Reform Movement was a conspiracy paid for by the CIA, that the Czechs were—what? A reactionary nation, as the Generalissimo (not Franco; this gentleman came from another country and, besides sharing the absurd rank with *el caudillo*, the monster is dead) described the Crimean Tartars? Or a stupid people seduced by foreign propaganda, whose government, as Bertolt Brecht once suggested, should have overthrown them long ago and elected another people? Which is what the government did, eventually, with Soviet help; only the newly elected people remain a shadow-people.

How can one speak about one Central European imagination after this very real image of a split in it? Surely there are two major imaginations here, opposed to each other. To the bearers of the one, it is important that the American soldiers who died on Central European soil were killed in action against a system that murdered and incarcerated millions of people because of crazy theories. And they remember that system, not in its abstract concepts, but in its concrete horrors. If they are too young to remember *that* system of dictatorship, they remember another one; it was different in some respects, but alike in others.

The younger half, the bearers of the other imagination, never went through the experience of any dictatorship. They know it only as a word. To them what's important about the soldiers killed in 1945 in Central Europe is that they were Americans. Americans are imperialists. American soldiers are mercenaries of imperialism. Whoever lays flowers on their graves is a Fascist. Many of these people still think that there is nothing wrong with syllogisms like this one.

And then there is another film; a short one, made with a hand-held camera, about the funeral of a youngster who went first east and then west to see for himself how things are, and then burned his living body to death in protest against the steel monsters. He was technically a Catholic, so the burial was Catholic. Great masses of people, encircled by the police with submachine guns, moved through Prague. Thousands wept. Sure, the occasion was hysterical, but isn't hysterical weeping a natural reaction to the, no doubt, very rational orders that sent the monsters to Prague? The day was chilly, misty. No red flags, of course, just national ones; and crosses. Not that this would be an immense crowd of true believers. It was the monsters that resurrected some of the meaning of the cross in that part of Central Europe.

The movie was shown in New York at a private screening. A rich young gentleman from West Germany was there. He remained calm. After the film was over, he proclaimed that now he knew why the Soviets had to come. Aside from an almost irresistible urge to hit him on his dry-look coiffure, I thought that this son of a reputedly methodically thinking people missed one point: the Soviets came first, and only then did Jan Palach burn.

So there is the West Central European imagination of the *Besserwissers*, who like all *Besserwissers* know perhaps better, but certainly not much. True, some people in that other part of Central Europe sometimes over-react: a Catholic friend of mine has recently been accused, at several underground gatherings in Prague—she is lawfully and legally married to a Frenchman,

so she enjoys the privilege of freedom of travel—of being a
"socialist agent". But this is just a reaction to what has been
forced on them as "socialism" by a foreign power that has never
known any sort of democracy, bourgeois or otherwise. They are
not *Besserwissers*; they just know better because they have had
the experience. Capitalism has no lure for them, as socialism
does for their West Central European counterparts. They have
just ceased to think in theoretical and abstract concepts. Their
way of thinking is like the one that brought citizens to lay
flowers on Yankee graves: not because they were Yankee, but
because they were soldiers who were killed, although they
wanted to live. These East Central Europeans don't give a damn
about labels. Their imagination is concrete: a society without
the nightmare of the doorbell ringing at 4 a.m., and with a
justice that has no adjectives ("class", "racial", "national", etc.)
Just Justice. That old blindfolded lady had been freed of her
blindfold in their part of Central Europe, only to have the point
of a pistol pressed between her shoulder-blades. They don't give
a name to their image of a good (not ideal, mind you) society;
but it is a very concrete image.

The imagination of the others? Hazy, I would say. Their
favourite image is Revolution, based on *wie sich es der kleine
Moritz vorstellt* (as little Moritz imagines it to be—a phrase denoting naivety), if you'll excuse me. Or on that most dangerous
illusion that if *they* make the revolution it will be different from
the ones which so far have always devoured their children. Of
course it won't be different, if it is a real revolution. Revolutions
are pretty well alike. Wonderful, for some time, as Hemingway
wrote. Then they deteriorate, as he also wrote.

So there is a double imagination in Central Europe. One
sees clearly the shadows of the sweet bloody dreams turned to
bitter bloody nightmares of European dictatorships—national,
proletarian, whatever; the adjectives don't matter much. These
shadows mark its novels, its film, and even its music with a
wisdom of, let's hope, the next century. Unfortunately the books
are written in exotic languages, so the marketing computers
will hardly recommend them for publishing in the West. The
films, true, are in the universally understood language of the
visual image; but whenever the political atmosphere gets a little
colder, they fall victim to bans; anyway, their message is usually

so well coded as to be indecipherable outside the context of country and experience. Likewise, the dissonances of its music make sense only in its officially harmonious context.

The other imagination is not able to see behind the tears of Jan Palach's pallbearers a just grief, a genuine human feeling undeserving of epithets ("reactionary", "demagogical", "hysterical", etc.) It may register (sometimes) the shadows of Buchenwald; but they are second-hand shadows, registered only as a background for a first-hand demand to create another system to which the reality of Buchenwald would not be entirely foreign. Its novels are very experimental; so although written in a major language, they are read neither in the West (being unreadable for most people) nor in the East (banned for being decadently experimental). Its music is full of novelty; its painting does away with the barriers between Art and Non-Art. The trouble is that when you remove these barriers all you get is Non-Art, and the screeching of bows against that part of the strings that is on the wrong side of the bridge makes much more sense when there is the context of an official stance on Music.

Sure, there are shades, semitones, transitions. Sure, I generalize too recklessly, I let myself be led by personal bitterness. But do I really distort the general tendencies of today's Central Europe so much? The whole damned thing would require research, but that could be undertaken only in one part of the region: the other part does not encourage research, for there they "don't bow to facts"—as a former President of Czechoslovakia, Mr. Novotný, once put it.

And it is all not even very new, just as the experiments of today's art are of the age of Abraham. That early and very great representative of the East Central European imagination, Joseph Conrad, saw the schizophrenic split fifty years ago. "All this was a sort of sport for him—the sport of revolution—a game to look at from the height of his superiority," muses Razumov, the unfortunate and unwilling associate of the revolutionaries, thinking about his meeting with the English Teacher of Languages. He is not being quite fair to him (as I am not fair to many), because the same Teacher, seeing two rather unattractive Swiss citizens, has the following thoughts about them: "...a solitary Swiss couple, whose fate was made secure from the cradle to the grave by the perfected mechanism of democratic institutions." They are, of course, Konrad Korzeniowski's own thoughts. The thoughts of the man who, at the age of six, had to make that non-exceptional but non-voluntary journey to Russia's north.

But there is also Miss Haldin, that child not so much of reality as of the great kind Pole's imagination. "I believe that the future will be merciful to us all. Revolutionist and reactionary, victim and executioner, betrayer and betrayed, they all shall be pitied together...pitied and forgotten." Which gets pretty close to the only abstract concept held by the people in East Central Europe during that very brief period of hope in 1968, as witness the proposed Law of General Reconciliation which was never passed, because of the advent of the monsters of class hatred, or so they say. This abstract concept may not be held by those people any longer; I don't know. I am afraid that their imagination has grown concrete even in this respect; that it may be a slightly mellowed version of Orwell's image: "If you want a picture of the future, imagine a boot trampling on a human face—forever." The sophistication of Stalinism may have transformed the image into a metaphor; nevertheless this is the dominating image of the East Central European imagination at the moment.

The future according to the other Central European imagination? Some sort of paradise, I guess.

THE GOOD OLD DRINKING POET

When the great Czech poet Jaroslav Seifert (1901–1985)
was awarded the Nobel Prize, three English academics
wrote The Times *protesting the award. According to them*
Seifert had produced only poems of "sentimental drivel"
and "mawkish self-pity" since leaving the Communist
Party in 1929. It's interesting to note that, according
to these three experts in East and Central European
literature, Seifert was almost as mediocre a writer as
Karel Čapek.

"YET ANOTHER OBSCURE East European," went the word around
on the cocktail circuit, and Marxist dons from Cambridge
University, in a letter to *The Times* (October 20, 1984), condemned the Swedish Academy's decision as another proof
that the Nobel Prize "is becoming more and more a reward
for...pussyfooting...mediocrity." The new Nobel laureate, deem
Messrs Brušák, Short, and Pynsent, is writing "verse of mawkish self-pity" and is a master of the "sentimental drivel expected
of poets incapable of devoting themselves to female tractor-
drivers". The reference to female tractorists may be an uneasy
acknowledgement of the civil courage with which the poet has
steadily refused state-imposed themes and styles; however, it is
a somewhat obscure reference—caused not, I hope, by the dons'
stylistic clumsiness. I can assure them that Jaroslav Seifert,
even in his self-pitying old age, is perfectly capable of devoting
himself to female tractorists, particularly pretty ones. Proof of
that ability was recently provided by a reporter working for the
Svenska Dagbladet who took a picture of the poet in his hospital bed holding hands with an eye-filling blonde. On the back of
the photograph she was described as his "wife", but I know Mrs.

Seifertová, and unless she has recently undergone radical plastic surgery she is definitely not the person in the picture. My
guess is that Seifert's handsome visitor is one of the numerous
Czech women who have always admired the Master and his poetry and have benefited from his predilection for the company
of the weaker sex. To put it bluntly, the Master, even in his very
old and venerable age, is still pursuing *Frauendienst*.

> I was lying on my side,
> my hands tied at the wrists
> but with my palms free:
> these a nurse was holding in her lap
> up by my head.
> I firmly gripped her thigh
> and convulsively pressed it to me
> as a diver clutches a slim amphora
> streaking up to the surface.
>
> (From *The Plague Column*)

These lines of, if you wish, "mawkish self-pity" are from a
poem written about 1977, when the author was seventy-six.
"Sentimental drivel" perhaps does not describe them accurately.
I would rather surmise that they are daringly erotic; among
other things, the sexuality of the patient etherized upon the
table is apparently stronger than the ether. The little poem
seems to me as remarkable a statement on the poetic power of
sex as the following one, written by the same man half a century
earlier:

> If I saw you naked in the bath-tub
> with your knees pressed tightly together
> your white body would look like an envelope
> with a black seal in the middle.

I apologize for my barbaric translation.

For the past few years the author of the above-quoted poems
has been enveloped in paradoxes. Ludvík Vaculík (author of
The Czech Dreambook, *The Guinea Pigs*, and *The Axe*), in a
feuilleton written on the occasion of the announcement of the

Nobel Prize, tells the following story. In 1981 he found himself in jail in the company of two other criminals: the older, a plumber, "unshaven and morose, kept shaking his head over the fact that fucking his own unwilling wife was regarded as rape." The younger, also a working-class type, had committed a drunken break-in at a tobacconist's. After they had told the writer their sad stories, the plumber turned to him and asked, "And what are you here for?" "I signed a letter to the Swedish Academy to give the Nobel Prize to Jaroslav Seifert," answered the novelist. Silence followed; after some time the plumber raised his head and queried, "Seifert? The poet?" Vaculík nodded. The youngster, walking across the cell, stopped abruptly and burst into:

> My dad used to smoke
> every night before he went to bed.
> I can still see him clearly
> pressing tobacco into his pipe's head.

Does this happen often to poets?

Vaculík's letter to the Swedish Academy has a story of its own. The conspirators around Vaculík intended to send it to Sweden by two French citizens, Mr. Thonon and Ms. Anies, but on their way to Prague the couriers were stopped at the border and their car was searched. It was a custom-made vehicle with a hidden container used for smuggling books and letters to dissidents in Prague. The guards went straight for the receptacle; they had been tipped off by an agent named Hodič who had gained the confidence of several émigré organizations. The two couriers and some thirty Czechs were arrested. After extensive interrogations the police were able to locate the letter, the books—most of them *samizdat* "Padlock" editions, and other materials in the garage of Jiřina Šiklová. Ms. Šiklová went to prison, where she was interrogated. She admitted that the books and letters were destined for the Swedish Academy as supporting materials for the deliberations of the Nobel committee. The lieutenant had apparently never heard of either Seifert or Alfred Nobel. He left the room and, after consultations with more knowledgeable colleagues, returned to tell the detainee that "even if that Seifert received three Nobel prizes, it would not change the criminal nature of your actions." In due course Ms. Šiklová was charged with "attempting to smuggle abroad texts of an anti-state nature". As far as I know, the trial never took place but the charges have not been dropped. To suggest someone for the Nobel Prize may still be a criminal offence in Czechoslovakia. It certainly was in 1977, when a journalist, Jiří Lederer, was actually sentenced to three years in jail for trying to send out of the country a manuscript collection of Seifert's poems and the memoirs of the pre-1948 socialist minister Prokop Drtina.

Shortly after the detention of Ms. Šiklová, Ludvík Vaculík, and the others, Mr. Jan Pilař and two other gentlemen came to visit Seifert in his apartment. Pilař is the editor-in-chief of the Writers' Union Publishing House and a notorious figure of the Prague cultural demi-monde, and I modelled the character of the "Chief" in my novel *Miss Silver's Past* on him. His two companions turned out to be high-ranking police officers, and the outcome of the visit was Seifert's first heart attack. Three years later, in October 1984, the same Jan Pilař came again—no real-life Miss Silver had had the guts to do him in, unfortunately—unaccompanied this time, to tell the poet, on behalf of the Writers' Union (of which Seifert is not a member), that he had received the Nobel Prize. At practically the same time, the *samizdat* and émigré editions of Seifert's works were still routinely confiscated during house-searches of political suspects, and the collection of materials found in Ms. Šiklová's garage was still being held by the Ministry of the Interior as a *corpus delicti* of criminal activities. And while the cops busied themselves collecting Seifert's books as evidence, there were three official Prague editions of the poet's works on the market—all tampered with by the censors, and all published years earlier, uncensored, in the Padlock series and by émigré firms. The memoir *All the Beauty of the World*, for instance, was brought out by our Toronto house, Sixty-Eight Publishers, almost two years before it came out in Prague with quite a few passages and some names (including Milan Kundera's) deleted. There are indications that the numerous editions smuggled into the country and met with tumultuous demand were such an embarrassment to the establishment that it grudgingly gave in and approved the printing of a few titles.

The poet was taken by surprise. "Isn't that awful?" he asked
Ludvík Vaculík, after confiding to him that the Union's publishing house was going to do *An Umbrella from Piccadilly*. Clearly
he did not feel at ease joining the ranks of the approved ones
while most of his friends continued to be banned, and appearing
on the same publisher's list with hacks who—on government
orders, but with envious initiative of their own—had expelled
Milan Kundera, Ludvík Vaculík, Václav Havel, Ivan Klíma, and
countless others from the writing community.

The Swedish Academy has twice presented the rulers in the
Soviet empire with a dilemma, by giving the prize to Pasternak and to Solzhenitsyn. The Soviet government solved the
dilemmas simply: it called the decisions political provocation,
condemned the two laureates as enemies and traitors of the people, forbade one to leave the country and deported the other. A
nice, clear-cut, Stalinist solution. Also boring. The Czech government wriggled out of the mess in a much more amusing
way.

When the bombshell of the prize descended upon Prague, via
Voice of America, Radio Free Europe, and the BBC Czechoslovak Service, the authorities could not make up their minds
what to do. For several days, while meetings were held in the
corridors of power, nothing but identically worded five-liners
appeared in various papers, stating the fact and refraining from
comment. A few booksellers did not wait for instructions but
displayed Seifert's photographs in their shop windows; these
were promptly removed by the police. Eventually the bosses decided to take the existence of the damned prize into account, and
a cautious commentary appeared in the Party organ *Rudé právo*
on October 13. It noted that as a poet and citizen Seifert "was
not easy, was even controversial, but the importance of his work
for our poetry is indisputable." To put a smokescreen around
the shameful treatment of Seifert during the past decade, *Rudé
právo* then went over to the attack. On October 19 it printed a
letter by the Czechoslovak ambassador to Paris entitled "The
Nobel Prize Manipulators" in which the envoy accused French
journalists of "attempts...to misuse the name of our poet in
their slanderous attacks on our country, and make his name
into a weapon in the psychological war against the socialist

countries!" It was not true, he asserted, that the poet was subjected to chicanery; on the contrary, his work was held in high esteem and President Gustáv Husák himself had congratulated him on the occasion of his eightieth birthday three years earlier.

And that was the truth—yet not the whole truth and nothing but the truth. When he turned eighty, Seifert received hundreds upon hundreds of letters from readers all over Czechoslovakia. Among them were two brief official congratulations signed by the President and by the Prime Minister. Since there were so many well-wishers, the poet could not answer them all by individual letters and decided to place an acknowledgement in the cultural sections of the daily papers. It turned out, however, that no paper had room for such an item. The poet then tried for a paid advertisement; the classified ads columns were also overcrowded. Seifert persisted, meetings were held, and after two weeks permission for the ad was finally granted. But shortly afterwards two colonels of the secret police came unannounced to see the poet and tried to convince him that, in addition to the ad, he should print an announcement thanking the President specifically. They had the text with them, all the poet needed to do was sign it. Seifert argued that the President was included in the ad which thanked *all* his readers. Communism was never egalitarian, however, and the colonels insisted on special treatment for the most equal. A heated ideological debate developed, in the course of which the stubborn egalitarian collapsed and eventually signed something he later could not recollect. His health rapidly deteriorated and he went back to the hospital with another heart attack.

In his article "The Nobel Prize Manipulators" the ambassador did not mention any of this.

In the next few days the government went to great lengths to present the laureate, both to its subjects and to the West, as its man. A hack by the name of Ivan Skála announced on Prague television, in militant tones, that "we shall not permit anybody to take Seifert from us." Thirty years earlier the same Ivan Skála, writing in the Party cultural weekly *Tvorba*, condemned one of Seifert's masterpieces, *The Song of Viktorka* (1950), in militant tones, and proclaimed that its author "had no right to use the honourable title of poet." At about the same time this vociferous moral judge also commented on the execution of the eleven defendants at the Slánský trial by wishing "a dog's death to the dogs". (In 1969 he would veto the publishing of my novel *Miss Silver's Past* by the Mladá Fronta publishing house—where he had just replaced the editor-in-chief because, among other things, the latter had given his placet to the novel. However, since by then times were no longer so favourable for a hardline decision, Skála offered me a bribe, a new printing of 80,000 copies of my collection of crime stories *The Mournful Demeanour of Lieutenant Boruvka*. That represented a nice bundle, for in Czechoslovakia the author is paid not for copies sold but for copies printed—in itself a form of bribe for well-behaved writers. I must admit I accepted—but then, I had no power to enforce the publication of *Miss Silver* anyway.)

As soon as Jan Pilař left Seifert's hospital room after officially congratulating him, two secret policemen in white doctors' coats seated themselves in front of the door and began checking the identity cards of readers who came to pay tribute. In Stockholm the Nobel people threw a party at a local Czech restaurant for Seifert's children Jana and Jaroslav, who arrived from Prague to accept the prize on behalf of their father. That restaurant is the meeting-place of Czech and Slovak émigré intellectuals and that evening many were present, including myself. Jana and Jaroslav were to meet the press at the party. However, we and the journalists waited in vain: neither Jana nor Jaroslav materialized. It leaked out that the Czechoslovak ambassador had warned the poet's children that if they decided to attend they would have to "face the consequences" back in Prague.

But in a way these about-faces and somersaults were to be expected, since Jaroslav Seifert has become anathema to everything Communist mythology holds sacred. At the same time his popularity (approximately equivalent to American movie-star worship), his venerable age, and his unshakeable courage have made him into a kind of untouchable national saint. Of the great Czech Communist poets born around the turn of the century— S.K. Neumann, Jiří Wolker, Vítězslav Nezval, Vladimír Holan, František Halas, Josef Hora, and František Hrubín—he was the only genuine proletarian, the son of a factory blacksmith; the rest were bourgeois pinkos and parlour reds. In the euphoria after the 1917 Russian Revolution they all joined the Social

Democratic splinter group which became the Communist party, and they all, to different degrees, diligently produced "proletarian poetry"—sometimes with the artistic results one can expect of such endeavours, sometimes creating poems of charm, sincerity, and enduring value. But unlike the leading personality of the group, S.K. Neumann, whose method of learning about the Soviet Union was purely deductive and who would later pass sharp judgement on the truthfulness and accuracy of André Gide's book on Russia without ever bothering to visit the land of his many encomiums, Jaroslav Seifert chose the inductive method based on observation of facts. He travelled to Moscow as early as 1925, and to make sure he had seen clearly he made another trip a couple of years later. Then he came to a conclusion which he never changed, never *had* to change, because the events of the next half-century of his long life have borne him out.

In 1929 Stalin's Prague agent, Klement Gottwald, grabbed power in the Party and effected its "bolshevization", changing it from a relatively independent Marxist organization to a totally subservient subsidiary of the Kremlin. On Seifert's initiative, seven prominent Communist writers issued a manifesto in protest against the ominous development. Five of them soon let themselves be bolshevized too; they recanted and humbly returned to Gottwald's deadly embrace. A quarter of a century later the deadliness ceased to be metaphorical: Gottwald, by then president, sent eleven of his lifelong friends and comrades to the gallows in the Slánský trial. (One year later Gottwald himself followed them to hell: he died of the "Moscow flu" only two weeks after Stalin.)

Two signatories of the 1929 manifesto did not withdraw their names from the document and were duly expelled from the Party: Josef Hora and Jaroslav Seifert. Both joined other leftist parties, Hora the Czech Socialists and Seifert the Social Democrats. Ideologically the Czech Socialists were more objectionable from the Communist point of view because they were mostly petty-bourgeois nationalists. But then, Hora was no proletarian, whereas Seifert was. The approved personal development of a proletarian was from the confusion of Social Democracy to the enlightenment of Communism; to take the reverse route was unheard of. Seifert thus became a

walking collection of gravest sins: instead of believing the revealed religion about Russia and its revolution, he, like a
doubting Thomas, went and put his finger into Bolshevik Russia's side. Then, instead of restricting himself to discussions
of Party issues behind the Party's closed doors, he seduced
six other comrades, went public, and persisted in his heresy
rather than recant and receive absolution. Finally he ceased
to be a Communist entirely, rejoined his working-class father's
old party, befriended many non-Communist poets including
Catholics, and joined the ranks of the admirers of Thomas
Garrigue Masaryk. Masaryk—another failed proletarian who
wasn't even a socialist—had written *The Social Question*, one
of the earliest criticisms of Marxism, had conceived the idea
of the Czechoslovak republic in Washington under the guidance of American history professors, had sent the Czech Legions
all over Siberia to fight Lenin's Bolsheviks, and had married
Charlotte Garrigue of New York, an American!

Horrible!

Had Seifert not become, in the course of the next twenty years,
the dearly beloved grand old man of Czech letters, his old
adversary Klement Gottwald might have added him to the
hundreds of unfortunates he handed over to the hangman
after the coup in 1948. But, to use a cliché which describes
the situation well, the love of the people shielded the poet—
and, more prosaically, he was well connected in the cultural
hierarchy of the Party. Among his protectors there were old
buddies František Halas and, above all, Vítězslav Nezval. This
epicurean and magnificent poet, who wielded much influence
with Gottwald, was willing to prostitute himself as an artist
in incredible ways: once, for instance, he wrote a eulogy to
Gottwald's wife describing her as if she were a combination of
Greta Garbo and Madame Curie. But he never betrayed old
friends, and his poetic genius was such that even the rhymed
ode to the dull and corpulent first lady is a piece of remarkable
artistry. And so Seifert survived the deadly years of Stalin's
decline, just as he had survived the even deadlier time of
Nazism.

It was during the Nazi era that Seifert first gained not just
popularity but the loving devotion of his readers. In book after

book of great linguistic beauty—and full of encoded messages clear to the Czechs, impenetrable to the Nazi censor—the poet boosted the morale of his nation and filled hearts with the perhaps sentimental but in those days so necessary love for the country and its ancient and picturesque capital, Prague. He also did such things as publishing under his own name a book by a Jewish writer, and helping the families of Gestapo victims.

Some character, this obscure pussyfooting mediocrity.

Ivan Skála's attack on *The Song of Viktorka* silenced Seifert, but fortunately for only a few years. In 1953 Stalin died, followed immediately by Gottwald. Emulating the mummification of the Georgian, the Party had Gottwald embalmed and put on display. But the Czech mortician, having no experience with embalming techniques, botched the job. The corpse spoiled, had to be replaced by a dummy, and eventually was removed from public sight. And after the Twentieth Party Congress in 1955, the sweet winds of heresy began blowing from Moscow, so that at the 1956 Congress of the Czechoslovak Writers' Union Seifert was able to break his silence. He did so in the shrillest way possible: accusing his colleagues among the establishment hacks of voluntarily keeping their mouths shut when police were arresting tens of thousands of innocent people, among them many writers, he proclaimed, "If an ordinary person is silent about the truth, it may be a tactical manoeuvre. If a writer is silent, he is lying...." He demanded that banned writers be invited back to the literary scene, that the cases of writers languishing in prisons be re-examined, and that, if found innocent (later, indeed, they were all found innocent), these writers be released. Even though the general mood at the Congress was critical in the extreme, Seifert's speech was too much, and earned the poet a personal attack from the Czechoslovakian president who had succeeded the mummy, Antonín Zápotocký. For the time being nothing happened either way: the writers remained in jail, but Seifert was not sent there. Soon the "Thaw" set in, and though it went through several reversals, eventually the writers (and most other prisoners) were freed and Seifert was nominated National Artist. If "national" in this Stalinist title means "known to and loved by the nation", then among the several dozen bearers of the title, Seifert is the only genuine article.

Things picked up in the short-lived Dubček utopia, but Seifert's private life got worse. Shortly after 1960 he fell seriously ill. He could barely walk and on the doctor's merciless orders his consumption of red wine was severely restricted. Yet whenever I visited him, the old sinner managed to disregard the orders and fill himself with the "milk of the oldsters", as he called his forbidden nectar. It didn't harm him—after all, the diagnosis was probably wrong—but it brought out absurd pricks of conscience. Once, sitting in his room with Zdeněk Mahler, a playwright-scriptwriter (you will find his name among the credits for Miloš Forman's *Amadeus*) and, then, a heretical Party member, we listened to the poet's tearful reminiscences of people, many of them friends, who had been either executed by the Party, such as Záviš Kalandra and the Socialist minister Milada Horáková, or condemned for long years to concentration camps, like the great Catholic poet Jan Zahradníček or Josef Palivec, or sent to their graves by suspicious suicides, like Konstantin Biebl and the surrealist theoretician Karel Teige. Suddenly the old man turned his beautiful face to Mahler and his voice broke; "Mr. Mahler," he wailed, "how can we ever reconcile it with our conscience that we were Communists?" It was laughable, of course, for Seifert had been a Party member in his green years and at a time when the mass murders of Lenin were still believed by many to be an invention of bourgeois propaganda. Yet, at the same time, it was characteristic of the poet. Some, not many, take their consciences seriously.

I have always felt that the Soviet invasion in 1968 had at least one good consequence: it literally put the incapacitated old poet back on his feet. The insult of the military intervention hurt his sensitive heart beyond endurance. He hailed a taxi, on crutches descended the staircase down which, on a memorable occasion captured so well in Milan Kundera's *The Book of Laughter and Forgetting*, he had had to be carried by fellow poets (yes, that helpless, wine-filled poet is the present Nobel Prize laureate), entered the Writers' Club, and had himself elected the union's chairman in place of Eduard Goldstücker when the old chairman, faced by virulently anti-Semitic threats, had to flee the country. For the nine months or so that remained of the life of that organization he firmly held off both the attacks and the overtures of the Husák regime. In the end they lost patience and ordered Seifert to proclaim, in the name of the membership, the union's support for the officially accepted version of the Soviet ambush ("brotherly help"). Seifert refused, claiming that the union was a democratic organization and he could do nothing in its name without consulting the members. Then he put the matter of brotherly help to the vote. Almost unanimously the union rejected the Orwellianism, whereupon it was promptly disbanded.

Seifert found himself a full-fledged member of the underground. In 1977 he signed the bold Charter 77 manifesto, damned by the Party in tones of mediaeval diabolism and followed by a witch-hunt. Once again his popularity, and by then also his venerable age, saved him from consequences more serious than the banning of his books and occasional interrogations.

All right. This may prove that the poet is an exceptionally courageous, politically clairvoyant, morally blameless man who irritates the Communist regime more than any other poet. But is he an artist great enough to justify the awarding of the great prize? As great as, for instance, another laureate, Pablo Neruda, that thief of an honest Czech name, that parlour Stalinist and admirer of the Georgian's chief executioner, Andrey Vyshinsky?

I have no doubt that he is. But unfortunately, the proof is in the poetry—and many, including myself, have serious doubts whether lyric poetry, particularly of the crystal-clear, onomatopoeic kind that Seifert mostly wrote, can really be appreciated unless its language is the critic's mother tongue. If it is true that the translation of prose, even by excellent and sensitive experts, is always a distortion, what can the translation of subtly rhymed, musical, lyric poetry be?

Even relatively simple things are hard to do well. Take the following lines from one of Seifert's early poems:

> *Slyším to co jiní neslyší,*
> *bosé nohy chodit po plyši.*

The literal translation is "I hear that which others don't, bare feet walking on plush." But the two lines are rich in recurrent affricates ("š" pronounced "sh") and spirants ("s" and "c" pronounced "ts") which evoke the sound of the steps. The effect of the entire poem is based on similar sound-play. I attempted a translation, for which I deeply apologize:

> I hear sounds that others do not hear,
> Bare feet on plush tiptoeing near.

All that is left is a rather ordinary rhyme, definitely a distortion of the elegant rhyming of the Czech original. A better translator would naturally do better, but would he be able to do absolute justice to even this simple ditty? I wonder. If translation of subtle lyric poetry is possible at all, it can only be done by writing new poems on themes borrowed from the original; of paraphrasing the original as closely as possible without disfiguring the texture, the idiomatics, the beauty of the second language—something in the manner of Edward FitzGerald's *The Rubáiyát of Omar Khayyám*. With all due respect to the existing renderings, Seifert has yet to find his FitzGerald.

Another difficulty, not linguistic but psychological, is that many of Seifert's main themes—Prague, Czech history and literature—are imbued with a vast richness of associational meanings that are simply not perceived by most foreign readers. Take *The Song of Viktorka*, for instance. It is a tribute to the memory of the most beloved and most interesting Czech nineteenth-century female novelist, Božena ("Betty" to her admirers) Němcová, a kind of Czech George Eliot—a courageous feminist before the word was known in Bohemia, a bold mistress of several lovers at a puritanical time when having lovers was suicidal for a married woman, and, last but not least, a celebrated beauty who died of tuberculosis at the age of forty-two. Several modern poets have written entire books dedicated to the memory of Betty Němcová; Seifert wrote two. The heroine of the second one, Viktorka, is a romantic rebel from Němcová's best novel, *The Grandmother*. Seduced and abandoned by a soldier, Viktorka goes mad, lives in the wild freedom of the forest, and is eventually killed by lightning. Romantic stuff, but my God, how mythopoeic! Seifert rendered the story in haunting, balladic, untranslatable quatrains that reverberate with crisscrossing Czech associations, linking the countryside to nineteenth-century literature, history to legend,

present tragedies to past ones, the lovely image of the mad girl
with the lovely image of her creator. The associative chains are
endless—for those who can grasp them.

The same holds true of such books as *The Stone Bridge*
or *Robed in Light*, lyrical slaps in the face of Nazism, with
their many historical echoes and coded meanings. But you have
to know Czech history to hear the echoes: know it, and be
moved by it. In order to be moved I guess, you have to be
Czech. But despite all these obstacles, much of the poetic power
transpires through the translation. The following is Seifert's
characterization of his friend Vladimír Holan's work, from a
poem written to mark the poet's death:

> In the wretched aviary that is Bohemia
> he tossed his poems around him
> with contempt
> like chunks of raw meat....

That was written in the mid-seventies. In the mid-twenties,
influenced by the freely associating surrealism of Apollinaire,
Seifert wrote:

> The acrobatics of roses
> in the clouds
> rise to the stars
> which are swallowed
> by the cushion of boredom
> poetry....

In the fifties, after *The Song of Viktorka*, he wrote these
verses of "mawkish self-pity":

> If the tyrant won't fall
> —even that is hereditary—
> the poet is sentenced to silence
> and the square palm of the barred window
> stuffs with its claws his singing mouth.
> But he shouts his verses through the bars
> while the tearers of books
> are busily at work....

In the sixties came *The Song of Hendele*, written in memory of a girl who died in Auschwitz:

> Little Hendele
> sometimes tells me
> what she has learned in kindergarten:
> "Cuckoo, cuckoo, tell me, please,
> Is there a life that I shall miss?"
> Oh, dove, shut up, no more sweet songs;
> here you cannot sweeten anything.
> Beat your wing against the stone,
> the rabbi should get up
> he's been sleeping too long....

And one more from the *annus mirabilis* of 1968:

> I want to believe the time has come
> when it is possible to tell murder to its face:
> You are murder.
> Meanness, even adorned with laurel,
> will again be meanness,
> lie will be lie as it used to be,
> and pistol will no longer be able
> to unlock innocent door.

For the last time I apologize for my barbaric translation; I am definitely not a FitzGerald.

And there is yet another difficulty. Something in most of Seifert's poems strikes a chord that the Czech intellectual has in common with the man in the street. That something, I think, has largely disappeared from the poetry of North America. There are exceptions—Allen Ginsberg, perhaps. But the bulk of poetry written today in North America is, it seems to me, largely unread by wide audiences, except on campuses. Unread poetry tends to develop codes that few can break; it permutates into something that can be appreciated only by a cabal of the initiated. It may be great and powerful poetry; its power, however, hardly grabs the fancy of the man from Main Street. Its very encodedness—together with a tone which, as a rule, shuns openly emotional overtones—becomes in the eyes of its few readers and more numerous critics the only mark of excellence. A poet who appeals to both highbrow and lowbrow readers, like Chaplin in film, seems an impossibility in today's North America, except in the marginal field of nonsense verse.

Seifert is precisely that type of artist, and Professor Lars Gyllensten of the Swedish Academy was right when, in his presentation speech, he said that Seifert "knows how to address both those who have a literary education and those who approach his work without much schooling in their baggage." This "Chaplinesque" aesthetics is not an accidental development but a program. In an essay written at the very beginning of his career in 1922 and called "A New Proletarian Art", Seifert, in agreement with the canons of a literary trend he subscribed to in those days called "poetism", demanded the destruction of barriers between lowbrow and highbrow art.

However, Czech men and women of literary education are somewhat different from their North American counterparts. History, experience, political climate, tradition—all these powerful factors have given their sophistication a different bent. Seifert's appeal to readers both with and without intellectual baggage may be largely lost on American audiences; the poems' very accessibility may prove a hindrance to their acceptance by the North American intellectual of today.

But then, not all of Seifert's poetry is of the "easy" kind, and should he find his FitzGerald even the songlike pieces might lose their flavour of open emotionality, so alien to the English-speaking Westerner. In such a translator's hands, the beauty of *Viktorka* may yet shine through all the thick layers of inaccessible associations and bring tears of Slavic emotion to the sophisticated eyes of North American student readers, at least in the privacy of their campus dormitories.

FRANZ KAFKA, JAZZ,
AND THE *ANTI-SEMITIC READER*

———

Like so many of Škvorecký's essays on literary subjects,
this one takes a very personal approach and is ultimately
less about Franz Kafka (1883–1924) than about Kafka as
encountered by Škvorecký. It was written for an issue of
Cross Currents *devoted to Kafka.*

ONE DAY, NOT so long ago, after being introduced to someone at
a party, I met with an interesting variation on the familiar
response to the usual question about my background. The
familiar line goes: "Oh, from Prague? I know! Švejk!" This
man, however, said in a tone of amused interest: "Oh, from
Prague? I know! Kafka!" Which may explain why I, of all
people, was invited to write this article. Facing such a task, I'm
afraid I share the feelings of Gustav Janouch when, after the
Second World War, Kafka-adorers from all over the world made
their pilgrimages to Prague and invariably asked Janouch to
show them the grave, which is among the smallest and least
ostentatious in that display of pomp and wealth called the New
Jewish Cemetery in Prague. "I often had to fall silent," Janouch
writes, "for they all knew Kafka's work...much better than I."
Truly I feel like Janouch, for I have never *studied* Kafka, I have
only read *some* of his books.

The little I know of Kafka's work is about as original as
my knowledge of Hašek's *The Good Soldier Švejk*. If Hašek
presented us with an analysis of the absurdity of ideological
orthodoxies, Kafka analysed for us certain mental situations
that everybody who "been there before"—as Mark Twain im-
mortally diagnosed the distinction between the Eastern and the
Western experiences—recognizes as only too familiar. But let
me begin my narrative with an evening in the summer of 1944,
by which time I already knew about Kafka, for I had read one

of his shorter works earlier that year. That evening I was in Prague, skipping work at the Messerschmitt aircraft factory in Náchod, thanks to a friendly doctor's certificate of infirmity. I was attending an amateur jazz festival in the big hall of the Lucerna, because the band from my native town, the Miloslav Zachoval Orchestra, was performing there. The occasion itself was a *kafkárna*—quite an experience—sitting in the beautifully gilded hall in a huge, enthusiastic crowd, sprinkled here and there with the *Feldgrau* (field grey) of the Wehrmacht uniforms, listening to the Jew Benny Goodman's "Sing! Sing! Sing!" in a good if amateurish rendition, presented as the work of that celebrated if nonexistent master of swing, Jiří Patočka.

That morning, when I arrived in Prague on an early train, I went for a stroll along the Moldau river. In the shop window of the Mánes building I spotted an unexpected book: *Zámek* (*The Castle*) by František Kafka. I couldn't believe my eyes— but should I really use this worn-out cliché for that perfectly normal, if Kafkaesque situation? I *did* believe my eyes. I knew that grim censors who were fooled by the one-hundred-percent Czech name Patočka attached to the patently Negro syncopations of "Tiger Rag" were hardly connoisseurs of art and would pass over a Czech name like Kafka without suspicion. I bought the book. Yes, it was the valuable first (and at that time only) Czech edition of Kafka's *Das Schloss*, translated by Pavel Eisner, a younger contemporary of the novelist in the Jewish community of Prague. It had been published in 1938, shortly before the Munich crisis, in a daring publishing venture prompted by the supposition that the recent successes of Czech surrealism had paved the way for the unusual author's acceptance. They had not. *Zámek* was one of the biggest flops in the history of Czech publishing. Why? Perhaps first of all because the situation of the protagonist, K., as he tries in vain to penetrate a dense web of red tape, was unfamiliar to people who, in 1938, had already forgotten the celebrated *k und k* (*kaiser und königliche*—imperial and royal) bureaucracy of old Austria, and did not realize that they would soon swallow another, far deadlier dose of that twentieth-century poison. Alienation was not common in the Czechoslovak liberal democratic state of Thomas Garrigue Masaryk, and if Hašek is a revelation of the absurdity of orthodoxy, Kafka, of course, is alienation: the alienation of the man in the street from society's institutions, beyond which lurk dark and dangerous powers, hard to pin down and far beyond his control.

That is how I read the book then. I was a graduate of the Protectorate's *reálné gymnasium*, where the Nazi authorities had reduced literary instruction to the minimum, and where, instead of Kafka, we were treated to *Schlageter* with its famous line "When I hear the word 'culture', I go for my gun," and to some very early examples of socialist realism. At the *reálné gymnasium* in Náchod, we complemented this mandatory reading with an incongruous collection of privately circulated books such as Nezval's by-then-banned surrealist poems *Absolutní hrobař* (*The Absolute Grave Digger*) and *Žena v množném čísle* (*The Woman in Plural*), and Čapek's brilliant translations of Baudelaire, Rimbaud, and Apollinaire; but we also read Margaret Mitchell's *Gone with the Wind*, and Richmal Crompton's saga of the naughty upper-class rascal, *William*.

Now tell me: how could a youngster reared on such an incongruous literary diet interpret *The Castle*? I simplemindedly thought the book was a strange but rather good satire on bureaucracy. Yet, in my innocence, I sensed some other dimension beyond the vain efforts of K. to have his job confirmed. I, of course, knew nothing about dimensions, about levels of meaning, about symbolism, about the art of interpretation. The university had been shut down by the Nazis in 1939, and neither *Schlageter* nor *William* is renowned for complex texture. But prior to *The Castle* I had read one other work by the same author. From it I had received my first instruction in the openness of meaning, and I read into the little story a very personal meaning of my own. But I shall come to that later.

That evening the Miloslav Zachoval Orchestra played, besides Duke Ellington's "Caravan" (announced as "An Evening in Turkey" by, naturally, Jiří Patočka), one genuine Czech swing hit, "V lednu je máj" ("May in January"), by Emil Ludvík. Ludvík was the uncrowned king of hot jazz, as swinging jazz was called then, in Bohemia. He was a dedicated jazzman and also a courageous man. Long after the enactment of the Nuremberg Laws in Bohemia, he employed in his big band a Jewish musician who later became legendary: Bedřich ("Fricek") Weiss.

Weiss was to lead the Ghetto Swingers in Terezín, and later perished in Auschwitz. But as long as he possibly could, Ludvík continued to employ him, first as an alto-sax man, and then, when Bedřich's Semitic features were too dangerous to be seen on stage, as an arranger. There was also a German trombone player in the band, Walter Paul, whom Ludvík shielded from the military draft as long as he could. Paul eventually perished on the Russian front.

Ludvík was also a personal friend of Pavel Bayerle, the half-Jewish first trumpeter in Zachoval's orchestra, and he often visited with Bayerle's family in Náchod. That evening in the Lucerna Hall he was a member of the festival jury, and after the concert he invited us to his apartment. There I produced my volume of Kafka and showed it around. As it turned out, Ludvík was the only one present who knew about Kafka, and not only that. He said, "I know Janouch, too. He's a chap who used to be Kafka's buddy. But you know of him as well. Wrote *Jazzová technika hry na basu* [*The Jazz Technique of Double-Bass Playing*] and *Solo jazz-kytara: od breaku k improvizaci* [*Solo Jazz Guitar: From the Break to Improvisation*]." Well, if I knew precious little about Kafka, I was familiar with at least one of those works. Jarýk Celba, Zachoval's guitar (later piano) player, owned the latter volume and had probably perused it.

So, early in my acquaintance with Kafka, a strong associative link was formed between what I loved most, jazz music, and the mysterious figure from Prague's Old Town.

Absurd? Perhaps. But such is life. Strange are the ways of the Lord.

Much later, when I read the first, incomplete edition of *Conversations with Kafka*, borrowed from Pavel Eisner, I recalled that nocturnal conversation in Ludvík's apartment, and I read the book much, much more avidly than I would have, had Janouch not been a member of my own jazz fraternity. In the absurd way of the world it was not Janouch who, in my mind, was glorified by his friendship with Kafka. It was Kafka who acquired an interesting feature by his acquaintance with the jazzman. Browsing through old publications preserved from the war, I came across an issue of an obscure journal called *List soukromých zaměstnanců svobodných povolání* (*Journal of Private Employees of Freelancing Vocations*) and remembered that

I had kept it because of an article entitled "Magie jazzu" ("The Magic of Jazz"), which contained a lovely memoir:

> In 1921, the enterprising owner of the Konvikt nightclub in Bartolomějská Street brought the first jazz drum to Prague. it was a big, red-painted monster, surrounded by sixteen pipes of the tubaphone, by four strings of bells and jingle-bells, by six cowbells, three cymbals, a tom-tom, a gong, and four smaller drums. In addition to these usual sets of pipes and noisemakers, this particular "jazz drum" was equipped also with a curious machine. It consisted in principle of six popgun barrels with six foot-pedals in the place of triggers, so that, during one composition, the drummer could fire them six times using his foot. That, of course, was a staggering sensation, and therefore the most popular hit of those times was something called "Indianola," during which the drummer metamorphosed into a wild gunman.

I remembered how inflamed my imagination had been when I read this message from the primordial era of jazz in Czechoslovakia. And as I reread it then, after the war, the name of its author acquired a meaning it had not had on the first occasion. The man who wrote "The Magic of Jazz" was Gustav Janouch.

I came across Janouch's name for the last time in Canada, in Toronto's Robarts Library. Reading his preface to the complete edition of *Conversations with Kafka* I realized how, on another occasion in my life, I came very close to meeting him. He tells about how he lost all means of support in the early 1960s when "the directress of a well-known Prague publishing house for whom I worked as an external lecturer and translator, had committed suicide.... I wasn't paid for a whole year's work, and when I defended myself against this injustice, I was deprived of all further opportunities for work." Well, no wonder! I knew this lady well, for I too had earned some extra money from that generous source. Her name was Šlechtová, and she was the wife of a minister who represented the Czechoslovak Socialist Party, one of the semi-existent shop-window parties in the Communist government. As privileged quislings, the couple enriched themselves by various ingenious means, for the

description of which there is no room in this article. The suicide
may have been the sort old Prussian officers used to commit,
when they were left in a room alone with their revolvers. But
if Mr. and Mrs. Šlechta were generous to themselves, they
certainly were not stingy with slightly unkosher figures like
myself and apparently Gustav Janouch, who after the Second
World War spent almost two years in jail. He belonged, I
suppose, to those German-speaking Pragers with clear political
consciences, who naively thought that revolutionary justice
harboured no dangers for them.

A warm feeling overcame me in the reading room of the
Robarts: for all practical purposes, I had been Janouch's accomplice in making those fast crowns so lavishly paid for our efforts
by the good crooked lady. I read on:

> At that same time I clashed with a few Nazis at the
> German book fair. They interfered with the publication
> of a book in which I revealed the spiritual consequences
> of racial persecution and jazz as an attempt by the
> racially oppressed to achieve psychic liberation. I knew
> not only black music, but also the *tönendes Brot* (singing
> bread) music of the young Jews in the Theresienstadt
> ghetto, whom my friend of many years, the composer
> Emil Ludvík, supported at great sacrifice.
>
> Naturally, these were facts which didn't suit erstwhile
> racial experts and half-baked, freshly minted democrats,
> and for that reason they delayed publication of my book,
> *Der Todesblues* (*The Blues of Death*), in an absolutely in-
> famous manner. And when I protested, my book *Prager
> Begegnungen* (*Prague Encounters*), the first edition of
> which had shortly before been sold out within a few
> weeks, was requested in vain by the University of Cal-
> ifornia, Berkeley, in the USA, the Russian University in
> Lvov in the Soviet Union, and the Paul List Publishing
> House in Leipzig; it was simply suppressed and no longer
> published.

Immediately I dispatched a query to C. Fischer Verlag: was
the book *Der Todesblues* eventually published? Could I purchase a copy? I never received an answer. The book is not listed

in any catalogues. The name Gustav Janouch does not appear in encyclopaedias. I don't know.

Poor Janouch. His *magnum opus* is by now very much discredited as an authentic source on Kafka. It seems the old swingman doctored his memories and puffed them up. But do we really have the moral right to condemn him for wanting to make a little money out of his acquaintance with the Master? And does he deserve the almost sneering tone of Eduard Goldstücker's devastating analysis of the *Conversations*? Goldstücker writes, "In order to make Kafka as credible as Cicero [in English one would say: in order to sell], he must emphasize Kafka's interest in the history of his own home town." Yes, sure, the poor bugger did all he could to sell his Kafka-ware, because in his later years, judging from several hints, Kafka was his main potential source of income. Mrs. Šlechtová's publishing house Svobodné Slovo-Melantrich was the last refuge for those eking out a living through translation and similar activities, people who, more likely than not, were elsewhere unacceptable politically. Yet at that time a rather well-known Kafka scholar, Josef Čermák, an ambitious and rather vainglorious man, had a very influential position at Odeon Publishers, the respectable place to sell yourself, and Goldstücker himself was not without influence. He stopped seeing Janouch in 1960. In 1962, the year of the Liblice Conference, Janouch was, as far as I know, the only man living in Prague who had known Kafka personally. Was he invited to the conference? I have found no evidence of it. With the single exception of old Otto F. Babler, it was a conference of Marxists, some of them with pretty awful Stalinist pasts and with equally awful neo-Stalinist futures. Dr. Jiří Hájek, for instance. It seems there was no room in this group for an old jazzman who, as a young greenhorn, had had the dubious good fortune of briefly knowing one of the great intellectuals of our century. At the time of the conference he was probably finding solace by associating with his old nightclub buddy Emil Ludvík, also more or less a nonperson in the 1950s and early 1960s.

And yet he did not squander the inheritance of his youthful gig with Kafka. All right, his book is to some extent—perhaps even mostly—the fruit not of diary entries and Dickensian memory, but of imagination. But it's not a bad book. It is a loving tribute to the Master which has inspired many readers, both scholars and nonscholars. But what of the many who have mistakenly assumed its accuracy and perhaps even based their hypotheses on pronouncements by Kafka probably authored by Janouch? Well, let's take it for a *kafkárna* and enjoy the book for what it is, if we love the Master.

At long last, then, I get to Kafka. Until I started working on this article I firmly believed that I first saw Kafka's name in another of those obscure wartime publications called *Protižidovská čítánka* (*An Anti-Semitic Reader*). This was an anthology of articles written, very probably, by one or two people under several pseudonyms who were also editors of the magazine *Arijský boj* (*The Aryan Struggle*), the Czech equivalent of Julius Streicher's *Der Stürmer*. I recalled distinctly how excited I had been while leafing through the book in the local library, because there I found verses which, in those days, would have been suppressed in any other publication: *Nezemřu já od práce, / nezahynu bídou, / nezalknu se v oprátce, / skončím syfilidou.* Which means: "I shall not die from overwork, / I shall not die from misery, / I shall not expire in a noose, / I shall die of syphilis." To understand the irresistible charm such boldly provocative verses had for a conventionally rebellious youth in the Nazi Protectorate, one has to have some knowledge of the atmosphere of moralistic puritanism pervading all bloody dictatorships, of the pathetic drivel of chauvinistic class-conscious or race-conscious "poetry" pushed down people's throats. Naturally, the poem was quoted in the *Anti-Semitic Reader* to convince the readers of the depravity of the Jewish mind. Its author was a Jew, the Czech anarchist František Gellner. The pedagogical effectiveness of this method was of course predictable: the "disgusting" lines by Gellner, from "Píseň zhýralého jinocha" ("The Song of the Dissipated Youth"), stuck firmly in my non-Jewish mind and made me yearn for more of the same.

The book, as I also recalled, contained an article which mentioned, as a particularly revolting example of decadence, a story by one Franz Kafka in which a man—a human being!—changes into a bedbug. The commentary explained that such a stomach-turning image could emerge only from the beastly, subhuman imagination of the Jew. But the image filled me, an aspiring poet then, with a sense of inferiority. I would never come up with such a brilliant idea! I felt depressed, but not for the reasons envisaged by the authors of the *Anti-Semitic Reader*, and my curiosity concerning one Franz Kafka was aroused.

Well, memory is both reliable and unreliable. Preparing to write this paper I tried to get hold of the *Anti-Semitic Reader*. It was not an easy task, but eventually, thanks to an Israeli friend, Mr. Erich Kulka of Jerusalem University, I obtained a microfilm of the book. It is a genuinely disgusting thing. Disgusting is not the right word. Horrifying is more appropriate. I shuddered when I read it. But I read on and, indeed, found the article on Gellner. It bears the title "Traviči duší" ("Poisoners of Souls"), and several of Gellner's poems are quoted—but my memory had failed me, at least partially. The lines about death by syphilis are not among the quotations. I had to correct my memory. What had inspired me in the public library in Náchod in 1944 were other lines, described in the *Anti-Semitic Reader* as Gellner's decadent life-credo: "*Svůj život rychle utratit, / nic nezískat, nic neztratit*" ("Spend your life fast, / gain nothing, lose nothing"). A nice and certainly an inspiring credo for a pubescent youngster, with its familiar mood of nihilism, of Apollinaire's "irreverence to any fame".

And yet, in early 1945 at the latest, I knew those other lines too. Those about syphilis. I quoted them in a poem I started writing in the summer of 1945. I must have read them elsewhere, possibly in a book by Gellner I had searched for and eventually found, having been prompted by the *Anti-Semitic Reader*. Yes, there they are, in my poem entitled *Nezoufejte!* (*Don't Despair!*), quoted imprecisely, indicating that I quoted them from memory:

> In the *Anti-Semitic Reader* I found the following magnif-
> icent lines:
>> *I shall not die of love I shall not perish of misery*
>> *I shall die of syphilis*
> The *Anti-Semitic Reader* was the most magnificent
> book of the time of the protectorate.

I read on, looking for the story of the bedbug. Alas, neither was this memory exact. To be sure, Kafka is mentioned in the book: "Among their Prague 'classics,' the Jews list the writers Franz Kafka and Franz Werfel. Their mysterious stories stink of the mustiness of the Jewish ghettos, especially Kafka's *Recherches de Dieu*." Apparently the author, one E. Peřina, did not dirty his mind actually reading Kafka. But that's all. Nothing about Jews turning into bedbugs in musty ghettos.

And yet, I *must* have read about it somewhere. I know that I already knew about the bedbug when I read *The Castle* in the summer of 1944. Possibly I came across some debunking article in *The Aryan Struggle*, through which I occasionally browsed because my father had been attacked as a *židomil* (Jew-lover) by someone in their circle, some *protižidovec*—a rather awkward neologism for "anti-Semite".

Yes, I must have known about Kafka because otherwise I would hardly have picked up a book which must have been *Beim Bau der Chinesischen Mauer* (*The Great Wall of China*), when I spotted it in the library of Pavel Bayerle's father, in the same treasure chest which yielded many a precious forbidden fruit to us, hungry for anything the Germans disliked. It has also yielded Hugues Panassié's *Le jazz hot*, which, however, like the *Book of Mormon*, was written in a tongue unknown to us; we could only use it for incantations of the holy names: Joe King Oliver, Kid Ory, Trixie Smith, Louis Armstrong.

My German—learned from the cantor of the local synagogue, who was the unwitting reason for my father's being labelled a "Jew-lover"—was excellent. I read and soon came across a story entitled "Der Bau" ("The Burrow"). It was right at the beginning...here I must make another digression. At the time I came to read this tale I was in a jam, perhaps the worst jam of my life. Shortly before I discovered the book in Mr. Bayerle's library I had committed an act of sabotage in the Messerschmitt factory where I worked as a draftee under the *Totaleinsatz* (total mobilization) scheme. Among other things, the factory produced something called "the lids" (*dekly*) for the Messerschmitt 111 (I believe that was the number) fighter plane. One of the great stories of the last war was the uninterrupted duelling between the British Spitfires and the German Messerschmitts. Because of that deadly competition, weapon after weapon was being added to new and improved variations of the same fighters. The last addition to the firepower of the Messerschmitt was a powerful, fast-firing cannon. It could not be fitted into the wing, so a metal housing for the gun, shaped like a small bathtub, was attached to the bottom of the wing, with the cartridge drum fastened to a dural cross by four screws with conical heads. These heads fitted conical holes in the cross, and it was my duty to drill these holes. They had to be made with precision because if they were too deep there was danger that as the cannon began to fire, the metal of the drum would break. I was issued a special device to measure the depth of the holes. My brilliant idea was to tamper with it so that I could drill the holes a few millimetres deeper. The metal would break but nothing could be proved, since my measuring device would show correct figures. I confess, my motives were not entirely patriotic. The real patriot in that scheme was the girl who worked on the drill next to mine. I did think of the sabotage independent of her, but she triggered the affair. I wanted to impress her, and she could only be impressed by heroic, anti-Nazi deeds, not by doodling on the saxophone.

Well, my idea proved stupid rather than brilliant. The faulty drillings were discovered, the foreman threw out the measuring device and raised hell. Fortunately he was Czech, the hell was raised in the privacy of his office, and he devised a way to camouflage the faulty equipment. Nevertheless, for the next three or four months I lived in a nightmare of fear, expecting that the Czech foreman would not remain alone in his discovery of my heroic stupidity.

In the Second World War there were basically two nightmarish situations: that of the soldier on the battlefield, and that of the victim, either conspirator or Jew, caught in the totalitarian cage of an occupied territory such as Bohemia, from which there was almost no escape. I was in the latter situation. Feverishly, during sleepless nights, I tried to figure out where to hide, how to get away, where to find a shelter should the Gestapo be on my trail. I was probably in little danger, for all this happened in the early months of 1944 when, in the chaotic conditions of the shrinking Reich, much of the equipment produced by the

Messerschmitt works in Náchod probably never reached its destination. However, that thought was no great comfort to me. I felt like a mouse locked with a cat in a cage.

And then I read "The Burrow".

Now, according to learned books, this story has had a variety of basic interpretations. Among them are: "The presentation of a problem of the author's 'literary existence'" (Heinz Politzer); "The animal is an image of the totality of empirical humanity in its relation to its true self" (Emrich); "The burrower is the symbol of an inner psychic experience in which man undergoes injury to his own being through a self-created 'counter order'" (Henel); "The burrower is an allegory of the spirit, which seeks to protect itself" (Marache); and so on. Well, my interpretation when, covered with cold sweat, I read the story, was nowhere near as sophisticated. It was quite straightforward and primitive. It was simply the story of someone caught in a burrow who is being slowly, implacably cornered by a powerful and deadly enemy seeking his life. The story was unfinished. The poor bugger in his imperfect hideout, I thought, was obviously killed in the end.

I don't think I have to explain why "The Burrow" belongs among the stories that made the deepest impression on me—indeed, among the few stories I have never been able to push out of my mind. And that is why, many, many years later when, as assistant editor-in-chief of the bimonthly *Světová literatura* (*World Literature*), I was cautiously preparing some of Kafka's work for publication under the guidance of my editor-in-chief, I suggested this particular story to him. The translator, Pavel Eisner, the same man who had rendered *Das Schloss* into Czech in 1938, was enthusiastic about the project. And so "The Burrow" became the very first story by Franz Kafka to be published in Communist Czechoslovakia after the February putsch of 1948.

Here let me make a slight correction in what seems to be a widespread idea about Kafka's reintroduction in his own country. It is generally believed that the gate for his reacceptance was opened at a conference which met May 27–28, 1962, at the Château of Liblice, at which the assembled Marxist critics and writers successfully defended the notion that Kafka was, after all, relevant to the socialist readership. Well, perhaps not a gate, but a small trapdoor, had been opened much earlier. If you recall, one of the reasons the publishers of the Mánes Club decided to do *The Castle* in 1938 was that it was hoped the success of surrealism in Czechoslovakia had paved the way towards an understanding of the enigmatic author. The editor-in-chief of *World Literature* was an old surrealist and pataphysician. He was also a member of the Communist party—otherwise he would not have been editor-in-chief. His name was Jan Řezáč. As far as I know, he wrote only one book in his life, and that came out as a very early piece of *samizdat* during the war; it was pataphysical rather than surrealist. Its title was *The Illustrated Guide to the Public Toilets of Greater Prague, Giving Their Histories and the Best Graffiti Found on Their Walls* (the title is not accurate, for I quote from memory). It was an impressive list of nearly a hundred of these important little buildings usually not mentioned in books on architecture. It included photographs of each of them, architectonic data, and citations of the more interesting graffiti to be found over the urinals.

Surely a man like that was no stranger to such mischief as reintroducing a decadent writer to a readership engaged in the building of socialism. From the very beginning—the first volume of *World Literature* appeared in 1956, only one year after the celebrated unmasking of Stalin by Khrushchev—my dealings with my remarkable boss resembled conspiratorial sessions rather than editorial meetings. For the most part we compiled lists of dubious authors, such as Evelyn Waugh, William Faulkner, Alfred Jarry, Henry Miller, and so on, and devised ways to smuggle them into the pages of our journal. We were helped a great deal by interpretations which had appeared in the literary journals of other socialist countries (preferably the Soviet Union). Evelyn Waugh's *The Loved One* was printed because some ingenious Polish critic saw in it a scathing attack on the irreverence of capitalism. *Fahrenheit 451*, Ray Bradbury's story about the burning of books, was of course a critique of Senator McCarthy, and if you dealt your cards shrewdly, no censor could object that the book was relevant to the widespread banning of books in Czechoslovakia as well. The method had been suggested to us by Sergei Nikolski, a young Soviet doctoral student who, in his thesis on Karel Čapek, saved the bourgeois anti-Communist storyteller for Czech literature by interpreting him as a humanist anti-Fascist. The distant roots of the method stem, of course, from scholastic references to *auctoritates* who were considered more important than empirical knowledge.

So we plotted Kafka's comeback carefully. The first step was printing, in the sixth issue of 1956, a short article by the "progressive" German writer F.C. Weisskopf, originally written in 1945. Its main thesis is a refutation of the existentialist interpretation of Kafka and it places heavy stress upon Kafka's links to the world of the Czechs. Half a year later we got together with the Germanist Rio Preisner, who had just been released from the "work battalions" of the army, and then with Pavel Eisner, and planned our strategy. That's when it was decided that "The Burrow" would be the sample and that Eisner would write a substantial essay on Kafka. He did, rejecting the psychoanalytical interpretation, accentuating Kafka's Prague roots, his social feeling, his knowledge of the Czech language, his kindness, and also the anti-Fascism of Milena, his unforgettable friend, a victim of Ravensbrück. It is an ironic commentary on the era that Eisner, quoting from Margaret Buber-Neumann's book *Kafkas Freundin Milena*, had to omit the author's name. "Her co-martyrs," says Eisner, "loved Milena so much that one of them, who wrote a report on her in Ravensbrück, contemplated suicide when Milena passed away." There is more irony in the fact that Eisner's essay was translated into Italian and published in an Italian Communist party cultural magazine with an editorial comment which states that this is the first Marxist study of Kafka to be written in a socialist country. Pavel Eisner was about as Marxist as I am Islamic. He was a charming gentleman of the pre–World-War-One school who actually bowed to ladies, and who reacted to lady editors' suggestions concerning alterations in his translations with the words, "Esteemed lady, I bow deeply to your charming emendations!"

Last but not least, one more important decision was made at that historic meeting sometime in the beginning of 1957, five years before the world-famous Liblice Conference. We would commission a portrait of Kafka especially for our première. Řezáč, the old surrealist, an unflinching admirer of *entartete Kunst*, said, "We'll ask Tichý!"

František Tichý was one of the very best modern Czech painters, certainly not much in favour with Party aestheticians in the 1950s. I was first exposed to his art when, as a boy before the Second World War, I read a translation of Poe's *The Narrative of Arthur Gordon Pym* with Tichý's illustrations. I cannot decide whether the agreeable shock of that book was due primarily to Poe's imagination or to the delightful morbidity of the drawings. I was sent to seek out the Master, and I found him at his favourite watering hole. At that time he already had the brownish complexion of patients suffering from cirrhosis of the liver. He died a few years later. I gave him several photographs of Kafka, and in a few days the portrait was on my desk. It was duly reproduced in the third number of the 1957 volume of *World Literature*. Since then it has become the most-often-reproduced drawing of Kafka's beautiful face.

In 1980, selected publishers, literary agents, writers' organizations, university libraries, and journalists were sent unsolicited copies of *Panorama of Czech Literature*, a glossy new literary magazine in English which poses as a journal of what is best in contemporary Czech fiction, poetry, and literary criticism. In fact it is a panorama of the bemedalled ones: national artists, artists of merit, winners of government prizes and awards. In Number 3 of 1981 this magazine, yours for the asking, brought an article entitled "Czech Literature in the World" and signed "Editor", although the name of that person is nowhere to be found in the journal. This anonymous critic begins by saying that only two writers from Bohemia are known to the average Westerner: Jaroslav Hašek and Franz Kafka. About the latter he opines: "Even if, perhaps, he felt and signalized in his works certain general tendencies in the development of the modern world, his stories have very little in common with the Czech character and way of thinking. Dubious attempts to identify the atmosphere of Kafka's books with the situation in today's Czechoslovakia are of course not worthy of discussion, for their political aims are transparently clear."

I am not so sure. In an essay written for *World Literature* at a time when the regimentation of Czech society was about as intensive as it is today, Pavel Eisner wrote: "That Kafka became the favourite writer of even non-snobbish and honest people in so many countries was made possible by an epidemic of existential anxiety. Kafka's vogue was not created by the cocktail-circuit aestheticians—that would be overestimating them. But the man sold by the Chamberlains and the Lavals, crushed by the boots of the Schickelgrubers and Hitlers, humiliated by a daily avalanche of lies and crookedness, oppressed by the devilish machinery of bureaucracy.... This creature...found his way to the monothematic author of life's anxiety." I wonder if the atmosphere of a country where anonymous people coined the untranslatable word *kafkárna* to denote the craziness produced daily by totalitarian *Besserwissers* cannot be identified with the atmosphere of the great Bohemian writer's stories. Anyway, I think there are issues much less worthy of discussion, and scores of them are to be found on the pages of *Panorama* and other literary journals of today's Czechoslovakia.

This, then, is the story of my encounter with Franz Kafka. As you see, I don't know much about him. The little I know I have offered here. I hope it has shed some little light on a little-known corner of the history of the books of my compatriot.

A DISCOVERY IN ČAPEK

—

Although Karel Čapek's (1890–1938) reputation has probably never been as high as it was during the 1930s, he is still a force within Czech literature and is still known in the West as the author of the plays The Life of the Insects *and* R.U.R. *(both with his brother Josef), and of the novel* The War with the Newts.

Škvorecký's essay, published in 1976, is a piece of literary detection practised on a little-known short story of Čapek's.

THIS PAPER IS going to be short. It does not have to be long to deal with a strange discovery—one I was able to make by applying, in part, the scholarly methods worked out by the doyen of crime writers, Mr. Rex Stout, in his research on the sex of Dr.

Watson. The credit for any results I may have obtained should therefore go to this gentleman, who is truly the Leo Tolstoy of crime fiction—as another resourceful researcher in the bloody field of letters, Professor Kathryn B. Feuer, has established. By applying Mr. Stout's celebrated method to his own name, she was able to decode its true meaning. *Leo* is Latin for "lion"— from time immemorial called *rex animalium*, "the king of the animals"—and *tolstoy* is the Russian word for "stout". And so it is only proper that my thanks go to Mr. Leo Tolstoy of West Thirty-fifth Street, Manhattan, New York, *rex of crime writers*.

The story of my paper is, as I have already mentioned, a strange discovery: a discovery in Karel Čapek, that eminent Czech writer who gave us the word "robot"; it was first used in his play *R.U.R.* (Rossum's Universal Robots), which secured him a safe place in the valhalla of science-fiction writers. First of all, I'd like to ask you to remember the correct pronunciation of Čapek's name—not for petty or chauvinistic reasons, but because the wrong pronunciation of our names can sometimes give us Czechs a severe shock; and since our nerves are not used to shocks, due to some forty-odd years of over-quiet life sheltered by our mighty protectors, a disturbance like that might lead to a heart attack. I am not speaking academically, but from personal experience. When I left my native country— after it had received overwhelming military help against itself from the Soviet Union—I spent a month at Cornell University in Ithaca, New York, as visiting fellow of the Society for the Humanities. Once, attending a party given by the Society, I was approached by a youngish woman with very strange earrings. They looked like some sort of lizard or crocodile, but before I could make up my mind as to what kind of nasty animal they represented, the woman leaned over to me and whispered in a conspiratorial manner, "I know Kapek!" I jumped, I saw black, and my heart began to beat like a doped rock drummer— the reason being that Mr. Kapek was one of the leaders of the ultra-Stalinist pro-Soviet group in Prague, and had, among other things, pleaded that dissident writers and journalists be extradited and handed over to the KGB. Mr. Kapek was also one of the reasons I left Czechoslovakia; after the international help arrived I gave a dissident talk to the workers in a factory, and he immediately afterwards became the general manager. So I jumped when I heard his name from the lips of the lizard lady, and for a second thought I would faint. Then the lady winked at me and said, "Which of Kapek's works do you prefer? My personal choice is *The War with the Newts*." She pointedly touched her earrings, and it dawned on me that the crocodiles were in fact newts—and that Mr. Kapek was in fact the late Mr. Čapek.

As I said, Čapek has ensured a place for himself in the science-fiction hall of fame because of his robots. What this paper proposes to prove is that he is entitled to a place in the crime writer's valhalla as well. Not because he comes from a nation which contributed another important word to the English language, "pistol"—a word very much in use these days—but because of a more personal achievement.

There are two ways in which the mystery story touches upon the absolute: it involves death, the absolute end of life, and it strives for an absolute of its own—the perfect crime, the unsolvable mystery. Karel Čapek tried to embody both these absolutes in that part of his work which can be classified as detective fiction.

This is obvious in his treatment of death. In a proper mystery story death is only a prop, with little or no metaphysical value. Here and there, however, one encounters a writer who attempts to turn the prop into an object of philosophical probing while at the same time observing all the rules of the game. Karel Čapek was such a writer, and he obtained results that are familiar in such experiments: philosophical art he did create, but not tales acceptable as mystery stories in the technical sense. In an essay entitled "Holmesiana, or About Detective Stories", which appears in his book *In Praise of Newspapers*, he admits his defeat:

> I will own that at one time I myself tried my hand at a volume of detective stories; I meant serious business, but when I had finished, a booklet called *Roadside Crosses* was the outcome, and I am sorry to say that no one recognized my detective stories as such.

No wonder nobody recognized these stories as belonging to the classical genre, for as William E. Harkins says in his excellent book Karel Čapek:

> ...there are only two typical examples of the genre [in Čapek's *Tales from Two Pockets*...in all the remaining stories] at least one element of the traditional detective story is left out. In "Dr. Mejzlík's Case" it is the logic of detection itself which is missing. In "The Footprints" there is no solution. In "The Coupon" the identity of the murderer is unimportant....

Professor Harkins goes on to enumerate further examples of Čapek's violations of the accepted canons, but let me just point out here that in the case of "The Footprints" he is not entirely right. This story is unique in Čapek's oeuvre: it exists—unlike any other of the tales—in three different versions. It is the version entitled "The Imprint", which appears in the Czech booklet *Roadside Crosses*, that does contain a solution, as I am going to prove. This solution also represents Čapek's crowning achievement in his striving for that other absolute of detective fiction—the creation of a perfect mystery.

To prove my point I will combine a method Čapek himself used, in one of the few stories of his that abides by the technical criteria of the genre, with the method I mentioned earlier employed by Mr. "Leo Tolstoy" in his sexological enquiries. The law-abiding story—which I have not seen in translation—is called "The Poet".

In this little yarn an old beggar-woman is killed by a reckless motorist who drives away without stopping. There are three witnesses to the accident. The first is a policeman on his beat, who runs to the old woman and tries to give her first aid before he thinks of noticing the licence number; when this idea occurs to him, it is too late. The second witness is a student of mechanical engineering, who notices only the sound of the engine and deduces from it that it must have been a four-cylinder motor; otherwise he is completely in the dark as to the make of the car, its colour, and of course its licence number. The third witness is the engineer's friend, a poet, who is in the dark about everything since at the time of the accident he was soused.

The case appears insoluble, and you will notice that the situation points to a kind of perfect mystery, the only clue being a four-cylinder engine. But then the poet remembers that after coming home, and before falling into alcoholic slumber, he wrote a poem. The detective in charge of the investigation is not too hopeful that the poet's artefact can provide him with a solution, but he reads it nevertheless. It is a somewhat modernistic poem, modelled after the French surrealists whom Čapek translated so well into Czech. In my inadequate translation it goes approximately like this:

> March on dark houses one two stop
> the dawn plays on a mandolin
> oh girl why do you blush
> we'll drive a car 120 HP
> to the end
> of the world
> or to Singapore
> stop stop the car is rushing on
> our great love lies in the dust
> girl broken blossom
> a swan's neck female bosom big drum and cymbal
> why do I weep so much.

Naturally the poem does not mean much to the detective, but eventually the poet interprets the imagery of the lines so that they make sense. The marching houses are the street in which the accident occurred; the blushing girl is the red sky of the morning (the two friends were on their way home from a nightclub); the 120 horsepower engine indicates that the car was driving very fast, as if it wanted to reach the end of the world. Up to this point the poem hasn't supplied the detective with any new information. Then comes the mention of Singapore, about the meaning of which the poet himself is not sure. "I don't know," he says. "Perhaps because Malayans live there." "But what connection is there between the car and the Malayans?" wonders the detective. "Well," suggests the poet, "maybe the car was brown. I'm sure there was something brown there." And that's the first material clue derived from the poem.

The next problem the prosaic mind of the detective encounters is the line "girl broken blossom". "That's the drunken beggar-woman?" he asks ironically, and the poet replies somewhat heatedly, "You don't expect me to write about drunken beggars, do you? She was simply a woman." And finally comes the line "a swan's neck female bosom big drum and cymbal", which baffles even the poet himself. But he thinks hard. "Wait," he muses. "These are free associations.... Something must have been there that reminded me of —listen, doesn't the numeral 2 look somewhat like a swan's neck?" And here we are.... In the same associative way, the "female bosom" is interpreted as the numeral 3 and the "the big drum and cymbal" is the numeral 5, which resembles a sketchy drawing of half of a jazz-band drum with a cymbal attached on top of it. The licence number of the murderous car later proves to have been 235 (we didn't have many cars in Prague after the First World War) and the killer is duly apprehended. Thus the detective has solved the case with the help of the poet, by decoding impressions and associations which penetrated the poet's subconscious mind and emerged again, transmuted into visual images.

We see, therefore, that Čapek was a believer in the associative method of psychoanalysis, which unravels the true meaning of the symbolic images of the subconscious mind. The story, in fact, may be taken as a tribute to Čapek's famous compatriot Dr. Sigmund Freud—which, I am sure you will agree, gives us some right to treat other mysteries in Čapek's tales by the same means.

In the story which is the subject of this paper, "The Imprint", two strangers meet on a country road after a snowfall, and in the empty and snowy field beside the road they discover a mysterious footprint. It is about seven yards from the road, and there are no other footprints or tracks leading to or from it. To you, experts of the mystery story, this phenomenon of the isolated footprint that defies any rational explanation is easily recognizable: John Dickson Carr used it in a book entitled, if I remember correctly, *The Problem of the Wire Cage*, and there must have been others—though Čapek's footprint, as I shall endeavour to prove, differs in its significance. Anyway, the phenomenon belongs to the same category as the corpse in the room locked from the inside, the unbreakable alibi, or the grotesque murder perpetrated by a "superman" who later turns out to be an orang-outang, in a lovely ancient story we all know. This is how Čapek describes the baffling footprint: "an imprint of a large shoe of the American type with a very broad sole and five strong nails on the heel."

Well, the two strangers, after examining the lonely footprint, attempt to explain it away rationally—which proves very difficult. Perhaps, suggests the first one, the shoe that made the imprint was left by someone in the field before it started to snow, and then, when the snow stopped, was carried away by a bird to be its nest. Please, notice the animal agent, the bird, which undoubtedly points to a subconscious awareness of that ancient story I mentioned earlier. But this explanation is rejected; there would have been a stretch of ground uncovered by snow under the shoe when it was lifted by the bird, and anyway the shoe would have been too large for a small bird to carry, and too small for a large bird to use as nest. The other stranger then opines that somebody played a practical joke on the world by descending to the field in a balloon, making the single footstep, and then drifting off again. The man immediately apologizes for sounding improbable, but stresses the need for a rational, or, as he puts it, natural explanation; and the balloon hypothesis is certainly rational, if improbable. Other equally possible though improbable eventualities are examined and discarded: a champion jumper—perhaps one-legged—who jumped from the road into the middle of the field without losing his balance, and then jumped back to the road. Even more improbable than the balloonist.

I hardly have to point out that these efforts by the two amateur detectives follow the method described by Dorothy Sayers in "The Omnibus of Crime": "When you have eliminated all the impossibilities, then, whatever remains, however improbable, must be the truth." Now the two strangers take the method to its logical conclusion. Since no "natural" explanation is found for the elusive footstep, and since, at the same time, any explanation has to be logical to meet the demands of the case, one of the searchers for the meaning of the imprint deduces that the footprint was made by a being possessed of supernatural powers—a deity. He gives a strange little speech at this stage: "Who knows...," muses the man, "maybe the next footprint is no longer in the snow but somewhere in society, mixed up with some event or accident that has already happened...perhaps a demigod walks this way...some sort of guide, or leader, to be followed...."

An imprint made by a demigod as the solution of the mystery? We, the aficionados, naturally feel uneasy about such a solution. Didn't the great S.S. Van Dine insist in "Twenty Rules for Writing Detective Stories" that "a reader...[who] must compete with the world of spirits...is defeated *ab initio*"? And didn't that eminent legislator, Father Ronald Arbuthnott Knox, decree in "A Detective Story Decalogue" that "All supernatural or preternatural agencies are ruled out as a matter of course"? Karel Čapek is not playing fair with his readers.

Now, fair play is something the reader has a right to expect from his mystery writer. And vice versa, of course: for instance, the reader is not supposed to guess, but to deduce logically. The writer has his obligations to readers, and the readers have their obligations to the writer. The relationship is mutual and very complex.

Laws are laws, and they have to be obeyed under any circumstances. A fine-sounding platitude—but is it really so true? Let's search our minds. Wasn't there a woman once, a certain Antigone, who broke the laws of men because she felt entitled, and indeed obliged, to follow the laws of the gods? And if this example seems too remote to you, or based on supernatural or preternatural agencies, as Father Knox puts it, let's open the Holy Script, where in the Book of Charles Augustus Milverton we find the following verse: "There are certain crimes which the law cannot touch, and which therefore, to some extent, justify private revenge."* What else does this maxim express—in the legal terminology of the nineteenth century—than the right of man to disobey the laws of human society in certain cases that call for an application of divine law? And doesn't that mean that under certain circumstances the rules of fair play may be disregarded?

I have said that the duty of playing fair is mutual, binding both for the writer and for his readers. In the course of these

pages I have referred several times to a story that contains
an orang-outang; in other words, I have reminded you of our
Founding Father, Edgar Allan Poe. But was Poe universally
beloved during his lifetime? We know that he wasn't. The
readers and the critics of America drove him to a sorry death,
a slow suicide. Had he been paid what he deserved for his
seminal works he would not have died in poverty, and we can
speculate that he would have died much later. His readers, to
tell the plain truth, did not keep their side of the bargain, did
not meet their obligation towards the writer. The readers of the
early nineteenth century did not play fair with Edgar Allan Poe.
These readers, in fact, murdered Poe.

But there are no laws for this kind of murder. Therefore,
according to the Book of Milverton, the man who wants to see
justice done can resort to private revenge. This will look like a
violation of the law, but in fact it will follow a higher law and
exert a higher justice. I contend that Karel Čapek was a man
seeking justice—not for himself but for a fellow writer—and
that in seeking it he followed a higher law.

Let's therefore return to Čapek's story, which seemingly vi-
olates one of the basic laws of our genre. As we have seen
it is full of indirect references to poor Poe, the victim of our
readers' crime. The two detectives employ the ratiocinative
technique of Chevalier Dupin. An animal is introduced as the
possible culprit. And the lofty speech of one of the amateur
detectives (remember that Dupin wasn't a professional policeman either) clearly points to—whom do you think? "The
next footprint...mixed up with some event or accident...perhaps
a demigod walks this way...some sort of...leader to be followed...."

All right, you may say, this is all very nice, but surely it is a
clear case of overinterpretation. Has it ever been established,
for one thing, that Čapek really *knew* Poe's writings?

On this point I can produce evidence without any difficulty.
First of all, Poe is *the* American author in Czechoslovakia. No
fewer than twenty-five different translations of "The Raven"
have been done to date—maybe more—and when in 1954 I
worked on a bibliography of Czech translations of American
literature, I found two hundred or so Poe titles published between 1891 and 1954. Moreover, in his rather interesting essay

"Holmesiana, or About Detective Stories" Čapek mentions Poe explicitly four times, and one reference to the master is especially significant in the context of this paper, for it proves that Čapek not only knew that lovely first story, but had a deep understanding of Poe's sarcastic treatment of the organized police; an attitude mirrored, by the way, in many of Čapek's own tales:

> The police would solve the murders in the Rue Morgue without much ado if on the basis of reliable experience it could be said that as a rule such murders are committed by orang-outangs.

Does that satisfy you? We have external evidence that Čapek knew Poe. We have internal evidence in "The Imprint" that Čapek was—consciously or subconsciously, it doesn't really matter which—patterning his story on the Dupin method and investing it with motifs from "The Murders in the Rue Morgue". This is certainly enough to form a working hypothesis. But since we are dealing with a mystery story, what we need is conclusive, irrefutable proof.

To find it, let us once more return to the tale and consider, first of all, its title. In Czech it is "Šlépéj", which means "footprint". But it is a slightly obsolete word; the word generally used in spoken language in Čapek's time (Čapek was the pioneer in replacing bookish language with the vernacular in fiction) and the word which predominates in modern Czech is its synonym *stopa*. This word is also a homonym for both "trace" and "clue". Well, in the name of Rex Stout, isn't this a clear indication that the footprint in the story is a clue to the solution of the footprint's mystery?

Let's therefore reread the description of that footprint, that trace, that clue. It was an "imprint of a large shoe of the *American* type with a very broad sole and *five* strong nails on the heel" (emphasis added). Well, in the name of Čapek's Freudian poet, isn't the associative interpretation of this clue—based on the fact that impressions and associations that penetrate the writer's subconscious mind have a tendency to emerge again in visual images—more than obvious, and quite unequivocal? What is an American shoe doing in the midst of the Bohemian countryside? And why exactly five strong nails?

Yes, the symbolic meaning, the sublimation of a suppressed guilt, is more than clear. "The Murders in the Rue Morgue", "The Mystery of Marie Roget", "The Purloined Letter", "The Gold Bug", and "Thou Art the Man" are universally accepted as the first five true mystery stories of literature, stories that laid the foundations for our art and that contain all the principal methods, patterns, formulas, and rules. The *five* strong nails in the shoe of an *American* perpetrator of a *practical joke on the world* which amounts to a *perfect mystery*. All that in addition to the fact that the name of our Founding Father in one of its forms contains exactly five letters: E.A. Poe.

And so I suggest that Karel Čapek wrote his little tale about the mysterious clue as a coded—perhaps subconsciously coded—tribute to the Master: it was EAPOE (to imitate the orthography of his biographer Daniel Hoffman) himself who stepped with his American shoe onto the snowy field in Čapek's Bohemia, leaving the imprint of the five strong, solid American nails which have provided us with our solution. Or if you are more mystically inclined—as Čapek himself was—it may have been EAPOE in spiritual form who used a spirit pen, like Dickens in *The Mystery of Edwin Drood Complete*, to pull this malicious joke on the descendants of the readers who had murdered him by their indifference. By creating a perfectly insoluble mystery which breaks the laws of our game while following the higher laws of divine poetic justice, he took his personal revenge on us, the money-making exploiters of his discoveries.

* *The Holy Script is, of course, the work of Sir Arthur Conan Doyle—in this case* The Return of Sherlock Holmes.

Introducing Bohumil Hrabal

———

*This two-part essay about the Czech short-story writer
and novelist Bohumil Hrabal (born 1914) is based on
two separate introductions. The first was to the English
translation of Hrabal's short-story collection* The Death
of Mr. Baltisberger, *and the second was to Hrabal's novel*
Closely Watched Trains. *The latter was made into a
motion picture, which won the 1967 Academy Award for
Best Foreign Film.*

*A historical note: Škvorecký published the intro-
duction to* The Death of Mr. Baltisberger *under the
pseudonym Daniel S. Miritz because the Czechoslovak
government objected to having Hrabal introduced by him.*

I

THE OCCASIONAL successes enjoyed by authors who write in one
of the world's "minor" languages often have unfortunate consequences for other writers who subsequently compose in that
language. Reviewers unfamiliar with the "minor" language
tend to create pigeonholes to use in classifying its entire diverse literature. They fall back on oversimplification, to the
general satisfaction of their readers, and to the trivial irrita-
tion of the authors thus pigeonholed. For example, any Czech
writer displaying even the lightest sense of humour is likely to
be classified as a successor to Jaroslav Hašek (*The Good Soldier Švejk*). But—although Bohumil Hrabal personally admires
this Czech classic—pasting the label "Švejk" across the entirety
of his own short stories is only a little closer to the mark than
describing William Faulkner as "Mark Twainian" because both
authors used folksy material.

There is yet another misconception that may attach itself to
Hrabal, though this collection should do much to remedy it.

The Academy Award–winning film *Closely Watched Trains* was based on a story that Hrabal wrote in the early fifties entitled "The Legend of Cain". I say this not as a criticism, but rather to indicate that the true Hrabal, the one who did much in the sixties to upset ideas about Czech literature, is to be found neither in Menzel's famous film, nor in the fact that Hrabal, like Hašek, likes to drink beer in taverns. The true Hrabal can be found in these stories. Works of art, they are a synthesis of "high" and "low", and the influences that formed them extend far beyond the borders of Prague, or of Czech literature.

What we have here is above all urban folklore, filtered through the author's own experiences. Born in 1914, Hrabal graduated from Charles University with a doctorate in law, but in the madhouse that was Europe around the middle of this century the closest he ever came to the bar was in any number of Prague's pubs.

His biography is what we in Europe used to think of as "American"; a jack of all trades, he has been a travelling salesman, a steelworker, a dealer in scrap paper, a stagehand. He married a charming waitress who appears to have stepped right out of one of his stories, and he stylized himself into the figure of a beer drinker who thinks like an intellectual but speaks in the language of the palavering populace. With the typical understatement of a writer subjected to an excess of critical attention, he refers to himself not as a writer but as a reporter, in the original sense of the word: a chronicler of beer-hall stories.

In 1968, at one of our last joint meetings with readers in Czechoslovakia, he complained, "I'm as good as done for. Those guys heard about the money I'm supposed to be raking in by putting their stories down on paper, and so now whenever I walk into a tavern, all I hear is 'Here he comes, the great writer! Wants to make another hundred thousand by just sitting and listening.' And they clam up and scowl in their beer."

Obviously Hrabal is not done for, not by a long shot, and this anecdote is just another example of his palavering. But we do find traces of folklore in his works, and the Western reader needn't look far to see that these stories have their roots deep in the same kind of soil in which the tall tales of America germinated. In one story, "Palaverers", an old man is blown

twenty feet into the air with a quarter-ton of excrement—isn't
he a not too distant cousin of Paul Bunyan, Davy Crockett, or
Pecos Bill?

Yet the sense of fun characterized by the Davy Crocketts
has long since transcended the borders of the United States.
Through silent film comedies—the forgotten art of the gag—it
joined hands with jazz to leave a noticeable mark on Czech art
as far back as the twenties, blending with the native folklore of
Prague's urban milieu to create an infrangible alloy. That is why
Hrabal garnishes his stories with scenes from the early two-
reelers of Charlie Chaplin, Buster Keaton, and Lupino Lane.
Take, for instance, the youth so extraordinarily absorbed in
reading that he even takes a leak with his nose in a book; or
the girl who breaks through a door panel with her head and
knocks down a neighbour lady snooping at the keyhole; or the
old geezer with a pot of sauerkraut in his hand, following the
splendid butt of a shapely beauty down the street....

But there are other unexpected clues to be found. In the title
story, the narration of Uncle Pepin—who, incidentally, is based
on Hrabal's real-life uncle of the same name—comes up with
an element from classical American literary theory, stripped of
the author's name and dropped a few notches to accommodate
the needs of tavern yarn-spinners: "[I] consoled her with the
thought that the poets say the most beautiful thing in the world
is a dead beauty." Could it be that the shade of Edgar Allan Poe's
radiant Lenore has somehow found its way to the distant tavern
where the Good Soldier Švejk used to tell his tales about dog
turds? Or was it perhaps imported by the erudite ex-stagehand
and admirer of Nelson Algren and William Faulkner? The
still untranslated novella *Dancing Lessons for the Elderly and
Advanced*, written in one book-long sentence, is a direct tribute
to Faulkner.

There is no telling. So far, all of this could be part of the
genuine folklore experience—including the pair of naked cary-
atids who meet during a performance of *Troilus and Cressida*.
And the common woman who reads Milton. For the fact is that
we are reading of Prague, a city imbued with culture, in a nation whose nearly extinct language was artificially revived by a
group of eighteenth- and nineteenth-century intellectuals using
translations of Milton, Byron, and Shakespeare...and Poe.

But as we look further into Hrabal, we find ourselves in pure literature. Consider the story called "Romance":

> she carried the hemisphere of the half-loaf of bread beside that black hair of hers and the white crust sketched her path in the darkness....

Or "A Prague Nativity":

> the black propman's green skull emerged from the black velvet backdrop...then, as black velvet drapes were slipped open by the green skull suddenly as it had appeared, it slipped back into the deep purple darkness....

Now we are close to Stephen Crane, both his impressionistic and his expressionistic aspects. Which is not to say that the author of *Maggie* and "The Monster" was Hrabal's model, but rather that they both had one supremely important source of inspiration in common: the fine arts. The key to Crane's imagination is impressionism, the trend that launched modern art. The key to the imagination that is Hrabal's is the most durable scion of modern art's family tree: surrealism.

"I don't actually write," Hrabal used to say in his talks with readers. "I cut, and then glue the cut-outs together into collages." Sometimes he does it literally, without using his own words: "The Reader's Own Mortuary Ballad" (from the untranslated collection *Mortuary Ballads and Legends*) is in fact a literary collage of fragments chosen from letters from his readers, without a single word added by the author. For the most part, however, Hrabal's collages are made up of stories that, having passed through a sophisticated imagination, are glued together by a poetic text. But collages they remain: forceful juxtapositions of images which—unlike Eisenstein's abstract montages—stress the concreteness of experience. Once removed from its accustomed contexts and placed by means of collages in the "liberated" context of dreams, palavering, and fantasy, this concreteness of experience becomes a reality more real than reality itself: a surreality. A reality that is *alcoholic*, a manipulation of its concrete elements basically unrestricted by any sort of realism—Dali's "critical paranoia", André Breton's black humour.

When a work of art transcends the frontiers of its homeland, it takes on a dual existence, as it were: its native existence, and its existence abroad. For the American reader, Hrabal will, I hope, appear as an interesting and original, perhaps an experimental, author of short stories. For Czechoslovakia, Hrabal was a revolution. In Czechoslovakia, Hrabal represents a category all his own.

Perhaps a brief excursion into the past would be appropriate. I met Hrabal under circumstances that sound like one of his own stories. In the early fifties when I was an editor at a publishing house, one of my duties was delivering obsolete galley proofs to the scrap-paper salvage centre. The fellow in the patched overalls there would examine my proofs with interest. Then he would launch into a fluent discussion of literature; Breton's *Nadja*, I think, was his subject that day. Later on this fellow and I would meet at the flat of poet and artist Jiří Kolář (best known in the West for his collages), a typical centre of the Czech avant-garde, where we discussed abstract expressionism or whatever else was in the air in those days. We also read aloud our verses and stories. It was at some of these sessions that I first heard "The Death of Mr. Baltisberger", "The Legend of Cain", "Jarmilka", and others.

But these were only private meetings; none of us was publishing anything. The literary taste of the times was different. It had to change before Hrabal's strange, unique tales could find their way to more readers than just the few people interested in what was not quite in vogue—at least with the publishers.

Eventually the taste of the times did change. And with the publication of *Lark on a String* in 1963 (Hrabal's first attempt to publish it, in 1958, did not meet with success), the revolution came.

To understand why it was a revolution is, perhaps, not easy for a Western reader, and an attempt to explain it would require something resembling a Ph.D. thesis. But perhaps such an explanation is not really necessary. Maybe it is enough to bring "The World Cafeteria" to the reader's attention. In this wonderful story he will find a character of key significance:

the artist of "absolute graphics". This character has difficulties finding a gallery willing to exhibit his work. But the workers in the factory where he has a job like his unconventional art and see to it that he has an exhibition right at the factory, despite the protests of the functionary in charge of culture—a man who shares the taste of the times. The workers come into direct contact with modern art for the first time, through the efforts of their fellow employee. They do not know anything about the taste of the times, hence they cannot see why this man and this kind of weird picture should not be shown to the public. This story is, once again, an incident that actually happened to a friend of Hrabal's—Vladimír Boudník—but at the same time it is a metaphor for Hrabal's own struggle, and for the struggle of modern art against misunderstanding.

I hope there is no misunderstanding now about how Hrabal brought a revolutionary new quality to Czech prose during the late fifties and early sixties.

II

In Czechoslovakia, Bohumil Hrabal is considered almost a national hero, a revolutionary of prose, an innovator, a revitalizer of language: in short, a man who has opened up new vistas for Czech writing, extricating it from the vicious circle of propaganda and setting it back on the path of art. *Closely Watched Trains*, the story of an adolescent boy with an intimate personal problem who commits an act of heroism that is more a consequence of sexual euphoria than premeditated patriotism, is undeniably an original work from the hand of a master storyteller. American literature, however, has a long tradition of what might be called deliberate "deheroization" of war—ranging from the ingenuous *The Red Badge of Courage* through Frederic Henry's valorous deeds while eating cheese in *A Farewell to Arms*, right down to Joseph Heller's *Catch-22*, and, for all I know, to works even less reverential—and therefore I'm not entirely certain that the adolescent tragicomedy of Miloš Hrma will seem bold enough in content and innovative enough in form to make Hrabal's apotheosis wholly comprehensible to the Western reader. I'm afraid one simply has to know the basic facts of socialist realism—not its theory, for socialist realism has no theory worth taking seriously, but its history.

When William Dean Howells was preaching realism, he advised American writers to concentrate on "the rosier aspects of American life, because they are the more American." He could have had no idea at the time that he was in fact articulating the starting point for a category of art that would take power much later and in another country altogether. In the beginning this category was genuinely intended to be no more than an emphasis on the "rosier aspects" of Soviet life; or, translated into Communist party cant: the old-style realism of the critical or bourgeois variety, despite frequently harsh criticism, was fundamentally just recording the status quo; socialist realism was supposed to present reality not merely as it actually was at the moment but also "in its revolutionary development and perspectives." In plain terms, reality was to be painted pink.

Whatever Maxim Gorky meant when he introduced the term to the Soviet public, the party bureaucrats—men whom the Ukrainian film director Alexander Dovzhenko, in his diary, labelled "cutthroats, know-nothings", and, most frequently, "dog-turds"—understood Gorky's ruminations on socialist realism as a call to eliminate from the reality of socialism anything that might cast a shadow over the rosy hues: first, any social criticism of the post-revolutionary status quo, and secondly, aspects that they considered "decadent and offensive to socialist morality", mainly violent death (except in the grand heroic mode) and sex (except Victorian-style innuendo). In the late stages of Stalinism things became so confusing that these "decadent" human affairs were even censored out of translated novels of social criticism from the capitalist world.

Perhaps it will now be somewhat clearer to the uninitiated why a story combining *ejaculatio praecox* and anti-Nazi sabotage hit the Victorianized and sex-starved Czechoslovak market like a bomb. A far less explicit blending of the sexual drive with war-time heroism led my own book *The Cowards* to be seized by the censor seven years earlier, setting in motion a landslide of bans that buried Hrabal's first collection of short stories, *Perličky na dně* (*Pearls on the Bottom*), which was withdrawn a week before publication. *Closely Watched Trains*, however, did not appear until 1965, in a period when the "thaw" was well under way, when the Stalinists were keeping a low profile and their literary and moralistic dogmas were no longer taken seriously. Moreover, *Closely Watched Trains* appeared in a form that from the censor's point of view was far more publishable than its original version, which Hrabal had written in 1949, a year after the Communist takeover, when he was still very much an underground writer.

Sometime in 1950 Hrabal read this original version, called "The Legend of Cain", at a gathering of Jiří Kolář's underground literary circle. It was there that I first listened to the dark tale of an existentially motivated suicide attempt that had taken place in a hotel in the midst of an apocalyptic war. Hrabal did not publish this original version of the story until 1968, the year of the Prague Spring, in a volume entitled *Moritáty a legendy* (*Macabrosa and Legends*). It has not been republished since.

There is a great deal less sex in "The Legend of Cain", and to the extent that it is there, the narrator has no particular problem with it. On the other hand, the story does contain a great many ordinary human deaths that have nothing to do with heroism. Shortly after delivering the coup de grâce to a mortally wounded German soldier, the narrator himself is shot by a Czech guard. This absurd ending, more typical of Albert Camus than of laureates of the Stalin Prize, is very unlike the socially significant demise of Miloš Hrma in *Closely Watched Trains*. The main characters of "The Legend of Cain" are utterly obsessed with death. The doctor who in *Closely Watched Trains* advises Miloš how to deal with his sexual problem commits suicide in "The Legend of Cain" by tying himself up—and it is not clear whether the narrator helped him in this—and jumping into a furnace: "Before the furnace a huddled black puppet was lying. It was charred all over, and its right eye, molten and fallen out of the skull, was staring at me. When I walked down a few steps, it burst open and began flowing out quietly on the floor."

The novella's black imagination reaches a peak with the hero's vision of a "beautiful suicide" worthy of the imagination of Edgar Allan Poe, in the terms of socialist realism an archdecadent who even appealed to Dostoevsky: "I knew a religious man who craved for holiness so much that one night he lifted the lid of a crypt in the local church, and having entangled himself in the shrouds and in the petrified intestines of that holy woman, he shot himself through the head and at the same time closed the lid so that he was not found until years later. Until he looked almost like that saint." The novella is bursting with such "unacceptable" passages. Moreover, Hrabal had not written it right after the war but after the Communist putsch in 1948, and it may not be irrelevant to recall that in Czechoslovakia that was the beginning of an era of "class liquidation" and "layered graves", as they were called: the executed, because there were so many of them, were buried one on top of the other, in layers, to save space. It was also a time when the police chauffeur responsible for scattering over the roads of north Bohemia the ashes of those twelve innocent men hanged after the Rudolf Slánský trial quipped in the canteen of the Ministry of the Interior that he'd never been able to fit twelve men into his car before. If there is any genuinely morbid post-war prose from Czechoslovakia, the "The Legend of Cain" is it. I would prefer, however, to say that the age itself was morbid. Good literature merely reflected that morbidity.

Despite the "thaw", then, "The Legend of Cain" was still too strong a book for 1965, and so Hrabal, in his own words "wove a braid" from it called *Closely Watched Trains*. Something of the horrors of "The Legend of Cain" remains—the cruel things done to animals, for instance—and Hrabal added others: the stories of the nurse, Beatrice, who eases badly burned German soldiers into death, and of the charwoman who cleans up the blood after executions. Nevertheless, it was an essentially different book, and it became the bestseller of the 1960s.

Many of Hrabal's old friends, particularly those who remained staunch nonconformists despite the liberalizing trend, were disappointed. They called *Closely Watched Trains* "prettied-up" Hrabal and regretted that the author had gone so far out of his way to appeal to conventional taste. I myself am not sure who is right, but two things seem beyond dispute. Formally, *Closely Watched Trains* is smoother, more masterfully executed than the raw "Legend of Cain". The author took what was essentially a linear story, despite some flashbacks, and subjected it to Joseph Conrad's "deliberate confusion"—or, if you like, Hrabal formally modernized it, though he did return to the chronological mode in the film scenario of *Closely Watched Trains*. On the other hand, it is also beyond dispute that, for all its freshness and originality, *Closely Watched Trains* presents a far more conventional literary representation of war than the Boschian visions of "The Legend of Cain". This difference, perhaps, can best be made clear in a key scene that occurs in both stories, in which Cain and Miloš are held hostage on the munitions train and confronted by the scarred SS captain. In "The Legend of Cain" this officer allows Cain to get off the train without noticing his scarred wrist:

> His narrow lips were seeking, in the last moment when everything would soon be lost, some object for which he would be forgiven.... I saw...that he knew I was not his enemy, but that I was his lucky chance, his good deed, which, perhaps, Providence would weigh up on its scales.... Besides, it was disagreeable today to sully the agreeable end of war.... He was smiling. His brutal soul received the first candy, and he was drunk with magnanimity.... I told myself: I am grateful to you, devil, because I accept my life from your hands. I am forced to declare you to be my angel. You are my God.... [The two SS men] threw down some cigarettes after me and smiled at me. Because why should they be angry when the commander is not? Why should they butcher me when the commander, out of perversity, does not wish me butchered?

This is a straight, dispassionate, and rugged treatment of a harsh war experience. The captain is not a man who, mellowed by the horrors of battle, is reminded of a common humanity. He is not made human by any sentimental solidarity with another comrade in death. He remains the whimsical, inscrutable Nazi. Compare how differently the same man with a duelling scar appears in *Closely Watched Trains*:

> The captain's eyes were gazing now at my wrist, where I, too, had a scar.... Perhaps this captain had already learned much more, perhaps he was looking at

everything now from the opposite viewpoint, and his eyes...were all staring at my wrist, and the captain stretched out his little whip, and with it drew back my other sleeve, too, and looked at the second scar. "*Kamerad,*" he said.

One can see why the nonconformist critics called this "braid" of a story a "prettifying" of Hrabal and of reality. Indeed, shifts like these smack dangerously of humanitarian, if not downright sentimental, clichés, of which Hrabal's early prose was remarkably free. One can sense that Hrabal was aware of what had happened to him, for in a self-deprecating conclusion to a later book of his called *Poupata* (*The Buds*), he wrote:

A cabdriver...drove me this year from the Barrandov studios, and suddenly he laughed and asked me, "Are you Mr. Hrabal?"
I replied, "Indeed I am."
And he said, "Ha, ha, they've outsmarted you, haven't they? You wanted to be a *poète maudit*, and they've turned you into a socialist realist. That's what I call a real achievement."

The nonconformist avant-garde, then, saw *Closely Watched Trains* as "prettied-up" Hrabal, but this harsh criticism of a bestseller must be understood in the context of the time and the country. Because an oppressive regime is always most unjust towards the creators of all sorts of "*entartete Kunst*", the avant-garde has a tendency to be unfair in its judgement of those whom the oppressive regime, however hesitatingly, tolerates. It is a narrow-minded view, and in the democratic world one can afford to be more liberal. Here, the small compromises one makes do not play into the hands of some Party cultural secretary who would be happier if there were no writers and no culture at all, just hacks and an entertainment industry.

Objectively, I don't think there can be much doubt that, compared to the dark and often excessively encoded and private world of "The Legend of Cain", *Closely Watched Trains* is a generally more accessible and dazzling display of storytelling. It still contains quite enough of human death, but here Hrabal balances it, as he does not in "The Legend of Cain", with something no less human, something that has annulled death for generation after generation: sex or, if you prefer, love—its splendour, its despair (as embodied in the stationmaster), and its evenly matched battle (so far) with the angel of Thanatos. I would say that in the literature of the so-called socialist states, *Closely Watched Trains* is, as far as I know, the only genuinely successful, genuinely persuasive "optimistic tragedy". In this sense it achieves what Gorky may have had in mind, and what Dovzhenko's "dog-turds" never have and never will understand. Witness the fate of Jiří Menzel's film version of *Closely Watched Trains*: awarded an Oscar for Best Foreign Film of 1967, banned after the Soviet invasion of Czechoslovakia, and never re-released. Witness also the fact that as I write this there has still not been a reprinting of the novella. Moreover, unlike "The Legend of Cain", *Closely Watched Trains* has that blend of tragedy and humour that is so typical of life in Central Europe.

Humour of a sometimes rather bawdy variety is inherent in the very names of the characters, which unabashedly belong to the tradition—or, if you like, the convention—of symbolic nomenclature. Miloš Hrma might be translated as Sweetheart Cunt-Hair; Hubička means Tender Kiss; Zdenička Svatá (she is called Virginia in the translation) is Saint Sidonia; Viktoria Freie elicits associations of Victorious Freedom, both in the general sense of the expression as it would have been used by resistance fighters and in Miloš's own private sense: moreover, the Czech pronunciation of the word Freie (*freye*) suggests a sexual and alcoholic frolic. Sex is thus a main source of humour, as it usually is and has always been, from *The Canterbury Tales* to *The Good Soldier Švejk*.

Hrabal's life story is typical of that of a writer who hides a lyrical tangle of nerves beneath a tough, Hemingway exterior. As such, of course, he is a misfit in socialist society, at least in the kind that existed in his country under the Nazis and exists today under the neo-Stalinists. He went unpublished during the 1950s, although everyone knowledgeable in Prague was aware of his existence, until 1956, when Jiří Kolář assumed the risk of issuing a semi-legal, not-for-sale Bibliophile Club edition of Hrabal's story "Conversations with People".

In the 1960s, when that strange socialism imported into Czechoslovakia from the Russian empire began to take on a slightly more human face, Hrabal became a literary star. The most important thing about him, however, was that he personified an ideal quality, one that in his memoirs, *The Oak and the Calf*, Alexander Solzhenitsyn ascribes to Alexander Tvardovsky: he became "a writer of the people...he wrote as freely as one breathes." Naturally, Hrabal supported Alexander Dubček and his ill-fated experiment with socialism in 1968. Consequently, after the Soviet invasion—when Dubček's now-deposed parliamentary chairman, the populist leader Josef Smrkovský, attended Hrabal's private birthday party—the secret police got their hooks into Hrabal. The poet's nerves did not hold out, and the result was a prolonged and critical period of hospitalization. Then he broke, or rather bent somewhat, as so many before him had done. He publicly declared his support for "socialism", which he took pains not to define—and how many different socialisms exist in the world today?—and he signed the Anti-Charter, a document forced upon the creative community by the Czechoslovak regime as a reaction to Charter 77, the human-rights manifesto issued by many of his old friends.

As a reward, the regime has officially published, so far, three new books by him. One is a collection of literary fragments; another is a charmingly idealized portrait of his mother, free of any explicitly sexual or existential connotations; and the third encountered the same fate as "The Legend of Cain", except in a far more drastic form. *The Town Where Time Stopped* is philosophically not far removed from "The Legend of Cain", but for the Prague edition, published as *The Beauty of Sadness* (the original manuscript was published under its original title without the author's permission by an exile publishing house), Hrabal altered his characteristically spontaneous diction so that, as the popular definition of socialist realism runs, "even the comrades from the Central Committee would understand it". Worst of all, he completely eliminated a long and powerful conclusion containing the book's main message. The passage is in fact a lyrical requiem, delivered in strong, Waughian tones, for the world of beauty which, in the perversion of "class justice", has been destroyed by the "new world"—that is, by Communism. This requiem culminates in a poetic report on the state of the author's soul during his "illness" after 1968, when he thought long about what he would still like to write:

> *Beloved*, this first (and future) book of mine, will be borne gently by the sensuous dynamics of Matisse's *Luxe, calme et voluptée....* It will be suffused with the brilliant pigment of light and space. The second book will be called *Surprise in the Woods*, and it will be full of fear and stress and vain efforts to adapt, like [Edvard] Munch's lyrical expressionism. In it I shall attempt something I have been thinking about for many years, something that, deriving from realistic drawings, gradually moves towards a state of deformation and at last becomes something that is the essence of action painting, as practised by Jackson Pollock.

I don't know whether Hrabal has written this work yet or not. If the situation in Prague, described by Heinrich Böll as "the graveyard of culture", persists, I am afraid that this story will join the other manuscripts in Hrabal's desk drawer—the best of his manuscripts: *The Town Where Time Stopped, I Served the King of England, Too Loud a Solitude*.

THE SPILLING OF THE BEANS

———

This is a much-expanded version of an essay which first appeared in 1985 in The New York Times. *Its focus is on translation and what the world of literature and culture looks like to writers from "small countries" and "small languages".*

Škvorecký's incidental comments on some of the problems faced by East and Central European translators of Sir Arthur Conan Doyle can be compared to Vladimir

Voinovich's anecdote (reported in The Anti-Soviet Soviet Union, *p. 226) about the Soviet film that had to be
shelved because Holmes mentions in it that Watson has
just returned from Afghanistan.*

A TRANSLATOR HAS received the commission to render into English
a five-hundred-page novel at five cents per word, with instructions to perform his task within three months. The author is
"hot": either a person who has just been awarded a prestigious
literary prize, or a celebrated dissident recently shipped away
to Siberia, or someone whose mistress has cut off his head because she figured prominently and unflatteringly in his current
bestseller. Right on page one our speedy worker comes across
the following line: "Sam has spilled the beans, and now we're in
a jam." The translator either knows the meaning of the idioms,
or looks them up in a dictionary. There he finds: "*Spill the beans,
Informal,* disclose a secret, either accidentally or imprudently,
thereby ruining a surprise or plan." "*Be in a jam, Informal,* to be
in a difficult situation." Working at five cents a word, and with
the deadline looming over him, the translator does not search
his memory for adequate phrases in his own language; he types,
"Sam has disclosed our secret, and now we are in a difficult situation." Then he rushes on. Eventually he meets his deadline
and comes up with a translation that contains no mistakes, for
he is a conscientious worker, and that (as his editor, ignorant
of the language of the original, assures him) "reads well", because he is a good English stylist. Nobody in the five hundred
pages spills any beans, nobody pulls anybody's leg. The smooth
text resembles a Van Gogh sunflower excellently reproduced in
black and white.

Certainly something of the power of the original travels
across to the foreign reader; sometimes quite a lot. Literature, though it is primarily an art of words, does not rely
entirely on the *mot juste*. A Theodore Dreiser is not as endan-
gered by translators as an Emily Dickinson. For it is when the
right word becomes the *sine qua non* of success—as in subtle
lyric poetry—that our fast-working, non-idiomatic, and under-
paid translator turns into the literary murderer described by
Vladimir Nabokov:

What is a translation? On a platter
A poet's pale and glaring head,
A parrot's screech, a monkey's chatter,
And profanation of the dead.

Muddled stylists, raconteurs suffering from verbal diarrhoea whose impact depends mainly on their vision, on some burning passion that shines through the convoluted verbiage, have little to fear from translators; occasionally a good stylist even improves on a visionary or a man filled with too much class hatred and little patience to fine-tune his words. The same thing sometimes happens with ancient writers; Chaucer in his original Middle English is inaccessible to the average English reader, but he changes into a profoundly readable entertainer in a good modern rendition into a foreign tongue. Judging by the complaints of some of my Canadian students forced to work their way through Dickens, the Victorian master, because of his nineteenth-century diction, has lost something of his spellbinding magic—yet if a good translation of *Little Dorrit* or *David Copperfield* preserves Dickens' original freshness, its effect on the foreign reader may be comparable to the enthusiasm of the crowds that, a century ago, used to wait at newsstands for a new instalment of Boz's latest melodrama. Not much harm is done to writers like Kafka, whose verbal art depends on aspects of German other than idiomatic usage; his was the language of the Prague Germans cut off from the German *Volk*, the main, sometimes the only, source of verbal inventiveness. And writers working in and influenced by the rational, not mimetic, tradition of literature, such as Milan Kundera, fare much better at the hands of their translators than, say, a Mark Twain.

That great improviser seems to have been aware of the dangers of dissolving a story into another tongue. In "The Celebrated Jumping Frog of Calaveras County" and "Private History of the 'Jumping Frog' Story" he ascribes the lack of success of his tale in France to a bad translation, and as proof offers his own retranslation of the French version.

Twain's original:

"Now, if you're ready, set him alongside of Dan'l, with his fore paws just even with Dan'l's, and I'll give the word." Then he says, "One-two-three-*git!*" and him and the feller touched up the frogs from behind, and the new frog hopped off lively; but Dan'l give a heave, and hysted up his shoulders—so—like a Frenchman, but it warn't no use.

Twain's retranslation:

"Now if you be ready, put him all against Daniel, with their before-feet upon the same line, and I give the signal"—then he added: "One, two, three—advance!"
Him and the individual touched their frogs by behind, and the frog new put to jump smartly, but Daniel himself lifted ponderously, exalted the shoulders thus, like a Frenchman—to what good?

It is all tongue in cheek, of course, and Twain too often cannot resist the temptation to anchor his fun in the transparent trick of literal translation, in slavishly keeping the French word order, and in similar primitivisms of which a professional translator is rarely guilty. Yet I hope the excerpt illustrates my point. Sometimes I amuse myself by imagining Mark Twain having been born a Sam Klemens in Bohemia—where he once tried taking a cure (see his "Marienbad, a Health Factory"). As a youngster he would have got involved in the revolution of 1848; after its defeat, like many others, he would have emigrated to America and tried his luck prospecting in California. There he would have written the story of Dan'l the Frog in Czech, and had it translated into English by one of the many German veterans of the Civil War. Well, he might have become the star author of the old August Geringer Bohemian Publishing House in Chicago; that, however, brought no national fame and no money. Mr. Klemens would have ended his days as a poor but respected raconteur, celebrated for his funny tales in all the Czech pubs of the Windy City.

Such are some of the world's injustices. It is unjust, if you are a writer, to be born into a nation whose language territory covers a piece of land slightly larger than New York City. If you have this kind of bad luck you'd better become a film director, for foreign films are essentially subtitled pictures that move, a sort of sophisticated comic strip in motion, and I don't suppose that success in that popular genre ever depended on what was in the balloon.

But we live in times that are acutely aware of such and similar injustices, and among people who are touchingly considerate, even self-deprecatory, in order not to hurt the feelings of a black, an ethnic, or a "broad". And yet there has never been much knowledge—and why should there be?—about that New York–sized strip of land I come from, that inland island of Bohemia. Chaucer undoubtedly knew about it; in his days it was a European superpower, and the bard was apparently inspired to his *The Parlement of Fowles* by the marriage of Richard II to the pretty Anne of Bohemia. But between Chaucer and the—one would hope—better-informed present-day scribes, there seems to be half a millennium of almost total obscurity. Shakespeare laboured under the impression that Bohemia was an island in the Mediterranean. Sir Arthur Conan Doyle apparently believed that in 1888 the ruler of Bohemia was a Jewish king by the name of Ormstein—clearly the stout Britisher's misspelling of Ohrenstein. Jerome K. Jerome presumably knew where he was when he was in Prague—he travelled before the age of the jet plane, that devilish modern invention which left Big Joe Turner, performing at a jazz festival in Prague, utterly convinced that he was in Warsaw—yet Jerome, in *Three Men on the Bummel*, theorized that Czech must be related to Chinese as it uses an alphabet of forty-two letters, whereas English has only twenty-six. With these and similar precedents, Neville Chamberlain's notorious public confession of ignorance of the land of the Czechs no longer sounds so shameful.

Americans fared a little better in Central European topography—in the old days at least. According to Cotton Mather's venerable *Magnalia Christi Americana* (1702), John Winthrop invited Jan Amos Komenský (Comenius) to come to America and become the first president of Harvard College. But Winthrop probably did not strike up his correspondence with the celebrated educator until Comenius was an exile in Holland, and God only knows whether the governor believed him to be

Deutsch or Dutch. I have already mentioned Mark Twain, who drank the waters in Marienbad and reported a parliamentary brawl in Vienna in which Czech deputies noisily participated— see his "Stirring Times in Austria". James Huneker, the music critic who, alone among American musical arbiters, did not like the *New World Symphony* when it was first performed in New York, made a thirsty pilgrimage to the springs of Pilsner Urquell, and is also responsible for the first appearance of Antonín Dvořák in fiction; the composer briefly enters the pages of Huneker's abortive novel *Painted Veils*. Hemingway, although he never set foot on Czech territory, obviously knew enough to support the Švejkian image of the Czechs in *A Farewell to Arms*, and of course Willa Cather knew everything—albeit only about American Czechs. After that things got progressively worse, and contemporary American authors writing about Bohemia not only seem not to bother—in this age of universal travel—to visit the setting of their novels, they do very little homework, with results that are amusing. There are honourable exceptions. Philip Roth, for instance, with his accurate topography and mood of Prague in *The Professor of Desire*, is one. To a certain extent Helen MacInnes is another, for she at least did some quick research in the Foreign News section of *The New York Times*, and consequently the heroes of her thriller *The Snare of the Hunter*, both positive and negative, bear the names of post-1968 ministers of the Czech government. But these are no more than exceptions.

On the whole, the peaceful Czechs seem to inspire American writers mostly to thrillers. A couple of years ago I became involved in the script for *The Amateur*, a film based on the best-selling novel by Robert Littell. To be fair to the author, he did apparently use a Czech adviser—but this person must have been a fifth-generation American Czech, or else someone with a predilection for practical jokes. Czech-American actors were cast in the roles of Czechs in this melodrama set in a totally unrecognizable Prague, but when they were given the script it puzzled them. For instance, a wife asks her husband something like this at the breakfast table: "My dearly beloved one, shall I please you by selecting some eggs and putting them into boiling water so that after a lapse of time they will be hardened and eatable?" The producer asked me to edit the Czech dialogues,

and I retranslated such gems into the vernacular. This aroused
my curiosity, and I purchased the novel and read it. The Prague
KGB resident of Mr. Littell's imagination is a Professor of
English at Charles University (which became the University of
Karlova in William Styron's *Sophie's Choice*) and the chairman
of the Prague Baconian Society. This is slightly inaccurate, for
any believer in such unscientific stuff would soon find himself
without tenure in Prague. One real "Baconian", a Professor of
English at the University of Olomouc, committed suicide after
finding that neither in academe, nor at the Party secretariat,
would anyone believe that he had discovered a coded message
in *Piers Plowman*. On the other hand, Mr. Littell's Prague CIA
resident is a pretty lady who makes a living running a private
business which produces guinea fowl. A private entrepreneur
in the Prague of the mid-seventies—if such a person could
exist at all—would surely be more than conspicuous, and a
very bad choice for the CIA. If Mr. Littell's city is Prague, it
must be the Praga Magica of Emperor Rudolf II, the alchemist,
where, according to Colin Wilson, John Dee and Edward Kelly
translated the *Necronomicon* from Enochian into English (and,
lest I forget, H.P. Lovecraft was another American who knew:
see his *The Case of Charles Dexter Ward*), and where Rabbi
Loew made his superhomunculus by the name of Golem.

Quite similar is the Prague of Robert Ludlum's *The Parsi-
fal Mosaic*. He too must have had a fifth-generation American
Czech for his linguistic adviser, for he places the headquarters of the KGB in a *veřejná místnost*. I never thought the
KGB would settle for a public lavatory as their residence when
the city has so many governmental palaces. Mr. Ludlum's
hero, a Michael Havelock, as a boy witnessed the annihila-
tion of his native village of Lidice by the Nazis, in retaliation
for Reinhard Heydrich's assassination, whereupon he joined a
"children's [guerrilla] brigade...whose members were used by
the Czech underground as couriers carrying dangerous plastic explosives." Again, I never knew that the rare Bohemian
guerrillas invented this weapon; I thought plastic explosives
came after the war, and not in Bohemia; but then, I am not
a historian. As for the "Children's Brigade", Mr. Ludlum must
have been reading Barbara W. Tuchman's *A Distant Mirror*,
which contains the story of the thirteenth-century Children's

Crusade. His Charles University professor, unlike Littell's, is not a spy but a guerrilla leader who assists the killers of Heydrich and then lives in hiding "in the cellars of the University". That would have been difficult: Charles University was closed down for the duration of the war and turned into various SS institutions such as the Institute for Race Research.

Do I ramble? Not really. All I wanted to demonstrate was that, even in this age of American considerateness and notorious guilt feelings, there are still residua—subconscious, no doubt—of a feeling of supremacy. I think I would be reprimanded if, in my novel-in-progress about the participation of the Czechs in the American Civil War, I equipped Harriet Tubman's Underground Railroad with diesel engines; but obviously one does not have to bother about insignificant details concerning a land some people know next to nothing about. Sixty-Eight Publishers, the Czech-language publishing firm for which I work, recently received a manuscript of a novel by Jan Křesadlo, *Fuga trium*, which, among other things, nicely satirized the kind of homework some Western writers do. In it, one such person decides to set his story in Bohemia, where he has never been, whose language he does not speak, about which he knows nothing, and in which he is not at all interested; he just needs what he believes is an exotic setting for his pornography. So he peremptorily consults an encyclopaedia. There is a scene in the brothel of a small Bohemian town—whose square, by the way, is adorned with palms. The bandleader of the local band is enjoying himself with the institution's prettiest prostitute, with whom the brothel's bouncer is madly in love. The method of enjoyment is remarkable and involves the insertion of a little ball in the bandleader's rectum. A string is attached to the ball, with a sort of yarmulka on the other end which the bandleader puts on his head, thus turning himself into a living bass viol. The prostitute then plays a composition of his on him, the conclusion of which coincides with the man's orgasm. But before that happens, the bandleader, hearing strange noises from behind the closed door, tiptoes to it, opens it abruptly, and catches the bouncer in the act of looking through the keyhole. He roars at him "Masaryk! Get lost!"

Do I have to explain? Well, perhaps. Thomas Masaryk (1850–1937) was the first president of the Czechoslovak Republic.

Křesadlo's Western writer liked the look of the name and followed in the steps of Helen MacInnes. Unfortunately, Masaryk's
name has connotations the writer knew nothing about. To him,
Masaryk was just another Czech name.

Well, not to be one-sided, harm is also being done to the
work of American writers, and unlike many writers in minor
languages they usually have no way of controlling their translators. Eudora Welty would hardly be pleased to learn that,
judging by the Czech rendition of her story "Powerhouse", her
knowledge of jazz music is flimsy at best. "Hell, that's on a
star, boy, ain't it?" asks the percussionist of the story's jazz
band, and he underlines his exclamation by a "crash of the dulcimer". The original word is "cymbal", of course, which happens
to be homonymous with the Czech word meaning "dulcimer".
Fortunately I was editing the translation for *World Literature*
magazine, and managed to save Ms. Welty's jazz reputation before the story went to print, but the blunder set me on the trail
of the lady translator, otherwise excellent, with just a lacuna in
her musical knowledge. In the course of the next few months
I discovered, among other things, one more dulcimer player—
this one in a British military band, marching right next to the
fellow with the big drum in a novel by Thackeray—and soon afterwards a postal coachman in Dickens who would whistle on
his key when approaching a tavern; in actual fact the man was
blowing his key-bugle. Which is probably negligible compared
to the lunatic who, in the Czech translation of Angus Wilson's
Anglo-Saxon Attitudes, went to a Medical School formal held in
a beach pavilion clad only in his trunks, whereas in the original a much saner person, dressed in trunks, played with a
medicine ball in a beach pavilion. And even this feat of imagination pales before the achievement of yet another word-artist
who made a striking historical discovery in a Negro spiritual
which contained the lines:

> Nevah was a prophet in the days gone by,
> he preached the Bible to the poor.

The translator added an explanatory footnote: "Nevah—a
less-known Old Testament prophet." Not trusting my biblical
knowledge, I consulted a concordance, but there was no trace of

the prophet Nevah. Then I urged the translator to bring me the original, and there was indeed a Nevah in it:

> Nevah was such a man befo'
> Preachin' de bible to de poo'.

What misled the translator was the fact that the Anglicized names of Hebrew prophets end in "-ah": Jeremiah, Jonah, Obadiah—whereas their Czech equivalents end in "-áš": Jeremiáš, Jonáš, Abdiáš, etc. If it were not for my vigilance, we might now have, in Czechoslovakia, baby boys christened "Neváš". Something similar actually happened to the late Harold Sonny Ladoo, an excellent West Indian writer and a student of mine (*No Pain Like This Body*; *Yesterdays*) who christened a son of his after a character in my novel *The Cowards*, Krocan Ladoo. "Krocan", however, is the character's surname, and it means "turkey". A little Turkey Ladoo is probably roaming the streets of Trinidad.

This is all pretty basic stuff, and gross misinterpretations of the meanings of individual words or phrases are not the worst disaster that can befall a piece of fiction rendered into another tongue. There is mismanaged syntax and style, word play, onomatopoeia, and the finer nuances of word order which, in some languages, can completely change the import of the sentence; there is the richness of the author's vocabulary reduced to unintentional Hemingwayese; there is a good novelist's virtuoso command of his instrument rendered into an étude for beginners. There is the hypnotic power the original exerts on the linguistic thinking of the unthinking translator, which gives birth to the mortal sin of "-isms": Anglicisms, Germanisms, Bohemianisms, Xhosaisms, etc.

Every language is rich, but in every language the richness is somewhere different. Sophisticated English has only four cases and no case endings; barbaric languages have as many as fifteen or more. Simple grammar is great, but so is complex grammar. It all depends on the man or woman who is using it. When Robert Jordan says to the Spanish girl, "I love thee and I love thy name, Maria," to an English ear I suppose the sentence reverberates with the beauties of the King James Version. This cannot be adequately transposed into

Czech, not with all its overtones; for Czech has never lost the second person singular. On the other hand, while Robert may like the girl's name, in English it suffers from an incredible poverty. How many forms of it exist? How many diminutives? Endearing variations? Mary, Marie, Molly—what else? The following is a partial list of names, all denoting "Mary", which are at the disposal of a Czech lover: Marie, Mařenka, Márinka, Mánička, Maruška, Marienka, Molly, Mollinka, Máří, Máry, Máňa, Maruše, Marika, Mařena.... Each expresses a different stage of intimacy, a different mood, a different depth of amorous intoxication or amorous hatred. If you hope to have your novel translated into English, never name your heroine Mary as I did in *The Swell Season*.

Although I love English, and only wish I could write fiction in it, compared to Czech it seems to me a hopelessly sexless language. I am probably wrong, never having had an English-speaking mistress, but—my God—what an erotic impoverishment it must be, not to have feminine endings. Martina Navrátilová's insistence on the prolongation of her long name by the feminine ending "-ová" may seem patriotic, but I think I know better. The fact that Czech women speak a language that differs slightly from that of Czech men is, for a writer (or for that matter for any erotically sensitive person), of crucial importance. A clever use of the differences creates a wealth of subtle associational thrills impossible to translate into a language where a Smith can be either male or female, and both say, "I am fond of you!" with the adjective not betraying the source of the pleasant announcement.

Many of the linguistic problems that trouble American feminists are of no concern to Czech girls. No neologisms like "chairperson" or "he/she" are necessary in Czech, and "man", that confounded noun which seems to exclude women from such important statements as "All men are created equal", is, in such pronouncements, replaced by a perfectly neutral but also perfectly natural and noble-sounding *člověk*, meaning both "man" and "woman". I suppose the Czech language harms the cause of Bohemian women's-libbers, for it deprives the movement of quite a few arguments. But the writer profits greatly from this eroticism of language, and I have played many a game with this sweet linguistic double-standard—no doubt to the chagrin of my excellent translator Paul Wilson, who had to transform them into his native language.

Milenka, my talkative go-getter in *The Engineer of Human Souls*, is nicknamed Blběnka by the book's Czech male community. In English she parades through the pages of the novel as Dotty. Not bad, I suppose—but Blběnka literally means "little stupid one", its diminuitive form turning the potentially insulting name into an endearing one, so that it has been adopted by many of my female readers who now sign their letters to me Blběnka Cabicarová, Blběnka Držmíšková, etc. In fact, I seem to have enriched my mother tongue by introducing this nickname into its literature. The truth is that I borrowed it from some Californian Czech barflies who revenged themselves on a vivacious, attractive, and very flirtatious married real estate agent by nicknaming the gorgeous butterfly Blběnka.

What a pleasure the coining of words is for a writer, or for a translator! I can still feel the intense joy that took hold of me when, for Sinclair Lewis's "booster" in *Babbitt*, I hit upon a perfectly natural neologism, *hiphurák*. Or when I derived the new word for "reefer", a marijuana cigarette in Warren Miller's *The Cool World*, from one of the forms of "Mary" and called it *márinka*. Marijuana smoking was unknown in Czechoslovakia in the early sixties, and so there was no word for "reefer". Well, there is now, as there is also one for another unknown object, the "zipgun"—*rourák* in my translation, derived from the Czech word for "pipe".

Words, words, words! There is no greater pleasure for a writer than words. In May 1945 I arrived in Pilsen with a group of friends, for rumour had it that the Yanks had opened a recruiting office in the Pilsner Beer Capital of the World for Czechs who desired to enlist and be sent to the Pacific— that was before Hiroshima, and while the war in Europe was over, Allied troops were still dying in the Far East. It was a false rumour, but I at least had the pleasure of observing the birth of a word. Lounging on the corners of the beer city, I gazed at the mildly sex-starved GIs engaged in girl-watching. From time to time they would call to each other, "Look at her!" when a particularly sex-bombish Pilsnerite passed by and made eyes at them. Soon Czech youngsters began commenting on the pretty girls walking by with exclamations like, "What a

luketa!" or "Isn't she a perfect *luketka*?" A new word was being
born out of the mouths of the people! Later I used the word
in several stories of mine and it caught on. Recently, like a
friendly greeting from a distant land, the word came back to me
in a novel by a Czech writer born in 1951. "She was among the
prettiest *luketkas* in town," muses the hero of the story. "What
is it really: a *luketka*? I have read it somewhere. Something like
a beautiful girl, a joy to look at...."

The *luketka* called Dotty in *The Engineer of Human Souls*
does not speak Czech: she speaks very consistent *American*
Czech, a language which was another pain in the neck for
Paul Wilson. The lingo is described in Mencken's *The American
Language*, but since Mencken's days, with the massive waves
of immigrants escaping from various totalitarian empires, the
language has greatly expanded, developed, even become sophisticated. Alas, it is untranslatable into English. It is Czech
beautifully bastardized by the language of Mark Twain, and it
is its English component that makes it such a charmingly funny
vehicle. But English cannot be translated into English.

By the same token, no Czech translator—and there are
some pretty good ones—can do justice to *For Whom the Bell
Tolls*. The "Spanish" effect of its dialogues—and it is there, I
suppose, no matter what Hispanic linguists say about Hemingway's inaccuracies—is based on the composite roots of modern
English, on its richness of synonyms of Romance and Anglo-
Saxon origins, a richness that does not exist in Czech. Romance
elements in that language are minimal, and to find a substitute...well, we tried once, in another book. The publishing
house where I was an editor was guided by the "scientific" approach of Marxism, and a brilliant translator, entrusted with
rendering three novels by Agatha Christie into Czech, decided
disparagingly that all previous translations had been "unscientific" because the translators made no effort to be true to the
original, and consequently Hercule Poirot talked like any other
character in the novel. In the original, of course, the clever Belgian speaks an extremely Frenchified English; not that he could
not speak like a Briton, but if he did he would alert the murderer. Speaking as he does, with all his "This is a lady most
beautiful!", he lulls his criminal adversaries into inattention,
for what danger can they expect from a stupid bloody foreigner?

So the woman set to work scientifically. But since there is no historical relation between Czech and French, she based her ingenious solution on the historical relations between Czech and German. The experiment backfired. Countless letters arrived at the editor's desk: "This is an outrage! How could you permit this to appear in print! The charming, the beloved Poirot, speaking like a Sudetengerman!"

A lesser storm followed the translation of Steinbeck's *The Grapes of Wrath*, in which the translator borrowed the East Bohemian mountain dialect to characterize the language of the Oakies. That, by the way, is the language Nadia speaks in *The Engineer of Human Souls*. Unfortunately the dialect is too well known, thanks to the popular humorous stories by Josef Štefan Kubín, and something clashed with the geographical associations of the readers. How come Oklahomans spoke like the hillbillies of Riesengebirge? Therefore, when I translated Faulkner I used only some elements of the countrified speech in the dialogues of his Negro characters. I had to; although there is a black Czech population, so far it has not developed a distinct dialect of its own.

However, all these things are more or less technical problems of the translator's craft. The art enters after he has solved them, or rather, it pours out of the book through many channels that circumvent the difficulties and impossibilities caused by radical differences between languages—and it is this component that a good translator has to capture. He can be forgiven his discoveries of new Old Testament prophets or an occasional dulcimer in a be-bop combo, but there is no excuse for transforming a thing of beauty into a wobbly story badly told. It is a difficult, difficult task, and also a very responsible one. A good writer does not rely only on the richness of his vocabulary, on style, on wordplay, on imagery. He often draws heavily on connotations, on associations which sometimes only readers with his own background, his own past history, can have. Ginsberg's *Howl*, although excellently translated by Jan Zábrana, lacks some of its important dimensions because to enter into them one must have been to Denver, to Frisco, one must have been initiated into the beat mythology; one must be North American.

Knowing all this, and more, one has to be grateful to the translators and to their watchful editors who, not being under the spell of the foreign language, correct their English. Working against heavy, often overwhelming odds, against impossible deadlines and for beggarly remuneration, the brave translators still manage to produce good copies of otherwise inaccessible originals. They succeed in giving their readers the sense of what it is to be a human being in distant, God-forsaken countries about which, before reading the book, they knew nothing. The translators thus help to create a spiritual condition in which any future Neville Chamberlains will be utterly ridiculous figures.

BETWEEN TWO WORLDS

—

The following piece combines a 1980 essay, "The East European Emigré As Writer: Some Personal Observations", and an unpublished speech, "Some Problems of the Ethnic Writer in Canada". As in "The Spilling of the Beans", Škvorecký deals with aspects of translation, with the important difference that in this case the concern is with the writer who has been "translated" from one place to another.

I

I HOPE IT will not sound like boasting when I, a novelist, say that literature, and specifically fiction, is the most complex of all creative arts. It shares some aspects with other disciplines—it works with motifs or with point-counterpoint like music; it uses striking visual images just as the visual arts do; the techniques of the flashback and of montage are its common tools, as in the cinema. To all that, fiction adds possibilities that are its own: it can encompass almost any content, render life in all its crazy

ambiguity, tell stories, show details and endless vistas, and at
the same time evaluate and comment on what is going on in the
manner of history and philosophy.

But at the heart of the art of fiction there is a paradox: the
tool for this all-encompassing craft, language, is the property
of almost everyone. There is therefore something dubiously
democratic about fiction, as there is something elitist about
music and the visual arts. Just look at our ethnic press—
or perhaps only our Czech ethnic press, for my knowledge is
limited to that area. Whenever (and it is not often) the Czech
papers carry an article on Czech music, Czech painting, or, to a
lesser extent, Czech films, what you get are not critical reviews
but mostly reverent eulogies. But when it comes to criticizing
Czech fiction published in Canada, everybody has a field day.
An amateur critic, if he could not read music and knew nothing
about harmony, would think twice before committing to the
printed page his opinions on, let us say, Leos Janáček. But the
same man or woman feels free to voice views on literature that
were outdated when Chaucer used scatological humour in *The
Canterbury Tales*. One such critic, writing about my novel *The
Tank Corps*, for instance, seemed to think that nobody before me
had ever used four-letter words in literature. Though this was
rather flattering, the man's main critical criterion was less so:
"It is not possible to read this novel while you are eating," quoth
the critic, without specifying the nature of the food consumed
while perusing my satire on army life. But I am used to such
approaches to my fiction. After all, Marie Majerová—a National
Artist of Czechoslovakia who, according to Prague gossip, was
Louis-Ferdinand Céline's mistress in her younger days—once
proclaimed, at a Writers' Union meeting which pilloried me,
that she had to wash her hands after not finishing my novel
The Cowards. (Then again, the reference may not have been to
the scatological qualities of that innocent book; Majerová was
a voracious eater of frankfurters and consumed at least four at
every meeting.)

However, the fact that novelists are easy prey for amateur
hunters who would be stuck for an answer if asked to define a
metaphor does not present a danger to the profession. The pre-
cariousness of the writer's tool becomes more of a problem when

he is forced to leave his native land for a country with a different language. Musician Oskar Morawetz had no difficulties (other than those faced by all Canadian composers) in establishing himself as a composer in this country. Painter Alfons Mucha was able to become not only a star in Paris but even a lover of the immortal Sarah Bernhardt. Director Miloš Forman is a household name among film fans in the West. The tools of their crafts have no need of translation, which always distorts the original (though in some cases for the better). They can talk directly to their audiences anywhere in the world, because they are not using words.

On the other hand, we have right here in Canada Jaroslava Blažková, the most popular and one of the very best Slovak writers from before 1968, yet—except for one story printed in the ethnic issue of *Canadian Fiction Magazine* (No. 36/37, 1980)— her charming stories and remarkable novels are unavailable to English-speaking Canadians. Her heroines do not make love to bears; she doesn't praise older women; her stories are just about what are called, in the dry language of our computer age, "human relationships".

Ethnic novelists like Blažková face enormous problems when they land on these shores. Who is going to publish their work? For a competitive publisher, the translation of a novel means an additional complication. And in an increasingly commercial market the chances that a translated novel by an unknown author will become a bestseller, or will even break even, are slim indeed. So unless they have already enjoyed international acclaim—like, let's say, Milan Kundera—nobody will touch their work. One cannot blame the struggling Canadian publisher; he (or his editor, if he can afford one) cannot read the manuscript, and has to rely on readers' reports by people fluent in the author's language. These, more often than not, are the author's compatriots (and may well be people who think certain books cannot be read while eating hamburgers), and the Canadian publisher naturally suspects them either of being biased in favour of the work or of lacking the acumen necessary to recognize literary value. And the publisher has good reason to be suspicious. I remember an editor in the CBC's Literary Department who was approached by a Czech émigré writer, one Bohumil Hrabal, and offered a novel entitled *Closely Watched*

Trains for radio serialization. The editor vaguely remembered some American fame attached to that title, and phoned me. When I heard that my old friend Bohumil Hrabal had also left the old country and chosen Canada, I was overjoyed. However, when the editor confronted me with the author, I could not recognize my old buddy. He had grown younger! By at least thirty years! He had grown fat! And he no longer shaved closely like an English gentleman but sported a Castro-like full beard. Yes, he did have a copy of the book in Czech, and yes, the name in his Czechoslovak passport was Bohumil Hrabal, but that was all he shared with the writer. I hear he moved to Yellowknife and enjoys quite a reputation there as a pastry cook.

Fortunately, Czechs are traditionally avid readers of fiction. Several factors have contributed to this phenomenon. The national awakening of the late eighteenth and early nineteenth centuries was effected, to a considerable extent, through literature, for the Czech language first came out of limbo by way of the printed page. Secondly, for the past forty years the Czechs have lived under several different kinds of dictatorships which have had one thing in common—they and books did not mix well. Books became paradise apples, and forbidden fruit tastes sweet. That is why books, even relatively difficult books, are more frequently than anything else the topic of Czech family conversation, and lovers may split up just as often because one of them adores Kafka and the other thinks he appeals only to snobs as because of incompatibility in bed.

Once people get involved with books, they tend to get involved in thinking. And thinking and being obedient subjects of an authoritarian regime make poor bedfellows. Consequently, after every major shake-up of the Communist party general line, people line up for defection. The last great wave came in 1968. Its participants had spent most of their lives trying to get a bite of the rare apples of the Tree of Wisdom, and therefore, once in the West, they created an unusually large market for Czech-language fiction and even poetry.

As a result, a considerable number of émigré publishing houses sprang up. Most of these businesses are doing well, some of them even exceptionally well. Just compare the sales: to date our firm, Sixty-Eight Publishers, has sold 7,000 copies of my novel *Tankový prapor* (*The Tank Corps*). The equivalent in domestic sales would be about 700,000 copies. That, in Czechoslovakia, has never been achieved by any book. It may sound like a purely theoretical computation, but I believe it rests on facts. If you exclude the second and later generations of exiled Czechs, who, if they know the language at all, are no longer able to enjoy it aesthetically, you arrive at a figure of approximately 100,000 potential readers, and even that is probably too high. Compared to that, there are ten million Czechs in Czechoslovakia. Therefore the sales of émigré publishers have to be multiplied by a factor of a hundred. If that is so, then even our average sales of 2,000 copies per book are much higher than comparative figures in Czechoslovakia, where the average is something like 10,000. Add to that the fact that we do not publish proven classical bestsellers like Karel Čapek or Alois Jirásek, but rather strictly contemporary works that have not been printed previously.

It's as well that we have a strong local market. Canada has a policy of support for ethnic cultures—a great, uniquely Canadian thing. Yet I sometimes wonder whether the priorities of the institutions that carry out this policy are in the right order. I am the last man to disdain—if you will pardon my chauvinism—pretty girls in short skirts dancing the *kozatchek* in nicely embroidered national costumes. However, when I come to ethnic events like Toronto's Caravan I feel as if I were in a time machine. I find myself in the nineteenth century—and not in Jules Verne's nineteenth century, but in the century of remote villages in north-eastern Bohemia. There, these merrily jumping hillbillies have been extinct for at least a century; young girls over there now dance to rock'n'roll, which emanates from ghetto blasters. And so I wonder: is not this particular form of ethnic culture falsifying the image of ethnic cultures for the enjoyment of Canadians whose knowledge of distant places is not always extensive? Aren't these pretty lasses in their lace drawers perpetuating an anachronistic image of the ethnic as a jolly but primitive semi-literate?

Yet those trying to obtain grants to found groups pushing folklore seem to encounter little difficulty. In my experience it is much more difficult, in fact next to impossible, to get money to help an ethnic publishing house. I tried once, and in spite of all the real and apologetic understanding of the people at the appropriate institution, there was simply no provision for such a thing. I don't know why that is so. Perhaps, when the ethnocultural policy was being formulated, ethnic publishing houses were simply not associated, in the Canadian mind, with the jolly hillbillies.

The hard fact of life is that, as an ethnic Canadian, you can retain elements of your culture and traditions, perhaps even customs, to some degree, but that the language is largely lost in the second generation, and entirely lost in the third. Naturally there are exceptions, but they are rare. Our government and our multicultural ministry cannot very well encourage New Canadians to forget about learning English or French and stick to their mother tongues—unless they want to create a force of ethnic labourers unable to hold any except the most menial jobs. Furthermore, ethnic groups who come to Canada for economic reasons rarely have writers among them. And if they do, such writers—if they are good—have no difficulty publishing their works in their old countries; in West Germany, say, or in Italy. To create publishing houses for such ethnic communities would be superfluous indeed.

But the communities that came into existence as a result of the political intolerance of totalitarian regimes do include writers—often quite remarkable ones—and the Canadian audience for such writers is usually too small to support a publishing house. These writers have a limited export market, thanks to the regimes in their home countries. And if they try to sell their work in translation, they are likely to come up against the obstacle of "Canadian content".

Believe me, for an ethnic writer coming to this country late in life, the issue of Canadian content is a difficult one. Once I was asked by CBC-TV to write a one-hour play. I did my best, and based it on a story contained in my book *The Swell Season*. The nice guys at CBC liked it and asked me for just a simple thing: to change the place of action from Bohemia to Canada so the film would have Canadian content. In my greediness I was not at all unwilling to oblige, but it proved technically impossible. The whole story hinged on a situation that never—except perhaps in Victorian times—existed in Canada; namely that when you planned to commit adultery in a hotel in Nazi-occupied Bohemia you had to rent two rooms. The desk clerk was obligated to check your *Kennkarte*, your identity card, and to refuse double occupancy to couples not legally married—legally married, that is, to each other. He couldn't be asked to close his eyes, since the Gestapo was fond of conducting midnight raids on hotels, and the fornicating couple would not be the only ones facing serious consequences for their immorality. However much I wanted to please the CBC, I was simply unable to deliver the goods.

II

There is a persistent tradition, or perhaps a myth, that a writer who leaves his native land, for whatever reason, is doomed as an artist and, consequently, as a human being. Behind this vision looms the Roman poet Ovid, that tragic, homesick wreck of a former playboy. In our own time, this paradigm is cunningly exploited by East European regimes that, often intentionally, create an atmosphere encouraging writers to leave. Czechoslovakia is especially well known for this type of duplicity, this hypocritical moral pose, this strong-armed cultural policy.

In the old days of Stalin, one wrote a novel, one disappeared, one was *pulverized*, as Orwell would put it. The West, then still living entirely according to the complacent philosophy of "It can't happen here," did not care very much. Even authors of the calibre of Isaac Babel could disappear without creating a stir, and were sometimes indeed branded as counter-revolutionaries by those incurable Western intellectuals who act as apologists for any kind of atrocity, provided the perpetrators use the simple trick of calling themselves "socialists".

The situation is now better in the West; we simply know more. But the police socialism of the East, for which its proponents have coined the term *Realsozialismus*, has, unfortunately, grown more sophisticated too. It is by now, I would hope, unheard of to be "pulverized" for a novel; and it is even uncommon to get locked up for one, though it still happens occasionally. Jiří Gruša, author of a truly exquisite novel, *The Questionnaire (Dotazník)*, has been indicted by the Czechoslovak authorities essentially for having written it. But Gruša may be an exception, perhaps because his book is so exceptionally good.

Normally, the police try to create circumstances that will encourage writers to choose the proverbial artistic death in exile instead of life in the bosom of the motherland. They do so through subtle forms of nastiness more often than through crude harassment. The police may poison your wife's lapdog, as in the case of Mrs. Jelena Kohout, the spouse of the well-known novelist and playwright. Or they may build a sentry box at your doorstep and block your sewer, thereby putting your bathroom out of use, as they did to another distinguished playwright, Václav Havel. If such methods prove too gentle, or the writer proves too tough, the police may take him for a ride, Chicago-style, and break his leg. They did that to the eminent actor and playwright Pavel Landovský. No wonder, then, that many people call it quits. Havel is still resisting, but Kohout, Landovský, and the filmmaker Jan Němec are now living in the West, and a considerable number of other people prominent in the cultural scene have given up the fight at home as well.

The cynical theory behind these curious expulsions, in which the expellee is often allowed to take along his entire family, is that a dissident author ceases to be interesting once he crosses the border. All too often this proves true. He can no longer create trouble for the government by forcing it to send him to jail, and consequently his newsworthiness abroad is reduced to zero. That is the *tacit* theory; the theory expounded aloud is the ancient one, based on the fate of Ovid. In the case of the Czechs, it is usually expressed in a line stolen from Viktor Dyk: "If you leave me [meaning the native land], I shall not perish: you will." A party hack named Zdeněk Pluhař even wrote a novel with that line as its title, at a time when, ironically, the opposite was closer to the truth. Egon Hostovský, the Jewish novelist, Jan Čep, the Catholic writer, and Ivan Blatný, the avant-garde poet, all left, survived, and produced their best work in exile, while those who stayed—the country's artistic lifeblood, so to speak—perished in various ways. Some, like Záviš Kalandra, the essayist, were executed; some, like Karel Teige, the theoretician of surrealism, were reported to have "committed suicide". Some really did take their own lives, like Konstantin Biebl, Jiří Pištora, and Stanislav Neumann, all of them poets. The survivors turned into artistic corpses, as did the brilliant visionary of *Edison*, the poet Vitězslav Nezval, who ended his days as a sort of court jester. A particularly piquant aspect of Dyk's phrase is that, had he been alive in the fifties, he would in all probability have joined Záviš Kalandra on the gallows. Politically this poet was very conservative, and personally very brave; it is a combination that qualifies a person for radical re-education in the next world.

The establishment parable that is hammered into the heads of citizens contemplating defection, then, is the parable of Ovid. Nobody mentions the example of another political exile of the writing profession who, as a child, received the kind of treatment now meted out to Czech dissidents. It is interesting to speculate what would have happened to his talent and to his life had he stayed in his native country, then under Russian domination. Fortunately he did not, and so we now have the fine oeuvre of Joseph Conrad.

Conrad is one reason why I call the theory of artistic decline in exile a persistent myth. Obviously a decline may set in, and one often does. Writers, like everyone else, react differently to changed conditions. But even if they are afflicted by a serious case of homesickness, it often brings about a flowering of creative powers, rather than leading to paralysis. After all, Ovid himself, before he died, managed to write something quite remarkable, the *Epistulae ex Ponto*. Had he continued chasing married women in the *forum Romanum*, who knows?...

It is true, however, that writers, unlike other artists, have a specific problem which I mentioned earlier, and for which Conrad is not a good example, the problem of language. The usual belief is that when a writer is forced to live in a linguistically alien setting, his mother tongue becomes blunted and stiff, and the richness of his vocabulary vanishes; in short, the verbal artist loses the tools of his art. The chances that he will master a foreign language well enough to write vivid fiction in it are extremely slim; and although Conrad was an exception, even he never freed himself from his heavy Polish accent.

But, as can be shown in the English of such expatriates as Hemingway, Fitzgerald, or Henry Miller, if a writer lives surrounded by the strange sounds of a foreign language he may develop a greater sensitivity to the beauties and subtleties of the language in which he feels at home. He becomes afflicted by a kind of beneficent nostalgia for his verbal homeland, and potentialities of his medium that he tended to miss while the acoustic milieu was familiar begin to dawn on him. Someone should, I think, try to discover to what extent Hemingway's style, which is in essence an English purged of clichés, slang, and the hypertrophy of colloquialisms and idiomatic usage—to what extent this most influential way of writing is indebted to the fact that, while the crystal-clear sentences were being pounded out on his typewriter, the author was daily forced to speak French, Spanish, and German. After all, Henry Miller recommends this cure to the word-weary writer: live abroad and you will soon feel a new energy permeating the sole language in which you are able to write.

And here is yet another point of view: the way non-English peoples speak their native language in North America is usually seen in the light of linguistic purism. Most people in exile condemn what they believe is corruption and, depending on their nature, either savagely attack, as unpatriotic villains, those who use the American idiom when speaking Czech, or apologize profusely for all the disfigured English words that have penetrated their Czech. But every spoken language is in a sense a corruption, a corruption of the schoolmaster's dream. What these old schoolmasters call "correct" Czech is a language deader than Latin. If you listen to the few extremists who actually try to speak that lingo, you feel as if you are listening to robots. The fact is that much beauty comes from corruption, and also much that is interesting. Paradise without Eve's sin would have been a dull place.

Looking at our problem from this angle, then, corrupted North American Czech becomes simply another dialect of our mother tongue. It is not a theoretical concept, as the language of normative grammars is. People on this continent actually speak it because it comes to them naturally, not in the form of a schoolmaster's ideological "must". If you are a realist Czech writer living on these shores, then why not use North American Czech in the same way that novelists who remain at home use Prague slang or the Moravian dialect? After all, this strange transatlantic Czech lends itself beautifully to humorous treatment, the only drawback being that you cannot translate it into English.

Imagine hearing a happy little Czech-American girl who has
just received a pink parakeet as a birthday present and is ad-
miring it with these words: "*Lukni, strejdo, jaký má ten birdík
krásný pinkový fedříčka!*" ("Look, uncle, at the birdie's beautiful pink feathers!") To my ears, what has happened here to both
Czech and English is beautiful because it is charmingly funny.
I love this sweet corruption.

To sum up: a writer does not have to perish in exile. On the
contrary; he may benefit both from the new sounds that daily
fill his ears, and from the new linguistic experience of his own
language. So much for the tool. As for the material shaped by
the tool, the case is simple and clear: why should the life of, say,
the Czech community in Toronto be less exciting than life in a
small Czech town of the size of the Toronto Czech community?
Why should it be less worthy of the writer's attention? It too
is Faulkner's pinhead on which a good writer can engrave the
entire history of mankind.

What, then, is the situation of the exiled Czech writer, unknown
to the general public in the West and ignored by his new
country's local police? My belief is that it is very good. He lives
in a setting that prompts him to experiment in language; he
has new experiences which he can mould into tales. Read the
novels of the late Egon Hostovský, many of which are available
in English translations, or read Jan Drábek's fine fiction written
in English, and you will see North America from a new point
of view. Read the Australian poetry of Stanislav Mareš, or the
English poetry of Ivan Blatný. Read the moving stories about
the sad Czech boys and girls in Switzerland by the exceptionally
talented Jaroslav Vejvoda—read the marvellous novel *Willy's
Dream Kit* by Jan Novák of Chicago, nominated for the 1986
Pulitzer Prize— and you will see what I mean.

Finally, and this is certainly most important, the exiled Czech
writer has a body of readers for whom reading a Czech book
is comparable to making love to the language. The intensity
of their reading experiences is quite incredible. The fruit is
no longer forbidden, but it is still rare. These readers rave
about books in a way comparable only to the enthusiasm of an
American reviewer who has a crush on a pretty editor whose
advancement depends on the book's success. These readers will

drive hundreds of miles to the provincial capital, through the blizzards of a Canadian winter, to hear a popular novelist read from his works. They are a truly Dickensian audience.

Personally, therefore, I have no reason to complain. In a way I am living proof of my theories. During my years in Canada, I have written and *published* more novels than in my twenty years of writing in Czechoslovakia—and there I was a freelance writer, whereas here I hold a job and write in my spare time. And I do not think my fellow Czech writers belong to the category of incurable complainers longing for the often imaginary and always idealized native ground. Given the circumstances created in my old country, I am happy to be a writer in exile. My cats are safe, my sewer always works. If it gets blocked from natural causes I call my plumber who happens to be a compatriot, a customer of my wife's publishing house, and a reader of my novels. He demands to be paid in books, which costs me nothing, for I make them.

THE INCOMPREHENSIBLE FAULKNER

—

Of the non-fictional books Škvorecký published in Czechoslovakia, the most important was probably O nich—o nás (About Them—About Us), a 1968 collection of essays on various American authors. Both a homage and a critical introduction, it contained chapters on Stephen Crane, Ernest Hemingway, William Faulkner, Ambrose Bierce, Dashiell Hammett, and Raymond Chandler. This is one of two devoted to Faulkner.

Like the chapters on Hemingway and Škvorecký's 1967 book on the detective story, Nápady čtenáře detektivek *(Thoughts of a Mystery-Reader), this is a defence of literature against Czechoslovak and other East European*

critics who approached it on the basis of the criteria of a
vulgar Marxist aesthetics or socialist realism.

I speak
to poets
who suffer guilt
Stop scribbling
verses for the poor!
For the ruling class
has no comprehension
Of great art
smaller than yourselves

Vladimir Mayakovsky

WHEN WILLIAM FAULKNER died and the pages of the Anglo-Saxon press were full of posthumous praise, the British *Books and Bookmen* published a letter of one reader who, in the midst of the deluge of odes, sounded like the voice of stubborn sobriety. The reader denied that Faulkner was a great author; he said that he was sombre and incomprehensible, that reading him was a worthless effort, and that even though Faulkner wrote about the racial issue, his novels left the reader cold. "He didn't contribute a thing to the improvement of the Negro's lot, in fact he didn't even ruffle the surface of the average American's mind as far as the question of race is concerned."

Several apparently unconnected memories flashed through my mind. Once I was sitting with a friend at a concert where they were playing Bach's *Art of the Fugue*. When the concert was over, I returned from that world of fantastically ordered freedom that is Bach's music, to the rattle of seats, and found that my friend had fallen asleep. Not because he was tired. "Forgive me," he said afterwards, "I don't have an ear for music. I don't understand it. I came with you because I didn't have anywhere to go."

A second memory: the fifties, when I used to repeat lines by Vladimir Mayakovsky like the Lord's Prayer while I read literary treatises of the time:

Let each of you raise up to the masses
an immensely superior culture.

Each book is essential and accessible
to farmers and workers and you and me.

And another one: of the author Kotrč-Kotalík, and a pre-war textbook of Czech literature used at the wasteland that was my high school during the Nazi Protectorate, and of the fragments of ideas of banned poets, inaccessible at the time, that gleamed in the didactic subject matter like rubies in grey dirt. They emerge in the paraphrase of memory: "You can ask a nightingale to sing. You can't ask him to solve the world's problems." And so the letter from the British reader once again reminded me of that eternal dispute about comprehensibility and incomprehensibility, popular and non-popular art, commitment and lack of commitment, active and passive art.

Anyone who wants to deal seriously with Faulkner cannot avoid that dispute, which I feel results from unclarified terms and from the somewhat romantic notion that writers are persons of a strange and *uniform* type, conspicuously different from non-writers—that a writer is primarily a writer, and only afterwards a human being.

There is no notion that causes writers more difficulties than that one; because of it, they are showered on one hand with undue attention and on the other with undue mistrust. If it were in fact true that the writer transcended his human existence, then literature would indeed be incomprehensible to everyone but writers. In reality, however, the human differences between one writer and another are far more substantive than the difference between a writer and a non-writer. Except for the ability to wield a pen, writers share everything with everyone else, and they are just as infinitely different one from the other as everyone else. Making some sort of universal demand on them—except for the universal one that society makes of all people, that they work to the best of their abilities—may be well intentioned but is pointless and self-deluding. Perhaps there are some nightingales capable of making a significant contribution to solving the world's problems, but the others just know how to sing; that is their way of responding to the world. If you were to force them into philosophy instead of singing, they might come up with a few hackneyed truths, but they would probably begin to sing off key, just as a psychiatrist forced to do a complex heart operation would probably kill the patient even though he made the incision exactly according to instructions. Because although it is true that the word is a weapon, the word is not solely and exclusively a weapon; or maybe we should say that weapons are not just heavy artillery, but can include an old man's fine force of spirit, or the defenceless beauty of a young woman.

And that is why I wonder if it is true that William Faulkner's novels could never move anyone to action. Perhaps a person speculating about racial injustice would be most taken by the fact that Faulkner writes about his black people exactly as he does about white people—that to him skin colour makes absolutely no difference, in the positive or the negative sense, not only in life but also in literature; that a Lucas Beauchamp (in the novel *Intruder in the Dust*) has exactly the same human dignity as any of the noble white Sartoris family. Of course, Faulkner's black men are not the attractive innocent victims of the neo-abolitionist novels. As for militant deeds towards the improvement of the blacks' lot, Faulkner is one of the outstanding American authors who took a fearless civic stand against racism, with public proclamations in specific cases of lynchings, and with articles in the press. And what about comprehensibility, about intelligibility? That friend of mine fell asleep at the concert—incomprehensibly to me—because *he has no ear for music*. Don't you think there may be something like an ear for literature? Is the fact that we have few adult illiterates a guarantee that the only ones who won't understand literature will be small children? Can we guarantee that everyone who can learn musical notation—something that almost all are capable of—will understand Bach?

No, the whole dispute about comprehensibility is like talking about apples and oranges. Just because literature is composed of words, there is the assumption that anyone who understands the individual words must understand their sum total, and that if he does not comprehend them completely and without fail there is something wrong, not with him, but with the author. Literature is not made up only of the rational meanings of words, however; at least half of it rests on their emotional or associative meanings, unusual combinations of words which create new qualities of sensations, fantasy, beauty, ecstasy, and multi-faceted meaning. Everyone but the deaf can listen to Bach, but only a person with an ear for music truly hears Bach. Everyone but the blind can read literature, but only a person with an ear for literature truly understands it. And I'm not just speaking of certain irrational, surrealistic texts, but even the realism of, say, Hemingway—seemingly so clear to everyone. Do you believe that a fourteen-year-old high school student will comprehend everything Božena Němcová's *Grandmother* stands for?

I think not. Moreover, Faulkner is not incomprehensible, he is just difficult. In essence he is a realist who makes things poetic, absolute, certainly not a non-realist of some paranoid school. He is only difficult the way Bach is difficult, the way Schoenberg is difficult, the way even undoubtedly "folksy" Shostakovich is often difficult. But to read Faulkner a person must have an ear for literature. For instance, the simple sentence that leads off the magical tale of the bird in *A Fable*, "It happened in America, at a remote place called by an Indian name I think...." exhilarates me the way the sharp and mellow encounters of contrapuntal melodies do, and I don't know why. Or consider the sketch of Reverend Tobe Sutterfield, the old black man in *A Fable*: "the serene and noble face of an idealized Roman consul...." Or this: "Through the bloody September twilight, aftermath of sixty-two rainless days, it had gone like a fire in dry grass—the rumour, the story, whatever it was...." I only know that when Faulkner describes the ordinary supper of an ordinary old man—and he is sure to describe it in detail—the wiped moustache, uncorked bottle, and every raised hand—it is a poem. With another author it would probably be descriptive, realistic filler; with Faulkner it is—to me—as full of suspense as the best mystery story, as resonant as a poetic symphony, as sensual as Zrzavý's colourful paintings.

In other words, no one who lacks an ear for music has the right to decry music, just as the person who has not made the effort to develop an ear for literature and who is unable to hear the harmony of words has no right to criticize literature.

As entities, as monumental representations of humanity—of its passions and virtues, foolishness and heroism, the wisdom and compassion of which it is capable—Faulkner's novels are clearly comprehensible to even the most unemotional rationalists. Not understanding them means not understanding concepts like love and honour and pity and pride and compassion and sacrifice—concepts basic to Faulkner, fundamental human concepts. They are like six notes on which he based his incomprehensible sextatonic symphonies.

A SORT OF TRIBUTE TO G.K.C.

—

Josef Škvorecký, a long-standing fan of classical detective stories, delivered the following address to the national meeting of the Chesterton Society, at York University in Toronto, on January 28, 1977. The Detective Borůvka stories that he refers to here are now being issued in English in a series of volumes, beginning with The Mournful Demeanour of Lieutenant Boruvka *(1987).*

THERE IS NOT very much to tell. But that is as it should be. Our truest loves live beyond words and defy analysis. So there is really not much to tell. I never studied Chesterton; vis-à-vis his pages I was always, luckily, only a reader—later, perhaps, a writer—but never a literary scholar.

My first experience of the theatre of the absurd occurred when, at thirteen or fourteen, I read the judge's summing up of a complex case in *The Club of Queer Trades*: "Oh, Rowty-owty tiddly-owty." It was one of those inexplicably strong impressions one acquires when the mind is still impressionable. The memory of the retired judge came to life many years later over a photograph, in *Books and Bookmen*, of the bulky, towering man standing on a rostrum, with one of his trouser buttons caught on the edge of his fly and clearly showing in the picture. That combination of dignified learning and comical domestic clumsiness was a visual suggestion of G.K.C.'s love for paradox.

Somewhere in between came the stories about the little priest. I was fourteen, fifteen by then, an ardent churchgoer suffering from an almost Joycean feeling of sinfulness, for no matter how hard I tried, my every confession contained a wide assortment of sins against all the Commandments except the one about adultery. Among the derivative guilts stemming somehow from "Thou shalt not kill" was also the reading of detective stories. Our religion instructor, Father Plocek, kept exhorting us against that vice, for at that time it became a veritable epidemic at the *Realgymnasium* of Náchod. The bacilli were neither Sherlock Holmes, nor Austin Freeman, nor Agatha Christie, nor Dorothy Sayers, but the obscure sleuths of Central European penny dreadfuls, which were printed on paper that yellowed within a week after the purchase, thereby giving the work an aura of almost classical antiquity. There was Tom Shark, a sort of tenth-carbon copy of the man from Baker Street—authored by one Pitt Strong who, in real life, was reportedly an impoverished German countess—and Detective Banggs, a pre-hardboiled school tough, one of whose many exploits stuck in my memory. A mad scientist invents rays which create an invisible wall, somewhat in the manner of the trick played years later by the cuckoos on the unsuspecting maidens of Midwich. In his madness, however, the scientist sells the gadget not to the Pentagon but to one of the soccer teams in danger of being dropped from the first league. From that point on, nobody can score against the former losers. Eventually Banggs—turned centre-forward for the sake of investigation—solves the case by a penalty kick that misses the goal but hits an inconspicuous photographer's camera standing on its tripod close to the goal posts. It is, of course, not a camera but the generator of the protective rays.

Is it any wonder that, given such marvels to admire, I too succumbed to the Shark-Banggs infection and suffered pangs of conscience twice a week during the philippics of Father Plocek? He probably never said, in so many words, that reading detective stories was sinful, but he was an enthusiastic preacher, and I was a susceptible youth. Like every saint, I sinned again and again. In my search for the stuff (two penny dreadfuls once a week did not suffice to quench the habit), I ransacked my

father's library and discovered that he too was a secret sinner. There, behind *The Complete Works of Alois Jirásek* and
K.V. Rais, both immaculately classical and serious, stood a row
of Edgar Wallaces and Bulldog Drummonds—and also a book
called *Moudrost Otce Browna* (*The Wisdom of Father Brown*).

I cannot say that, there and then, I liked G.K.C. more than
Wallace. I was too young for that. But the detective was a priest!
How did a priest fit into the brotherhood of Shark and Banggs
and Bulldog Drummond?

I took my problem to Father Plocek—not in a spirit of yearning for enlightenment, I am afraid, but in a slightly rebellious
mood of challenge. The good Father was embarrassed. He apparently had never read the Father Brown stories; he had
probably never even heard of them. I felt sorry for him as he
bungled about for arguments, and I was ashamed of myself. I
realized that I had brought the book to Father Plocek with an
evil intention.

He was the village priest. When, at Mass, he raised the Host
high towards the ceiling of our twelfth-century parish church
of St. Lawrence, his black trousers showed under the chasuble
and revealed black laced boots and also the ends of white laced
underpants of the kind the mountain people of north-east Bohemia used to wear year in and year out to protect themselves
against the chilly mornings. He was a helpless being; I remember the dismal way some of us used to torture him in later years
when religious instruction was no longer mandatory—the nasty
questions about Jonah's whale and other "lapses" of Holy Writ.
His face would redden with anger which he valiantly—and
unsuccessfully—tried to suppress; his quiet voice would repeat
the usual explanations—how it was the translator's error—but
there was frustration in the blue Bohemian eyes set like a pair
of cornflowers in his countrified face. The face was kind, big and
round; the Father's head looked like a watermelon. Naturally,
he was nicknamed Father Meloun (Melon). Again I must confess: I was one of the torturers. This happened during my phase
of heresy, of blasphemy.

My heresy phase over, I used to meet him, from time to time,
on my infrequent visits to my native town. He was retired—
involuntarily, for this was already after the Communist coup
in 1948—and he said daily Mass at the hospital chapel for

the Franciscan Sisters whose "useful" vocation saved them—for some time—from being sent to the "concentration cloisters", one of the little-known Stalinist inventions in social engineering. His person exuded a mildness, a goodness, an innocence. I did not know precisely what it was, but it attracted me to him, and I regretted my blasphemous antics of the years past. Somehow this meek, inconspicuous, unimportant servant, lost in the cruel wilderness of Stalinism and doomed to die soon of cancer, grew in my mind to a strange sort of greatness. It was hard to explain. But after another lapse of many years, I found this sentence in Graham Greene's *A Sort of Life*, in which he comments about Father Trollope, also a victim of cancer: "I was facing the challenge of an inexplicable goodness." That defines what I felt. Without being able to express it myself at the time, I nevertheless slowly realized that Father Meloun had been a much greater influence in my life than I had ever assumed. And finally—I had launched on my literary career by then—he merged in my memory with that other inconspicuous Father, much smarter than he, but also a humble servant. As "Father Meloun" he started to appear in my books: in *The Cowards*, in *The Menorah*, in *The Swell Season*. And then I wrote the detective stories.

Father Meloun was not a detective in them; he could not be, for there are certain limits to imagination, and he, in real life, would not have been able to solve the simplest riddle. The detective was Borůvka, my alter ego (in many respects) at the age of fifty, a layman. Yet I felt that these two men complemented each other and that somehow, in the background, there lurked the dusty shadow of the little sleuth in the clerical hat who once embarrassed Father Meloun and, perhaps as a result of that, brought me closer to the Christianity which shone from the naive eyes of his moon-shaped face. Working on the first book of my Borůvka stories, I felt that the tribute to Father Meloun which I had paid in a couple of previous books was incomplete without a tribute to the shadow in the background. The feeling prompted me to write a story entitled "Whose Deduction?"

In it, the fifty-year-old and married lieutenant is in a state of infatuation with a young policewoman and is about to commit the one sin to which I did not have to confess in my soul-searching young days. At the last minute, before the departure for the decisive rendezvous, however, he overhears a telephone conversation which clearly indicates that a murder is planned somewhere. The clues are more than inadequate. To trace the call is next to impossible—and yet, after a series of events that have all the appearance of chance happenings, the lieutenant catches the murderer before he is able to commit the crime, and in the course of an all-night investigation unravels several other minor offences. But the young policewoman, who is waiting for him in a wine tavern, is eventually forced to leave at closing time. The lieutenant is saved. The chain of chance events was of course really the finger of God, which carefully led him away from his uniformed Eve back to his wife and children.

Would Chesterton have written such a story? I don't know. But I did write it as a tribute—indirect perhaps, certainly feeble, probably old-fashioned, yet a tribute nevertheless. Can I be forgiven for my conceit? Anyway, no matter how good or bad or conceited my story is, in one respect it constitutes a paradox. The obvious fact that the "deduction" is God's escaped the Party censor-editors. They worried about another story in the collection, "Death of an Old Tomcat", a yarn concerning a prosecutor who is involved in one of the many political frame-ups of the times. They did not even mention God's deduction.

If nothing else, this might have caused Chesterton to chuckle. And maybe he did, somewhere in heaven, if he still takes an interest in detective stories.

POLITICS

Railway station, 1959; Zdena Škvorecký takes
her husband's manuscripts to a hiding-place in the
mountains, as Prague police raid bookstores for
The Cowards

PRAGUE WINTER

—

When in 1983 The American Spectator *asked Škvorecký to review* The Writing on the Wall: An Anthology of Contemporary Czech Literature, *he used the occasion to reflect on the Prague Spring, the Warsaw Pact invasion of Czechoslovakia in 1968, the nature of totalitarianism and historical memory. Almost in passing, he left the reader with a strong impression of the state of contemporary Czech writing.*

SUPPOSE AN AIRCRAFT designer talks Boeing Aircraft into financing an airplane which, according to its creator, is guaranteed to be faster, safer, and more comfortable than any ever built. In the course of a century the company goes on to build several dozen prototypes, but they all prove slower and more uncomfortable than the previous models, and able to return to Mother Earth only by crash-landing—yet the company continues to turn them out. Certainly, the originator of such an insanity would be recognized as a genius—not of aircraft design, perhaps, but of conmanship.

This year, 1983, marks the hundredth anniversary of the death of Karl Marx. The ironic result of his dialectics seems to be Poland, where the workers' party has been replaced by an alliance of the army and special units of storm troopers, where class justice has been superseded by martial law, and where the folksy party leader has given way to a ramrod general who looks like a South American junta boss envisioned by Costa-Gavras. As Marx and Lenin predicted, the state has withered away: first into the country-wide jail of martial law, then into the universal barracks of military discipline imposed on the industrial work force, with everybody drafted for an indeterminate length of time.

The past twenty-five years or so have witnessed other crash-landings of Marxism, and the story is becoming a bore. Consequently the year 1968 does not ring many bells, and the publication of *The Writing on the Wall* will go unnoticed by most North Americans.

In the distant days when I still attempted to explain things to left-leaning North American acquaintances, I invariably asked, "If you are interested in Communism because you think it would be good for this country, why try to find out how it works in Albania, Angola, Mozambique, and other conveniently unverifiable places? Wouldn't it be more logical to study what it does to old Western cultures, like those of the Czechs and Slovaks?" They could well begin by reading the stories in *The Writing on the Wall*. But note that the gory events of the fifties do not find their way into this volume; this is not a book about Communism's past but about its future. It will move only those readers who, in this land of soft bodies and pampered souls, still believe that to oppress the mind is as reprehensible as to oppress the body.

A remarkable tale by Eda Kriseová, "Our Small Town", illustrates the impact of Marxist social engineering on a society where problems of literacy were solved in the previous century. Its intellectual female narrator quietly observes the daily habits of the contemporary villagers, who spend their free time gorging themselves on smoked pork and drudging on the building sites of private retreats. No music, neither folk song nor symphony, resounds against the strangely barren landscape. Only the smell of wieners seeps through an atmosphere of devastating senselessness. A metaphor, of course, for what Czech Party ideologues have come to call *reálný socialismus*. This recent addition to the Marxist lexicon cannot be translated as "real socialism"—English lacks the decidedly pejorative connotations "reálný" has acquired in Czech, and "real" in English can also mean "true". But *reálný socialismus* means a deadpan general, or toneless country gluttons...never a busy workers' council or a thriving contemporary culture.

"Really? And what about those wonderful concerts in the Renaissance Rudolfinum Hall in Prague? What about the lavish Shakespearian productions?" say my left-leaning acquaintances, fresh from a flying visit to Prague. "And although we can't read Czech, we are told that not everything in the bookstores there is trash."

Well, all dictators love fiddlers, but they suspect pen-pushers—except those who are safely dead or those willing to omit certain facts and details from their work. Let's imagine a young Mark Twain who grows up in the Old South in the days of slavery, but under conditions of literary censorship as strict as those in today's Czechoslovakia. This hypothetical Sam Clemens is as obsessed by literary fame as any budding writer anywhere, at any time. He gets the idea for *The Adventures of Huckleberry Finn*. But he faces a dilemma. If he builds his novel around the issue of slavery, the book will be seized by the censors and its author, quite possibly, by the police. Yet the call of the printer's ink is irresistible. So young Clemens does a little focus-shifting—away from the immorality of taking a man's freedom, to, let's say, offences against proper Southern table manners—and his "sivilized" *Huck Finn* is soon on the market. It is a funny, entertaining, well-written book. It's just that something is missing from the story.

In a feuilleton or short essay by Vlastimil Trešňák, a man badly in need of money sells a few drawings in an art shop; an artist-friend gave him the pictures in better days. The manager displays the new acquisitions in his shop window. The police soon arrive, equipped with a secret list of undesirable artists; the manager is reprimanded and the drawings are confiscated. The police ask for the address of the seller, who is then apprehended and accused of trafficking in anti-State art.

Nothing much, is it? Just a little unpleasantness. Multiply it by ten million, though, and perhaps you will begin to sense the quality of daily life under *reálný socialismus*.

One aspect of this daily life is a kind of schizophrenia. In Pavel Kohout's story "Trouble", two secret policemen use electronic bugs to tape the goings-on in the apartment of a dissident writer. What is going on is perfectly normal: the writer has breakfast with his wife, they are seized by sudden lust and make love on the floor, the man then goes to the toilet and has a bowel movement (at this point one of the policemen discreetly turns down the volume); then the woman says goodbye, the writer retires to his room, and for the rest of the policemen's shift he pounds on his typewriter.

What goes on between the policemen is also perfectly normal: the younger complains about his unfaithful wife, and the older gives him advice about how to deal with females in general, and with fickle ones in particular.

In short, it's just a perfectly normal, unremarkable day—for that kind of society.

Some of the pieces are more ominous. When Ludvík Vaculík leaves home to attend the funeral of Professor Patočka, a seventy-year-old philosopher who has died during a twelve-hour police interrogation, he is picked up and driven to the police precinct, where he is kept until the funeral is safely over. In the meantime, on a track adjoining the cemetery, a group of motorcycle racers begins intensive training, and the priest's funeral oration is drowned out by the unmuffled exhausts. A police helicopter hovers a few feet above the open grave. This is not an attempt to emulate Kafka; it is not even a story. It's just a piece of reportage.

These little clashes with "real-socialist" power accumulate, and eventually become nauseating. But there is little blood in the stories; only the soul bleeds occasionally. Prague, these days, is simply uninteresting. News-unworthy.

Or is it? This city of ancient Western culture, crushed by the Marxist steam roller? All right, the stories so far have been about intellectuals, who—if American experience is any indication—have a tendency to grumble. What about the ordinary folks, who are believed to be better off—perhaps because the Western liberal presumes such types can live by bread alone—than they were in the oppressive old days of the Thomas Baťa Shoe Company? In Ivan Klíma's story "A Christmas Conspiracy", a former writer, now working at odd jobs and occasionally finding a "front" for his television plays, gets a temporary job selling Christmas carp for a grocery store. The job becomes his initiation into socialist entrepreneurship. One of the shopgirls tells him about a number of tricks, based mostly on mixing cheap stuff with more expensive stuff, which brings the store a nice profit. The profit is split up among all the employees, who work as a team. Or rather, a gang: the penalties for betraying the collective are forbidding.

But this is small change; the girl has a more grandiose dream. She tells the writer about gas stations where one can "pull in ten thousand a month if it's a halfway decent pump." There is just one hitch: such a franchise costs, in bribes, at least 25,000 crowns. The girl is so obsessed by her vision that she drags the writer into a big crate in the storage room and offers to sleep with him if he'll promise to become a partner in the scheme. "Mr. Ivan...your friend told me about you, that you write for the TV and make a nice bundle...Mr. Ivan, for a man like you twenty thousand means nothing. I've already saved up the rest, I know about a great pump, in six months it would be paid off and from then on it would be all gravy...in two years we'll save up enough for a house...we'll take trips to the seashore, won't that be great?"

Yes, ordinary folks are definitely better off under *reálný socialismus*. To the amazed writer, who compares them to himself and his fellow dissidents—officially described as "antisocialist conspirators"—their lively community appears as a "world full of real conspirators...an all-penetrating conspiracy of people who saw the futility of all ideals and the murderous ambiguity of human illusions...a determined fraternity of true materialists who knew that you could count only those things that can be counted, that money can buy anything and anyone—except Death (which they don't worry about) and except a few isolated fools whom they clap into prison, kick out of the country or shove into cellars to stoke furnaces and indulge their idle cogitations."

This is perhaps more useful reading for the Western left-leaning man than news items about poetry workshops recently organized for the Nicaraguan police force. We had them too, thirty years ago. This is a story about the future of the future, and how it works.

The final metaphor for the metamorphosis of the working class and their leaders in *reálný socialismus* is Vaculík's feuilleton "First of May". The date is a traditional socialist holiday in Europe, commemorating the victims of the Haymarket Riots in Chicago. In Czech literature, its mood was first captured in a piece by the poet and journalist Jan Neruda (a nineteenth-century Czech liberal whose surname was misappropriated by the twentieth-century Chilean Stalinist Ricardo Reyes). Apparently one is not permitted to quote from Neruda's account in today's Czechoslovakia; it alludes to the Prussian invasion of the country in 1866, and a surrealistically associating reader might be reminded of something the Soviets did in 1968. But Neruda writes about the silence of the marching workers and about the dedicated speeches of their leaders. In Vaculík's description of the same day's celebration a century later, a worker waiting for the march to begin calls to a busy functionary, "Mr. Organizer, mark me present!" The difference between what Neruda saw many years ago and what Vaculík witnessed in 1975 stands revealed: you have to be marked "present" if you happen to have a daughter, and she wants to go to high school.

Eventually, Dr. Gustáv Husák, the Czech president, is about to make a speech when all of a sudden the public address system fails. No sound comes out of the amplifiers, so the crowd resumes talking "quite loudly" about what interests it most; mainly soccer. In the past the workers listened silently and attentively to their leaders; in the future of the future, the leader performs the pantomime of a television announcer rendered mute, and the workers, not giving a damn about him, twaddle about trivialities.

The Writing on the Wall is a book of ruins, of hopes "grotesquely betrayed, ideals caricatured" (Joseph Conrad, *Under Western Eyes*). Only readers who once lived among those ruins are likely to pick it off a bookshelf. This, I suspect, is the fate of most such works published in the United States. Aimed at readers who will never know of their existence, they end up in the libraries of people who do not need their message, because they know it by heart.

Quite a few unread volumes describe and analyse 1968, the year of the Prague Spring, of the glorious temporary insanity that befell the Czechoslovak Communist Party. To me (and I was there) this *annus mirabilis* remains something of an enigma. What led the Dubčekists—all of them, for years, dedicated Marxist-Leninists, in many cases with a shady Stalinist past—to create a situation that was bound to become explosive, and eventually unmanageable? Were they serious about their promises? Did they indeed intend to hold free elections, convinced, as some of them said, that the people, out of gratitude to the Communist party for giving them back political freedom, would return it to power? How grateful can you be to a thief who, for unclear reasons, returns your stolen property? And do you trust him in the future?

Such naivety in people as politically hardened as the Dubčekists seems incredible. In my own simplified view, it all started in the early sixties, after official revelations of Stalinist "excesses" began spilling out. These confessed horrors, smacking of the Gestapo rather than of noble revolutionary violence, shook the idealists among the comrades—the former young activists and hotheads who had been lured into uncritical acceptance of an unexamined ideal. I remember them after these revelations, talking excitedly into the wee hours over empty bottles of slivovitz, swearing, weeping, even apologizing to some of their victims. At least a portion of such carryings-on may have been genuine.

In 1963 Alexander Dubček, a bona fide working-class boy, signed one of the most horrifying documents on the unspeakable crimes of the fifties, the report of the Kolder Commission "investigating the violations of socialist justice." The report describes innovative methods of Marxist penology, such as keeping prisoners' hands in tight rubber gloves until their fingers begin to rot away, or a spectacular variation of the age-old hunger torture which leads half-crazed prisoners to offer their eyes for medical research in return for a piece of bread, or to eat their own excrement. Dubček was also familiar with the content of the later Piller Report, which cited the recommendation of the Ministry of Justice that the passing of death sentences be slowed down because too many in a brief span of time affected the sanity of the executioner. All this, mind you, in an official Party document available—in Czech—in the West as well—not in some John Birch Society pamphlet.

As I see it, this was the eye-opener. Then came Ludvík Vaculík's famous speech at the Writers' Congress in 1967, contrasting optimistic visions of socialist reality with actual achievements. It followed a long, fierce, outspoken struggle within the Party, between those who were not shocked—the convinced Stalinists and the cynical opportunists—and those who were. Although Communism creates an elitist society and there is no democracy for the citizen, there is something called "inner Party democracy" (a Leninist heritage) which enables high Party functionaries to indulge in frank discussions behind closed doors. Naturally, they are required to change back into parrots for the public stage, no matter how openly they have quarrelled *in camera*.

But the shocked ones got used to this private-club democracy, and slowly, with the Stalinist guard weakening and the opportunists changing sides, some of it spilled over, first to the cultural weeklies, eventually to general periodicals. The public was puzzled, then amused, and finally excited. The Stalinist president Antonín Novotný, along with his cohorts and censors, tried to curb the flow. Savage battles were fought over such grave ideological issues as the nakedness of the protagonist in Miloš Forman's *Loves of a Blonde*, about the resemblance to Lenin of the leading actor in Jan Němec's *Report on the Party and the Guests*, or about the wasting of food in Věra Chytilová's *Daisies*.

So far, so good. Unfortunately, the process created new illusions. The shocked ones, having once succumbed to the illusion of a just dictatorship, now began to see themselves as the natural leaders of a democratic movement; in fact, as pioneers of some kind of democracy. In the heat of battle, it slipped their minds that other leaders had once been duly elected, and then—often with their help—silenced, forced into exile, or even liquidated. They forgot also that the majority of the public had never subscribed to Communism. In the end, they laboured under the illusion that they were spokesmen for the entire people, loved and esteemed by the masses, while in actual fact the common people supported them only because they knew—having learned the hard way—that in a totalitarian state decisive change can come only from above.

The rest was almost all a bad miscalculation by the politicos, who, despite their many years of speaking in the name of the masses, knew nothing about the real and often vengeful spirit of the democratic crowd. They expected, for instance, that the enforced discipline of Stalinism would continue even after the total abolition of censorship, but the lure of uncensored freedom proved too tempting. Ivan Sviták, now a professor of philosophy at California State University, drew attention to the case of Jan Masaryk—the half-American son of Thomas Garrigue Masaryk—who, although he owned a revolver and a wide assortment of sleeping pills, was said to have committed suicide by jumping out of a third-floor window. A nurse revealed that a priest, Father Toufar, arrested after a cross had miraculously moved in his village church at Čihošť, had died on the operating table from numerous internal injuries suffered during police interrogation. A criminologist showed me, without commentary, police photographs of a hanging judge from the fifties who had just hanged himself from a tree, his legs bent stiffly at the knees. An old butler of a former non-Communist politician fell into a well and perished. The director of my publishing house, the one-time secretary of the Stalinist president Klement Gottwald, died in Prague after a prolonged visit to Moscow, of a heart attack during a stroll in the park; his body was never seen by anyone, even his widow—just a sealed coffin in the crematorium. The commander of the Czechoslovak armoured forces put a bullet through his head. The Communist reform movement was quickly assuming the characteristics of a cheap thriller.

And people literally got drunk on freedom. Political prisoners organized themselves into a vociferous club. Non-Communists started the KAN, a club of non-Party activists. Those window-dressing parties listed in the *Encyclopaedia Britannica* as proofs of pluralism in Communist Czechoslovakia made efforts to come to real life. Father Plojhar, the quisling priest who for twenty years had been chairman of the Catholic People's Party, had to resign in disgrace.

By then, completely flabbergasted by the incredible *commedia*, I saw with absolute certainty how this experiment would end—but I thought it would be with a bang, not with a whimper. Just as in *The Sorcerer's Apprentice*, the reformists had brought to life the dangerous spirit of democracy and now they were unable to get rid of its logical consequences. For too long they had been shouting meaningless slogans which no one had taken seriously. But this time people did take their words seriously. And so did the Soviet Union.

For a brief time after the armoured ambush the public supported the Party leadership as their acknowledged leaders; perhaps even loved some, above all the kindly, innocent-looking, and so obviously suffering Mr. Dubček. Emotions naturally swelled under the impact of Soviet violence, cruelty, cynicism, primitivism, and murder. The fact that close to a hundred people died in Prague alone during street fighting (including, allegedly, the black actor from my film *End of a Priest*) is often overlooked; Czech resistance was not entirely passive. A general strike saved Dubček's life. Instead of shooting him, as they did Imre Nagy, the Kremlin masters returned him to office—to office, mind you, not to power. Then—with the help of a fifth column, an anti-Semitic pressure group of old Stalinist storm troopers called the Jodas Men (Jodasovci), and also of the surviving Stalinists in Dubček's Central Committee, and of the opportunists on all levels of the Party apparatus—the Soviets began to undermine the reformists' position. Popular emotions reached their peak after the self-immolation of Jan Palach, a non-Communist Charles University student, and then, in true Czech style, after two consecutive victories of the Czechoslovak ice hockey team over the Soviet *kommanda* during the 1969 World Championships. Crowds shouting anti-Soviet slogans filled Wenceslas Square, drivers honked their horns; a victorious pandemonium expressed the joy of a small nation over the justice of games, where an ant-sized David can beat a brontosaurus of a Goliath. Then somebody smashed the shop windows of the Soviet airline Aeroflot.

The Soviet commander responded with an ultimatum: either the Dubček government show itself in control, or he would move his forces from twenty miles east of Prague to the capital. Dubček resigned; he lingered on as chairman of the National Assembly, a powerless club of yesmen, then as ambassador to Turkey, then as a clerk in a forestry office in Bratislava, eventually as an old-age pensioner. His supporters from among the shocked emigrated or submerged. Some ended up in jail, others as professors at American universities.

The people, disgusted, frustrated, oppressed more than ever before, mostly came to the conclusion that the entire Prague Spring was just another case of one set of Communist rascals fighting another set, and that since non-Communists would never again have a say in anything, anyone in his right mind should not concern himself with these gang-wars, but instead give all his energies to the building of private retreats of well-furnished apartments, well-stocked wine cellars, and well-chosen country cottages. Eventually—quite soon, in fact—only a tiny group, which in time produced Charter 77, was still willing to combat the plague rather than just abuse it over a glass of beer. The group had the sympathies of most people; some even sent anonymous donations. But most also regarded its members as daredevil idealists; yes, even as not quite right in the head.

For, in a perverted way, Soviet psychiatry is correct: civil disobedience in the Soviet empire is indeed a symptom of mental abnormality. But there is a hitch here, a subtle demagogic trick, a shift in meaning. The demands of the dissidents are perfectly legal: respect for the Constitution, which guarantees personal liberty and all the human rights specified in the U.N. Charter and reaffirmed by the Helsinki Agreement, which was signed by the Czechoslovak government. But to make such demands in a Soviet colony exposes the demander and his family to untold miseries, to the dangers of socialist prisons, even death. So, while the dissidents' demands are *legally* normal, in terms of the Constitution and of valid laws, the act of demanding them is *psychologically* abnormal; it is in conflict with the instinct for self-preservation. Naturally, Soviet psychiatrists never ask the interesting question, "What *makes* such actions abnormal?" Bertolt Brecht knew the answer when, in *Galileo Galilei*, he has one character exclaim: "Unhappy is the country that needs heroes!" And he was being hypocritical when he got mad at Orson Welles for telling him the play was anti-Stalinist.

Of course, every citizen of Czechoslovakia is aware of the answer. He knows that he owes his relative safety and prosperity to his civil obedience—which, in the context of totalitarian dictatorships, translates as cowardice. Few people who feel like cowards relish the power that makes them feel that way. Judging by the manuscripts smuggled to me from Prague, the vast and truly silent majority is now past even hating Communism. And I am not speaking of known dissidents, but of authors who are university students, members in good standing of the Communist Youth, "progressive non-Party citizens": in short, not the third- but the second-class citizens. On the outside these "conformists", the Grey Zone of real-socialist society, have become "normalized", as Party lingo has it; that is, they conform to the post-1968 political climate. They express their thoughts and feelings only in intimate circles of the most trusted friends, otherwise they follow the nauseating rituals of "socialist progressivity".

But occasionally the accumulated frustration spills over into clandestinely penned pages, delivered then by courageous emissaries to distant Canada. The feelings about Communism captured then are much more critical—to use a polite word—than those in books by such dissidents as are represented in *The Writing on the Wall*. The dissidents (they themselves don't like this label, since it's not they but rather the government that dissents from the Constitution) either continue to consider themselves democratic socialists, or, understandably, are somewhat inhibited by the fact that they are not and cannot be—their literary styles are easily recognizable—anonymous. Out of frustration and disgust, some have become apolitical. But the non-normalized voices of the "normalized" are anonymous, and they therefore often speak without caution, without the hard-to-overcome consideration for one's political past (they have none), and without illusions. They are *jenseits von Kommunismus und Kapitalismus* (beyond Communism and capitalism). They don't even hate Marxism-Leninism. All they feel for it is boundless contempt.

A REVOLUTION IS USUALLY THE WORST SOLUTION

—

In October 1981 Škvorecký participated in an international conference held in Toronto, on the subject of "The Writer and Human Rights". The participants included Margaret Atwood, Stanislaw Baránczak, Joseph Brodsky, Allen Ginsberg, Nadine Gordimer, Susan Sontag, Michel Tournier, and many others.

Škvorecký's speech was a disturbing reminder that "human rights" can be and have been abused by regimes

of the left as well as of the right. To some left-leaning
members of the audience, it was not what they had come
to hear.

FRANKLY, I FEEL frustrated whenever I have to talk about revolution for the benefit of people who have never been through
one. They are—if you'll excuse the platitude—like a child who
doesn't believe that fire hurts, until he burns himself. I, my
generation, my nation, have been involuntarily through two
revolutions, both of them socialist: one of the right variety, one
of the left. Together they destroyed my peripheral vision.

When I was fourteen, we were told at school that the only
way to a just and happy society led through socialist revolution.
Capitalism was bad, liberalism a fraud, democracy bunk, and
parliamentarism decadent. Our then Minister of Culture and
Education, the late Mr. Emanuel Moravec, taught us this, and
then sent his son to fight for socialism with the Hermann
Goering SS Division. The son was later hanged; the minister,
to use proper revolutionary language, liquidated himself with
the aid of a gun.

When I was twenty-one, we were told at Charles University
that the only way to a just and happy society led through
socialist revolution. Capitalism was bad, liberalism a fraud,
democracy bunk, and parliamentarism decadent. Our then
professor of philosophy, the late Mr. Arnošt Kolman, taught us
this, and then gave his half-Russian daughter in marriage to
a Czech Communist who fought for socialism with Alexander
Dubček. Later he fled to Sweden. Professor Kolman, one of
the very last surviving original Bolsheviks of 1917 and a close
friend of Lenin, died in 1980, also in Sweden. Before his death,
he returned his Party card to Brezhnev and declared that the
Soviet Union had betrayed the socialist revolution.

In 1981 I am told by various people who suffer from Adlerian and Rankian complexes that the only way to a just and
happy society leads through socialist revolution. Capitalism is
bad, liberalism a fraud, democracy bunk, and parliamentarism
decadent. Dialectically, all this makes me suspect that capitalism is probably good, liberalism may be right, democracy is the

closest approximation to the truth, and parliamentarism a vigorous gentleman in good health, filled with the wisdom of ripe
old age.

There have been quite a few violent revolutions in our
century, most of them Communist, some Fascist, and some nationalistic and religious. The final word on all of them comes
from the pen of Joseph Conrad, who in 1911 wrote this in his
novel *Under Western Eyes*:

> ...in a real revolution—not a simple dynastic change
> or a mere reform of institutions—in a real revolution
> the best characters do not come to the front. A vio-
> lent revolution falls into the hands of narrow-minded
> fanatics and of tyrannical hypocrites at first. Afterwards
> comes the turn of all the pretentious intellectual fail-
> ures of the time. Such are the chiefs and the leaders.
> You will notice that I have left out the mere rogues. The
> scrupulous and the just, the noble, humane, and devoted
> natures; the unselfish and the intelligent may begin a
> movement—but it passes away from them. They are not
> the leaders of a revolution. They are its victims: the vic-
> tims of disgust, of disenchantment—often of remorse.
> Hopes grotesquely betrayed, ideals caricatured—that is
> the definition of revolutionary success. There have been
> in every revolution hearts broken by such successes.

I wonder if anything can be added to this penetrating analysis? The scenario seems to fit perfectly. Just think of the
Strasser brothers, those fervent German nationalists and socialists: one of them liquidated by his own workers' party, the
other having to flee, first to capitalist Czechoslovakia, then to
liberal England, while their movement passed into the hands of
that typical "intellectual failure", the unsuccessful artist named
Adolf Hitler. Think of Boris Pilnyak, liquidated while those
sleek and deadly scientific bureaucrats he described so well—
who were perfectly willing to liquidate others to bolster their
own careers—bolstered their careers, leaving a trail of human
skulls behind them. Think of Fidel Castro's involuntary volunteers dying with a look of amazement on their faces in a
foreign country where they have no right to be, liquidating

its black warriors who for years had been fighting the Portuguese. Think of the German Communists who, after the Nazi *Machtübernahme* (the grabbing of power), fled to Moscow and then, broken-hearted, were extradited back into the hands of the Gestapo because Stalin honoured his word to Hitler; the Jews among them were designated for immediate liquidation, the non-Jews were sent to Mauthausen and Ravensbrück. It is all an old, old story. The revolution—if you don't mind another cliché—is fond of devouring its own children. Or, if you do mind, let me put it this way: the revolution is cannibalistic.

It is estimated that violent Communist revolutions in our century have dined on about one hundred million men, women, and children. What has been gained by their sumptuous feast? Basically two things, both predicted by the so-called classics of Marxism-Leninism: the state that withered away, and the New Socialist Man.

The state withered away all right—into a kind of Mafia, a perfect police regime. Thought-crime, which most believed to be just a morbid joke by Orwell, concocted when he was already dying of tuberculosis, has become a reality in today's "real socialism", as the stepfathers of the Czechoslovak Communist Party have christened their own status quo. The material standards of living in these post-revolutionary police states are invariably lower, often much lower, than those of the developed Western democracies. But of course, the New Socialist Man has emerged, as announced.

Not quite as announced. Who is he? He is an intelligent creature who, sometimes in the interest of bare survival, sometimes merely to maintain his material living standards, is willing to abnegate the one quality that differentiates him from animals: his intellectual and moral awareness, his ability to think and freely express his thought. This creature has come to resemble the three little monkeys whose statuettes you see in junk shops: one covers its eyes, another its ears, the third its mouth. The New Socialist Man has thus become a new Trinity of the post-revolutionary age.

Therefore, with Albert Camus, I suspect that in the final analysis capitalist democracy is to be preferred to regimes created by violent revolutions. I must also agree with Lenin that those who, after the various gulags (and after the Grand

Guignol spectacle of the Polish Communist Party exhorting
the Solidarity Union to shut up or else the Polish nation will
be destroyed—and guess who will destroy it), still believe in
violent revolutions are indeed "useful idiots".

In the Western world, such mentally retarded adults sometimes point out, in defence of violence, that capitalism is guilty
of similar crimes. Most of these crimes, true, have occurred
in the past, often in the distant past, but some are happening in our own time, especially in what is known as the Third
World. But to justify crimes by arguing that others have also
committed them is, to put it mildly, bad taste. To exonerate
the Communist inquisition by blaming the Catholic Church for
having done the same thing in the Dark Ages amounts to an admission that Communism represents a return to the Dark Ages.
To accuse General Pinochet of torturing his political prisoners,
and then barter your own political prisoners, fresh from psychiatric prison-clinics, for those of General Pinochet is—shall we
say—a black joke.

Does all this mean that I reject any violent revolution anywhere, no matter what the circumstances are? I have seen too
much despair in my time to be blind to despair. It's just that I
do not believe in two things. First, I do not think that a violent
uprising born out of "a long train of abuses and usurpations,
pursuing invariably the same object" which "evinces a design to
reduce" men "under absolute despotism" should be called a revolution; because when such a revolution later produces another
"long chain of abuses and usurpation" and people rise against
it, to be linguistically correct we would have to call such an uprising a "counter-revolution". In our society, however, this term
has acquired a pejorative meaning it does not deserve.

Second, I do not believe that any violent revolution in which
Communists or Fascists participate can be successful, except
in the Conradian sense as quoted above. Because, quite simply,
I do not trust authoritarian ideologies. Every revolution with
the participation of Communists or Fascists must eventually
of necessity turn into a dictatorship and, more often than not,
into a state nakedly ruled by the police. Neither Fascists nor
Communists can live with democracy, because their ultimate
goal, no matter whether they call it *das Führerprinzip* or
the dictatorship of the proletariat, is precisely the "absolute

despotism" of which Thomas Jefferson spoke. They tolerate partners in the revolutionary effort only as long as they need them to defeat the powers that be—not perhaps because all Communists and Fascists are radically evil but because they are disciplined adherents of ideologies which command them to do so, since that is what Hitler or Lenin advised. The Fascists are more honest about it: they say openly—at least the Nazis did—that democracy is nonsense. Lenin was equally frank only in his more mystical moments; otherwise the Communists use Newspeak. But as soon as they grow strong enough, they finish off democracy just as efficiently as the Fascists, and usually more so.

All this is rather abstract, however, and since individualistic Anglo-Saxons usually demand concrete, individual examples, let me offer you a few.

In Canada there lives an old professor by the name of Vladimir Krajina. He teaches at the University of British Columbia in Vancouver and is an eminent botanist who has received high honours from the Canadian government for his work in the preservation of Canadian flora. But in World War II, he was also a most courageous anti-Nazi fighter. He operated a wireless transmitter by which the Czech underground sent vital messages to London, information collected by the members of the Czech Resistance in armament factories, by "our men" in the Protectorate bureaucracy who had access to Nazi state secrets, and by Intelligence Service spies such as the notorious A-54. The Gestapo, of course, was after Professor Krajina. For several years, he had to move from one hideout to another, leaving a trail of blood behind him, of Gestapo men shot by his co-fighters, of people who hid him and were caught and shot. After the war, he became an MP for the Czech Socialist party. But his incumbency lasted for little more than two years. Immediately after the Communist coup in 1948, Professor Krajina had to go into hiding again, and he eventually fled the country. Why? Because the Communists had never forgotten that he had warned the Czech underground against cooperating with the Communists. And he was right: he was not the only one to flee. Hundreds of other anti-Nazi fighters were forced to leave the country, and those who would not or could not ended up on the gallows, in concentration camps, or, if they were lucky, in menial jobs. Among them were many Czech RAF pilots who had distinguished themselves in the Battle of Britain and then had returned to the republic for whose democracy they had risked their lives. All this is a story since repeated in other Central and East European states. It is still being repeated in Cuba, in Vietnam, in Angola, and most recently in Nicaragua.

In a recent article in the *New York Review of Books*, V.S. Naipaul tells about his experiences in revolutionary Iran. He met a Communist student there who showed him snapshots of Communists being executed by the Islamic Revolutionary Guards and then told him about his love for Stalin: "I love him. He was one of the greatest revolutionaries.... What he did in Russia we have to do in Iran. We, too, have to do a lot of killing. A lot.... We have to kill all the bourgeoisie." For what purpose? To create a Brezhnevite Iran, perhaps? To send tens of thousands of new customers to the Siberian Gulag? But obviously the bourgeois don't count. They were useful when they fought the shah, as the Kadets had been in 1917 while they fought the czar. Now they are expendable. They have become "Fascists", just like the Barcelonian anarchists denounced in the Newspeak of the Communist press decades ago in Spain, as described by Orwell in *Homage to Catalonia*. They have become nonpeople. James Jones once wrote, "It's so easy to kill real people in the name of some damned ideology or other; once the killer can abstract them in his own mind into being symbols, then he needn't feel guilty for killing them since they're no longer human beings." The Jews in Auschwitz, the *zeks* in the Gulag, the bourgeoisie in a Communist Iran. Symbols, not people. *Revolutionsfutter*.

When Angela Davis was in jail, a Czech socialist politician, Jiří Pelikán, a former Communist and now a member of the European Parliament for the Italian Socialist Party, approached her through an old American Communist lady and asked her whether she would sign a protest against the imprisonment of Communists in Prague. She agreed to do so, but not until she got out of jail because, she said, it might jeopardize her case. When she was released, she sent word via her secretary that she would fight for the release of political prisoners anywhere in the world except, of course, in the socialist states. Anyone sitting in a socialist jail must be against socialism, and therefore deserves to be where he is. All birds can fly. An ostrich is a bird. Therefore an ostrich can fly. So much for the professor of philosophy Angela Davis.

So much for concrete examples.

In his *Notebooks*, Albert Camus recorded a conversation with one of his Communist co-fighters in the French Resistance: "Listen, Tar, the real problem is this: no matter what happens, I shall always defend you against the rifles of the execution squad. But you will have to say yes to my execution."

Evelyn Waugh, whom I confess I prefer to all other modern British writers, said in an interview with Julian Jebb, "An artist must be a reactionary. He has to stand out against the tenor of the age and not go flopping along; he must offer some little opposition."

All I have learned about violent revolutions, from books and from personal experience, convinces me that Waugh was right.

ARE CANADIANS POLITICALLY NAIVE?

—

One of Škvorecký's most powerful political essays, this lament was written in response to a series of articles published in The Winnipeg Sun *by a Canadian who made an "official" visit in 1983 to The World Assembly for Peace and Life Against Nuclear War held in Prague. It should be read by all North Americans who think that a brief visit to East or Central Europe qualifies them to offer a report on "over there" because they have "seen it with their own eyes".*

YOU WON'T LIKE this essay, but let it be a comfort to you that the question in my title is stupid. If you do not subscribe to collectivistic hypotheses—as I most vehemently don't—you will know why. What, after all, is the *only* thing that Canadians have in common? Not even the language; just their citizenship. Apparently there are some naive Canadians; some are downright silly. Others are sophisticated, knowledgeable, talented. A truistic observation that can be made about any nation.

The question should read: are many Canadians politically naive? As much as I hate to hurt people's feelings, I am afraid I must answer yes. Unfortunately, many are.

As long as such men and women are not members of the academic or mass media communities, their naivety is pardonable. In this country we don't have mandatory indoctrination sessions for everybody, and the majority of our citizens are preoccupied with the good old Yankee business of pursuing happiness. The cab driver who has never had a totalitarian experience cannot be blamed for not reading scholarly treatises on history and politics. Inexcusability begins with people in the mass media and in university lecture rooms. In this day and age, it is not just naive to express uninformed opinions and judgements publicly, it is *criminally* naive.

To be accurate: Canadian political naivety, as I see it, has nothing to do with the way Canadians view our domestic political issues; in that respect they are admittedly and understandably much shrewder than citizens who came to this country late in life. Neither has it anything to do with the way they view Nazism (though they rarely distinguish it from Fascism). Nazism was blatantly evil, anti-humanistic, racist, supremacist. It would have been dangerous to the world—and therefore to Canada—had it won the war. Fortunately the Nazis lost, and in my opinion they present no danger at all to the world at large; they can only endanger individuals. The Nazi ideology never could have any appeal except to Germans, the nation of supermen (and certainly not to *all* Germans), to some individuals in nations that deemed themselves racially first class, and to cranks in other nations: to the Sir Oswald Mosleys, or to the Emanuel Moravecs of Bohemia. Today, the influence of the Nazi ideology is limited only to cranks. But what about the estimated 2,000 ex-Nazis living in our midst? Do they not present a danger? How can they? For the past thirty-eight years they have kept not just a low profile, but utter silence. None of them has ever tried to stand up and defend their past and their ideology publicly. They know better than we do about the crimes they had committed before this country gave them—unwittingly—shelter. Now, after Rauca, they must be shaking with fear.

Unlike the Nazi ideology, which had charm only for members of the *Herrenvölker* and for deviants, the Communist ideology sounds sweet. It is antiracist, uses humanistic clichés, talks a lot about peace (while conducting little surreptitious military interventions, wars, and proxy-wars in Hungary, Czechoslovakia, Poland, Afghanistan, Angola, Ethiopia, etc.), about international solidarity, brotherhood, even love. Vis-à-vis things Soviet, the political naivety of quite a few Canadians is brought to oppressingly fragrant bloom. Let me discuss a concrete and recent example of this blooming at its Stakhanovite best.

In the spring of 1983 a World Assembly for Peace and Life against Nuclear War was held in Prague. The Brobdingnagian length of the name betrays the inspiration behind the gathering: where else but in Soviet Russia does one find dailies with titles like *For the Lasting Peace, For a People's Democracy*! But one cannot ask Canadian delegates to do extensive homework in semantics first, and only then head for Prague. So they went without having done their homework. Once there, they were wined and dined, guided through the countryside on Potemkinian excursions, and allowed to witness a peace rally of—according to their estimate—a quarter-million people. They also met some Soviet VIPs. Back home, some wrote about the events in Canadian papers. One such writer was Ms. Lesley Hughes from Winnipeg.

I have read three reports from her pen. One, headlined "A Prague spring without tanks", appeared in *The Winnipeg Sun* on June 22, 1983, and tells about how, on arriving in Prague, she suffered "a shock when [she] discovered the sophistication of life in Communist Czechoslovakia." Her second shock came when she realized the "similarities to Western life. First there were teen-agers. All in denim...a few given over to punk-rocking...defying the system just like the ones at home." In another article (July 6), "Why we don't have peace", Ms. Hughes recounts some personal chats with Valentina Tereshkova, the world's first woman cosmonaut, and with "a high-placed Russian". This gentleman even entrusted her with a few state secrets, namely that the American delegates to the Geneva Peace Talks had "been told [by their government] to offer only impossible suggestions for disarmament." Ms. Hughes opines that "we have been seduced out of our ability to see beyond appearances to reality" and expresses a wish *"to see for ourselves"* (Ms. Hughes's italics). Finally, she gives advice to Western leaders: they should act "to prevent [war] first, and worry about the communist threat to our way of life when life itself is secure."

Her other article (July 4) is a meditation on the untruths of anti-Communist assertions, entitled "Repression? It's certainly well hidden." Here the Winnipeg author tells her readers about "phone calls from New York...where newspapers have reported riots, suppression and arrests" in Prague, and about some "bad press" from Western radio according to which the Peace Assembly would grant "freedom of expression to communists only." She also confesses that, on her way to Prague, she was anxious not to "be seen as today's Neville Chamberlain, shouting Peace in Our Time!" but was eventually reassured that this would not be the case when she spoke to "Czechs she met on the street, in obscure shops, in bars," and they all "said they attended [the Peace Rally] gladly, and not just for the tourist money but for hope." There was some more dining, vodka drinking, and dancing, a "full day group tour [through] factories, schools, day care centres and a collective farm", and the exhilarating (and certainly hectic) days culminated with the Peace Rally in Prague's Old Town Square, packed to capacity. "Do you really think," asks Ms. Hughes, "the communists could have driven the citizens from their homes to line the streets 10 deep, forced them to weep and take our pictures, shake our hands?"

Finally, the Winnipeg reporter concludes: no, we Canadian delegates were no "Lenin's fools" to support the conference. (Lenin's term was "idiots".)

A depression descends on me: can I hope to get the space in *Canadian Literature* necessary to analyse in detail this gargantuan collection of misconceptions? Hardly. I cannot ask the editor to reject other contributors whose themes are more relevant to the issue of literature. How many people read

Canadian Literature anyway? Possibly fewer than those who read *The Winnipeg Sun*.

All the same, perhaps one should not give up. If I cannot go into all the details necessary to rectify the myopic vision of our Alice in the Czech Wonderland, let me at least try to be systematic.

Ms. Hughes' articles display some naiveties of the Canadian psyche which I would describe as follows.

1. *The Canadian Insensitivity*

It strikes me as odd that none of the Canadian delegates found it odd to travel to a *peace* conference held in a country which only fifteen years ago fell prey to a *military* ambush of gigantic proportions (about seven times as many soldiers as the entire Canadian army, plus hardware, took part in it). During that military adventure about a hundred civilians died, and ever since the country has lived under virtual Soviet military occupation. The main of several Soviet military bases is only twenty miles east of Prague, at Mladá, a mere hour's drive for armoured vehicles. Missile sites (with atomic warheads, naturally) loom behind many a Czech village, though the delegates saw none near the collective farm where they spent a few minutes, probably snacking and wining. It could not have been more than a few minutes since, in the course of one single day, they visited "factories, schools, day care centres and a collective farm". Ms. Hughes saw Bohemia—as the Czech saying goes—from an express train.

But if I find all this odd what am I to think about the sensitivity of the woman who titled her article "A Prague spring without tanks"? Apparently, the word she chose was just a word to her, with no reality behind it. A useful gimmick to coin a catchy phrase for her headline. For the millions of Czechs, however—including the 70,000 who now live in Canada—Ms. Hughes' chosen word has a more material meaning. For there are thousands of their loved ones in Czechoslovakia who lost their jobs, their professional careers, their social status, their personal liberty, and even their lives as a direct result of the action of the metaphorical tanks. But Ms. Hughes did not meet any of those. She was a friendly visitor; friendly, that is, to the government.

2. *The Canadian Ignorance*

Here part of the blame should probably be placed on the shoulders of our ethnocultural institutions which financially support folk dancing, pork feasts, and other extinct forms of European village life. In the minds of some people, the jumping about of sexy girl Ph.D.'s in "national costumes" creates the image of a universal East European as a simple-minded, semi-literate hillbilly. This was apparently Ms. Hughes' idea of the typical Czech. She seems never to have heard of sophisticated Czech literature and film; names like Čapek or Kundera tell her nothing; neither do words like Martinů or Mucha or, for that matter, the Bren gun, the Škoda AA cannon, the *Panzerjäger*—but that, perhaps, is because she loves peace. When, instead of simpletons in mud huts, she found English-speaking denim-clad youths, who very probably know much more about Mick Jagger than herself (and possibly more about Faulkner), she was shocked.

She also met the punk-rockers, "defying the system *just like* the ones at home" (italics mine).

3. *The Canadian Inability to See the Importance of Quantity in Quality*

I love—that is, I hate—the phrase "just like". When Václav Havel, the playwright, was arrested for the first time for having smuggled the manuscript memoirs of an ancient socialist minister to our Czech publishing house in Toronto, I met a Canadian colleague, and when I told her about this she uttered: "Just like Daniel Ellsberg."

Well, yes. Both Havel and Ellsberg committed, in a way, the same crime: they leaked documents their governments wished to keep secret. There were some differences, though: the difference between the private memoirs of an octogenarian former politician, and military documents labelled Top Secret; the difference between sending the material abroad with no demands of remuneration, and selling it for a handsome price to the rich American papers. Then also the difference between Ellsberg's later fortunes: acquittal, a lecture circuit; and those of Havel: four years in jail and now round-the-clock police surveillance.

Even more illuminating of this Canadian failing was another encounter I had with another youngish lady, this time over the frame-up of the socialist leader Milada Horáková which resulted in her execution. "Just like Angela Davis!" my interlocutor commented on the frame-up trial. Now, *that* made me mad, and I lost self-control. "Oh really? But that trial was in California, wasn't it?" I cried. "I thought the Yanks put Angela in a gas chamber!" The lady has avoided me ever since.

Similarly with the Czech punks. Yes, they do defy the government. But instead of permitting them to hold monster concerts in big halls and stadiums, the government—only about a month after Ms. Hughes' departure from Prague—clamped down on the punk-folk, disbanded dozens of punk-rock and New Wave bands, took away the licences of their musicians, fired the entire editorial board of the only pop-music monthly, *Melodie*, and apparently is about to dissolve the Jazz Section of the Musicians' Union, the chief spokesman for the punks. Not "just like" at all. Just "a little like".

4. *The Canadian Neglect of Pertinent Literature*

Ms. Hughes was taken through all the stages of subtle brainwashing described in detail (with many examples) in Paul Hollander's *Political Pilgrims*, one of several books Canadians intent on travelling behind the Curtain should read. With all due respect to her, Ms. Hughes is a provincial Canadian journalist who dines with "high-placed Russians" and with the female stars of the universe only occasionally. In Prague, however, she received VIP treatment. The high-placed KGB man even gave her a piece of interesting information, and she, overawed by the friendly kindness of such greats, believed his information just as strongly as she disbelieves the information offered to Canadians not only by us, biased exiles, but also by scholarly books and acclaimed novels readily available in Canada. Some were even written by Canadians, such as the books on Czechoslovakia by the eminent Professor H. Gordon Skilling of the University of Toronto. Disregarding such works of scholarship, Ms. Hughes expressed a wish to "see for herself", not through the eyes of propaganda. After seventy years of totalitarian trickery, however, the primitive methods of Count Potemkin have been vastly improved. Travelling to a totalitarian country in order to "see for yourself", without having done substantial homework first, guarantees the very opposite of what Ms. Hughes wanted to achieve by "being there". It guarantees that you will be unable "to see beyond appearances to reality."

5. *The Canadian Inability to Realize that the Totalitarians ARE Different from Us*

"Prevent war first, and worry about the communist threat afterwards!" A nice-sounding slogan. It reminds me of a graffito I found on a wall at the University of Toronto under a Communist party election poster: "Vote Now, Pay Later!" The trouble here is that it is impossible to separate peace from freedom. By freedom, naturally, I mean not national independence but the individual liberty of the citizen. In the sense of national independence, one of the "freest" nations was certainly Germany under Hitler. However, individual freedom in Herr Hitler's Reich is best characterized by just one word: Auschwitz.

There does exist a genuine, non-government-sponsored peace movement in Czechoslovakia. But its delegates were not admitted to the dining-and-wining parties, nor were they permitted to speak. This movement stresses the indivisibility of the question of peace and the question of freedom. To simplify this matter for our Alices: the civil freedoms and human rights that exist in our Western society guarantee that people like Ms. Hughes can, quite effectively I'm afraid, fight for disarmament—in our part of the world. The lack of such rights, such freedoms, in totalitarian countries of whatever political stripe can lend effective support to Ms. Hughes's fight for disarmament—in our part of the world. If the Ms. Hugheses have their way—and there is a chance they may—there will be disarmament—*in our part of the world*. The long word for this is "unilateral".

Now, the experience of both remote and recent history teaches us that the autocrat, the tyrant, the dictator, the totalitarian ruler understands, unfortunately, but one international language: that of material strength. He is unmoved by the presumably human feelings that move Ms. Hughes. After all, the men who lead a state which has killed between 30 and 70 million of its own citizens can hardly be soft-hearted. But they do understand the language of military strength. The Nazis in the Second World War, for instance, never used poisonous gas, yet

a gas-mask box was attached to the belt of every German soldier from the first day of the war to the last. For the Allies too
had gas, and would have used it had the Germans started gas
warfare. It was solely this knowledge which prevented Hitler
from resorting to the diabolic invention of his predecessors in
the First World War. But if the Allies had not been in possession
of the chemical weapon is it reasonable to assume that Hitler,
from humanitarian considerations, would have refrained from
yperiting the Yanks, the Tommies, the Bolshies, all of them?

A more recent example from the same category of killing:
the North Vietnamese certainly had access to Russian-made
gas during the war in Vietnam—but they used it only after the
Americans had departed, against the primitive tribesmen in the
mountains, who do not even possess bazookas.

This is the reason why people of my experience, both personal
and bookish, think it important that Western atomic defences
not be weakened, let alone abandoned altogether. We do not
want to die in an atomic war, just as Ms. Hughes doesn't.
However, we have reason, supported by logic and history, to
fear that if the West were to disarm atomically, we would have
not peace but war. Non-atomic perhaps; but if the conventional
forces of NATO put up stiff resistance, we probably would live
to experience even the atomic variety. Limited, perhaps, but
atomic nevertheless. Did you read Sakharov's report on the
party and the guests in that remote top-secret Siberian place
where they celebrated the successful completion of the Soviet
bomb? Sakharov, the father of that weapon, proposed a toast:
"That this terrible bomb may never be used!" To which one of the
jolly-looking, rotund Soviet generals responded: "Thank you,
comrade Sakharov, for delivering this baby. As to how it should
be used, please, leave that to us!"

It is, unfortunately, impossible to secure peace first and
worry about Communism later. You cannot separate the two
endeavours. It would be nice if you could, but you cannot.

No, I have no ready-made advice to give to those who want
to preserve peace. I only know—because history has taught me
this lesson—how peace can go to pieces. Pacifism, the naive or
cowardly efforts to extricate ourselves from our common North
American destiny in a world of powerful totalitarianism, is a
guaranteed road to war.

6. *The Ahistoricity of Canadian Observations*

How often, in our Canadian newspapers, have you come across sentences like: "Mr. Jaruzelski, the leader of the military junta which grabbed power in Poland a year ago, said..." or "Mr. Arafat, the leader of the anti-Israeli guerrillas, declared...," etc.? Apparently it is presumed that Canadians have either a pathologically short memory, or a lamentable lack of knowledge of the affairs of the world.

Ms. Hughes asks her rhetorical question about the Communists' ability to drive their citizens into the streets in support of a Pax Sovietica. Yes, such a thing would be impossible in this country. But Ms. Hughes does not seem to know that people now living in Czechoslovakia have a past very much different from the past of people now living in Canada. The Czechs are the veterans of six years of Nazi occupation, with its fear-enforced mass gatherings (in the same Prague square) protesting the "perfidious assassination of *Herr stellvertretende Reichsprotektor, Obergruppenführer der SS und General der Polizei Reinhard Heydrich*"; they have lived through Stalinism with its 300-500 political executions (including the above-mentioned Milada Horáková), with about 100,000 political prisoners mining uranium ore for the production of Soviet A-bombs; with hundreds of thousands of intellectuals, lawyers, clerks, small businessmen, farmers, teachers, and scholars sent to the mines, to the "black [working] battalions", to the factories and state farms for "re-education"; with widespread screening, police surveillance, harassment, "voluntary" mandatory weekend brigades, etc. These people are the fathers and mothers of children who would have very little chance of being admitted to higher schooling, not to speak of university, if their parents refused to "fight for peace". In short: Ms. Hughes seems to be unaware of the very concrete, non-metaphorical bloodiness of the Communist system in the first years after its coming to power, and of its unabated repressiveness ever since. After the unleashing of their holocaustic actions, these regimes do not have to drive people to rallies with whips. The fear of their power and of their readiness to crack down on you, Jaruzelski-like, suffices. You are slowly manoeuvred into a frame of mind where you no longer give a damn about anything. You say to yourself: so what? We rallied against the criminal British paras who killed our good socialist friend Obergruppenführer Heydrich. We rallied to demand death sentences for the criminal defendants in the Slánský trial, and later were told that the hanged comrades had been innocent—so what? We rallied against the lies of the imperialist Kennedy about the presence of Soviet missiles in Cuba, and a few days later we rallied in support of the peace gesture of Nikita Khrushchev when he removed non-existent missiles from that island. We rallied in support of the good Communist Dubček, and we rallied when the Soviets invaded to depose him; only a couple of years later we rallied in support of the Brotherly Soviet Help and against the bad Communist Dubček. So what? Why not rally for peace? It's just another Kremlin trick, and you'd better be present.

Two more things Ms. Hughes does not seem to know: mostly, these mass demonstrations are held during working hours, with no loss of salary. In this sense, the participants are paid for participation. If the rally falls on a holiday, the above-mentioned powers of persuasion still function. And usually one has to have one's name marked off on lists checked by foremen and other bosses in the side streets where the voluntary demonstrators gather. Then one marches down Paris Street, in the direction of Old Town Square—a huge river of humans. Through the side streets, rivulets of people, their banners and flags rolled up, flow in an opposite direction. They are headed for the many pubs in Old Town Prague, to celebrate a sunny day spent on an enjoyable walk and crowned by a convivial beer-drinking party in the colourful medieval rooms where, a thousand years ago (who knows?), Good King Wenceslas himself may have dined and beered with sexy bathing-house attendants.

Had Ms. Hughes known all this, would she be so surprised that people with whom she obviously did not speak in Czech, though possibly through an interpreter, expressed such orthodox views in the presence of an apparently fellow-travelling foreigner?*

7. *The Canadian Habit of Judging Others by Ourselves*

Reading in US newspapers about protests and arrests in Prague, Ms. Hughes expected to witness something on the scale of US riots, but she failed to notice anything of that sort. Once again, she did not take into account the well-developed fear which is the best guardian of civil obedience, a fear stemming, in this case, also from the claustrophobic situation of a small nation living under a police regime. There is simply no way of escape. An American draft-dodger easily slips across the border to friendly Canada, sometimes even in his car. The criminal rents a hotel room under an assumed name, and puts on a false moustache. Even when caught by the police, a youngster who has just smashed a window at the American embassy will have no problem continuing his studies at university.

No such possibilities exist in Czechoslovakia. To slip across the Iron Curtain is rather difficult—and if Ms. Hughes thinks that the Curtain is just a metaphor invented by the old reactionary Winston Churchill, she should have travelled to Prague by car and, while still in Germany, taken a walk along the border. As for hotels, you cannot rent a room without showing your identity card to the desk clerk, who has to present the list of guests to the police on demand. A false beard will not help you. And if you are a student and smash a window in the Soviet embassy, well....

That's why Ms. Hughes did not observe any huge crowds of protesters, battalions of police, and dozens of patrol wagons overloaded with beaten-up humans. But there *was* a protest march in downtown Prague, not only reported in the Western media but also acknowledged (privately) by the Reverend John Morgan, who was dining and wining in Prague at that time. Only about three hundred people marched, mostly very young, and they were handled with ease by the police. What the future has in store for them, I don't know. The totalitarian press never informs its readership about such matters.

And then there was the meeting, much written about in West German and British papers, of the representatives of Charter 77, the Czech peace and human rights movement, with delegates from the German Green and Social Democratic parties. It took place on the White Hill, on the outskirts of Prague, where three hundred years ago the Czechs lost their freedom to the authoritarian rule of the Austrian Hapsburgs. The historical hill, on this later occasion, was surrounded by police, the participants were rounded up, cameras were taken out of the hands of Western peace delegates, and films were torn out of the cameras and exposed to the shining sun. But Ms. Hughes has neither seen this nor read about it. Canadian papers did not cover the event very much; Czech papers did not cover it at all. Ms. Hughes does not read German and probably ignores the British conservative press.

In the end, as predicted by the Americans, freedom of expression was indeed granted "to Communists only"— certainly in the final document of the conference. Does this document protest against the two main atomic arsenals in the world with equal vehemence? Does it protest against one of the two at all? Or does it just rave against the warmongering Yankees, those inefficient trigger-happy militarists who, for at least a decade, had a monopoly on atomic weapons and yet somehow failed to launch a war on the then non-atomic and therefore defenceless Soviet Russia?

Ms. Hughes, presumably, voted for that document. I am afraid she fits Lenin's description rather well after all.

Oh my! I wanted to write about this beautiful land; about its golden skyscrapers silhouetted against the skies of Indian summer; about the joy of its libraries; about the sweet charm of freedom I and my wife and all my good old countrymen found here, under the protective umbrella of the Yanks. But damn politics got me like the blues, and the naivety of so many of my fellow Canadians does not help me out. I am far from being of the stuff that Sisyphus was made of, and yet, again and again, I push this boulder up the steep slope of incomprehension.

How silly of me!

In December 1983, the Czechoslovak News Agency CTK, in a press release, informed the world that "hundreds of thousands of demonstrators welcomed the decision of the Supreme Soviet and of the Czechoslovak government to place Soviet missiles with atomic warheads on Czechoslovak territory." Apparently these were the same crowds that only six months earlier had demonstrated for peace. Now they rejoiced over the fact that their country had been made a target for American atomic missiles. What a strange people, the Czechs!

TWO PEAS IN A POD

—

Here Škvorecký again insists that whether a totalitarian state is of the "left" or "right" it is still totalitarian. This extended comparison of Nazi and Communist songs and propaganda may be one of the few essays of the past few years that will offend individuals on both the left and the right. It has been published twice: first in 1982 in Západ, *then in 1986 in* The Idler.

THERE ARE VARIOUS ways to anger a bull. According to tradition, the best way is to use a red rag. Marxist-Leninists, and particularly those in power, are angered by any kind of criticism. But the most reliable way to enrage them is to point out certain similarities between their doctrine (and the system deriving from it), and the doctrine and system of German National Socialism. Should the upstart who suggests such a thing be under their jurisdiction, they will lock him up. If he happens to be beyond their imperial reach, they will pronounce him to be an arch-reactionary, and, if he is an academic, they may inundate him with indignant disquisitions on all the ways in which the two theories and practices differ.

It is true that they differ in some ways, but they have at least one important thing in common: the pillar of both Communist and Fascist regimes is the devoted party member, the so-called "healthy core", at whose own core is a certain kind of pathology. The conflict between these people and the world of liberal democracy—or, to use the language of personal experience, between party members and the world of decent people—is not a struggle of the proletariat against indecent economic conditions. It is rather something non-collective, purely individual, and private. The "healthy cores" consist of people scarred by private hatreds, grounded in deeply negative personal experience. Their trauma may be political in origin (such as racial prejudice, or the execution of Lenin's brother); its roots can be the family (the rebellion of children against wealthy parents); or it may spring from feelings of inferiority (the artistic frustration of Hitler, or the unrequited sex-drive of the storm troopers and their cult of male companionship). More often than would appear, the cause is a physical inadequacy or even handicap: here the classic example is Dr. Goebbels, to whom we shall return later.

Alfred Adler is practically unknown outside academic circles today, yet it was he who scientifically explained a phenomenon known to everyone who has ever had anything to do with organizations like the Hitler Youth, the League of Young German Women, the Czechoslovak Union of Youth, or the Komsomol: the disproportionate number of members with physical or psychological malformations. Adler concludes—to put it briefly—that every instance of "inferiority complex" (based on some kind of inferiority of the physical organs, often quite hidden) is somehow compensated for in the psychological superstructure of the personality. "Cerebral compensation" can even explain the birth of philosophical systems and "world-views".

Adler, in fact, paints the picture of "ideological man". This creature is distinguished by a strong tendency to hide his inferiority, or to present it as the consequence of some form of heroism (a natural limp may be passed off as a war wound, and so on). He is haunted by a feeling of insecurity, as though he were constantly surrounded by enemies ("party vigilance"). Often he tries to contain his uncertainty with arrogance, or by playing the fool. Thus there may be a smooth transition from a feeling of inferiority to a belief in one's own superiority and exclusivity; so smooth, in fact, that the victim is never aware of it. His fictive view of the world gives rise to hypotheses that become dogmas. He considers them to be real, even as reality itself is receding from his view. Soon he begins to place exaggerated demands of faith, discipline, etc., on himself and others. He exploits ideas and movements to achieve a feeling of self-worth, and to devalue other people. Ultimately, he becomes the prisoner of an ideology.

As we know, this is what Friedrich Engels called "false consciousness". It is an idea that meshes wonderfully with Adler's. According to Engels, ideology is a process through which the so-called thinker passes, consciously, but on the basis of a consciousness that is false. His real motives, the concrete forces that lead him, remain hidden; he persuades himself of motives that are false or merely apparent.

Engels believed that, in the final instance, the concrete forces were economic; Adler, that they were the individual's negative personal experience. But this variance is, I think, only apparent, since economic factors are not the only source of false consciousness. This is confirmed by a certain well-known phenomenon. In Communist (Fascist) parties—alongside the various "radishes" (red on the outside, white on the inside) and "careerists"—there have always existed those of whom ordinary people say, "He may be a Communist (Fascist) but otherwise he's a decent sort," and those whom they tend to describe as "Communist (Fascist) swine". Only the latter—if we discount the simple gangsters among them—are real carriers of false consciousness. They are ideological in the real sense of the word, and their genesis is not in the general social or national misery, but in nocturnal incontinence.

The "otherwise decent" types join radical movements out of genuine social or national feeling, but soon find themselves at war with the ideology; they end up being shot, or expelled from the party as traitors, revisionists, Röhmists, Titoists, cosmopolitanists, Gang-of-Fourists—the repertoire of labels is almost endless. It all means simply that these unfortunates are quite normal people who have been led astray by sincere emotions and by the critical state of public affairs. We must realize that a certain form of inferiority (the painful collision between inexperience and the intense desire to improve a world that is imperfect and frequently evil) is also a simple fact of youth and immaturity. This explains the mass occurrence of radicalism among young girls whose breasts are just beginning to sprout, and young boys who secretly use anti-pimple creams; when their breasts attain their proper proportions and the pimples disappear, they are surprised at themselves for having been so silly.

Let us return to Dr. Goebbels, an archetypal illustration of
Adler's theory. As perhaps everyone knows, he was a person
of extremely small stature. Moreover, he had a limp, a defect
which was obviously congenital, but which he later ascribed to a
childhood accident. There were clear Adlerian reasons for this,
but there was the added factor that as a cripple from birth he
would scarcely have fit the prevailing racial ideal. He had an
enormous head that stood in unpleasant contrast to his almost
childlike body.

Goebbels compensated for these shortcomings in two ways.
The more innocent way was in bed, a field in which he excelled
not only because of his status as a minister, but also because
he made up for what he lacked in height by cultivating the
gifts of speech, of those black eyes, and of his beautiful, well-
groomed hands. So successful was he that these compensatory
charms hid from young maidens not only his limp, but also the
fact that when he kissed them he had to stand on tiptoe. The
other field of compensation was more dangerous, and had tragic
consequences for far more people. That was politics.

Several factors were very probably decisive here. In the
first place, Goebbels had volunteered for military service when
the First World War broke out, and the medical commission,
naturally, turned him down. He locked himself in his room for
several days and, to his friends, threatened to commit suicide.
This frustration, combined with what, as an intellectual, he
saw as the disgusting petit-bourgeois environment of his law-
abiding and God-fearing family, led him immediately after the
war to a passionate study of Marx and Engels, and later of
Lenin as well. He never ceased to admire the last, and if one
were to undertake a thorough analysis of his rhetoric, I think
that more than an insignificant influence would come to light.
The scholars of institutes of Marxism-Leninism do not write
about such things, but it is a historical fact that can be proven
easily, by examining Goebbels' surviving speeches.

After entering the National Socialist German Workers' Party,
Goebbels joined its ultra-left and violently socialist wing, led
by the Strasser brothers. He became editor-in-chief of their
organ *Nazionalsozialistische Briefe*, a Nazi periodical that is
extremely interesting for the insight it gives into a chapter
that has been erased from the official history of Nazism, first

by Hitler, and later by Marxist-Leninists. Goebbels wrote editorials for the *N.S. Briefe* that were particularly outstanding for their ceaseless propagation of the notion that the fates of revolutionary Russia and revolutionary Germany were linked together. Sometimes he was quite prophetic:

"We look to Russia because it will walk with us as our closest partner on the path to socialism, because Russia is an ally given to us by Nature against the devil of temptation and the corruption of the West."

Or again:

"There is far less linking us with Western capitalism than there is with Eastern Bolshevism."

And further:

"If it came to the worst, we would rather die along with Bolshevism than live eternally as slaves of capitalism."

According to Strasser, Goebbels at one time even saw in Hitler, whose concern from the very beginning had not been socialism but power, a traitor to the National Socialist revolution, and once, at a stormy meeting of Strasserite party groups and trade unions in 1926, he is said to have shouted out in the heat of debate: "I move that the petit-bourgeois Adolf Hitler be expelled from the party."

Very soon, however, he sensed that the future did not belong to Strasser, but to the charismatic demagogue Hitler. He became Hitler's intimate friend. Soon after he had suggested the Führer's expulsion from the party, he delivered one of his most subtle speeches, which shows, among other things, how close to Communism the ideological Nazis (and not the pure gangsters like Goering, who always win out in the end over ideologues) were at the beginning of the movement. The title of the speech, "Lenin or Hitler", might tempt one to conclude that Goebbels was presenting Communism and Nazism as irreconcilably exclusive. But that is not the case. The entire speech is infused with admiration for Lenin and his work. Far more space is devoted to Lenin than to Hitler, and Lenin's work is analysed in far more detail. But Lenin's historical achievement, says Goebbels, is Communist Russia, and German Communists like Thälmann or Rosa Luxemburg are merely minor Russian agents. Over and against the revolutionary creation of the Russian Lenin, however, an equally valuable or even better creation can be made by someone who is just as great as Lenin, but who will be thoroughly German. Such a man exists, and his name is Hitler. Just as Lenin carried out a violent Communist revolution and thus changed the course of world history, so Hitler will carry out a violent National Socialist revolution and thus he too will change the direction of history. Goebbels—unlike most liberal and even many social democratic politicians—understood the historical consequences of 1917. His speech is full of undisguised sympathy for the Bolshevik revolution; he calls it an important step forward for mankind. The Strasser brothers had already warned German politicians not to look at developments in Russia through the eyes of White emigrants; Goebbels was a passionate advocate of co-operation. He believed an alliance with the Soviets to be the only possible guarantee of the German national future: social revolution in Germany, he thought, would work only if Russia was Germany's ally. Hitler's pact with Stalin, which so surprised a world ignorant of Nazism, was not, in fact, the illogical consequence of some incomprehensible wheeling and dealing by Ribbentrop.

In Germany itself, Goebbels distinguished three main political currents: first, the centre, "the bloc of the status quo and reaction, a conservative bloc that is rooted in the system." He included in it all political parties from the Social Democrats to the German Nationalists, "for all of them stand under the protective umbrella of democracy, liberalism, and capitalism: the values which they consider holy and inviolable." On either side of this "reactionary" bloc stood two revolutionary movements: the Communists and the National Socialists, "who have clearly recognized one thing and understood it thoroughly: we will not achieve the State of the future through reform, but through social revolution. The system of liberal-capitalist democracy is internally so eaten away and so rotted from within that it can no longer be repaired or reformed. It must be destroyed to its foundations."

Thus the common aim of both the Communists and the Nazis was the destruction of the bourgeois democratic state. Afterwards, of course, there would necessarily be a conflict between these two allies but—listen closely—"this conflict must be carried on matter-of-factly, without demagogy and without a view to momentary advantages. We must get together with you of the left," Goebbels cried. "After all, we essentially want the same thing. Our goal is freedom.... For us, the central problem of our time is the resolution of social questions. But not social questions like higher wages and less work.... Germany will be free the moment that thirty million on the left come to an understanding with thirty million on the right.... The social question is not a matter of bourgeois sympathy, but state socialist necessity. We know that our way does not lead through the ballot box, but through a complete destruction of the system, through revolution."

For our purpose it is not important that the Strasserite trend lost out. Nor did it matter that the conflict between Nazism and Communism was, in the end, more than demagogical (it ultimately resulted in one of the greatest blood-lettings in modern history). The longing for an unlimited monopoly of power drowned out the rhetoric of social justice, and not only in Germany (what, after all, is at the bottom of the Sino-Soviet conflict today?). I mention all this to show that, even in some aspects of its theory (and I have not discussed the party organization, the system of cells, the cell leaders, the informers, etc.), Nazism has a good deal in common with Communism. More than this, it was, from its beginnings, very much like Communism, a radically idealistic reaction to an unhappy, concrete reality, in the name of a utopian ideal. Fascism draws that ideal from the past, from an idealized, mediaeval organization of society; Nazism goes so far as to idealize prehistoric myth. Communism has a utopian vision of the future. If there is, theoretically speaking, an essential difference, I don't know what it is.

These none-too-familiar circumstances can help us to understand a number of apparent contradictions; for example, Goebbels' speech at a meeting of German film actors and directors, in 1933. The Minister of Propaganda held up Eisenstein's famous film *The Battleship Potemkin* as a model to Nazi directors and declared that Eisenstein (a Jew!) was an example of a true artist. Poor Eisenstein was so upset that he published an "Open Letter to Josef Goebbels". From what we now know of Soviet cinematography, and of Eisenstein's own bitter fate, some of its formulations sound considerably ironic:

> How can you dare ask that your film artists truthfully
> depict life without first asking them to appeal to the
> conscience of the world about the thousands who are
> being tortured to death in your own prisons? Where do
> you get the insolence to speak of truth at all, you who
> have raised a Tower of Babel of falsehood and lies?

Eisenstein wrote those words in 1934, when the first huge
wave of Stalinist terror was getting under way and when
the last remnants of artistic freedom in the Soviet Union
were crushed by the proclamation of socialist realism. But it
seems that his indignation was sincere, so much so that he
returned to Goebbels once again, on the occasion of completing
Alexander Nevsky in 1938. In an article entitled "My Subject Is
Patriotism", he launched an even more fiery attack on Goebbels,
only to be embarrassed by Stalin's pact with Hitler—in the
interests of which his chauvinistic anti-German melodrama
about the wise czar who bravely slaughters hordes of idiotic
Teutonic knights was banned for eighteen months.

Goebbels is not the only Nazi who ever flirted with Communism,
nor was the traffic scarce the other way. The scriptwriter of the
famous film *Das blaue Licht* (*The Blue Light*), in which Hitler's
favourite actress and later director Leni Riefenstahl shone in
the main role, and which Susan Sontag convincingly interprets
as emphatically proto-Nazi, was the Hungarian Communist
Bela Balász.

The German Communist director Kurt Junghans, after making the swan-song of the socially critical silent film *Takový je
život* (*Such Is Life*) in Prague in 1929, worked for several years
on the production of an anti-American super-film in the Soviet
Union (which was scrapped only after Langston Hughes declined an invitation to take part, saying that the scenario was
utter nonsense). Junghans returned—after 1933—to Germany,
where, in 1939, he directed an official documentary on the history of the Nazi party, *Die Jahre der Entscheidung* (*The Years
of Decision*). In the end, he thumbed his nose at both ideologies
and ran to Hollywood, where he opened a photo supply shop.

The core of the notorious Flemish SS Division *Wallonien*,
led by Léon Degrelle, was, except for a handful of men, wiped

out after a heroic battle on the Eastern Front. It was formed by several hundred former Communists, and members of the militant socialist organization *Jeunes gardes socialistes*. In the shadow of their apocalyptic defeat, Degrelle declared, "If Europe were once more to become a Europe of bankers, and fat, corrupt bourgeoisie...then let Communism conquer and destroy everything. Rather let everything be blown up, than to see here once again the triumph of decay."

Mussolini's official ideologist in the so-called Italian Social Republic, Argento Soffici, said, "If the Axis powers were to lose the war, most real Fascists, if they survived, would go over to the Communists. Then we will have bridged the gap that has separated the two revolutions."

In reading the speeches of Hitler himself, we discover much that is a mere translation of Leninist principles into National Socialist jargon. One graphic example is the Führer's exceptionally short speech at the Nuremberg Party Congress in 1934 (available in English in the published script for *The Triumph of the Will*). Here is an excerpt:

> At a time when the Party had only seven members, it declared two principles. In the first place, it intended to be a truly ideological movement, and in the second place, it intended to be a movement that knew no compromise, that intended to gain total power in Germany and share it with no one. As a Party, we had to remain a minority because we mobilized only the most precious elements in the nation, those capable of struggle and self-sacrifice, and they have never been in the majority. But because these men, the best men in the German race, grasped the leadership of the empire and the nation proudly, confidently, daringly, and bravely, the people in ever greater numbers joined this vanguard and submitted to its leadership.... The Party will always be only a part of the nation, it will consist only of genuinely active warriors, on whom greater demands will be made than on the millions of their fellow citizens.... The Party will always represent the élite of political leadership. It will be unwavering in its ideology, as hard as steel in its organizational discipline, supple and flexible in its

tactics.... Our aim must be for all Germans to become National Socialists. Only the best National Socialists, however, will be members of the Party.

All of which is essentially a paraphrase of Lenin's notions: the Party as an élite vanguard of the proletariat; the strict differentiation between ideology and tactics; the need to rule the Party by iron discipline, and the rest of it.

Let us now leave the sphere of high political theory. If we look, as the Stalinists would say, "below", we discover that the picture there is very similar. Let us take the political song, for example. Here too, the basic laws of false consciousness apply: reality projects itself into the song-writer's consciousness in a distorted form, which he and his listeners take to be a reflection of reality.

Here are two examples, in which false consciousness of reality has changed it into utter fantasy. The first is a song by Wolf Biermann, an East German Marxist dissident, about the West German left-wing radical Rudi Dutschke. The first verse reads:

> *Drei Kugeln auf Rudi Dutschke—*
> *ein blutiges Attentat.*
> *Wir haben genau gesehen*
> *wer da geschossen hat.*

(Three bullets for Rudi Dutschke—
A bloody assassination.
We all saw very clearly
who fired the shots.)

In the following verses, he identifies the three gunmen. The first is the Springer press, the second is a spokesman for big business, and the third is the chancellor, a former Nazi who

> *Schoss Kugel Nummer drei*
> *er legte gleich der Witwe*
> *den Beileidsbrief mit bei.*

(Shot bullet number three
and then sent the widow

a letter of condolence.)

A listener who knew nothing about Rudi Dutschke, or the attempt on his life in 1968 (which was not made by any of the three above, but rather by someone called Josef Bachman), would conclude from the song that Rudi had been killed. He would get a vague impression that the deed was done by a group of hired assassins, with connections leading straight back to big business interests. But Dutschke was only wounded. He died years after. There was no widow, and the only one who lost his life in relation to the incident was the would-be assassin, Josef Bachman, who hanged himself in prison. The need to replace reality with an obsessive fiction was, in the mind of the ideological song-writer, more powerful than reality, more powerful than truth.

Authors of ideological songs are not, in any case, concerned about either truth or reality, but about emotional impact. For this purpose, Rudi Dutschke is more useful dead than alive.

Even more instructive is a song called "Lied für Angela Davis", sung by the West German group Bonner Songgruppe. The song begins like this:

> *Sie hassen dich, weil du*
> *des Volkes Zukunft bist.*
> *Sie jagen dich, denn du*
> *bist schwarz und Kommunist.*

> (They hate you because
> you are the future of the nation.
> They persecute you because
> you are black, and a Communist.)

In the verses that follow, the fate of Angela is identified—note well—with the fate of Joe Hill, Sacco and Vanzetti, the victims of the Ku Klux Klan, the "mass murders of imperialist gangs". In other words, Angela appears in the dispatches among dead heroes. Like Rudi Dutschke, she is more useful as a slain martyr, and when the American jury failed to send her to the gas chamber, the Bonner Songgruppe killed her for its own purposes.

It is no less amusing to discover that songs coming from apparently opposite ideological camps are, with very minor alterations, sung by both. They resemble each other like peas from the same pod. In the Germany of the twenties and thirties, the SA troops regularly traded songs with members of the Communist party. This apparently surprising circumstance can be explained by the fact that there was not so much enmity between the two camps as competition. They fought over souls, but the common enemy was liberal democracy, whose "terror" was a feature common to the songs of both camps. Here is an SA song:

> *Wir leben in einem freien Staate,*
> *jedoch von Freiheit keine Spur.*
> *Statt dessen herrscht in unsrem Lande*
> *der Terror der roten Diktatur.*

> (We live in a free state,
> yet there's not a trace of freedom.
> Instead of this, our land is ruled
> by the terror of red dictatorship.)

The Communist version goes like this:

> *Wir leben in einem freien Staate,*
> *jedoch von Freiheit keine Spur.*
> *Statt dessen herrscht in unsrem Lande*
> *der weisse Schrecken, Schrecken—der Terror!*

> (We live in a free state
> yet there's not a trace of freedom.
> Instead of this, our land is ruled
> by White horror, horror—Terror!)

There are only two differences between the two texts: the colour varies in the last line, and the Communist version is shriller in tone.

And two more examples: sad, funny, frightening. The Communists sing:

Fasse schritt, fasse Schritt,
Hakenkreuz schlag entzwei!

(To the left, to the left,
Smash the swastika to bits!)

The Hitlerjugend reply:

Die rote Front, schlag sie entzwei!
H.J. marschiert, die Strasse frei!

(Smash the red front to bits!
The Hitler Youth are marching, clear the streets!)

The SA sings:

Sprung auf die Barikaden, der Tod
besiegt uns nur, ja nur!
Wir sind die Sturmkolonnen der Hitlerdiktatur!

(Leap on the barricades, only death,
yes, only death can lay us low!
We are storm columns of Hitler's dictatorship!)

And the Communists reply:

Sprung auf die Barikaden, heraus zum
Bürgerkrieg, ja Krieg!
Pflanzt auf die Sowjetfahnen zum blutig-roten Sief!

(Leap on the barricades, onward
To civil war, yes, to war!
Raise the Soviet flag for a bloody red victory!)

Everything in the lyrics is either extremely misty or extremely generalized: hatred, joy, the enemy, blood, battle, sacrifice, terror, flags, hope, glory, victory, all of it verbal ballast that can be used for this cause or that, left or right. The fundamental characteristic of ideological poetics is precisely that: the result of its creative process is essentially acceptable to all ideologies. The identity of these and similar songs can be explained not only by the vagueness of the wording, but by the actual migration of both singers and songs from one group to another. This process is described in a book called *Lieder machen Geschichte (Songs Make History)*, by Hans Bajer, a composer of songs for the masses, and a member of the SA.

> The bar brawls and street battles between the SA and the Marxists, in which the latter very often outnumbered the former, frequently resulted next day in a large number of subdued Marxists presenting themselves to the *Sturmführer* and asking to be admitted to his *Sturm*. At first they were drawn by their respect for the men who were braver and could fight better. Soon, however, they became infused with the ideas of National Socialism, just like their other comrades in the *Sturm*. Horst Wessel was a master at attracting the best fellows in the Marxist formations and finding a place for them in his *Sturm*, much to the anger of the Communists. Obviously, these people brought with them the songs they were used to singing in the Red camp. But after a few alterations to the lyrics, the SA men were soon singing them as well.

Here is a little case of left-right symbiosis in the singing of the Internationale. Bajer writes:

> One Sunday our *Sturm* held a propaganda march through North Berlin. One of the songs in our repertoire was a revolutionary song we called the Hitlernazionale. No sooner had we begun to sing it than windows began to open and people leaned out to shout a welcome to their, i.e. the Red, columns. It is impossible to describe how their faces fell when, instead of their own people, they saw our tight columns in brown shirts. The words of the Internationale were at once sung from the windows: *"Völker, hört die Signale! Auf zum letzten Gefecht! Die Internazionale erkämpft das Menschenrecht!"* But we shouted them down with all our might with the words of the Hitlernazionale: *"Schon jubeln Siegessignale! Schon*

*bricht der Morgen herein! Der Nationale Sozialismus
wird Deutschlands Zukunft sein!"*

The whole propaganda march was then concluded with the
SA men singing a very revealing song:

*Einst waren wir Marxisten, Rotfront und SPD,
heut sind wir Nazionalsozialisten,
Kämpfer der NSDAP.*

(We used to be Marxists, Red Frontists, and SPD
Today we are National Socialists,
Warriors of the NSDAP.)

The ease with which people transfer from right to left and
vice versa, both in song and in life, finds a more natural explanation in Adler than it does in theories of conversion. The
ideological person does not convert, he merely shifts his alle-
giance in another, equally ideological direction. Many people
have an instinctive need to live in a world that is clearly organized, emotionally exciting, and, in a word, ritualized. It is
an ancient need, reaching back beyond the dawn of human history, and mankind has worked hard to overcome it. And now,
paradoxically, in our own twentieth century,

> ...perhaps not a single phenomenon from the prehistoric
> era of the human family is missing. Through all the
> efforts of ideologists, all the intellectual fossils are re-
> suscitated and become influential once again. Rituals,
> magic costumes in the form of uniforms, fetishism, taboo,
> the influence of medicine-men, charms and curses in the
> form of slogans and petrified clichés, the totemistic wor-
> ship of symbols, etc., etc. A cultural regression is taking
> place, characterized by the large role in the manipula-
> tion of people played by hypnotic suggestions that reach
> into the subconsciousness of the objects of indoctrina-
> tion, without their really being aware of it. At the same
> time, however, these sophisticated interventions on the
> part of ideologists into the unconsciousness of mass man
> are themselves directed by subconscious forces. We are

living through the final phase of the total collapse of the Enlightenment.*

We must, therefore, distinguish between ideas and ideology. But what is the criterion for this distinction?

It is the truth of the socio-critical reflection. A song that is born out of a powerful, personal, and therefore direct experience of social injustice or repression contains within it the moral force of truth. A song which rather derives from ideological, that is to say secondary, experience, or which is simply made to order ideologically, though its content may not differ from songs deriving from genuine experience, cannot touch the pathos of truth. That is why old blues about anonymous lynchings have the power to move us even today: they, by contrast, contain the truth of concrete reality.

Falsehood is the final outcome of all ideologies. No ideology was ever born of true feelings. Ideologies are indeed formed of feelings and ideas about value, but these are warped to solve the lacerating personal problems of certain people who shoot or box their way to the head of ideological power formations or, at the local level, to the head of a hierarchy of functionaries. Because this psychological law is the same for all ideologies, it is hardly surprising that the consequences are invariably similar.

I quote from Vladimír Karbusický's Ideologie im Lied, Lied in der Ideologie. *Most examples of songs are also taken from this book.*

THE CZECHS IN THE AMERICAN CIVIL WAR

———

This previously unpublished essay about Czechs who fought (or tried to avoid fighting) in the American Civil War resulted from Škvorecký's research for a forthcoming novel on that subject. It was written in 1986.

I WOULD LIKE to be able to say that the Czechs who began leaving Austria for America after the defeat of the 1848 uprising against the Hapsburg Empire volunteered *en masse* to fight with the Union Army against a system that must have reminded them of conditions they had left behind. In actual fact, Czech participation in the war was not very impressive numerically. True, no precise statistics exist, neither army listed soldiers according to their ethnic origin, and so one has to rely on guessing by the names as they appear, often in distorted spellings, on company rosters, and in collections of veterans' narratives, some assembled by Josef Čermák in his invaluable *History of the Civil War*.

Recently, though, one scholar, W.P. Hewitt, has done research in various archives on Czech soldiers from Texas, and has been able to come up with more reliable figures. According to his unpublished dissertation "The Czechs in Texas", about a hundred Czechs served in the units of the Confederate Army. Since by 1861 fewer than a thousand Czechs lived in Texas, this appears to be a relatively high number: close to 20 per cent of the entire male population. But as the situation of the South progressively worsened, Texas combatants ceased to be volunteers and were conscripted, more often than not, by coercion, frequently verging on blackmail; consequently the figure does not tell us anything about the motivation of these Czech warriors.

Although no such research has been done for the North, one can safely infer from what reckoning has been done that the percentage of Northern Czechs who served in the Union Army, was considerably lower. When the war broke out the Czechs in the North may have numbered 20,000 to 25,000; the sources are unreliable but in the 1870 census, five years after the war, with renewed and strong immigration, there were still only 36,000 Czechs in the country. In 1861 they almost certainly did not yield the 2,000 or 2,500 combatants which would have been equivalent to the Czech contingent in the Southern army. My guess is that fewer than a thousand Czechs shouldered muskets to fight for the preservation of the Union. Until scholars take on the painstaking labour of researching military archives, we must be content with this extremely rough estimate.

These humble numbers pale when compared with the figures given for other nations of the Austro-Hungarian Empire. About 4,000 Poles, out of a total 30,000 Northern residents, fought in the Union ranks, and even boasted two generals. The Hungarians also yielded remarkable numbers to the service of the North, among them many experienced professional officers, veterans of the 1848 uprising who lived in the States in involuntary exile. Compared to this the Czechs, as Thomas Čapek quips in *The Czechs in America*, "provided the United States Army with more musicians than generals," though he fails to give more specific information on the number of musicians. The reasons for this are not difficult to deduce. The last great military conflict in which the Czechs had taken an active part *en masse* was the Thirty Years War, and that had taken place more than two centuries before the war in America. Among the Poles, with their history of fighting the Germans and Russians throughout the eighteenth and nineteenth centuries, and among the Magyars, who traditionally provided the Austro-Hungarian army with an elite officer corps, the martial spirit was simply much more alive and widespread than among the Czechs, who in 1620 were deprived of their aristocracy, the traditional bearers of military tradition, and turned into more or less passive subjects of the Austrian emperor. Furthermore, the participation of the intelligentsia and of the military in the events of 1848 was also greater and more intense among the Poles and Hungarians than among the Czechs; consequently, incomparably more intellectuals and professional soldiers left the country.

Most Czech immigrants were poor people of rural background who came to the New World simply to make a better living (which of course also meant a freer life). They had been in the country for only a few years when the conflict exploded into war, and were without much security, with many private problems, and mostly ignorant of the language and of American history; their dilemma as to whether to enlist or not must have been much greater than that of the old settlers of Anglo-Saxon stock. And yet quite a few joined and fought bravely; unlike the Polish generals and the Magyar colonels, they were mostly rank-and-file privates or noncommissioned officers. The highest commission achieved by a Czech that can be verified from the official register was that of a lieutenant-colonel, but its owner was certainly atypical of the Czech Union warrior: he was Count Edward C. Wratislaw. Čermák mentions another colonel, one Procházka, but there is no official confirmation of this. So we shall do best if we reconcile ourselves to the rank-and-file Czech combatant, and give him his due. Although he did not enlist by thousands, he fought bravely and in some cases achieved high distinction.

In spite of Thomas Čapek's assertion, it is hard to decide whether the Czech musicians in the regimental bands were indeed numerous. As far as one can establish, only a few appear by name in the documents: a P. Miller who was bandmaster of the Twenty-Second Iowa Infantry; Jan Šála, a drummer with the same unit; František Chadima, active as a "musician" with the Army of the Potomac; and V. Rott, also a "musician" in a unit of General Fremont's army. Čermák mentions two company bugleboys: V. Froelich from Mirotice, who also fought under General Fremont and was killed in the battle of Memphis, and Frederic Vogel, "the sound of whose bugle gave the signal to the memorable attack of Captain Lyon's cavalry on the units of General Price."

As for fighting Czechs, one finds them in practically all major engagements of the war. Five served in the Thirty-First Company of the Thirteenth Regiment which was General Sherman's bodyguard, and took part in the legendary "March Through

Georgia", a strenuous effort which left only four hundred survivors of the original regiment. It was vividly described by
another of Sherman's Czechs, František Stejskal, who was later
seriously wounded and, helpless, captured by the Confederates. He spent some time in the notorious Libby prison and
then in various POW camps where he experienced the famous
"dead line", the crossing of which—most camps had no fences—
was punished by death. He survived all these ordeals, was
exchanged, rejoined the Union Army, and stayed with it until the end of the war. Another Czech, František Kouba, left a
chilling description of an even more notorious Southern POW
camp, Andersonville, from which he escaped by appropriating
release papers from another prisoner who died before he could
use them.

The crucial battle of Gettysburg appears in letters written
by a number of Czech infantrymen; they mention several of
their compatriots who were wounded, and one asserts that
"many Czechs were killed but I no longer remember their
names." Similar descriptions of first-hand battle experience
were left by one František Renčín from Grant's army which
conquered Fort Donelson; Renčín also reported on the battle of
Shiloh. Other personal testimonies tell about the engagements
at Fredericksburg, Atlanta, Chattanooga, Bull Run, and the
campaigns through South and North Carolina, and mention
many Czech casualties.

In a few companies that took part in the major battles
Czechs even seem to have been in the majority. Company
K of the Twenty-Second Iowa Regiment was known as the
"Czech" company: Čermák enumerates thirty Czechs among
its soldiers, three of whom were lieutenants and one—the
already-mentioned Pavel Miller—was the bandmaster. All, apparently, showed bravery and were often cited in the company's
documents. Another "Czech" unit was Company I of the Twenty-
Sixth Wisconsin Regiment. It was organized by František
Landa, who obtained a commission and had twenty-five Czechs
on his roster; the company distinguished itself at Gettysburg.

Occasionally one finds stories that, though perhaps enhanced
by soldierly boasting, apparently contain a kernel of truth, since
they can be verified in non-Czech sources. Thus Jan Klíma of
the Twenty-Second Iowa reports on an unusual battle fought

under the fortifications of Vicksburg: "We were engaged in digging a tunnel under enemy ramparts which we intended to blow up. The rebels, without our knowledge, were doing the same, in the opposite direction. By chance we met, and a bloody fight ensued: we fought with shovels, hoes, everything that came to hand, and so we experienced also a bloody engagement underground." The heroism of two Czech gunners is mentioned in a pamphlet entitled "Company I, Fourth Massachusetts Regiment". The two men, Kašpar and Kučera, manned a small field-gun which they had to drag into position themselves since they had no horses. They faced a fierce attack by a Southern detachment at the village of Berwick and, with a handful of comrades, refused to retreat. Due to their courage and skill in handling the gun, it was the rebels who finally had to withdraw. Kašpar was later seriously wounded, and developed a Huck Finn–Nigger Jim relationship with a young black auxiliary who apparently saved his life by faithfully nursing him.

Some Czechs appear on marginal but not negligible battle-fields. In Iowa, Minnesota, and Dakota, the local Indian tribes used the opportunity offered by the war to settle accounts with white settlers. One of the prominent Czechs, J. Švehla, enlisted with several friends in company D of the Sixth Iowa Cavalry. He helped build Fort Rice, whose garrison had to watch over the movements of the Indians, and took part in many battles with the mutinous tribes. Only after the tribes were finally conquered in 1865 did the president discharge the Czech Indian fighters, so that they were able to return to their farms.

It takes all kinds of people to fight a war, and Czechs were no exception. There seem to have been a few whose motives were more or less mercenary. An Antonín Vlk emigrated to New York when the war was already raging; he joined the army, collected $500—a large sum for the times—which he sent home to his wife, took part in some skirmishes around Petersburg, and then left the army and returned to Bohemia. Others enlisted for idealistic reasons but took a liking to military life and turned professional. But most were and remained idealists. Some, like Antonín Macal, were quite colourful. Macal took an active part in the uprising of 1848, then left Austria and learned the craft of a machinist in Paris. When Garibaldi raised the banner of revolt against Austria, Macal joined his army, and was wounded and made a prisoner of war; he subsequently escaped, rejoined Garibaldi, and after the war returned to Paris. When the war against slavery broke out in America, Macal crossed the ocean, and in 1863 he volunteered to serve in the Twelfth New Jersey Infantry. He remained in active service until the end of hostilities and was present at Appomattox when Lee surrendered to Grant.

Most Czech volunteers, though their careers were not as adventurous as Macal's, were made of similar stuff, and their personal narratives tell movingly how, when the good work was done, they returned to their farms and professions neither getting nor expecting any rewards. Some of their stories are tragic; others are moving or even humorous, and help to bring the modern reader near the day-to-day reality of combat. H. Sládek, one of the twelve courageous men who remained with the Lincoln Rifle Company when it went into battle, lost his life due to his ignorance of English. Ordered to haul some planks into camp, he was challenged to give the password. Sládek did not understand and walked on; he was challenged once more and then shot dead. Sládek's linguistic incompetence was by no means exceptional. In isolated farming communities, people could spend their entire lifetimes without learning more than a few English words to designate articles they bought or sold. In fact, it was the Civil War which enabled many first-generation Czechs to acquire a working knowledge of English. Full English literacy came only in the second or even third generation, especially after English schools were made mandatory.

One moving leitmotif of almost all narratives by Czech veterans is food, the sufficient supply of which was not something the struggling early immigrants took for granted. The description of the horrors of war often pales before the way the veterans tell about the terrors of eating various near-inedibles in order to quell nagging hunger. Although František Stejskal served as a bodyguard to General Williams, in his report he barely mentions the general but complains bitterly about the stomach-turning repasts such as "the nigger-beans which we had to devour with burnt corncobs." Private Čížkovský writes about another gourmet feast: "My companion found a half-buried, half-eaten leg of the carcass of a cow. We dug it up, washed it in a nearby river, cut it up, and started to make soup. Unfortunately there was no salt but we figured out a solution: we sprinkled the brew with gunpowder, and soon ladled the soup with appetite although it resembled ink rather than anything else." And nothing annoyed the brave musician František Chadima, marching with the Army of the Potomac, so much as when "one sunny afternoon we had just sat down to enjoy our dinner, with plates of soup and spoons at the ready, when suddenly the thunder of the cannonade broke out and 40,000 projectiles from guns and rifles hit our ranks so that we had to abstain from eating. I shall never forget that spoiled dinner."

So much for the Czechs of the North; let us look at the South. Among the slavery states only Texas had any significant Czech community, fewer than a thousand, as mentioned above. Both the history of these Czechs and their social circumstances made them very bad stuff from which to shape Confederate soldiers. The very first Czech known to have reached Texas before 1850, when immigration in larger numbers began, was a democratically minded nineteenth-century liberal, Anthony M. Dignowitý. He had fought with the Poles in their unsuccessful revolt against Russia in 1830, and after defeat fled to America. There, after adventures on plantations and among the Indians, he studied medicine at Cincinnati College, and eventually settled as a physician in San Antonio. Speaking up against secession and slavery, he barely escaped lynching and had to leave Texas on horseback. He went to Washington, where he made various suggestions about invading Texas from the sea, and eventually he became a wealthy manufacturer and writer. His two sons were conscripted into the Confederate Army, but both managed to escape and enlist in the Union Army.

Though Dignowitý's story is not characteristic of the Czech immigrant, since he was an intellectual, a well-to-do man married to an American woman, and had lived in the United States for almost thirty years when hostilities opened, a similar resentment of slavery filled the hearts of most Texas Czechs. In the old country the majority had been farm labourers or cottagers, and the old and the middle-aged still remembered serfdom, with its compulsory work and its many other restrictions of personal freedom, for this had not been fully abolished until 1848. None owned slaves, and many were ardent readers of the St. Louis-based paper *Národní noviny*

(*National News*), which espoused strongly abolitionist and anti-secessionist views. The paper's main distributor in Texas was the leader of the first immigrant groups, Josef Lidumil Lešikar, a self-educated intellectual, admirer of Karel Havlíček Borovský, the liberal hero of the 1848 uprising, and a friend of Božena Němcová. He pushed the paper and its cause with such intensity that he, too, barely escaped hanging by an angry mob.

At first the general situation in Texas was favourable for the immigrants who held pro-Union views. The large German community was also in no mood to support secession. When the authorities began conscripting young men in 1863, the mood became so rebellious that things almost got out of hand and General Magruder, commander of the Texas department, was forced to declare martial law in several counties, including those with significant Czech populations. Thereafter enlisting officers, often accompanied by the fierce, pro-secessionist cavalrymen of the Texas Rangers, roamed the country, enrolling immigrant men by force, threats, or blackmail. Many Czechs refused to serve and tried to avoid the service by hiding in the woods or in cellars or by working in the fields disguised as women. However, the Rangers often stayed at the farms whose young men were missing, harassing the womenfolk and children, so that eventually a hundred or so Czechs unwillingly joined the army. There were, however, quite a few defectors to the North, not always successful. One Jan Kroulík was prevented from defecting by General Grant himself, the supreme commander of the Union Army. As a conscript in the Texas Wolf Legion, Kroulík fell into captivity after the battle of Vicksburg. He managed to get a hearing with Grant and asked to stay in the North—whether he intended to enlist or just settle in the North is not clear from his narrative—arguing that as soon as the prisoners of war were exchanged, the Confederates would force them back into their army. Grant, however, thought that such a favour would constitute a breach of the agreement he had with the Confederates, and regretfully withheld his permission. There was nothing left for Kroulík but to escape again and hide until the end of the war. He was captured by the Rangers several times, once even threatened with execution, but he managed to regain freedom each time and survived the war. Some sixty young Czechs and Germans who planned a

massive defection were less fortunate: they decided to go to New
Orleans and seek out Union recruiting officers, but when they
were resting on the Nueces River about forty miles from the Rio
Grande, a unit of Texas irregulars ambushed them, massacring
and hanging almost all of them.

But there was one relatively safe way of avoiding conscrip-
tion. The South's main export was cotton, and after Yankee
ships began to blockade Southern ports, the only way to get
the commodity out of the country was by wagon to Mexico.
Teamsters were officially exempted from military service, and
numerous Czechs used this opportunity. But it was a dangerous journey; roaming bands of armed thieves often attacked the
convoys, and some Czechs died while thus avoiding the hated
service.

Some of these teamsters may have come into contact with
Czech soldiers of the expeditionary forces of Emperor Maximilian of Mexico. Before he set out on his fatal expedition—he was
eventually executed in 1867 by the rebellious Mexicans—the
Austrian prince had collected a volunteer army of 12,000 men,
mostly conscripts from the regular Austrian forces. It seems
there were quite a few Czechs in Maximilian's units, some of
whom hoped to undertake this government-sponsored journey
to America only to remain there after discharge or through defection. Some may even have defected intending to enlist in the
States—a few Czech short stories indicate that there were such
cases.

It is these stories (and at least one novel) written by American
Czech writers of the second half of the nineteenth century that
demonstrate how strong the anti-slavery feelings of the Czechs
were at the time of the great conflict, and how proud they were
of the exploits of those who took up the sword. Practically all
such stories were printed in the yearly issues of *Amerikán,
národní kalendář* (*American National Calendar*), published by
August Geringer in Chicago. They were very popular with farm
readers in Illinois, Nebraska, Oklahoma, Iowa, Minnesota, in
the big cities with strong Czech communities like New York,
Boston, or Chicago, and in Texas. They constitute a body of
fiction that, although of no great literary value, is an invaluable
source of information about the lifestyles and ways of thinking
of the early American Czechs caught in the storm of the war.

The literary models of their authors were American writers of similar Civil War fictions, novelists who wrote before Stephen Crane and Ambrose Bierce and who shaped their stories in the form of Victorian melodrama. In the Czech fictions, the story develops in terms of individual adventures, mostly amorous, full of unbelievable coincidences and private settlings of accounts set against a background of more or less realistically drawn battle scenes. In *Na hrotě bodáku* (*On the Tip of the Bayonet*), Pavel Albieri deals with two mortal enemies, the Czech Bořický and the Prague German Urban, who meet on the field of battle at Gettysburg. Back in Prague, Bořický was swindled out of his position with a bank and deprived of his fiancée by the villainous Urban, and had to emigrate to the United States in disgrace. He now fights in the ranks of the Union Army. Urban, whose crimes finally undid him and who also had to flee to America, is, as one might expect, a Confederate soldier. Bořický pierces Urban with his bayonet and kills him, but before he dies the villain confesses everything. By a stroke of Victorian luck the fiancée happens to be in a "Gettysburg hotel", and the story ends in a happy reunion of the lovers. This tale of good and evil illustrates well the political sympathies of practically all Czechs.

One obvious source for these tales was Čermák's *History*. In that book František Stejskal, the soldier who marched through Georgia with Sherman, recounts the story of a remarkable meeting of a few Czech soldiers with an old man in a village near Decatur. When he realizes that these Sherman soldiers are Czech, the oldster breaks into joyous weeping and, calling them "Czech Yankees", tells them about his woes: as a Lincoln supporter he suffered all kinds of harassment from his neighbours, and even from his wife who is a Southern woman. A narrative from Čermák's *History*, reshaped slightly for the purposes of fiction, appears in a novella by Albieri, *Pro starou vlasť* (*For the Old Country*). There an old man, a widower who is a staunch Lincoln supporter despite the persecution of his Southern neighbours, agonizes over the fact that his two children, Mary and Frank, not only prefer English to Czech but are enthusiastic defenders of slavery. Needless to say, by the end of the piece we find both children reformed, though not through any process of study or enlightenment: Mary becomes engaged to a gallant Czech Union soldier, and Frank to the soldier's strongly abolitionist sister.

To sum up: although the Czech participation in the Civil War was not prominent as far as numbers are concerned, it was apparently first class when it comes to quality. In this respect it seems to have set a pattern for future wars in which Czechs played a part. In both world wars, while the majority of the Czechs either did not fight at all or rendered Švejkian service to the wrong armies, large groups of men of high idealistic convictions and great personal courage saved the good name of the nation on bloody battlefields—the Czech Legions fighting the Bolsheviks in the First World War, the Czechs in the RAF in the Battle of Britain, the Czechs in the British Eighth Army at Tobruk, the Czechs (and Slovaks) who assassinated Reinhard Heydrich, the fighters of the Czechoslovak Unit on the Eastern Front. Last but not least, there were also Czech GI Joes, descendants of the nineteenth-century soldiers of the Union, who fought bravely in all the major theatres of the last world war and whose stories are told by gravestones in cemeteries in many Czech villages in Iowa, Minnesota, Illinois, Nebraska, Oklahoma, Texas, and everywhere Czechs live in the United States.

NATAŠA AND THE PEACEMAKERS

—

Not quite a footnote to "Are Canadians Politically Naive?", this short piece is also about travellers and fellow-travellers. It appeared in The Idler *in 1985.*

ONE OF THE very last decisions of our former prime minister, Pierre Trudeau, was to approve the establishment of an institution called "The Canadian Institute for International Peace and Security". Inspired by this project, Mr. Koozma Tarasoff, from Saskatchewan, the chairman of the Ottawa Branch of the "Canada-U.S.S.R. Association", suggested the creation of a "Centre for East-West Dialogue" in Canada. He received a letter from Mr. Trudeau from which he quoted the following to a meeting of the Sub-Committee of the Standing Committee on External Affairs, on May 3, 1984:

> In order to ensure that your very thoughtful contribution is properly considered as the designed work for the government-sponsored centre is carried out, I have passed on your paper to the officials most concerned with the creation of the centre. I hope that it will be possible to establish an institution with the creativity and practicality which you envisage.

Mr. Tarasoff's "creative and practical" proposal would be housed in the Château Montebello in Quebec. There, as Mr. Tarasoff put it, officials of the United States and the Soviet Union could "meet together, relax, eat and talk." The running of this peacemakers' club would cost around three million dollars a year; but in order to provide guests from Moscow with the luxuries they are accustomed to, it would be necessary to renovate the Château at a cost of "perhaps seven million". It would be a "hands-off structure funded by the government, yet independent". If I understand correctly, this means that the taxpayers should pay, but they should not expect to have a say in what goes on at the champagne-and-brie parties. Mr. Tarasoff envisages wise men assembled there, who will, in an unbiased, unprejudiced manner, clarify issues that threaten world peace because they are being constantly and systematically obscured by the Western media—things like the Soviet invasion of Afghanistan, the shooting down of a Korean passenger airplane, or the incarceration of Andrei Sakharov.

And yet, despite these wonderful intentions, Mr. Donald W. Munro, MP, protested the presence of Mr. Tarasoff and his colleague Mr. Lewis M. Leach of Ottawa before the Sub-Committee when it next met (June 26, 1984). He argued that members of a "group with such a record should not be given access to our parliamentary proceedings."

The record of the "Canada-U.S.S.R. Association" is quite colourful; but Mr. Munro had one particular item in mind: the exploits of the president of the association, Mr. Michael Lucas of Toronto. Just five days before the appearance of Messrs. Tarasoff and Leach before the Sub-Committee, Mr. Lucas had become the centre of a very interesting news story.

It all started two years earlier, on June 29, 1982, in Prague, Czechoslovakia. A group of Canadian students had arrived the previous day on a tour organized by the International Student Exchange of Urbana, Illinois. They were given a guided tour of the ancient city. Upon their return to Canada, one of them, Mr. Ronnie Evanoff, complained to Mr. Lucas that their Czech guide had "used every opportunity to throw extremely bad light on the Government, on the Communist Party, and on the whole aspect of Socialism in the C.S.S.R.," thus doing "a tremendous lot of harm to the cause of peace and understanding". On January 17, 1983, Mr. Lucas wrote to Mr. Jiří Sysel, Head of Overseas Department Five of the Czechoslovak Tourist Agency (Čedok). He asked him to "look into the matter and draw the proper conclusion". He identified the guide as one Anastasia.

On February 15, 1983, Mr. Sysel wrote back regretting that so far he had been unable to draw the proper conclusion because no guide by the name of Anastasia was employed by his agency. Would Mr. Lucas provide him with more detailed information?

Mr. Lucas promptly obliged. After some quick sleuthing he determined that the guide's name was not Anastasia but Nataša. He communicated this further nugget by mail, February 26.

On March 11, greatly relieved that he could now wash his hands of the unpleasantness, Mr. Sysel replied that his agency was innocent of employing any such character; it was Sporturist who had organized the Canadian students' tour, and who had hired Nataša. Therefore he was handing all correspondence to Mrs. Vlasta Křížova, the Deputy Manager of Sporturist.

Confident now that the proper conclusion would be drawn, Mr. Lucas turned his attention to other matters. But while the case was closing for him, it was of course just opening for Nataša Bayerová, a twenty-eight-year-old Prague newlywed, the wretched Jewish girl who had so dangerously harmed the cause of peace and understanding. Just to be sure that the guide would be punished, Mr. Lucas sent copies of his correspondence to Mr. Emil Ondruš, at that time in charge of the Canadian desk of the Czechoslovak Ministry of Foreign Affairs. Mr. Ondruš had been Second Secretary to the Czechoslovak embassy in Ottawa, a post usually held by a member of the Czechoslovak Secret Service.

The affair turned into a combat between the nasties, who immediately ordered an investigation, and the decent people who even today may be found in shady corners of the institutions of what President Reagan has so aptly called "The Evil Empire". These latter slowed procedures so as to give Nataša a chance to save herself. They also leaked copies of Mr. Lucas's letters, so that they eventually reached the *Globe and Mail* in Toronto, which, commendably, published news items and an editorial on the matter in May and June of last year. One such person— understandably Nataša is unwilling to reveal his name—called her to find out what had happened. He drew the conclusion that Nataša was okay, but that there might be something wrong with Mr. Lucas (who, by the by, was born at Humenné in eastern Czechoslovakia). According to Nataša, speaking later to an interviewer from *Západ* (a Czech bi-monthly published from Ottawa, in its issue for December 1984), this good Communist "became quite agitated about the fact that there are still some bastards who would not spare the effort of writing three times across the ocean to destroy an innocent human being."

The girl panicked. "I asked around what kind of food inmates of our gaols were getting, and how often they get beaten up.... Also, very cautiously, I asked lawyers what are the legal consequences of what I had allegedly done. None of the information I received was optimistic."

With the results of their research in hand, Nataša and her husband decided to flee. The decent people took three months to push the papers through the bureaucracy, and with the help of other decent people the young couple were able to purchase a seven-day trip to Yugoslavia. It cost them 22,000 crowns, or about a year's salary for a shop attendant. It was to be their "honeymoon trip"—for though they had applied earlier to take a honeymoon journey to Paris, it had been only "half-approved" (i.e., Nataša could go this year, and her husband could go the next).

"I had to leave my parents and all my friends," Nataša told *Západ's* Otto Ulč. "I lost my country, I lost Prague, a city I loved deeply, and where I had a job in which I was very happy. Mr. Lucas made me lose my parents and friends. Not only am I deprived of their physical presence, but they are afraid to write to us. My husband's career as a sociologist is in ruins."

The bus to Yugoslavia passed through Austria. The couple, travelling together for the first time, got out there.

What happened back on that summer day in 1982, that jeopardized the peace and security of the world?

"The Canadian students arrived in Prague on a Wednesday," Nataša remembers. "In the evening, between eight and nine, they heard a lecture on socialism, and then they invaded the Prague nightclubs. I got them the next morning at nine o'clock, most of them under the influence. They asked me the standard questions about wages and labourers and university profs, or how much money my superior makes.... Or, what does it mean to become a member of the Communist party. Or, what about censorship, travel abroad, availability of apartments, etc. " To these standard questions Nataša gave the standard answers she had been taught in the special courses that tourist guides must attend.

After two hours of sightseeing, the girl got rid of her Canadian charges and, off duty, hoped to hitch a ride to the town of Teplice, where she intended to visit her mother. In Czechoslovakia, as in Canada, it is not difficult for a slim, attractive girl to hitch a ride. As it happened, the Canadians were on their way to East Berlin, their next stop, and their bus would pass through Teplice. Pleased with her performance, they offered her a place on the bus. It was a warm summer day. The off-duty guide spoke a charmingly accented but fluent English, and she was more relaxed than when, a few hours earlier, on duty with a bullhorn, she had spoken more primly. The Canadians were young and male. This time the girl told the Canadians the truth as *she* saw it, not as she was supposed to see it.

But as Pilate said, What is truth? For Mr. Lucas and the members of the "Canada-U.S.S.R. Association", truth is *Pravda*. It was just last year that the association organized and hosted a tour of Canada for Mr. Victor Koryakovstev of the

FILM

With (left) Eva Pilarová, star of *Crime in a Night Club*, Jitka Zelenohorská, who became notorious as the girl with the stamped bottom in *Closely Watched Trains*, and director Jiří Menzel

VENICE BIENNALE

—

Škvorecký's broadcasts dealing with the Venice Biennale of November 1977 showed him in a melancholy, shoulder-shrugging mood. Counterpointing his own memories of "over there" with reports of recent cultural and political developments in East and Central Europe—and with some curious West European responses to them—he was both bemused and confused by the almost wilful miscomprehension he found in Venice about "over there".

I

ONCE, WHEN I was a little boy, I saw Mussolini speak. I was about eleven, and I had gone to Yugoslavia on an excursion sponsored by the Thymolin Company; thanks to a truly extended family, I had sent in so many Thymolin brand toothpaste caps that they had awarded me a free four-week trip to the famous seaside resort of Grado. A Jewish uncle of mine came to see me there one day and took me for a trip to Venice, and that was where I saw Mussolini.

I didn't know very well who he was, and when I recall that strange experience today I'm not certain whether the image that remains in my mind is actually that of the commander-in-chief of all true Fascists, or that of American comedian Jack Oakie in the role of Benzino Napaloni, who outshone even Chaplin in some scenes of *The Great Dictator*. In my memories it is as if *il Duce* were imitating Benzino Napaloni: he is so mobile, both vertically and horizontally, that the silly kid that I was at the time sees him more as a bald-headed puppet, with a look so stern that he seems to belong in the world of cartoons. He stood there, on one of the balconies of the Doge's palace, and after each sequence of mercurial gestures he put his hands on his hips, stuck his massive chin out over St.

Mark's Square, and waited for the applause. The men in black shirts standing under the balcony applauded, and the jowly commander proceeded with another comic, though far from silent, sequence. The tourists in the cafés that bordered the square—mostly British and American, but including me and my Uncle Mintz—did not applaud. We were not expected to. We watched the leader of all the Fascists and we looked like the audience in a movie house. Uncle Mintz said, "This fellow here is more for fun. His colleague in Germany, he's the one who scares me."

Uncle Mintz and Aunt Marie died together on March 15, 1939, on the day that that colleague in Germany brought international assistance to Czechoslovakia. I am quoting my uncle's statement, not to call attention to his political astuteness, but because it stuck in my mind, creating the awareness that there was not just one Fascism but two: one more for fun, and a second more for tears. The fun one was bloody, but the one for tears was, I would say, a lot bloodier.

To help you understand, let me remind you of a scene from *Amarcord*, Fellini's film about growing up under Italian Fascism. The Fascists are holding a meeting in the square; when the meeting is in full swing, suddenly the strains of the Internationale sound from the local bell tower. The Fascists didn't like that song, and so a bunch of the most zealous ones climb the bell tower and determine that the song is coming from a phonograph that someone has set there. They soon find the culprit; he is the town's staunch old socialist. They drag him off to the party secretariat and punish him in a manner characteristic of that hot-blooded nation with its sense of fun: they order him to drink a bottle of laxative, and then they let him go. Although the old socialist runs very fast, he doesn't make it in time.... It's not too difficult to imagine what their German colleagues would have done to him for a provocation like that. Had the old socialist been lucky, he might have ended up in one of their correctional institutions.

In short, all Fascisms are not alike, but because Fascism is a fine, sonorous word it became the general term for right-wing dictatorships. When I consider the exploits of the National Socialists, it seems to me that such a generalization is almost unfair to Italian Fascism.

All of this went through my mind in November 1977, when I found myself in Venice again, after all those years, to take part in the traditional Biennale. The theme that year was "Cultural Dissent", and I arrived the day after a meeting of historians and philosophers had turned into a monumental dispute between the delegates of the French Communist Party and the so-called new philosophers, who were very popular in Paris just then. The two most prominent were Andre Glucksmann and Bernard-Henri Lévy, whose book *Barbarism with a Human Face* was a huge bestseller in France. Both were former Marxists—well versed in Marx and the others, with quotations all over the place—but they had crossed the floor, and were contending that Communism was a very dangerous thing, hardly reformable, and comparatively unconcerned with things like intellectual and civil liberty. According to the new philosophers, people would do better to avoid it.

Of course, they said it far more elegantly, but the French and Italian Communists there were still very annoyed, and the discussion was transformed into an "orgy of anti-Communism" in which they compared, of all things, "Communism and Fascism!" These are not my words; they were spoken by the French Communist film critic Martain the first morning I came to the session, and his tone implied that both "anti-Communism" and any comparison of the two totalitarian systems were somehow improper at the Biennale. Then a Mr. Rotschild, an Austrian Slavist and journalist, asked for the floor, and declared that he, as a Marxist, agreed absolutely with the previous speaker; Communism could not be compared with Fascism. In order to clarify that, he said, he would like to read an article about the Biennale from that day's edition of a large daily paper in the East—and here I must apologize, for I have unfortunately forgotten the name of the newspaper. Nor can I quote Mr. Rotschild verbatim, but I think I am quoting the spirit of that text faithfully. It said something like: "International Zionist gangsters, with the support of the Mafia, are meeting at this time in Venice, to try to sweep into a single pile the contents of the garbage cans that they call dissent and samizdat." The article went on along those lines. I looked around. The fact is that there were a few Jews present in the Napoleonica Hall in Venice. There was Arnošt Lustig from Washington, and Ludvik

Aškenazy from Munich, and a few Russian émigrés who had arrived from Israel and were probably Jewish. And there was Andrey Sinyavsky, the Russian writer who got into trouble in 1966 because he authored a lovely study about socialist realism, and published it not in the USSR, but in the West; was he a Jew? I didn't know. He looked more like the model of a Russian moujik, straight out of Gogol: short, with the kind of turned-up nose common in Czechoslovakia. His face was bearded the way only Russian faces can be bearded, so that the only thing peeping out of that jungle was a pair of little eyes, displaying an incomparable, perhaps dialectical, unity of merriment and sadness; the end of his beard pointed slightly outwards, like the beard on a Disney dwarf. But certainly there were Jews there—Mr. Rotschild himself, for example. He finished reading the newspaper article and then said, "This is not the vocabulary of Fascism. It is the vocabulary of National Socialism. *That* is what should be compared...."

I stopped listening to Mr. Rotschild; my mind turned to thoughts like...what about the kind of "anti" you have to avoid, otherwise a Western Communist won't even talk to you? And I remembered—I don't know why—the time before 1948, when I graduated from university, and the period that followed, and how almost everyone I liked to read suddenly disappeared from literature and the arts, while the few who remained began to write as if they were turning out schoolroom compositions. Then I thought of all those friends who were sent away, at the age of eighteen, to various institutions where they were to be reformed. Then I thought of the sixties, and how the names that had disappeared began reappearing in literature, and how those friends started coming home, possibly reformed. Then came 1968. There was an interlude, pleasant if rather rash, but unfortunately a brief one—only nine months, and then the child died—and again names were stricken from literature, people lost their jobs, magazines perished of heart attacks and were replaced by a single new one that wrote about literature but sounded more like a religious incantation, quite uninteresting. And I wondered if, after all that in a single short lifetime, it was possible not to be at least a little "anti" (even anti-Communist). I supposed it was—assuming you were the kind of person who gets pleasure out of getting thrashed with a whip.

But I didn't say that at the Biennale. I spoke about my experiences with the Great Barrandov Council of Dramaturges, when Miloš Forman and I delivered the script for a musical comedy that took place at the time of the Protectorate, and how it exploded in our faces. In the evening I went to the Canale Grande, Harry's Bar, and sipped whisky and stared at the photograph of a bearded man that hangs there right next to the bar, in memory of the fact that he used to sit there. No, not Sinyavsky. It was Ernest Hemingway, old Papa. The coloured lights of the gondolas rocked on the canal outside the window of Harry's Bar, and at the next table sat Viola Fischerová, that pretty girl from the sixties whose poem Bohumil Hrabal quotes as the epigraph of his book *An Ad for a House I Don't Want to Live in Any More*, and as those thoughts went through my mind a little dwarf straight out of Gogol stuck his beard out of them, and I had the feeling that I was not "anti" after all, and that I was no dissenter. I am simply a writer, with no attributive adjectives—the kind they describe as, in some ways, never having quite grown up. And it occurred to me that it would probably be a lot better if nobody ever quite grew up, never turned into Jack Oakie gesticulating on the balcony of the Doge's palace, or into those other various incantators pronouncing magical formulae about Zionism and passing judgement with terrible ease on those of us who never grew up.

II

Venice in November is not exactly the place I would recommend for a trip in search of sunshine. It rains, it drizzles, and when the rain stops St. Mark's Square is like a swimming pool. So the congress resembled an assembly of drug users, everyone popping pills and swallowing them with the potent Italian coffee that was served free. Still, for ten days I returned to the time of my youth in Náchod, when I used to go to the movies every day. And for the first time in years I enjoyed films again— films that for the most part had never been shown in the lands of their origin, and in some cases had never been shown at all. Most of them seemed even better than the ones I generally attend in Toronto.

For example, they showed *Josef Kilián* by Pavel Juráček, that poetic Kafkaesque piece about a cat-rental store—beautiful surrealism. But they also showed Juráček's *Case for a Rookie Hangman*, which many people in Czechoslovakia probably haven't seen. It is a fantasy based on one part of Swift's *Gulliver's Travels*, an allegorical tale, I might say, about the alienation of some governments from their subjects. We also saw two of Věra Chytilová's older films, *Something Different* and *Daisies*. I am happy to say that *Daisies* hasn't lost anything with the years; it is still the same beautifully disrespectful tribute to the cinematic art, old American film comedies, Abel Gance and Méliès, still the same wonderful super-montage that Věra took from the somewhat didactic hands of Sergei Eisenstein and filled with impertinent life.

A.J. Liehm and his wife Mira, who wrote the very successful book *The Most Important Art*—a history of film in the countries of the so-called Soviet bloc—introduced an extensive series of films that in the sixties made Czechoslovakia famous in the Western, and to some degree even in the Eastern, world. It began with Forman's *Black Peter* and *Firemen's Ball*, his film about firemen who admitted to their wrongdoings, and then weren't certain whether that admission had helped or harmed the cause of firefighting. Miloš himself was unable to come to Venice, because he was shooting a megafilm in New York based on the famous musical *Hair*. Nor could Vojtěch Jasný be present at the screening of his film *All My Good Countrymen*, because he was shooting a film about Herbert von Karajan. I saw *All My Good Countrymen* for the first time, and I would say that it is a more than worthy epitaph for the Czech New Wave of the sixties. Although it is ostensibly about the forming of collective farms, the film is in fact about human destinies. A melancholy, lovely film.

Similar in tone but entirely different in form was Slovak director Dušan Hanák's film *322*, about a man who faces diagnosis number 322, which in Czechoslovakia means cancer. The hero of the film once did something he shouldn't have, and now, in the shadow of the diagnosis, he reflects. Even old Papa Hemingway who used to sit around at Harry's Bar here in Venice knew well that, in the shadow of the inescapable judgement, each of us finds his values falling beautifully into place. But the film was above all captivating for its camera work and editing; it seems to me that not since *Last Year in Marienbad* has any motion picture displayed such amazing camera work. There isn't a single shot that is a cliché.

But my most impressive experience at the festival was another Slovak film which wasn't actually shown at the Biennale, but was screened for me privately by an Italian producer friend in a little screening room on the Canale Grande, because I stubbornly insisted on seeing it. The film had the provocative title *See You in Hell, Gentlemen!* and it was shot in 1969 by Slovak director Juraj Jakubisko. Unfortunately, I have to say that Jakubisko is an irresponsible director. When the picture had been shot in Slovakia, my friend the producer took the exposed film to be developed in Rome. The director was supposed to go there to edit it, but he never came. It has been seven years now, and Jakubisko has still not shown up to edit his film, so the poor producer has had to give the job to local film editors and he is terribly apologetic that the film is not what the director wished. As a result, it hasn't been released to movie theatres. I do feel the government of the Slovak Republic should force Jakubisko to travel to Rome to finish what he started.

What is the film about? I don't know if it is about anything. It is a pure cinematographic spectacle, with the screen always full of picturesque things in motion, so that there is constantly something to watch. The characters misbehave with total freedom—or rather, they behave as if they were free of all laws of dramaturgy, aesthetics, and society. There is an entire series of sophisticated parodies, and towards the end some sort of police force tries to step in, fortunately unsuccessfully, in a sequence that is absolutely basic: the classic chase scene of the great D.W. Griffith. I might say that it is a film about freedom, with all its risks, dangers, and cruelty. Above all, however, it is about the hypnotic power of freedom, which binds you to your seat in the theatre so that you can't tear your eyes away from the screen.

What was it that great newspaper whose name I still can't remember said? Something about "Zionist gangsters sweeping into a single pile the contents of garbage cans"...? Well, apparently by accident, people have tossed some very beautiful things into those garbage cans.

III

One of the topics that came up at the Biennale was socialist realism. Alberto Moravia was of the opinion that socialist realism
is actually the bourgeois realism of the twentieth century, akin
to the realism of second-rate nineteenth-century bourgeois authors. They have several characteristic traits in common, above
all the fact that they avoid the fundamental questions of the
time, and that they depict reality in such an unreal manner that
it doesn't resemble itself at all. The true expert on socialist realism, of course, is Sinyavsky, but he spoke about how art is, in a
certain sense, more important than life—which sounds provocative, but there may be something to it. Sinyavsky claimed that
only those societies that have created works of art—great books,
works of architecture, sculpture, music—have left behind ineradicable testimony to their existence, and in that sense live
on. Societies that merely waged attacks on foreign soil exist only
as names of dubious repute in textbooks: Avars and Vandals
and all those purveyors of power and "aid". Perhaps without realizing it, Sinyavsky approached a concept of E.M. Forster. To
Forster, art is supremely important because, as he put it in "Art
for Art's Sake", "Ancient Athens made a mess—but the *Antigone*
stands up. Renaissance Rome made a mess—but the ceiling of
the Sistine got painted. James I made a mess—but there was
Macbeth."

Anyway, Sinyavsky didn't say anything about socialist realism at the Biennale. So that although I had hoped that I would
finally find out what that movement is, since no one had ever
been able to explain it to me, I still didn't know. Socialist realism
has always reminded me, personally, of cowboy novels.

But I know, I know—that was *old-fashioned* socialist realism:
they don't write like that any more in Czechoslovakia, and
maybe not even in the Soviet Union. How they write today
in Czechoslovakia was described at the Biennale by Dr. Igor
Hájek, Dean of Cartmell College at Lancaster University in
England, formerly editor for foreign literature in Czech literary
weeklies, and translator of Graham Greene and other authors
into the Czech.

In the first place, Dr. Hájek noted, authors of the aforemen-
tioned category—the socialist western—with a few exceptions,

no longer publish in Czechoslovakia, but have been replaced by other authors. "I have no intention," said Hájek, "of sneering at such professional writers. They have their useful place in the literary life of society. They fulfil the needs of a broad range of readers with professional skill, but without that spark of originality that separates the artist from the craftsman. By their very essence they are unable to play the role of the avant-garde, the role of explorers. But it was just this role that was offered to them after 1970, with the establishment of the new Union of Writers." Dr. Hájek proceeded to discuss, entertainingly and in detail, the strange phenomena that accompanied this important change. One was that average work was once again officially proclaimed as exceptional, while productive diversity was replaced by a uniformity. Special attention was ostensibly paid to young authors, but because the literary magazines of the sixties have been discontinued and replaced by a single one, the *Literary Monthly*, young writers didn't have a platform on which to test themselves, and instead published collections. These young authors wrote a lot about rural life, about the establishment of collective farms, but because in the forties or fifties they were either children, or not even alive, many pages of their novels sounded as if they had been copied from the old-fashioned works I mentioned earlier. Meanwhile the better ones filled their writing with a kind of lyrical, generalizing romanticism, bordering on sentimentality, which made village life seem like the traditional refuge of ancient, undistorted values.

An entirely contrary approach to reality was that of what Hájek labelled the Northern Bohemian school, whose authors, Jiří Švejda, Václav Dušek, or Arnošt Heřman, display evidence of the influence of the only surviving master of the sixties, Vladimír Páral. In their novels, people don't simply climb into a car, but always into a Simca, a Renault, a Mercedes, or a Škoda. Nor do they ever take a drink of just plain whisky; it is always Johnny Walker, Black and White, or Vat 69. Judging by these novels, Czechoslovakia has become a land of chain smokers—at least twice on every page, a Winston, Pall Mall, or Rothman's is lit. "In this obsession with symbols of social status," said Dr. Hájek, "in this immense and detailed attention to things, there seems to be some sort of message. Could these imported things be the only way to realize, to emphasize a person's identity?

Or is it just a matter of a belated imitation of American prose from the affluent fifties and sixties, which also displayed a consumerist pleasure in items of daily use?"

So much for Dr. Hájek. That evening, treating my cold with drinks at Harry's Bar, I contemplated what would happen to American literature if all at once somebody struck from it Faulkner and Fitzgerald, Arthur Miller and Tennessee Williams, Robert Frost and Wallace Stevens, in short all the authors whose work contains that spark of originality that separates the artist from the craftsman. And if the only one left—Hemingway, say—was forced to rewrite *For Whom the Bell Tolls* so that it glorified the Falangists. Little would change in bookstore windows. Books would keep being published; there would always be someone receiving the Pulitzer Prize for something, because it has to be awarded; newspapers would still publish reviews. American literature would continue to exist, but it would be American literature without Faulkner, Fitzgerald, Sinclair Lewis—American literature without a spark of originality. In short, a sort of extinguished American literature.

One evening I boarded the boat that is used in Venice as a taxi to the airport, and took the evening plane to Rome. I arrived at my hotel quite late and the dining room was almost empty; there was just one party at a table. I sat at a neighbouring table, to save the waiter some running around, and as I listened I realized that the gentlemen at the next table were talking Czech. That hadn't happened to me in a restaurant for a long time, except in Toronto's Czech pubs. It was a group of some sort of delegates from Prague, and they were in the process of an odd experiment. Each had ordered a different brand of beer (there were eight of them), and now they were presenting their evaluations. I drank two Manhattans. I ate my soup, then the main course, then my dessert, and finally I drank four Cointreaus. I was obliged to stop there because that is the limit of my capacity for alcohol. At the table beside me, they were still discussing beer. Knowledgeably, enthusiastically, as if they were delving into the mysteries of human existence. They were at it when I paid my bill and staggered off to my room.

When I came down to breakfast the following day, they were still there. Or there again, perhaps, because they were drinking coffee now, and spreading rolls with butter and jam. But even over their breakfast they were still talking about beer. Now it was beers they had tried during an official visit to Denmark. They knew them all by name, Tuborg, Heineken—they were experts. Although it was early in the morning, I ordered a Manhattan, which startled the waiter. Echoing in my ears were Dr. Hájek's words about that stylistic peculiarity of the Northern Bohemian school in whose novels people don't smoke cigarettes but Winstons or Pall Malls, and the message that this conveys.

Anyway, that is how the Venice Biennale ended for me. I went to the airport and took a jumbo jet to Toronto. As unsure as ever about the meaning of socialist realism.

JIŘÍ MENZEL AND
CLOSELY WATCHED TRAINS

As was mentioned in the introduction, Škvorecký was closely associated with several of the directors of the Czech New Wave of the 1960s. He wrote scripts for Miloš Forman's banned film The Band Has Won, *Jiří Menzel's* Crime in a Girl's School *and* Crime in a Night Club, *and Evald Schorm's* End of a Priest. *He was also a bit player in several films.*

The following essay is from Jiří Menzel and the History of Closely Watched Trains, *his 1982 book-length tribute to Menzel, and it should be read in conjunction with the earlier essay "Introducing Bohumil Hrabal", which discusses the novella on which Menzel based his award-winning film.*

IS *CLOSELY WATCHED* Trains, Jiří Menzel's 1966 film, a dilution and simplification of Bohumil Hrabal's original story, and not such a great movie after all? In spite of its Oscar for Best

Foreign Film, and in spite of its continuous success with student
audiences in the West?

Much depends on one's criteria. In my opinion, it is an
excellent, perhaps great film, although it may have distorted
an excellent novella.

For the radically avant-garde critics even that novella was
a step back: a "prettifying" of the harsh "The Legend of Cain",
and a move in the direction of the traditional. It had a clearly
defined plot, a platitudinous political moral—in fact, it had a
"message" acceptable even to the establishment. In the atmosphere of Central European avant-garde—greatly alien to the
atmosphere of the individualistic, pragmatic, and much more
liberal North American literary scene—these are sins, if not
crimes. A writer capable of absolute originality, of high intel-
lectualism, and free of clichés, becomes a traitor to the cause if
he makes compromises with less radical attitudes. Such compromises are explained as attempts at being accepted by the
general public and by the establishment. Viewed more liber-
ally, of course, they make an original author more accessible
to interested and intelligent non-specialists who are capable of
appreciating good art but not of enjoying extreme products of
what may very well be honest efforts to find new and better
ways of expression. But that doesn't count with the orthodox
avant-garde.

If this is roughly true about the literary life of, say, West Germany, where people have access to all kinds of art, it is doubly
true of the hermetic cliques in the underground of authoritarian dictatorships; there, to lecture on *Finnegans Wake* does
not just expose one to the danger of being called an egghead,
but may actually lead, during periods of freeze, to arrest and
time in camp. I was present at clandestine lectures by fanatic
surrealists whose Bretonian orthodoxy did not allow them to
acknowledge any merit at all in commercial hacks like Hemingway or Fitzgerald, who anyway stole all their goods from
Goddess Stein. It was morally hard to argue with those speak-
ers when there were several obvious police informers among
those present. To this very day there are at least two critics in Prague who swear that the only thing of any value I
ever wrote was a dark novella of sexual frustration set in an

abandoned cloister in the forlorn region of the Sudetenland after the Communist coup called *Zákony džungle* (*Jungle Laws*, 1950), not really much different in mood from "The Legend of Cain". I never published it (though I read it to the Kolář circle) because in spite of the genuineness of its frustration it seemed to me embarrassingly amateurish. In order to survive the stresses of sophisticated modern police states many people have to develop strong, unchanging convictions, and even fanatical beliefs. Including art theoreticians. The old maxim *épater le bourgeois*, metamorphosed into *épater le communiste*, is sometimes the primary motive for creation and criticism, and whatever does not *épater* the establishment to outbursts of anger is not regarded as good enough.

Since the oppressive establishment is unjust to the avant-garde, the avant-garde tends to be unjust to all those the regime extols, and even those it only oppresses less severely. This is also the attitude, for instance, of some of the former political prisoners to whom everybody who was not "there", i.e., in the camps, is a bloody Communist. Theirs is a narrow view, and in a democratic world one can afford to be more liberal. There one does not play into the hands of some Party cultural secretary who would be happier if there were no writers, only hacks, and no culture, just an entertainment industry.

One could invent similes for the evolution of the subject matter from "The Legend", through the novel, to the film. It all started with undiluted blackness which, among other things, reflected the mood of the adult author who had just survived the war. Sixteen years later it was transformed into a sort of twilight: the morbidity of the war receded in memory, the bloody cruelties of the fifties were still vivid, but political changes made it possible to enjoy more freely the pleasures of life and its bittersweet minor sorrows. Thus the novel is also a reflection of the times. The then young man, unscarred by both holocausts—at the time of the mass executions of the Slánský trial and the deportation of old-age pensioners from Prague to the deserted Sudetenland he was only fourteen—got a hand in the project. What remained was almost purely the joy of life, and of laughing at the frustrations of which very few people die. An ode to life's innermost source.

He filmed it superbly. The camera of Jaromír Šofr never calls
attention to itself, never intrudes: it reveals. This *is* how life
looks at a tiny station somewhere in central Bohemia. One can
almost smell the smoke of locomotives. This *is* how the seasons
pass; this *is* how it feels to stand on the platform on a grey day
and watch a simple, sweet proletarian girl in a clumsy uniform
come on duty. This is how a dinner can turn into the despair
of tragedy for an ageing man who sips his soup opposite a wife
with her charm and interest gone, while downstairs the hated
satyr is romping about the Elysian Fields with a carnal Venus.
What we see revealed here by the stationary camera is the
essence of the visible reality. André Bazin would have loved this
film.

Objects, sounds, little happenings talk, few of them have only
one meaning, yet none of them is an overt and premeditated
symbol. The tearing of the sofa is no Scarlet Letter. It is an
example of how rich in content and linkages a simple, common,
unspectacular thing can be in the hands of a perceptive artist.
Although the puncturing of it in sexual derision is a rather
direct suggestion of the "torn hymen", the object itself and its
placement, in the stationmaster's private office, evoke so many
associations that the directness of the suggestion does not for
one moment appear primitive or vulgar. When the sofa is torn
for the first time, the sound prevents a kiss which was to be
a prelude to Miloš's and Máša's loss of innocence. When that
sound resounds again, it is the woman who tears the couch
with her boots, and the man—Miloš—"grins happily". He has
at long last got rid of his uncherished unmanly state. He is
now like his idol, the First Tearer; in the shot following the
scene, standing on the platform with their backs to the camera,
the two men are indistinguishable. Miloš even cleans his ear
and whistles in direct imitation of his preceptor. All this is a
rather complex linkage developed from the little mess made of
the furniture—and the poor mooner Lánský gazes sadly at the
tear. At the moment the sadness is not the trifling dejection
of an owner of damaged small property. Its sources are pre-
capitalistic, pre-socialistic. They are prehistoric, universal. This
is how art differs from simple pornography. For precisely this
reason Henry Miller's books did not belong on Forty-Second
Street.

Several other objects in the film perform services as complex as the hole in the sofa. The rubber stamps in the hands of the quisling Zednicek represent armies on his torn map with the holes in it (the Führer has fucked up the war, if you want to stretch the hole association yet a little further). Next time the stamps appear on the screen they are pressed to a girl's bottom: the armies are heading for the ass, which in Czech is a juicy idiom for disaster. The contact of rubber and unmentionable (and unrevealable) flesh constitutes, in Zednicek's words, not a sexual but a political offence, "an abuse of the German language"; the stamps are bilingual. But at the same time, all this is perfectly natural. No raisins in this beautiful pudding of a movie. Just as Hemingway wanted it to be: if a thing is described (and filmed, I should add) well, it may have many meanings.[1]

The railwayman's cap, the most conspicuous part of his uniform, has such meanings. After the ritual coronation of Miloš by his mother, the cap becomes indeed a crown of thorns, when Miloš does not take it off during his near-fatal failure in bed. This links the uniform with sexual failure, a linkage which is indirectly exemplified in the oversexed stationmaster's preoccupation with his own uniforms and emblems of service status. In a society that, in the course of one generation's life-span, went through three heavily uniformed foreign regimes (Austrian empire, Nazi Protectorate, Soviet occupation), and to people who helplessly had to watch so many eager columns of big-assed men in differently coloured breeches—which, as Wilhelm Reich knew so well, are invariably a compensation for more natural but repressed yearnings—the game with uniforms in the film may be more meaningful than to audiences in predominantly civilian societies. The stationmaster's highest ambition is to become the Director of State Railways—but one feels that he would unhesitatingly exchange the fancy chair of a director's office for his own poor torn sofa if on it was lying, ready for him, Hubička's blonde "cousin". In one small but important scene—one of the many additions to the book—the subconscious interdependence between uniform (and implicitly careerism) and suppressed sex is translated into cleverly audio-visual terms: the Tailor "fishing between the stationmaster's legs" says, "Let's loosen it a bit there, in the crotch, so that it won't feel so oppressive." A man's balls squeezed by his uniform—could one invent a better, more folksy, more natural and healthily salacious metaphor for Reich's analysis?

And then there is the soundtrack, full of clicking, ticking, chiming, tolling, signalling, and time-measuring machinery. The meanings of these telegraphs, watches, clocks, and ball-clocks shoot out in even more directions: erotic, philosophical, poetic. Their role is strongly suggested in the novel but in the film their complex functions work towards effects that reverberate with allusive depths and audio-visual beauty.

And again everything is perfectly natural: clocks are machines for the measuring of time, essential in a railway station; time is essential in life. Clocks measure the time of life. Time, because it limits life, is death's close relative. Clocks, time, life, death: in this linking of images lies the best compensation for the lost dimensions of the novel.[2]

There, the relationship between time and death as symbolized by clocks appears directly in an introductory scene, omitted in the film. Miloš, inspecting a shot-down German fighter plane, finds the dead body of the pilot under the wreckage, notices that the clock on the instrument panel is still going, and compares its time with his own wristwatch. In the film, this missing chain is replaced by a scene in which Mr. Novák, holding the dead rabbit, comments on the sound of the stationmaster's clock. The chiming of this particular clock becomes a leitmotif which marks the action whenever it assumes portentous or sexual overtones. The clock strikes when the tailor is about to loosen the stationmaster's crotch in the office where, on a commode, stands the beautiful time-piece, with its massive, slowly revolving golden balls. It strikes again when Hubička stretches out his hand to place the bilingual stamp on the saintly bottom of Virginia: Hubička pauses, waits for the machine to finish chiming; then, with the last knell, it is midnight, the time of day's death, and simultaneously of a new day's birth; the virgin's initiation is about to culminate, her virginity about to be destroyed. Later a similar sparkling cluster of associations is once again introduced by the chiming of the well-balled clock, when Victoria Freie offers herself to Miloš. Significantly, while Miloš is rapidly becoming a man, Hubička in the next room is examining the time-bomb, another clock: the clock of death. The juxtaposition links time machinery directly with death, and also sex with death, and prefigures the concluding cross-cut sequences in which the same contrasting effect is spread across a longer time span and across a more complex structure. And the clock strikes for the last time when the explosion shakes the station and blows the—by now—dead Miloš's cap into Máša's lap. The beautiful chime becomes here the death-knell, a moving funeral hymn without words; a bell whose challenge could almost be translated into the famous words of John Donne popularized by Hemingway (whom, by the way, Hrabal knows very well). After all, like Robert Jordan's, this too is a story of a tragically brief affair in the shadow of wartime death; its hero has a slightly longer life than Francis Macomber, but a similarly happy one.

A substantial part of the director's art is his casting. Much of Miloš Forman's initial fame rested on his discovery of the amazing bandleader Mr. Vomáčka, who in the role of Black Peter's father became a national image. There is a lot to say for Eisensteinian *typage*, and Menzel proved himself to be a good pupil of yet another great tutor.

Non-actors appear in seven of the ten main parts, and almost all bit parts were also given to amateurs. It is, of course, not easy to define a non-actor; what I mean here is simply people with no professional training in acting. Originally the director wished to play Miloš himself; a wish that I, knowing Menzel, consider not purely artistic. Although he did not cut his wrists, the depth of his dejection after he got the sack from Máša, after *Crime in a Girls' School*, was scary. That is why Jitka Bendová fits the role of the conductress so well. In her case it was not just type-casting but love-casting: the proletarian girl in a clumsy uniform who can be "as clean and fresh at the end of a shift as if she'd just come on duty". I have rarely seen a better screen personification of a writer's suggestive image than the scene of the train entering the station and the clean, fresh, pretty girl approaching, standing on the steps of a dirty car.

When Menzel failed to provide himself with an opportunity to go to bed with Máša, if only in the studio ("What a shame!" he cried, according to Hrabal, when he saw he looked too old for the part), he compensated himself with another role: that of the doctor-confessor. Those who doubt my partly Freudian interpretation of the director's casting methods will be more inclined to agree with me if they look at the still which shows the doctor giving advice to his patient. These are not only faces of two men suffering from identical problems: the two—like Miloš and Hubička in a later scene—even look remarkably alike.

In the days when singers had to change their names from Gumm to Garland, Václav Neckář, whose name (washtub maker in Czech) is only slightly less ridiculous than Miloš Hrma's, could not have made a career in the pop-music industry. Yet he is one of its most durable stars, and in *The Trains* appeared on the screen for the first time. Like Forman's bandleader, he became a national prototype of the pubescent youth, and although he later appeared in several other films he was too much the Miloš Hrma of *The Trains* to achieve remarkable success as an actor in another story.

Besides Neckář's superb performance and the professionalism of Vlastimil Brodský in the role of the quisling Zednicek, two men stand paramount: the stationmaster and the dispatcher.

Vladimír Valenta—and for Czech audiences he will for ever remain the stationmaster—is not an actor but a very distinguished scriptwriter. In the sixties he wrote one of the most daring scripts for a political courtroom drama directed by Elmar Klos and Ján Kádár (of *Shop on Main Street* fame) called *Obžalovaný* (*The Accused*). It saw the debut of Jiří Menzel as an actor, in the part of a shy defence attorney. Much earlier, in 1949, Valenta had written the screenplay for *Svědomí* (*Conscience*), which remained one of the very best Czech post–Second World War films for about a decade, during which the studios were turning out socialist realist trash and Valenta was serving time in a concentration camp for having been too explicit about what was going on in the studios. The stationmaster made him as actor: since then he has appeared in numerous films, first Czech (including *Crime in a Night Club* and another movie I wrote, *End of a Priest*), then Canadian (the latest being *The Amateur*) and American (*The Unbearable Lightness of Being*). His performance in *Trains* is flawless; I doubt if one could find a more fitting voice to intone the lavatory-shaft exhortations than the wailing, reproachful, self-pitying shout of this Prague intellectual.

And as for Mr. Hubička, the dispatcher, played by Josef Somr, I don't think I have anything to add to John Simon's description of Somr's achievement: "If Czechoslovakia does not have an Oscar...one should promptly be created for Somr. There is something so spontaneous, unconcerned, and complete about such a performance that it affects our entire sensorium— fingertips, nostrils, and palate no less than eyes and ears."

A film miles removed from the original black story of Cain, and much different from the tragicomedy of the novel—but a film with subtle complexities of its own, beautifully executed, revealing the visible reality of a small corner of the world, and demonstrating the universal reality of man's joyfully dirty masculine soul through its fine script and actors. A film that makes people laugh by its intelligently farcical exaggerations, rooted in closely watched details of multifariously revealed reality. It was not an expression of undue humility or an attempt to flatter the director when Bohumil Hrabal wrote: "I like the film better than my novel."

My relationship with both creators of this funny thing of beauty, and particularly with Jiří Menzel, was very close, very personal; one of the things in my life that I gladly remember. As Hrabal wrote: "Mr. Menzel [although] only half as old as I was, still managed to find a common denominator with me." During a memorable car ride I was cast in the role of Dr. Brabec, Miloš's confessor—but I wrote about that in *All the Bright Young Men and Women*, so I shall not dwell on it here. That, however, is the reason why I did not obey Menzel when he sent word to his old friends in the West that, should they try to go and see his new films, they would no longer be his friends. I went and saw them. They are not bad, particularly *Seclusion near a Forest*. But....

There is a difference between art and craftsmanship. It is not easy to describe and it is less easy to define. But it is easy to feel. After sixty years of experience with art in the Soviet orbit, it is a truism to say that whenever a society becomes really closely watched all one can hope for is craftsmanship. Art, by its very nature, cannot survive close surveillance. In his more recent works Menzel, the receptive pupil of Griffith, Eisenstein, and Vávra, displays his accustomed skill, and perhaps even improves on it. But that he will make another *Trains....*

[1] *Daniel López, in an unpublished essay on* Closely Watched Trains, *suggests a parallelism between the marks on Virginia's stamped bottom, and Miloš's suicide scar: both of these are a kind of mutilation and indicate that sex initiation can be either torture or pleasure. I am indebted to López's essay for some observations on sex and time in the film.*

[2] *I have always been intrigued by the similarity of the watch/clock symbolism in Menzel's film, and in the Quentin section of* The Sound and the Fury, *especially since both stories end in the death of the protagonist and include a suicide. In all probability, neither Menzel nor Hrabal had ever read that book, though both of them knew Faulkner from Czech translations.* The Sound and the Fury *had not been translated at that time, but several Czech essays on Faulkner were printed in the sixties, some of which dealt with* The Sound and the Fury *and may even have contained quotations from Sartre's well-known analysis of the function of time in that novel. Hrabal expressly mentions Faulkner in an essay entitled "On the String between the Cradle and the Coffin" in* Homework.

ON THE INTRICACIES OF ADAPTING FICTION FOR THE SCREEN

Written in 1982, this essay represents Škvorecký's third engagement with Josef Conrad's Heart of Darkness *within a space of six years. As his own political and historical vision darkened through the 1970s, he began to refer more frequently to that other East European exile; Conrad figures prominently in* The Engineer of Human Souls, *in the 1982 essay "Why the Harlequin?" (*Cross Currents, *1984), and in the essay "A Revolution Is Usually the Worst Solution".*

Here Škvorecký directs his attention to Apocalypse Now, *Francis Coppola's very free adaptation of* Heart of Darkness.

A FEW FACTS about the relationship of film and fiction are well known: that film is much closer to fiction than to drama because the filmmaker, like a novelist, is free to move from place to place and from the present to the past and back again, whereas the playwright is limited by the imperatives of the stage. Neither of these assertions is quite true: the filmmaker's use of the time machine is somewhat hampered by the perpetually present tense of the visual image, and the modern playwright can hop, just like Shakespeare, from Toronto to the Kerguelen Islands simply by demanding more from the imagination of the audience. But even Shakespeare was almost completely dependent on words, words, words, whereas the filmmaker can almost completely depend on pictures—just as the novelist can build on the evocative concepts of which printed words are voiceless carriers.

All in all, film is pretty close to fiction, and rather remote from drama. That much, I suppose, is at the moment the *consensus omnium*.

One hears from time to time, however, other truths whose validity is less assured. It is known that some of the best films have been made from some of the worst novels, and vice versa—like for instance the unforgettable nightmare of Orson Welles's *Lady from Shanghai*, based on an obscure thriller; or on the other hand, Hemingway's *A Farewell to Arms*, whose main charm, its magically quintessential style, eluded the filmmaker, resulting in an uninspired melodrama.

So far, so good. The trouble begins when people try to extrapolate from this. There is a famous syllogism that all birds can fly, the ostrich is a bird and thus it is possible for an ostrich to soar to heaven. Similarly, some people have deduced that undistinguished novels make better sources for distinguished films than do literary masterpieces.

Every translator is familiar with the first axiom of his craft: one must be more loyal to the spirit of the original than to its words. The worst crime against a poem, whose effectiveness rests on rhyme and onomatopoeia—a crime, alas, frequently committed in English-speaking countries—is respecting every word of the original as defined in the dictionary, and consequently, of necessity, ignoring the rhymes and the word music. But the translator who respects the beautiful sounds in which the original's power is embedded, and ignores other aspects of the work such as the order of the lines, the completeness of its verbal content, and the taboo against additions, commits no crime. In the terminology of his craft, he has compensated for the charms of the foreign tongue by invoking the music of his own. In the very beginnings of American literature, Edgar Allan Poe already knew that "Music, when combined with a pleasurable idea, is poetry". Therefore to translate "The Raven" without rhyme, without inner rhyme, without the bells of its sounds, would be the equivalent of creating uninteresting nonsense. And therefore, by the way, none of the twenty-five or so Czech translators of this astonishing poem ever tried to ignore its music.

And that is precisely what the filmmaker must do with a novel: he must free himself from the exact wording of the printed page, and translate the spirit of the text into the mother-tongue of the cinema.

This, of course, is easy to say—but how does one go about doing it?

Henry James, in an essay entitled "The Art of Fiction", has the following passage:

> I remember an English novelist, a woman of genius, telling me that she was much commended for the impression she had managed to give in one of her tales of the nature and way of life of the French Protestant youth. She had been asked where she learned so much about this recondite being, she had been congratulated on her peculiar opportunities. These opportunities consisted in her having once, in Paris, as she ascended a staircase, passed an open door where, in the household of a *pasteur*, some of the young Protestants were seated at table round a finished meal. The glimpse made a picture; it lasted only a moment, but that moment was experience. She had got her direct personal impression, and she turned out her type. She knew what youth was, and what Protestantism; she also had the advantage of having seen what it was to be French, so that she converted these ideas into a concrete image and produced a reality. Above all, however, she was blessed with the faculty which when you give it an inch takes an ell,...the power to guess the unseen from the seen, to trace the implication of things, to judge the whole piece by the pattern....

This, *in nuce*, is James's "germ" theory. I suggest that the compensation process, which must be at work in any successful effort to transform a novel into a film, is a search for the germs in fiction from which flowers can blossom on the screen. However, the adaptor must possess the power to judge the whole piece by the pattern; he must see the implications of developing his germs into much larger units in the film.

Let me stay with James. One of the triumphs of his subtle, ironic, and complex genius is a short novel called *The Aspern*

Papers. Its hero, a wealthy American dabbler in literary criticism, is faced with a difficult dilemma: he can become the
possessor of the immensely precious letters of an early American poet, long since dead, if he marries the "niece" of the poet's
still living mistress. The trouble is that the mistress will never
see a hundred again, which makes her "niece" a woman of very
ripe age. The inner struggle of the protagonist between his literary obsession and his male instincts permeates the entire,
beautifully evoked chiaroscuro of nineteenth-century Venice
with a very modern counterpoint, and infuses the wealthy dilet-
tante's hour of decision with a deeply felt (though barely hinted
at) sense of human tragedy. This, I believe, is the essence of the
tragicomical story; this is the germ from which a scriptwriter
must start, if he is thinking of translating the novella into a
film.

Somebody in Hollywood did think of it, in 1947, and the film
was released by Universal Pictures under the title *The Last
Moment.* Commendably, the creators of this opus did not try to
put onto the screen everything in the novel; they selected a germ
and made it blossom. The protagonist remained a youngish and
wealthy American *littérateur.* The age of the poet's mistress was
also faithfully conveyed, by doing up a much younger actress
to resemble a mummy—somewhat in the manner of the horror
movie of the same name. But James's pathetic, overripe "niece"
metamorphosed into a beauty in her late twenties, thus nicely
demolishing the essence of the novella and leading to the stock
matrimonial happy ending. The multifaceted germ of James's
fiction had blossomed into a kitschy flower of pink nylon.

So much for the forgettable "niece" of *The Last Moment.* Let
us now pick up another relative of fiction, the young female
"cousin" of the dispatcher Hubička in *Closely Watched Trains.*
In Bohumil Hrabal's novel, this young woman is only the tini-
est of germs: an anonymous "certain lady" who is mentioned as
having participated in the ripping of the stationmaster's couch
some time earlier, while making love with the philandering railway employee. The whole affair is told in half a sentence. Yet in
the film the "cousin" becomes the hub of one of the most telling,
best executed, and quite extended episodes. She is both a con-
vincing character, fully at home in the world of the story, and a
device that tightens the plot and gathers several of the novel's

particles into one coherent sequence. She also becomes a foil for the climactic defeat of the stationmaster in his continuing duel with Hubička, and a witness of his tragedy when the old lecher's dirty joke is trumped by the dispatcher's much dirtier one. The ordeal is then further intensified when the poor, elderly bugger assists his faded wife with her skein of wool and has his arms symbolically shackled by it: a devastating humiliation absent from the novel, or present only in the form of fleeting hints. The sequence, with all its liveliness and reality, functions perfectly in the plot structure. It sparkles with Hrabalian humour, manages to make the on-screen telling of a vulgar anecdote palatable (a very unusual achievement), and, using elements of farce, beautifully renders the feeling of one of man's greatest frustrations—unfulfilled sexual desire.

That entire sequence is wholly invented in the script. But because unfulfilled lust is also the essence of the story of the protagonist, an adolescent suffering from *ejaculatio praecox*, the coarse ribaldry is not a violation of a good novel, but a translation of it into the medium of the screen. Out of this germ blossomed a fragrant blood-red rose.

Sometimes, however, I am glad for the author when I see a wildly distorted adaptation of a book. Even the best of writers occasionally produce works below their usual standard, and these are sometimes elevated into memorable films by filmmakers who simply build upon the aspects best suited to their medium. Such is the case of Hemingway's poorest performance, *To Have and Have Not*, which—surprisingly, for this superbly original artist—displays many trendy clichés of the time. I do not have exact information about the respective contributions of the director, Howard Hawks, and his scriptwriter, William Faulkner; but only what is best in the novel—and there is not much there of Hemingway at his best—was retained; the fatalistic mood, the oppressive atmosphere, and the trademark love story expanded into sparkling verbal exchanges between Humphrey Bogart and Lauren Bacall, set off by the haunting music—and screen presence—of Hoagy Carmichael. The result is a delightful film full of atmosphere, music, wit, sarcasm, and cynicism. Besides, the political implications of the film are not in radical opposition to the message of the novel.

All in all, I am pleased with Faulkner and Hawks's treatment of Hemingway.

On the other hand, I regret what Francis Coppola did to Joseph Conrad.

Not that *Apocalypse Now* is a bad film made from an excellent novel. It is a good film made from an excellent novel. Uneven, yes; philosophically befuddled, maybe. Rather Hollywoodish in its final sequences—they smack too much of all the melodramas featuring white jungle-goddesses, from Van Dyke's *Trader Horn*, to the various Tarzan sagas, to their Italian imitations of the forties which displayed the voluptuous Isa Miranda. But *Apocalypse* is still a remarkable and in places strikingly cinematic film that captures much of the anguish of American conscripts sent to fight for a good cause in a bad place.

What I hold against it is partly pragmatic, partly philosophical. The pragmatic objection: was it really necessary to use the skeleton of this early-twentieth-century novel for an interpretation of the war against political despotism in Vietnam? I do not think so. But it was done, and that drastically diminishes the chances that, in the foreseeable future, we shall see a screen adaptation of *Heart of Darkness* that is true to its spirit. Miloš Forman was contemplating a film based on the novella but abandoned the idea when it became known that Coppola was using it. Orson Welles wanted to shoot it after *Citizen Kane*, but failed to raise sufficient capital; would he succeed now, after *Apocalypse Now*? Yet, given the political wisdom he so amply demonstrated to Bertolt Brecht, Welles obviously knows much better than Coppola what the nightmarish story is all about.

Which leads me to my philosophical objections. Coppola's alterations were not aimed at what was not suitable for film—almost everything in the novel is supremely photogenic—or at adding material to help translate the book in all its complexity. The alterations were made without respect for Conrad's concepts, in order to bring out Coppola's own message. That in itself would not be objectionable—if this updating of an old, essentially political story did not run *contrary* to the political implications of the novel. Furthermore, these implications have not lost but rather gained validity in our own time. I wonder if such an updating of a tale's philosophy is defensible—especially since Conrad's vision of darkness and of the heart of it is not embedded in some inferior opus, but in one of the great examples of the art of the novel.

Among the numerous interpretations of Conrad's dark tale, I have not found one that has seen the forest of its meaning, and not just the various trees of Freudian, Jungian, Dantean, etc. significance—not one, except for a brief essay by Professor Lewitter of Cambridge University, and that did not even appear in print, but was only broadcast on BBC radio as part of a popularizing series on literature. No wonder, then, that Ronald R. Bogue, in his article "The *Heart of Darkness* of *Apocalypse Now*", can write that Conrad's "harlequin...does not impose the same ironic filter on the...events that the photographer [the film's equivalent] does." To me that simply indicates that most Western readers of the novel have missed the sarcastic presence and the crucial importance of the Russian "harlequin" in the novella. And yet, both Conrad's life and his prophetic "Russian" novel *Under Western Eyes*—extremely popular in Russia between the two revolutions of 1905 and 1917—provide an obvious clue to this problem of the presence of the "improbable" (as he is called by many interpreters) son of an orthodox priest in the heart of darkness called the Belgian Congo. Let me try to explain.

First: neither the harlequin nor his terrorizing mentor Kurtz should be examined separately; each is a complementary part of a meaningful unity. Taken separately, they will not render up their mystery.

Kurtz, as we know from various references in the novel, is a fallen idealist, a university-educated man who went to Africa to help the blacks achieve civilization, but who eventually concluded his scholarly report to the International Society for the Suppression of Savage Customs with the chilling recommendation that all those "brutes" be exterminated. Between his hopeful initial project and its horrifying conclusion he "raided the country", made the native chieftains "crawl" in the unmentionable "ceremonies used when approaching him", and adorned the fence around his dwelling with the skulls of his victims. His obedient Russian disciple interprets these trophies to Marlow as the heads of "rebels", only to elicit from the sarcastic Britisher other definitions which, to a contemporary reader,

sound as if a biased editor has updated Conrad's 1902 book:
the ornamental heads on Mr. Kurtz's fence are, according to the
English captain, the skulls of "enemies, criminals, workers".

Updated? Yes—because who is Kurtz? A journalist who ought
to have been a politician "on the popular side". A public speaker
who "electrified large meetings" and "could get himself to believe anything—anything. He would have been a splendid
leader of an extreme party.... Any party...." In other words:
whatever other meanings the enigmatic monster may carry,
Conrad has quite intentionally made him one of the earliest
portraits of the modern dictator. Some of the personal characteristics of this imperfect superman evoke further associations
for the modern reader. Mr. Kurtz, for example, used to recite
"poetry, his own, too", as have some of the bloody Marxist rulers
in Vietnam, China, and elsewhere in Asia. Mr. Kurtz's ultimate
fate—he is buried in a "muddy hole", not as a man but as a
"something"—brings to memory the "something" that lay in the
courtyard of the *Führerbunker*, or the putrefying mummy lifted
out of the glass coffin on Red Square and now rotting away in
the Kremlin wall, next to the corpse of that confused American,
John Reed.

And Kurtz is the man who has "enlarged the mind" of his
most devoted follower, the nameless (and thus representative)
Russian. What sort of enlightenment filled the soul of the Fool?
"We talked of everything.... Of love, too," says the disciple,
and contemporary associations, springing from the proximity
of "love" and Kurtz's threats to kill his loving admirer, are
Orwellian, especially since the two did not discuss love as men
usually do among themselves, but "in general". Furthermore,
we also learn that the Master made his pupil "see things—
things". One wonders what things.

The extreme vagueness of these intensely remembered but
contentless conversations—held in a hut surrounded by a pole
fence crowned with round knobs that were "not ornamental
but symbolic"—smells of ideological indoctrination. "You don't
talk with that man—you listen to him." Naturally, because
to the "son of an Orthodox arch-priest" Kurtz is the voice
of undisputed authority, and is to be followed with absolute
unthinking and unquestioning devotion. This is precisely what

the harlequin does: "He," Marlow tells us, "had not meditated over it."

Mr. Kurtz "could be very terrible" and yet the tribe, with the Russian at their head, "follow him...adore him", because, says the disciple, "You can't judge Mr. Kurtz as you would an ordinary man. No, no, no!" And so it is perfectly logical that, although this Belgian czar once wanted to shoot his Russian subject, the harlequin states helplessly, "I don't judge him." Reading this, the modern reader can hardly avoid images of countless *moujiks* in military uniforms defending their bloody despot against Napoleon, or dying for the mass-assassin of their fathers and sons with his name on their lips. A scene may even emerge in such a reader's mind from a recent novel— Solzhenitsyn's *The First Circle*—where, after Stalin ominously asks one of his court jesters, Abakumov, whether he isn't afraid he will be the first one shot if the death penalty is reintroduced, this historical but equally improbable harlequin gasps, "Josef Vissarionovich! If I deserve it...."

I call these insights of Conrad prophetic, but they have nothing in common with clairvoyance or any other sort of magic. They are just manifestations of Conrad's deep knowledge of the "Russian soul", which has not been changed even by Marxism; which, in fact, has adapted this fruit of Western enlightenment to the darkness of its Eastern orthodoxy.

The case, I believe, is clear. On the one side we have a one-time progressive politician turned monster, an idealist reformer metamorphosed into a terrible killer-despot. On the other we have a fanatic crowd crawling before him in an unspeakable ceremony of utter self-abasement, led by a man intoxicated by *el lider*'s charisma beyond any capability of judgement. The whole setup is just one huge sarcastic caricature of the reality more realistically depicted in *Under Western Eyes*: the reality of an autocratic police state, anathema to everything Conrad believed in.

All this, the true heart of this novel about the heart of darkness, is entirely lost in *Apocalypse Now*. True, *Heart of Darkness* is also a critique of nineteenth-century colonialism, and—one should not forget this—specifically of its worst excesses under the Belgian King Leopold. But Vietnam was not a colonial but an ideological war; the soldier who shot the people in the riverboat in *Apocalypse Now* was the very opposite of Conrad's trigger-happy "pilgrims", and Coppola, unlike Marlow, found the meaning in a dubiously applied surface "kernel" (to quote Conrad), not in the "outside" layer "enveloping the tale which brought it out only as a glow brings out a haze." As a result *Apocalypse Now* changes a complex work of fiction, presenting a critique of a complex evil still existing in the world, into a film which is blind to and in fact helps to obscure some very important roots of this evil in our own century. Coppola, of course, had a perfect right to his vision: all I wonder is whether he had a right to ignore, and thereby suppress, the vision of the author in order to serve his own purpose. It is as if somebody were to make a film based on Hemingway's *For Whom the Bell Tolls* (and that masterpiece, unlike *To Have and Have Not*, is one of the complex political novels of modern American literature) resembling Augusto Genina's *L'Assedio dell'Alcazar*, that cinematographically beautiful evocation of heroic men under fire—heroic men who happen to be General Franco's Falangists.

WAR & PEACE AT THE CBC

—

This short commentary, first published in 1985 in The Idler, *is another attack on Canadian political naivety. The object of Škvorecký's criticism is a television drama slightly shaky when dealing with political nuances and implications.*

"WIE SICH DER kleine Moritz die Welt vorstellt." This old Jewish saying, which I used to hear often as a boy, means approximately: "This is how little Moritz imagines the world to be." It would be a fitting subtitle for the CBC television drama aired March 2, 1985. Called *The Front Line*, it was written by Ken Mitchell, and directed by Sturla Gunnarsson.

Briefly, the content of the *kitsch*: it opens with what the Czechs call a *double-Krushchev* of a young Jesuit priest named Ellis and the Ontario Jesuit General Seaton seen embracing "old comrade style" (says the script) at the Toronto airport. Ellis is fresh from somewhere in South America, and he intends to return there; but Seaton—quite easily—convinces him that he is more needed in suburban Toronto. In South America they may be killing Ellis's parishioners, but in Toronto, the souls of Catholics are at stake. "People are falling away from their faith," says Seaton. A good, sane, Catholic argument, straight out of Evelyn Waugh.

After such an introduction, one would expect a religious drama about a priest's struggle against growing doctrinal indifference among the affluent bourgeoisie. Well, nothing of the sort. Instead, we are treated to a pacifist melodrama, which clearly betrays two layers of a first authorial, then dramaturgical intent, with an added third layer caused by an external factor.

In his new parish, the young Jesuit meets Roxy, an attractive Franco-Ontarian in her menopause, who immediately has a crush on him, disguised, as such things usually are, as religious fervour. She is so infatuated that she follows the handsome divine along the questionable path he soon takes. There is a factory in the suburb that produces gear for nuclear missiles. Ellis decides that to work in that factory is to be an accomplice to murder, and calls upon his parishioners to disrupt production.

Roxy's Polish husband soon diagnoses his wife's lovesickness, and strongly opposes her eros-induced political radicalism. Their marital crisis reaches a head when Roxy decides to join a sit-in in front of the factory gate, and leaves, followed by this frustrated outcry from her husband: "Go and be faithful to your priest! Go and make *him* happy!"

At the factory, a representative assortment of peaceniks— an old Waspish gentleman, an old ethnic lady, a Japanese survivor of Hiroshima, and Casimir, a Polish worker from the factory who is also Roxy's brother-in-law—join hands to prevent a company truck from getting through the gate. Babies, an otherwise mandatory ingredient of such works of art, are missing, probably because they would have to be carried by their mothers, and that would break the human chain. The

truck is stopped, and the demonstrators joyously break into
the old Negro spiritual "Zekiel Saw de Wheel". But they are
in Canada, which is a Fascist country. A sinister group of riot
police, plastic shields and all, appears on the screen, waving
their big sticks. There is a freeze, to encourage the imagination
of the viewers, who have seen so many similar scenes in news
footage from Poland. We are left to imagine what will happen
to the nice ethnic lady and the even nicer Waspish gentleman.

The above represents more or less the first layer of authorial
intent, the first draft of the script, which I had a chance to read.
Superimposed are distinct dramaturgical changes that work in
two directions. First, they play down the erotic overtones so
that the sudden radicalization of Roxy (the wife, don't forget,
of a political refugee from Poland) is seen to be motivated by
a Christian conscience, and not by her glands. Secondly, the
changes stress the Communist message of the movie, its call to
"democratic" action.

While Roxy is being "de-eroticized", the Poles are being made
into idiots. These chicken-brains are made to display "male
chauvinism". Casimir, for instance, advises Roxy that instead
of protesting against nuclear weapons she "should be in the
kitchen". If this piece of characterization lacks subtlety, the
following goes contrary to demonstrable facts. Stefan, Roxy's
husband who fled Poland, has a peculiar reason for objecting
to his wife's radical involvement. He wants her to stay away
from the peaceniks not because he knows (as all Poles, Czechs,
Tibetans, etc., know) that the peace movement in its rigorous
one-sidedness undermines the defence efforts of the democracies. No, this Polish idiot is simply afraid of the police. Which
police? The Canadian police. And why? Because they are the
"same as everywhere", says Stefan, i.e., the same as the Polish
Zomos, the Czech StB, the Soviet KGB, etc. This is a commonplace of Communist propaganda, directed at the West: that
there is no "essential" difference between a Daniel Ellsberg
selling classified documents to the *New York Times* and experiencing a little legal trouble on his way to a well-paid lecture
tour, and Václav Havel experiencing four and a half years in
jail for smuggling memoirs of an old socialist politician (Prokop
Drtina) to Sixty-Eight Publishers in Toronto. No difference, for
that matter, between the posthumous rehabilitation of some of

the executed victims of Communism and, say, Angela Davis's release from a California jail by a white jury. Apparently Roxy's imbecile husband shares such opinions.

To be sure, the peace movement has grudgingly acknowledged that the Yanks are not the sole possessors of nuclear weapons. While hundreds of thousands yell, "Fascists!" in front of American embassies around the world, a few dozen polite reminders assemble in front of the odd Soviet embassy to suggest cosmetic changes in the May Day parade. This libation to the gods of objectivity also appears in *The Innocent* (as the film was called in the script). Casimir, hearing Roxy's anti-American sermon, asks, "What about the Russians?" Roxy replies, "We'll have to set a Christian example for the Russians." Had Roxy lived in thirteenth-century Europe, she would have sent (no doubt under the influence of some Benedictine) her only son on the Children's Crusade. The Turkish armies, too, were shamed by Christian example.

A few more editorial changes. When the Canadian Zomos appear on the screen, the ladies and gentlemen of peace sing not "Zekiel Saw de Wheel", as they did in the script, but "Study War No Mo'". This, I would say, is a characteristic of CBC dramaturgy. "Study War No Mo'" has been an anthem of Communist-organized gatherings since the days of Stalin, and his black prophet Paul Robeson. Poles, Czechs, Hungarians, etc. associate Mr. Mitchell's "Zekiel" with Louis Armstrong; they associate "Study War No Mo'" with Stalin's mass murders.

As far as I know, special police squads were used when a Canadian terrorist cell called "Direct Action" attempted—with partial success—to blow up Litton Systems. But at all the peace demonstrations I have witnessed in Toronto, there were regular, polite, Canadian cops, with their neatly trimmed moustaches. No plastic shields, no Martian helmets, no bone-crushing sticks. *The Innocent* is silent about real-life terrorism. Its use of riot police against frail lady protestors is, I suppose, attributable to *licentia poetica.*

Last but not least, a most commendable editorial emendation. The title was changed from *The Innocent* to *The Front Line.* The CBC dramaturgists may have sensed that some viewers would be familiar with Mark Twain's famous book about some other "innocents". By changing the title they removed the chance of a double meaning.

Thus far I have dealt only with the dramaturgical work on the script. When it went into production, an unexpected obstacle emerged. The casting director approached the Polish community in Toronto and asked for a couple of amateur Polish actors to play Casimir and Stefan. The Poles insisted on reading the script first. When they had read it, they refused. The director then approached the Czech New Theatre in Toronto, and I must admit with shame that he found volunteers. To be fair to them, the Czech extras claim that they were not shown the script, and some are willing to say so under oath. It is possible: given his experience with the Poles, the director may have just told them that *The Front Line* was a Catholic film about religious faith. The only featured actor, who played Casimir (renamed Tomáš for there are no Czechs named Casimir), may have felt that, since he is the one who reminds Roxy about the Russians, he was not really acting as an accomplice. And for Stefan the director had to use an Anglo-Canadian who, in the film, mispronounces a few Czech words. It is symptomatic of the art of this CBC drama that no harm was done by switching one nation for another. Except for the names, no changes in characterization were deemed necessary.

One Czech, Mr. Tomáš Heřman, got wind of what was happening and went to the location to challenge his compatriots to quit. But extras playing the riot squad were already dressed for the final scene, and expected remuneration. When Mr. Heřman persisted, the casting assistant, Ms. Michelle Metinier, called real police to remove "the trouble-maker" (her words) from the scene. The cops obligingly arrived, but, after familiarizing themselves with the case, found no reason for intervention and departed. Well, the police "are the same everywhere", as Stefan says in the movie.

The way Poles were to be—and Czechs are—portrayed in the film is clearly insulting. Tomáš and "a bunch of Czechoslovaks, carrying lunch pails, who represent quite a remarkable concentration of village idiocy", as Mr. Heřman wrote in his letter to Mr. Pierre Juneau, president of the CBC, are an insult to the intelligence of Canadians of Czech and Slovak origin; they are mocked vis-à-vis their bitter political experience in the old country, now under Russian occupation. The film spits in the face of the many former political prisoners of Communist regimes now living in Canada.

We have laws in this country to protect the dignity of so-called ethnic citizens. I think that, in the case of this CBC abomination, these laws might have been used. I am sure they would have been if the object of ridicule had been some more temperamental ethnic Canadians.

An Interview in Toronto

An Interview in Toronto

—

This very informative 1983 interview with Geoff Hancock, the editor of Canadian Fiction Magazine, *shows Škvorecký in a relaxed, expansive mood. As in the autobiographical essay "I Was Born in Náchod...", he covers a wide range of subject matter, from personal reminiscences through the political situation in Europe to comments on his work. Note that the novel he was completing at this time was* Dvorak in Love.

JOSEF ŠKVORECKÝ now lives in a white house in a row of houses on a quiet street in Toronto's Cabbagetown. This interview took place in his bookish living room on a chilly February day, with jazz records from the forties playing quietly in the background. Josef puffed on the Cuban cigars I brought as a small gift, but he claimed they were stronger than the brand he normally smoked. An old cat sprawled on the sofa, and Josef sat comfortably in his writing chair beneath a painting of himself as a jazz musician. The painting is also reproduced on the cover of *The Swell Season*, his poignant recollection of a jazz- and girl-obsessed teenager in Nazi-occupied Czechoslovakia.

Josef, do you like to do interviews?

I have mixed feelings. On one hand, it certainly gives me a chance to speak my mind. But on the other hand, because I am limited in time and space, I tend to present to the interviewer conclusions that are based on lifetime experience, or that come out of a long process. But I cannot talk about the whole process, about how I arrived at those conclusions. People read it or hear it and label me immediately. For instance, if I say that I'm an anti-Communist, that throws a very bad light on me, because anti-Communism is a bad label. At least, people think it's a bad label, and I'm rejected right out of hand. But I was not born anti-Communist. I arrived at that position as a result of many experiences. It's sometimes quite discouraging. And that sometimes happens with people who read interviews. You say something provocative, and they just stop reading it. They put a label on you and you are finished.

Hemingway said, and you've quoted this often, that the job of the writer is to tell the truth. You've written novels, short stories, film scripts. You're an essayist, a broadcaster, a professor of American literature. Is part of this job of telling the truth to tell it in as many ways as possible?

Yes, but truth may be very complex—truth about what? Hemingway said that the writer must tell the truth about his own feelings at the moment they exist, which can be translated, simply, into sincerity. The writer must be sincere about how he feels, and that is his truth.

That was the stumbling block on my first published novel, *The Cowards*. I simply tried to be absolutely honest about my feelings during the events of May 1945, the end of the war, which in Czechoslovakia was called a revolution. I don't know why they called it a revolution; it was simply the end of the war, an uprising against the Nazis. This period in recent Czech history was the subject of many stories and novels. But all of them, before my novel, were written from the point of view of "socialist realism". The writer did not really present the events as they happened, as he saw them, but tried, I suppose, to colour them by using certain ideological concepts and putting them on reality. For instance, in a classic entitled *A Silent Barricade*, about the uprising in Prague, most of the heroes are workers and the traitors are invariably bourgeois. That is an ideological concept because there were as many bourgeois among the rebels as workers. The soldiers of the Red Army in those proper novels were always immaculate, chaste heroes who played accordion and sang songs. They wouldn't touch a girl, and that is simply not true. The Red Army soldiers were like any other soldiers, and they had just survived a very deadly war, so they did touch girls—because in a war you don't know if you will be living the next day. You don't have so much respect for proper behaviour, and they were dirty because they had just been through battle.

So my first quarrel with the establishment in Czechoslovakia was an artistic one. I tried to be true to my artistic convictions. They criticized me from the government point of view, they wanted writers to be hack writers, fulfilling their orders and describing reality as the government saw it. When *The Cowards* was banned, I received hundreds of letters from people all over Czechoslovakia who testified that they had been through the same thing, that it was exactly like what I said in the novel. So I had obviously struck a chord.

Is that why now you've continued to write your version of the truth in as many ways as possible?

I always tried to adhere to my feelings. I never strove for any great variety. I just belong to those writers who base their writings on personal experience. I never had any trouble finding my subject matter. I just described episodes in my life. That goes for what I may call my serious fiction. I also wrote detective stories and obviously I've never been a detective, so that's imagination. But in my serious fiction, I never looked for subject matter. That's probably due to life in Czechoslovakia, where everybody went through so many different experiences within a lifetime that it's not hard to find something to write about.

I still remember the Great Depression. The Nazis came when I was fourteen, and they stayed for six years. I was twenty when they left, and that was a very dramatic time. My father was arrested by the Nazis. After the war the tensions in Central Europe were very high. Many people sensed or knew or suspected that we had just got rid of one troublemaker and we were headed for trouble of a very similar kind: a totalitarian dictatorship. So there are the years between '45 and '48, the year of the Communist takeover. That was a dramatic time of political fighting, even attempts at killing ministers. Then came the Stalinist years and the mass arrests and executions and the class discrimination.

Later I was drafted into the army, which is an experience anywhere, but especially in those years. A Russian military system was imposed on the Czech army, which was absurd because the Russian military system was based on an entirely different tradition. It was designed for units that serve for two years somewhere in Siberia where there are no towns. Though the camp I was in was only about twenty miles from Prague, we were not permitted to leave it for one year. We just boiled in that little camp, bored to death.

Before my military service, I taught school. They sent me to the border regions, to a town called Braunau. This town was in ruins because the German population had been shipped out. It used to be a town of fifteen thousand, but when I came, only about a thousand people were living there. There was nowhere to live. So I got accommodation in the local cloister. I spent half a year in one of those monk's cells without heating in winter. There were so many strange and funny events.

After my military service, I got a job in Prague in a publishing house, in the Anglo-American Department, which involved me in all kinds of interesting squabbles with censorship. I published my first novel which caused a big scandal. So my life was full of things that in Central Europe are quite ordinary, but in fact are quite adventurous if you think about it.

Was your father a cinema operator?

He was a bank clerk by profession, but he also managed one of the two local cinemas. That was voluntary work. He was an operator, a projectionist, and he also sold tickets and ordered films. I helped him in the projection booth. I became a film addict. For five or six years, I literally saw a film every day, and on Sunday, two. The other cinema, our competition, also gave us free tickets. They changed programs three times a week in both cinemas, so that made six films a week, plus two on matinées on Sunday. So I saw everything. I am probably the greatest expert on Nazi cinema, because this was during the war and most of the films were German or Czech or Swedish. I became a film buff of the first magnitude.

Not much is known about the films of the Third Reich.

No, very little is known about them. In the post-war frenzy in which I unfortunately took part, I burned all the Nazi novels I had to buy as a student. I went to a high school during the war and had to study new German literature so we had to buy German books. So I'm probably the only person in Canada who read *Schlageter*, which was *the* Nazi drama about a guerrilla fighter in occupied Ruhrgebiet who is sentenced to death by the French and executed. That was a real historical person. That's for instance the play where you find that famous sentence *"Wenn ich das Wort 'Kultur' höre, da entsichere ich meinen Browning"* (the usual English version is "When I hear the word 'culture', I go for my gun"). This sentence is sometimes ascribed to Goebbels or Goering, but that's not true: it's in this play. And I read a novel called *SA Baut eine Strasse (The SA Builds a Road)* which read like any socialist realism. It was about the building of the Autobahn, the first highway in Europe. It was built by Hitler. In the frenzy of the post-war elation, I destroyed them all, and now I am sorry because they can't be replaced. There are no new editions, and they are valuable documents.

I'm afraid the same thing happened to many of the films. I don't think they were destroyed, but they were shelved. The only film that is always being shown is *The Triumph of the Will*, because it has become a classic. But Nazi films were not very political. They started making political movies before the war and at the beginning of the war. I remember the first war film was called *Stukas*, about dive bombers and their bombardment of Warsaw, but these films were not successful. Nobody during the war wanted to see films about war. The Nazis soon sensed that, so they started turning out musical comedies, and entertaining films, but very few political films, just because they were interested in getting some escapist stuff to the people who were terribly tired by the war, especially when the raids came. Some of these so-called Nazi films were really very good. I remember one which was called *Friedemann Bach*, a film about one of the sons of Johann Sebastian Bach. Maybe my memory makes it even more beautiful than it actually was, but I don't think I've seen a better musical film since.

From being a film buff, you became an actor in films; you were involved with the Czech New Wave during the 1960s.

I never was a professional actor. I appeared in a few Czech movies, but as a token appearance. All these young Czech moviemakers of the early sixties were graduates of the Film Academy, and they were among the few people who had a chance to see classical Western films. They picked up Alfred Hitchcock's signature idea and put me in films based on my stories. I never really acted. I just spoke a few lines.

But I was involved with the New Wave as a novelist. It all started with Miloš Forman, whom I had known since the war. After my novel was banned, the two of us wrote a script based on a story of mine called "Eine kleine Jazzmusik", and eventually the film was banned by the president himself. The banning of my novel made me very popular; that's the best publicity you can get. I was then approached by almost everyone in the film industry to give them something to film. Eventually I had five feature films based on my books. I saw and knew personally all those famous directors like Forman and Menzel, Chytilová, Němec, etc. Czechoslovakia is a small country and the film industry is concentrated in Prague. Once you start working in the studios, you meet everyone.

The Czech New Wave is much better known than modern Czech literature, although this movement of sincerity, of real realism, not socialist realism, started in literature with my *Cowards*. But books have to be translated, and that means additional expense for the publisher. Film is much more suitable for world distribution. All you need is a few subtitles. The impression was created that the film people were the avant-garde, but that's not true. The avant-garde were the writers. But they were not known. *The Cowards* was not published in America until 1970, although it was originally published in 1958. Whereas films were shown a year after they had been made, at film festivals in the sixties, and they became known immediately. But if you remember Czech films made by Forman, such as *Peter and Paula* and *Fireman's Ball* and *Loves of a Blonde*, and Menzel's *Closely Watched Trains*, and compare them to *The Cowards*, you will see that it's the same anti-ideological approach, showing people as they appeared to the filmmaker. The script of *Peter and Paula*, which is the first film by Forman (and was released here as *Black Peter*), had an epigraph, a motto, taken from *The*

Cowards. Forman was quite open about one of the sources of inspiration.

What made The Cowards *different? Was it the new style of writing? The little guy who became the main character?*

In the first place what made it different was the vision. I simply described the events as they appeared to me, and as they appeared to most people. Secondly the style. I used slang in dialogue. Slang was taboo in the 1950s because Stalin wrote a piece in which he said that slang was an invention of the bourgeoisie. In the translation of *The Pickwick Papers* the censors corrected Sam Weller and made him speak like an educated man, because for them "cockney" was non-existent.

Czech literature has a great lyrical tradition. Lyrical poetry achieved a very high level in the nineteenth century. But Czech fiction lagged behind: that's what happened in all world literatures. Every literature starts with great poetry, and fiction comes later. Between the First World War and the Second World War, there were probably only two or three really excellent fiction writers. One was Hašek, the author of *The Good Soldier Švejk*. His excellence is of a special sort. He was simply a natural-born genius who didn't care about how he wrote, he just put it on paper. The second was Karel Čapek, who is for some reason known here mainly as a playwright. He was a lousy playwright, but he was an excellent short-story writer. Some of the stories were translated years ago, but he's unknown. The third one was Karel Poláček, who has never been translated. He was a great Jewish writer who died in the camps. But I don't think he'll ever be translated because his Czech vernacular is difficult to translate. Czech fiction reached the standards that could be labelled international only in the sixties.

Do you feel at home in Canada? Or do you still feel in exile?

I feel very much at home in Canada. I don't even like to travel to Europe as Canadians do, because I have become so attached to this country, to the atmosphere it has. Because—this is probably hard to explain—in my life, since I was fourteen, I have never experienced this atmosphere of liberal freedom. I have always lived under some kind of dictatorship where you had to turn around if you had to say something aloud. If you wrote anything, you had to think twice before you formulated a sentence, because you knew this would be tough for the censors. The secret police were always after you, and you were taken in for interrogation because of some stupid thing. So I value the atmosphere of liberal freedoms that most people here don't realize they have, because for them it's like the air. To me, this was such a great thing when I came.

So we feel very much at home and also we both found interesting work which gives us fulfilment. We have made friends here, both Canadians and Czechs, and some old friends from Prague are here. The Czech community in Toronto is quite lively. The Prague that I knew and liked does not exist any more. It's a different city, different people. Most of my friends are either in the underground or in exile or in jail. It's not the same city I left.

Do you feel an empathy for the internal exiles—those writers in Czechoslovakia who must smuggle their works out? Who risk harassment by the police simply for writing?

We publish their works, and I have a great respect for them. Most of them are my personal friends, so I feel strongly about them. I will do whatever is humanly possible to help them. Just try to imagine that these people have been living for fourteen years now in a sort of semi-legal existence. They are interrogated literally every week. What possible questions can be put to them week after week? For fourteen years? That is beyond me. The questions make no sense. It's simply that the secret policemen have to do some work. So they just molest them. But it's not as innocent as that. Sometimes they are arrested for a few days, released, and so on. But it's a miserable existence. They have no jobs because they simply won't be given any jobs, so those of them who have wives who work are supported by them. People send them money anonymously. It's quite encouraging because most of the people of course adapted to the new situation. That doesn't mean that they love the government, but they have families and they have jobs, and they don't want to lose them. Few people are made of heroic stuff. So they just adapt. They say the proper things at the proper places, but of course they don't change internally. But the writers can publish in the West.

For reasons that are very hard to understand—there are many interpretations—so far the government has molested them, interrogated them, but they have not jailed anybody for publishing in the West. They tried to send Jiří Gruša to jail. He's a Czech writer who published a novel with Sixty-Eight Publishers called the *The Questionnaire*. The novel is now in English and it was published by Farrar, Straus and Giroux in New York. They arrested him, and said he would be charged with writing an anti-government novel. They even had readers' reports. I read them, they were incredibly funny. There were protests in the West. Writers in England and France signed petitions, so they quietly released him. But they have interrogated all the dissident writers and warned all of them: if they continue publishing in the West, they will all be charged with publishing anti-state, anti-socialist propaganda. But I think they are bluffing, because it would be very unpopular to put dozens of people into jail because they write. But who knows? They are capable of doing it.

They are now expelling dissidents. They came to the conclusion, because they unfortunately can learn, that if you sentence a writer to jail, it is counter-productive, because of Amnesty International, and writers' organizations. They raise hell, and they sign petitions and protests. It's bad publicity for Communism. It's much better to expel, to just send them out. So the writer makes a few statements and then he disappears. Because there are so many in the West nobody is interested. A voice is really silenced by the lack of interest. But if the same man is in jail! Havel is in jail, the playwright, and from time to time you still read a little article about him. But he was not arrested officially for what he had written. Of course the real reason was his writing, but he was arrested officially for slandering the government, some trumped-up reason. I feel very strongly about my friends there, because they are our real heroes. It's not an easy life.

Do you see dangers in nationalism? Canadian or otherwise?

Nationalism, like everything in the world, can be dangerous or useful. That depends on who, and under what circumstances, is a nationalist. The worst is big-power nationalism. If a strong, numerically big nation like the Russians or perhaps the Americans gets nationalistic, that's a tragedy, because it very soon changes into chauvinism. They may not use that slogan "My country—right or wrong," but that's what the Russians are doing. So if a nation that has a huge army at its disposal and can really threaten the world becomes nationalistic, that's a tragedy. That's what happened under Hitler. The Nazis were simply chauvinists. But if an oppressed nation becomes nationalistic, that's a way to survive. If a small nation which lives under foreign oppression becomes indifferent to its nationality, then that nation is lost. So it depends on the situation.

Nationalism is okay, but if you are not in the situation of a small oppressed nation, it should be pro-something, not anti-something. Here in Canada some people are anti-American. I'm not saying everybody has to love America; there are reasons you can criticize the States, and good reasons. But in the mind of a nationalist, it becomes generalized. "Anything the Americans do must be wrong, because they did us some wrong." That's where the trouble starts. Then you become anti-American and just reject everything, including democracy, because it came from the States. I had a discussion with a student about it just this week, and it's dangerous. In Canadian literature, it's true that undue preference is given to American books, because they are published by wealthy publishers and they are much better promoted, and not necessarily better than books written by Canadians. So certainly Canadian books, Canadian fiction, should be given every help. But what should be stressed is more the quality than the fact this has been written by a Canadian. That leads to a literature where every third-rate writer becomes an important writer simply because he is of a certain nationality. Then somehow the really good ones do not differ very much, in the mind of the reading public, from the bad ones. They are all Canadians. So there is another danger. That is a thing that happened in the States at the beginning of the last century. There was also this tendency, "Let's support American writers, don't let us read the British, we have our own literature, we must read the American writers." As far as I know, one of the few great American writers who criticized this attitude was Poe, who said, "Yes, I am also for American writers, but first they must achieve the same level of quality as Charles Dickens, and then I will prefer them to Dickens. But you can't ask me to prefer some third-rater to Dickens just because he's American." It's an intricate question, and certainly I'm not speaking against support for Canadian literature, because I profit from it myself. But I want to point out this danger, that sometimes people become so nationalistic that they would reject a Faulkner because he was American.

With that in mind, what can Canadians learn from your work?

I don't know, let them find out for themselves. I don't like to evaluate myself. All I can say is, I always try to do my best. Whether it's good enough or not, that's for others to judge. What they can learn from my work—if it ever gets translated, not in its entirety, but at least the main novels—is about life in Czechoslovakia under the dictatorships. It's a source of information, I hope in entertaining form, not a scholarly work that nobody reads.

My ambition, really, is to be an entertainer. Entertainment can be on pretty high levels. Charlie Chaplin was certainly an entertainer in the first place, and he was not a negligible artist. I'm not saying I just want to be a clown who does a few cheap tricks in the hope people laugh. But I want to appeal to a great variety of people. I'd like to flatter myself that my books appeal to every intelligent reader, not necessarily an intellectual, and not necessarily a boor.

So you don't see yourself as a human rights activist or a fighter?

To me the word "activist" means someone who attends meetings and speaks at public gatherings. I always add my signature to protests and, if I have to, I go to meetings and give speeches. But I do other things that help the same cause. I can probably help the cause much better if I write novels than if I attend and speak at hundreds of meetings. Other people can do this much better.

Can literature combat a dictatorship, compared to non-literary writing?

I'm sure that good fiction is dangerous for a dictatorship. Otherwise they wouldn't be so much against it.

What is the threat in fiction?

The threat to totalitarian regimes is that good fiction simply tells the truth, without ideological spectacles. Every totalitarian regime wants to turn writers into hack writers, into people who carry out an assignment according to the rules laid down for them by the men who pay for it, the government. So that's their idea of a writer. Most writers who are honoured by totalitarian regimes are hack writers.

Graham Greene once said that the totalitarians give the writer everything—no Western society can give him as much—in exchange for his ceasing to be a writer. That's very true. So the danger is that a writer who is not willing to accept such an assignment simply presents reality as they don't want to have it presented. Truth about reality is alway dangerous to any totalitarian ideology, because every ideology is false consciousness, as Engels knew. It is a consciousness that is false because it believes that its biased *conception* of reality *is* reality. Some people who have this ideologic bent start believing this is reality. This is something that a good writer cannot do, and that is why they are so much against writers. The interesting thing is that in every totalitarian regime, the first victims are always writers.

You like your work to operate on two levels: the story you tell and the message you convey. The occupation, whether it's Nazi Germany or Soviet Russia, is always in the background. Is that a deliberate strategy?

I don't think it's a deliberate strategy. I lived under dictatorships, so they are always in the background. That's one difference between a liberal democracy and totalitarian state. Here you can spend your life without realizing that there is something like politics. What is presented as politics here is simply local politics. There is no ideology in Canada. None of the leading parties is an ideological party. They represent certain views, interests, and so on, but none of them has a strict, well-defined, and compulsory ideology. Whereas the totalitarian states are based on clearly defined, very oppressive ideologies. They poison the entire life by the presence of aggressive politics. So if you lived in Nazi Germany you couldn't escape politics. It was simply interwoven in your life all the time. The same is true about the Communist state. So if you write a realistic novel about Czechoslovakia, you cannot omit political pressures. You cannot ignore the existence of the Communist party. But you can write an absolutely honest and truthful novel about life in Toronto and not mention the Progressive Conservatives or the Liberals or the NDP because they don't oppress you. If you are interested you can become a member, but if you are not you can just forget about it. But in a totalitarian state you cannot forget about it, because it reminds you of its existence all the time: censorship, compulsory meetings, screenings, questionnaires, and direct intervention by the police.

Do you see history as something that trespasses on the lives of your characters? Especially in Czechoslovakia, a nation at the crossroads of European history?

Yes, very much so. All my "major" novels, if I may use the word, are based on important historical events, or set at a time when something historically important happens. *The Cowards* is at the end of the war, which meant a complete change of the political system. *The Miracle Game* is set in 1968, when Dubček tried to reform Communism and of course met with disaster. And *The Engineer of Human Souls* is a re-examination of the past thirty years in the life of Czechoslovakia, which is framed by the Nazi occupation and the year 1968. These historical, crucial moments had a deep impact on society, much more so than in the West. In the West, the Second World War certainly meant some changes, but basically the system remained unchanged. Every system develops, of course, but there was no radical change. Whereas in Czechoslovakia the transition between the First Republic, which was a liberal democracy like Canada, into Nazism, was nightmarish. We fell from a liberal democratic regime into the cruelest dictatorship possible. So such a change, which came literally overnight, must have an impact on everybody, both mentally and in the literal meaning of the word. People got arrested, Jews were sent to the gas chambers: that's an impact of history.

Then in 1948 there was a change from a democratic socialist system into a Stalinist tyranny, which again meant concentration camps and the so-called class approach. This class approach is a very dubious thing because theoretically it should mean that the workers are preferred, and the non-workers are simply oppressed or tolerated, depending on their behaviour. But in actual fact, if you joined the Communist party you were safe. So the class approach is a strange thing. You can easily avoid it by joining the Party. You don't even have to join the Party if you are active and a sort of fellow traveller.

It's difficult with Communism. Nothing can be taken for granted. It is unpredictable. Then the question is, what happens to the children of the suppressed bourgeoisie whose fathers are sent to factories and made into workers? In the questionnaire their children state their origin as "working class". And that's the truth. But now they've introduced a new category in Prague. Class origin now has three categories: worker, non-worker, and a person in a worker's job. A "person in a worker's job" means that originally you were a shopkeeper or something and sent to a factory. You are not a real worker.

Is writing easy for you?

It depends very much on what I am writing and what mood I am in. I usually write the first draft very quickly. But then I work on it for several years, so I always do three, four, five drafts. I always write in longhand. Then I type it up. Then again I correct it in longhand and change it and cut and add, then I retype it. This I repeat sometimes two, three times.

Occasionally—two or three times only—I have written a novella which I did not have to rewrite at all. I wrote *The Bass Saxophone* in three days. I was at home with the flu and I wrote it in a fit of inspiration. I had had the idea for it for many years, and I somehow felt that someday I was going to write it. Then I sat down and wrote it in three days. I don't think I changed anything in retyping it. But it was exceptional. That occurs in literature from time to time. Stevenson wrote *Doctor Jekyll and Mr. Hyde* in three days. There is so much that is mysterious about the creative process.

Do you do a certain number of pages a day?

I put in a certain number of hours per day. When I was younger I used to write at night, because I had a job. I would come home at six and eat dinner and then sit down at seven and write until midnight. I can't do that any more because I am too tired evenings, so I write during the summer months when I don't teach. I usually start at nine in the morning and keep writing until four, four-thirty. On the average I do the same number of pages. When I retype it, it amounts to about twenty double-spaced pages per day. But that's the first draft, so let's say I spend seven hours a day and I produce twenty pages, then I spend another twenty hours on every page. It's hard to tell.

Do you write on this coffee table? Do you like being by a window?

I sit in this chair, by the window. I write on my lap with my feet on the table. I write in little scribblers, so it's almost unreadable, illegible. I think I can decipher it, but most people can't. Because as you write for so many years, you develop a sort of script that is almost like shorthand. I suppose a researcher could learn to read it, but it's not easy.

You're writing a more complex book now, with flashbacks and parallel time lines, as in The Engineer of Human Souls *and* The Miracle Game. *That's a departure from the novel and the chronological story that you've been writing in the past. It's also a departure from the interlocked story sequence in* The Swell Season. *Is structure affected by the time span of the novel?*

The Bass Saxophone or *Emöke* or even *The Swell Season* covers a brief span of time. *The Bass Saxophone* is one evening, *The Swell Season* is one year, and *The Cowards* is one week, so there is no need for an innovative structure. Remember *The Bass Saxophone* is also very diverse, digressive, because the associations just branch off. But *The Miracle Game* covers many years, and *The Engineer of Human Souls* covers about thirty years. So how to put that in chronological order? And it's interconnected. In *The Engineer*, the central story is set in Canada in the seventies and one of the things that happens is that Danny is teaching young Canadians, including young Canadian girls, and suddenly he realizes young people are not very different in different countries. They go through the same emotional upheavals and they even act in similar ways. So that reminds him of his own young years, when the girls who are now fifty were eighteen. So the putting together of episodes which in actual life were divided by thirty years has a logic. It forces the reader subconsciously to compare. But the main reason for that multi-level structure is simply that the novels cover so much time.

Is The Swell Season *an important book for you?*

For me, it is a very important book. It is what books should be written about, the really important thing in life: emotional relationships. The political and historical things unfortunately are a necessity that we cannot avoid. I wish we could avoid it, but we cannot. So *The Swell Season* is the book of all my books which is probably closest to my heart, because in a way it is pure. This is about a young boy who is after the girls. He cannot get any, but he never gives up, and he's happy and unhappy. And from time to time from the background comes this danger because I couldn't ignore it: the war. But this is how we lived.

If you are seventeen, eighteen, you just live, and you are interested in girls and you are happy because of the girls, which doesn't mean that you like the Nazis or that you do not yearn for another sort of life. But this is how it was.

Could you tell me about your interest in jazz, the Swing Era, Ella Fitzgerald, orchestras, obscure musical instruments? That all happened at the same time.

Well, that was a coincidence. I was fourteen when the Nazis came, and the swing craze came to Czechoslovakia about a year before that. As in the rock craze, students would start little bands, and there was a jazz band or a swing band in every town. Then came the Nazis, and they were against jazz music because it was American. And since they were so much against it, that was one additional reason for us to play it. But in the first place, we simply loved it, as the youngsters now love hard acid rock or whatever. Music also has some political connotations. They love it because it speaks for them. Young people are very emotional. They need music that expresses their emotions, their mental states, their feelings, and every generation finds such music. So when my father was young, they had brass bands, march music, and in the old times it was folklore, all these dulcimer bands and violin bands and bagpipes. So every generation has it. If it happens that the music, that generational expression, is being suppressed by the authorities, they love it even more.

You were in a band. Is that how you discovered an interest in more obscure instruments like flexatones?

That's part of the love affair, because you seem to love anything that has a connection with the object of your love. It's a sort of fetishism. If you love a girl and she forgets her gloves— she puts them on your night table and leaves them there— then it's simply part of her. When I became an aficionado, I searched for books about jazz. At that time there was only one book in Czech about jazz, by E.F. Burian, written in 1932 and full of mistakes. In the twenties, in the early Chicago days—Paul Whiteman and all that—they used very strange instruments that later disappeared, like the flexatone and something called the sarrusophone. They even had something called the kastophone, which was a set of drums, tuned drums, like timpani, but it was really like a xylophone or a vibraphone but made of drums. They had Hawaiian flutes and cowbells and all kinds of things. I became fascinated by it all because it was part of that beloved music. I bought a flexatone but it's very difficult to play. You have to press your thumb on it and shake it at the same time, so you can imagine that to play "Sweet Georgia Brown"—which is fast, full of syncopation— while shaking your hands and pressing your fingers is very difficult. You can play a slow melody like "Deep Purple" maybe. So that's part of my image of this strange, beautiful music. I became quite an expert on musical instruments. I developed an interest in them, even in classical music.

When I started learning to play the saxophone, I had a textbook that listed all the saxophones that exist, all the tunings. So I learned that there was a sopranino and a soprano—soprano is quite common, but sopranino is very rare. I saw it for the first time in Italy in a military band. It's very short and it's very high. Paul Brodie is a marvellous sax player and he plays classical music in Toronto. I have a recording where he uses a sopranino. There was something called a C melody, which was between alto and tenor. It was used in the thirties and it has a beautiful tone. I don't know why they abandoned it. Baritone was available in Czechoslovakia. There was a bass; I'd never seen it at that time. There was a contrabass and a sub-contrabass. To me it was so exciting to imagine what a sub-contrabass saxophone must look like. I've only seen one, in a museum, and it's just huge. It's like a kettle. I don't think it's even manageable. I read that in one of his operas Wagner asked a tuba player to hold a note over eight or ten or twelve bars, which is physically impossible. In a slow tempo, you simply cannot blow one tone on a tuba for ten or twelve slow bars. You'd have to have additional lungs. So I read they constructed a special device, a sort of foot pedal that pumped air into the corners of the mouth of the tuba player so that he could stay playing the note. I don't know if it's true. I became a specialist in musical instruments because they fascinate me. I always correct everyone who says that the famous *largo* in Dvořák is a solo for oboe, because it's for the English horn. Not many people know that. Well, it's part of my love for music.

How does music, especially jazz, operate symbolically in your work? Is it because it requires improvisation, which runs contrary to the rigid rules of an ideology?

That's really for you to say, because I have never been able to start thinking about symbols when I write something. My mentor was Hemingway and he said that if something is written well, then it may have several meanings. Obviously *The Bass Saxophone* can be interpreted in a symbolic way. The struggle with the bass saxophone is really a struggle for expression that every artist has to undergo. So the huge saxophone player at the end of the novella takes the instrument from Danny and starts blowing it. I think he symbolizes the efforts of any honest artist who tries to express what he feels about life and himself and so on.

Music functions in your work as inspiration, it's a lifestyle, it's a metaphor, it's a social ritual, it's a catharsis too at times, it's vital to being alive.

I always wanted to become a jazz musician. That was my sincerest wish when I was young, but I simply didn't have the talent to become a professional musician. Fortunately I realized that in time. I also had problems with breathing because of that early pneumonia, so I really couldn't play the saxophone. I started writing about it, but the love remained. Subconsciously in some of my books, I try to somehow express musical feelings in words. That was not very conscious. It was more like subconscious. But whenever I come across a passage about music, it's always what I enjoy most in my writings. I think it shows.

What makes Danny and his friends cowards?

To be quite honest, I don't know why I called that novel *The Cowards*. I think I subconsciously wanted to make fun of the concept of the hero, because in those days you had to have a hero. In the literary criticism of the Stalinist years, you never used such terms as the "central character". And the hero, usually, was really heroic. So there was an inflation of heroes. But I presented these absolutely normal youths and I called them cowards [*laughs*]. So that is probably why I called the novel *The Cowards*, because they are not particularly heroic, and they are not particularly cowardly. They just are caught in that situation and somehow get out of it.

So your books say something about our existence in the contemporary world. That makes your work so universally appealing in the dozen or so languages it's been translated into.

If that is true, that would mean my books are not so bad, if they have universal appeal. That every honest piece of fiction is in a certain sense universal, because the basic human situations and feelings are no different from two thousand years ago, and no different from America to South Korea. People are people. They are simply a species: the same, identical. So the basic emotions are the same. If you capture the specific variation of that human situation in a specific setting, it can be understood. It can be valid and paradigmatic.

I read a book about the tomb of Tutankhamen, the Egyptian pharaoh. They opened the gold coffin and there was a silver one. Then four or five coffins, and everything was inlaid with gold and emeralds—very rich, pharaonic luxury until you get to the mummy. On the breast of the mummy was a bunch of field flowers, very simple ordinary field flowers, which were obviously placed there by his young wife. Now this gesture is timeless. Modern girls will give you a bunch of field flowers. So that convinces me the relationship between these two people, the pharaoh and his wife, although they were demi-gods, was very normal, was really the same. He probably courted her and told her sweet stupid silly things like any ordinary boy and any ordinary girl in any time. Good literature that captures this essence is universally understandable and speaks to people.

Danny appears in so many of your books. Could we talk about him as a character? Over the years, his persona has changed from observer to participant. His reaction to Czech history is almost a counter-cultural guide to history. And Danny's version of post-war history is presented to history's subjects, that is, the readers of his stories. Who is Danny? Is he an alter ego, a persona, a symbol of the new man, a self-conscious character?

Obviously, he is a semi-autobiographical character: a sort of alter ego. The first book I wrote about him was *The Cowards*. When I started writing the book, intuitively I created this "I", this Danny, who is certainly myself, but of course like every literary character he is a composite. "Composite architecture" I believe Mark Twain called it. So there is part myself, part idealization, part imagination. But in the context of Czech literature, Danny used to be compared to, let's say Švejk, who was also a counter-culture figure. He is simply a non-ideological man. He never subscribes to any official ideology. He goes after his things, which is what most people do. That's probably why he was so well received by the readers, not by the government critics.

I was always so irritated by this talk about Danny's cynicism. To me, cynicism is in the acts, not in the words, the attitudes that one expresses. The so-called cynicism in Danny and similar people is a self-protective pose, because if you live in dreadful times you develop this seemingly cynical attitude towards murder, but you yourself would never murder anyone. The guy who murders talks about lyrics and very noble ideals, and then he goes and kills somebody. So who is a cynic? The man who talks about nobility and beautiful ideals, or the man who, because he has to face the results of these idealists' deeds, develops a sort of cynical, thick hide? So that's the cynicism of Danny. It's a protective mask. He doesn't want to get sentimental about things, and he doesn't want to express any noble ideas because he resents the results of such things. Danny never has done anything bad, really. Well, maybe he harmed some girl, although the girls harm him much more. He develops because he grows older, but I think the basic attitude remains. He's an intellectual and he very often associates with non-intellectuals. In *The Tank Corps*, which unfortunately has never been translated into English, he is in the army and is surrounded by non-intellectuals, soldiers, so he observes their behaviour and has some cynical comments. But obviously he speaks out of the hearts of many readers. In Czechoslovakia there are even women who baptized their children Danny because of that character.

I'd like to talk about your detective stories. You've done some very unusual things with detective stories. You translated Chandler and Hammett. You've written essays on detective stories, and you also made various alterations to the form: for example, the murder occurs at the end. In Sins for Father Knox, *you tried to violate the ten rules of Father Knox. You have a lady cabaret singer who's a detective. You have a society where the police are the criminals. You have moral detectives, who have to find a compromise with themselves when the criminals cannot be identified, perhaps because of political connections and so on.*

My interest in detective stories started when I was seriously ill. I had hepatitis. I almost died. I spent four months in an infectious ward where books were allowed to be sent, but you couldn't send them out. They had to remain there, because they were afraid that they would spread infection. So my friends sent me detective novels, because they could part with them, not serious stuff.

I discovered that this debased genre may be very useful in such situations, and they can be well written. I realized I could tell quite serious things through the genre. The name of my detective is Josef Borůvka. The first book about him was published in English in England: that's *The Mournful Demeanour of Lieutenant Boruvka*. At first he's just a regular grey detective who's sad because he is a humanist. He's sorry for the killers because they are so bad. Not because they are locked up, but because they are so bad. Then I started playing with the genre, so for instance in the first book I tried to get two stories past censorship and I succeeded. One of them is called "Whose Deduction?" and that's a tribute to Chesterton, because the deduction is really God's. Borůvka is led to the solution of the crime through a series of accidents, coincidences, which should not happen in a detective story. Coincidence should never help the detective. But in this case, the coincidences help him. You can also see the coincidences as the finger of God, who is leading him away from a sin, because at the beginning of the story he's about to commit adultery. Fortunately the censor didn't understand it. He thought it was an interesting story. And the other one is about a political prisoner who is suspected of murdering someone. It turns out that the murderer was the prosecutor who had sent him to jail years ago.

In the second book, *Sins for Father Knox*, the idea was that you have this famous decalogue by Father Knox about what must not be done in a detective story. I decided to write ten stories and each of them would violate one of the rules. So the task for the reader would be the normal task: to figure out who the murderer is, and also to figure out which rule has been broken. So that was a sort of game.

What were some of the rules broken?

One rule says there must be no Chinamen. That refers to the cliché that existed in bad detective stories in the twenties, where the murderer was always a Chinaman with a knife in his teeth. So I had a Chinaman in the story. Another rule is that there must be no doubles, so I had doubles. Another one is that the solution must not depend on some scientific or other specific knowledge, so there is a story that depends on your knowledge of mathematics.

Borůvka appears in these *Father Knox* stories, but the main character there is the singer, and he falls in love with her in the end. The third book, *The End of Lieutenant Boruvka*, is set in 1968, after the invasion. The fourth book, which is called *The Return of Lieutenant Boruvka*, is set in Toronto. He escapes from Czechoslovakia and is now a parking-lot attendant in Toronto. He of course solves a case. It features a woman who owns the first all-female detective agency. But she's very incompetent. It's told by a narrator who is a Canadian and who for some reason has very much to do with the Czechs. He doesn't really know why, but there are always some Czechs surrounding him. It's an opportunity to make fun of the Czechs and at the same time criticize some of the naiveties of Canadians.

There's a key worry and concern in The Engineer of Human Souls *that North Americans may be either ignorant of or indifferent to political oppression. There's a poignant scene in which a homesick Czech girl sings a song over the campus radio station, but there's no one to listen. Is that ultimately your deepest concern?*

Of course it is. This political naivety may be funny, but it's also a very dangerous thing. People who have never been exposed to any real political oppression simply have no way of realizing what it is and what it means. That leads to an underestimation of the danger. There is also what I call "selective indignation". That's not my expression; Kingsley Amis coined it years ago. If something happens, let's say in Afghanistan, a very cruel murder—they burn some village—it doesn't really result in too much excitement in the West. You read a story about it, but it's soon forgotten. When a much less cruel thing happens in Chile, there is an explosion and people protest. I'm not against protests against crimes committed by South American dictators. But there should be some balance, because the Soviets are as bad and worse and more dangerous to the world and to peace than some small dictator in Chile. The South American oppressors are certainly nasty people, but they don't present any danger to the world whereas the Soviet regime presents a very grave danger to the world. Attention should be paid to Soviet crimes. At least as intense attention as is paid to South Africa or some of the Latin American dictatorships. But here all you read about is the nasty Americans who support these nasty regimes and who govern their part of the world imperialistically. This is simply not true objectively. If you compare American dominance in South America with Soviet dominance in their sphere—there's no comparison. Do you think that the Soviets would ever permit a Nicaragua to happen on their territory? Never. There would be a Soviet army there at the beginning.

What I am irritated by is this saying, "It's exactly like." It's not exactly like. If you say something about the KGB and how brutal they are, they say, "It's exactly like in the United States. Did you read how they beat up this man or that man?" Again, policemen are similar everywhere, but the difference is in the political system. In America, some of these policemen are as brutal as any other policemen. But they have to play it safe because if they do some nasty thing, they are in danger of being written about and discovered and eventually forced to retire, or even punished, because we still have a free press. Whereas in the Soviet Union the situation is such that if you are a KGB man you don't have to be afraid of being written about in the papers and fired for beating up somebody because that's part of your job, and nobody has the right to criticize you.

The important thing is the system. Human nature is the same. The Russian policemen are probably the same type of people as the American secret policemen. But the systems are very different. The totalitarian system simply gives a much better chance to the lunatic fringe, to the bad people. We have Nazi people here in North America. They are given so much publicity and are presented as something very dangerous. They are not at all dangerous. They are the lunatic fringe, a few crazies who dress like SS men. They have a leader in Chicago who is half-Jewish. So that only shows what type of people they are: lunatics. In a liberal democracy, they will always remain a lunatic fringe. In Toronto, we had this Western Guard. I don't know if they still exist. They never presented any real danger to the society as a whole. They could do nasty things to individuals, certainly, but they like the Nazis have simply been discredited by history. Racism, obviously, is unacceptable.

The Nazis were supremacists, the Master Race and so on, and it appealed only to the Germans. How could it appeal to anyone in Czechoslovakia? We were a secondary race. So it appealed only to the lunatic fringe, the quislings, who in Czechoslovakia were maybe one per cent, even less. They were typical lunatic fringe people, they were pro-Nazi although they were not top-quality Aryans. Whereas Communism—if you forget about its practice, about the murders they commit, about the Gulag, about Cambodia, about Afghanistan—as an ideology it's nice: brotherhood, equality, social justice. For some reason, because the ideology is so appealing, people have a tendency to close their eyes to what they are doing. Some say this or that was a historical necessity. That's bullshit. We are human beings, we are not animals to be moved by some necessity. We have reason. We can solve problems without resorting to mass murder and locking up hundreds of thousands, millions of people. I don't subscribe to historical necessity.

But the feeling is that Communism as an idea is somewhat more acceptable. That leads people to this selective indignation. These South American dictators, they aren't even Fascists. I don't think they have an ideology. They're just autocrats who want to hold power and who are against Communism. But because they either don't have an ideology, or are leaning more towards the right, nobody likes them. Everybody's proud about being an anti-Fascist. But to be an anti-Communist, that's not so good, because you are suspected of being a rightist, a reactionary, maybe a Fascist. But this of course is a mistake.

I read a novel by Amanda Cross. She's a professor of English who wrote a novel called *Death in a Tenured Position*, a dreadful novel, highly praised by all the critics. At the end of the novel there is a university gathering, and a student gives a speech, and he speaks about the necessity of order and respecting the law and all these things, and everybody applauds. The professors applaud because it's law and order. After the applause subsides, he says, "This is what Adolf Hitler said in 1933." The professor thinks this is an argument against law and order. Well, this is *argumentum ad hominem*, which a professor should never use. Secondly, Hitler very probably also believed that one plus one equals two. Was he wrong? So this is demagogy of the first magnitude. Because Hitler said that one should respect law and order, it's bad. But that's not true. Hitler said many things that are quite acceptable, even true, apart from the things that are not, that are inhuman.

This is simply the attitude of many people: because the Americans do something, it must be wrong. The Soviets, after all, are different people. There is no unemployment, which is not true. People find all kinds of reasons to make excuses. These days they are building a pipeline across Czechoslovakia. Who builds the pipeline? Vietnamese. And who are these Vietnamese? People from the south, including, apparently, some boat people who never made it to the boats. How many of them volunteered to be taken from their homeland and sent to Czechoslovakia where they've never been, which is a country so different, to be placed in barracks and to work for much less than Czech workers? That's exploitation of the first magnitude. It's really indentured labour. Have you ever read about it? It's ignored. Imagine if Americans imported people from South Korea without their families, and housed them in barracks and forced them to work for half the pay of American workers—and that not a private firm, but the government did this. It's unimaginable. What a furor that would cause! So this is what I call selective indignation.

I wrote a letter to *Maclean's* about the Canadian bishops' statement on unemployment. It's nice they are interested in the fate of unemployed people, but I have never read any statement in my fourteen years in Canada about the situation of the Church in the Communist states. These are Catholic bishops. They should show some interest in what happens to their fellow Catholics in Communist states.

I don't like to talk about these things, because people always label me as a sort of rightist, Fascist, reactionary. But I am a reactionary in this sense. I believe some values are important and they are now almost forgotten or not respected or not valued. Who is interested in liberal freedoms? Many people just sneer at them. And lawfulness and order, these are not bad things in a democracy. I am reactionary because I believe there are certain traditional values that should not be forgotten, and if they are forgotten the results may be tragic. As Evelyn Waugh said, a writer must be a reactionary because at least someone must go against the tenor of the age. At least someone must offer a little resistance. And that's counter-culture for me.

Acknowledgements

——

Every effort has been made to contact copyright holders; in the event of an inadvertent omission or error, the editor should be notified at Lester & Orpen Dennys Ltd, 78 Sullivan Street, Toronto M5T 1C1.

"I Was Born in Náchod...", originally published in *Contemporary Authors: Autobiography Series*, ed. Dedria Bryfonski (Detroit: Gale Research Company, 1984), is reprinted by permission of Gale Research Company. "An Interview in Prague" was originally published in *The Politics of Culture*, ed. A.J. Liehm (New York: Grove Press, Inc., 1971); copyright © Grove Press, reprinted by permission of the publisher. "Red Music", tr. Káča Poláčková Henley, was first published in *The Bass Saxophone* (Toronto: Anson-Cartwright Editions, 1977; Toronto: Lester & Orpen Dennys, 1980) and is reprinted here by permission of Lester & Orpen Dennys. "Talkin' Moscow Blues" was originally published in *The New Republic* (May 9, 1983). "Hipness at Noon" first appeared in *The New Republic* (Dec. 17, 1984). "An East European Imagination" first appeared in *Mosaic*, Vol. VI, No. 4 (Summer 1973). "The Good Old Drinking Poet" was first published as "Czech Mate" in *The New Republic* (Feb. 18, 1985). "Franz Kafka, Jazz, and the Anti-Semitic Reader" first appeared in *Cross Currents* 1983. "A Discovery in Čapek" first appeared in *The Armchair Detective*, Vol. VIII, No. 3 (1970). "Introducing Bohumil Hrabal" combines two separately published introductions: one, tr. Káča Poláčková Henley, is from *The Death of Mr. Baltisberger* (copyright © 1975 by Doubleday and Company, Inc., reprinted by permission of the publisher); the other, tr. Paul Wilson, is from Hrabal's novel *Closely Watched Trains* (copyright © 1981 by Viking-Penguin Inc., reprinted by permission of the publisher). "The Spilling of the Beans" appeared originally as "A Translator

Bibliography

Camus, Albert. *Notebooks 1942–1951*, tr. Justin O'Brien. New York: Harcourt Brace Jovanovich, 1978.

Čapek, Karel. *In Praise of Newspapers and Other Essays on the Margins of Literature*, tr. W. and R. Weatherall. London: George Allen and Unwin, 1951.

—*Povidky z jedné kapsy*. Prague: Čs. Spisovatel, 1967.

Čapek, Thomas. *The Cechs in America*. Boston: Houghton Mifflin, 1920.

Čermak, Josef. *History of the Civil War*. Chicago: Geringer, 1889.

Chandler, Raymond. *The Simple Art of Murder*. Boston: Houghton Mifflin, 1950.

Conrad, Joseph. *Under Western Eyes*. London: J.M. Dent, 1911.

Doyle, Sir Arthur Conan. *The Return of Sherlock Holmes*. London: John Murray, 1924.

Faulkner, William. *A Fable*. New York: Random House, 1954.

—*The Unvanquished*. New York: Random House, 1938.

Forster, E.M. *Two Cheers for Democracy*. London: Edward Arnold, 1951.

Greene, Graham. *The Heart of the Matter*. London: William Heinemann, 1948.

Harkins, William. *Karel Čapek*. New York: Columbia University Press, 1962.

Hašek, Jaroslav. *The Good Soldier Švejk*, tr. Sir Cecil Parrott. London: William Heinemann, 1973.

Hemingway, Ernest. *A Farewell to Arms*. New York: Charles Scribner's Sons, 1929.

Hrabal, Bohumil. *Closely Watched Trains*, tr. Edith Pargeter. New York: Penguin Books, 1981.

—*The Death of Mr. Baltisberger and Other Stories*, tr. Michael Heim. Garden City: Doubleday and Co., 1975.

James, Henry. *The Future of the Novel*, ed. Leon Edel. New York: Vintage Books, 1956.

Janouch, Gustav. *Conversations with Kafka*. New York: Praeger, 1953.

Karbusický, Vladimir. *Ideologie im Lied, Lied in der Ideologie: Kulturanthropologische Strukturanalysen*. Cologne: H. Gerig, 1973.

Knox, Ronald A. "A Detective Story Decalogue", in *The Art of the Mystery Story*, ed. Howard Haycraft. New York: Grosset and Dunlap, 1964.

Liehm, A.J. and Kussi, Peter, eds. *The Writing on the Wall: An Anthology of Contemporary Czech Literature*. Princeton: Karz-Cohl Publishers, 1983.

Liehm, Antonin J. and Mira. *The Most Important Art: Eastern European Film after 1945*. Berkeley: University of California Press, 1977.

Pound, Ezra. *The Cantos of Ezra Pound*. New York: New Directions, 1970.

Puzo, Mario. *The Godfather*. New York: Putnam, 1969.

Sayers, Dorothy. "The Omnibus of Crime", in *The Art of the Mystery Story*, ed. Howard Haycraft. New York: Grosset and Dunlap, 1964.

Seifert, Jaroslav. *The Selected Poetry of Jaroslav Seifert*, tr. Edward Osers; ed. with additional translations by George Gibian. New York: Macmillan Publishing Company, 1986.

Škvorecký, Josef. *All the Bright Young Men and Women: A Personal History of the Czech Cinema*, tr. Michal Schonberg. Toronto: Peter Martin Associates, 1971.

—*The Bass Saxophone*, tr. Káča Poláčková Henley. Toronto: Anson Cartwright Editions, 1977; Toronto, Lester & Orpen Dennys, 1980.

—*The Cowards*, tr. Jeanne Němcová. Harmondsworth: Penguin, 1970.

—*Dvorak in Love*, tr. Paul Wilson. Toronto: Lester & Orpen Dennys, 1986.

—*The Engineer of Human Souls*, tr. Paul Wilson. Toronto: Lester & Orpen Dennys, 1984.

—*Jiří Menzel and the History of the Closely Watched Trains*. Boulder: East European Monographs, 1982.

—*Mirákl*. Toronto: Sixty-Eight Publishers, 1972.

—*The Mournful Demeanour of Lieutenant Boruvka*, tr. Rosemary Kavan, Káča Poláčková Henley, George Theiner. London: Victor Gollancz, 1973; Toronto: Lester & Orpen Dennys, 1987.

—*The Swell Season*, tr. Paul Wilson. Toronto: Lester & Orpen Dennys, 1982.

—*Tankový prapor*. Toronto: Sixty-Eight Publishers, 1971.

Solzhenitsyn, Aleksandr I. *The Oak and the Calf: Sketches of Literary Life in the Soviet Union*, tr. Harry Willets. New York: Harper and Row, 1980.

Starr, Frederick S. *Red and Hot: The Fate of Jazz in the Soviet Union 1917–1980*. New York: Oxford University Press, 1983.

Van Dine, S.S. "Twenty Rules for Writing Detective Stories", in *The Art of the Mystery Story*, ed. Howard Haycraft. New York: Grosset and Dunlap, 1964.

Waugh, Evelyn. "Interview", in *Writers at Work: Third Series*. New York: The Viking Press, 1967.